INTERVIEWS

Talk to Her

KRISTINE McKENNA

Edited by Matt Silvie & Gary Groth

Art Direction and Design by Unflown

Promotion by Eric Reynolds

Published by Gary Groth & Kim Thompson

7563 Lake City Way | Seattle, WA 98115

Located worldwide at www.fantagraphics.com

First Fantagraphics edition: August 2004

ISBN 1-56097-570-9 | Printed in Canada

Fantagraphics Books has been publishing books and magazines specializing in the work of cartoonists since 1976. Receive a free full-color catalogue by calling 1-800-657-1100. Many books by cartoonists who appear in this book—as well as countless others—may be viewed and ordered from our website.

Distributed in the USA by
WW Norton
tel: 212.354.5500

Distributed in Canada by
Raincoast
tel: 800.663.5714

Distributed in the UK by
Turnaround
tel: 011.44.208.829.3009

INTERVIEWS

Talk to Her

Kristine McKenna

SIDE
2

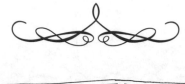

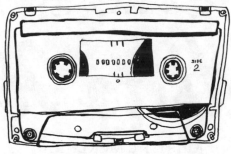

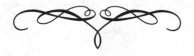

Contents : | *Illustrated By :*

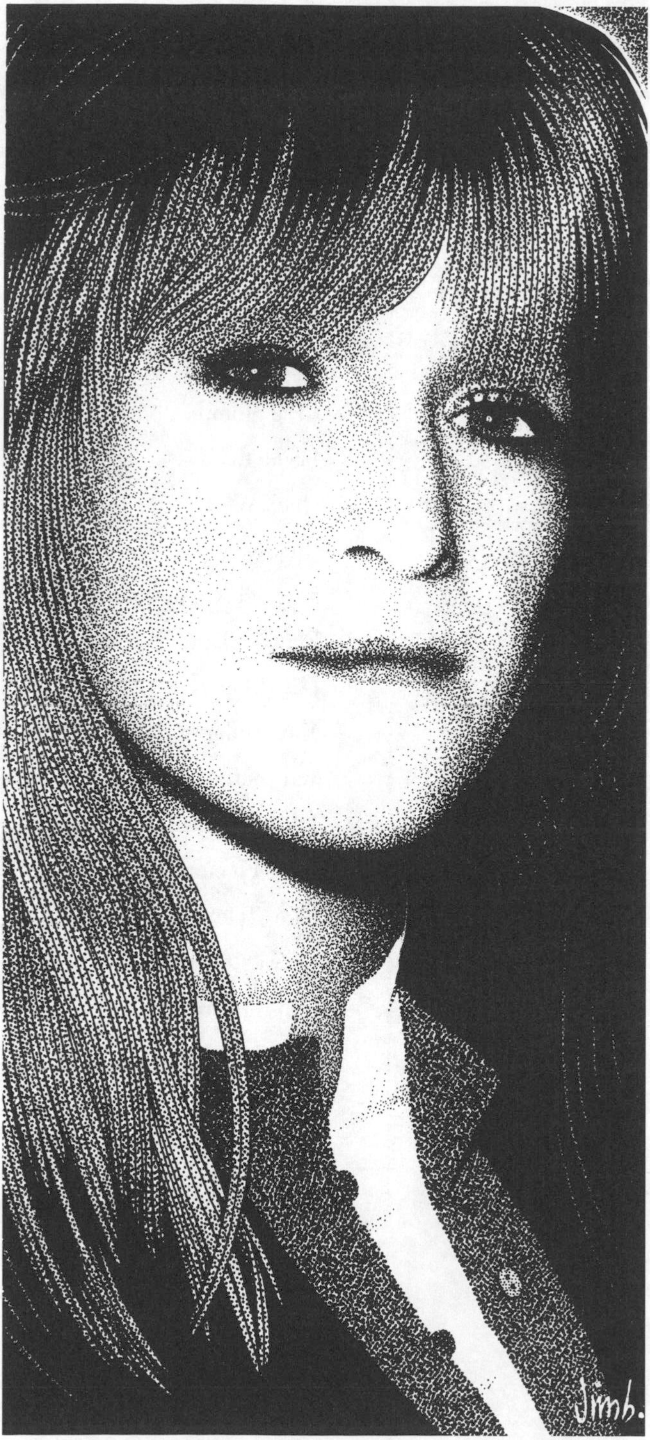
Jimh.

This book is an addendum of sorts to a volume of my interviews published by Fantagraphics Books in 2001. Titled *Book of Changes*, that book came to be when my friend Artie Shaw suggested to Gary Groth, the king of Fantagraphics, that a collection of my interviews might make a good book. Gary kindly invited me to put such a book together, and my plan was to include all my favorite interviews from my 25 years as a journalist. When the number of interviews reached 38, however, the book began to get crowded, and I knew I'd have to leave out some things I'd hoped to include. In fact, I wound up leaving out quite a few interviews I thought stood up to repeated readings, and I've done several new interviews since 2001, when the last book was published. I felt that a few of those were worth saving, too, and thus was born this volume. A friend of mine had a look at an early draft of this book and said, "Gee, it's kind of lumpy. Some things are really long, others are short – you'd better include some kind of explanation or something." I can't justify this text! All I can say is that each interview is as long as it needs to be. My plan was to call it *Book of Changes II*, but Gary Groth said nobody would buy a book with that crummy title, and he renamed it *Talk To Her*. I protested that that sounds like a phone sex service, but I nonetheless defer to his expertise in the marketing of books.

I must confess that I've always asked lots of questions, and it's an aspect of my personality some people find quite annoying. But I can explain! I figure that when you're trapped in a boring conversation – and who among us has not had that pleasure – you might as well take control and drag the conversation in a direction that interests you. I've discovered that if you always ask people about the things that really interest you then you'll never be bored, and you'll learn amazing things about people. One thing I've learned as a result of my endless interrogations is that there's a unique internal architecture to every life, and that the arc of every life is beautiful. I'm always moved by the ways that people transform and build on the events of their lives; that process of transformation demands imagination and courage; it's astonishing what people are capable of. The highly accomplished people in this book succeeded in transforming the events of their lives into art, which is surely the most astonishing achievement of all.

Thank you: Doug Aitken, Nick, Kathy and Andrew Asolas, Jay Babcock, Miles Beller, Shirley and Tosh Berman, Charles and Barbara Brittin, Diane Broderick, Gideon Brower, Nick, Meg, Steve, Linda and Penny Chase, Jack Cheeseborough, Catherine Coulson, Michael Duncan, Lianne Halfon, Walter Hopps, Gary Groth, Adrienne Levin, Lance Loud, Tom Lutz, David Lynch, Susan Martin, Bill, Beverly and Jennifer McKenna, David Meltzer, Glenn Morrow, Jonathan Omer-Man, Don Opper, Steve Randall, Margy Rochlin, Kati Rocky, Steve Samiof, Artie Shaw, Ridley Schruers, Marc Sirinsky, Lesley Taplin, Laurie Winer, and all the artists who contributed drawings to this book.

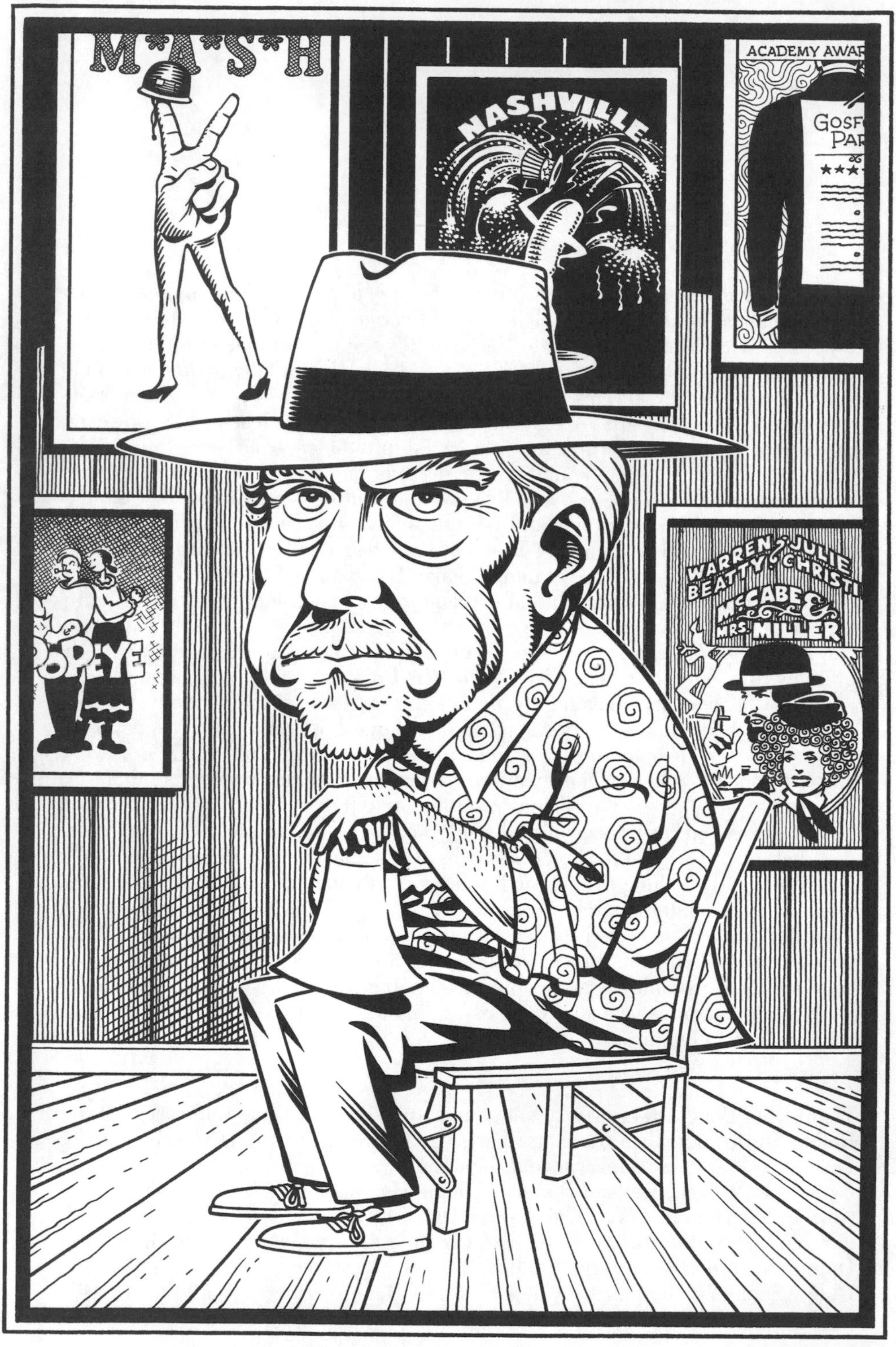
M*A*S*H
NASHVILLE
WARREN BEATTY
McCABE & MRS. MILLER

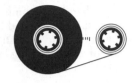

Robert Altman

Robert Altman was born in Kansas City on February 20, 1925. As a teenager he served as a pilot in World War II; then, when he returned to civilian life, he tried his hand at magazine journalism and radio. That led to a job producing industrial films for a small Kansas City firm, and he spent nearly a decade with the company mastering the nuts and bolts of filmmaking. He made his official directorial debut in 1957 with The Delinquents, a low budget movie he wrote, produced and directed. The film didn't fare too well, but it did lead to work in television, and Altman spent the next ten years directing installments of series such as Alfred Hitchcock Presents, Combat, and Bonanza. His career shifted gears dramatically in 1970 with the release of M*A*S*H, a phenomenally successful film that introduced the blueprint of Altman's mature style. Rejecting linear narrative, Altman developed an approach to storytelling that's comparable to a jazz musician riffing on an American pop standard. Life doesn't move forward towards a resolution in his intimate, multi-layered studies of the human animal; rather, it hovers in an odd time warp as his characters are placed under the microscope for examination by the viewer. "I'm not telling stories — I'm handing over a tray of stuff," Altman explained the first time I interviewed him in 1993. "What appeals to me is the idea of lifting up the roof of a house and watching the behavior going on inside. The idea of relating a story in A-B-C terms never interested me at all."

My first conversation with Altman took place on the occasion of the release of his adaptation of the writings of Raymond Carver, Short Cuts. We spoke on a summer afternoon at his Malibu beach house, a sunlit place hung with vibrantly colored abstract canvases, and Altman was great company. He's a refreshingly blunt person who immediately cuts to the chase in response to any question you ask him, and it's a startling thing to hear somebody in the film business tell the truth and name names. Obviously, he's a tough man in certain regards, and I'd hate to be on his bad side. But he's also a compassionate observer of the passing parade, he's easily moved by beauty, and he adores actors.

Talking that day about Carver, Altman observed, "Infidelity was one of Carver's central themes and his only comment on it was that it exists. Carver was a pragmatist and he never wrote about things the way he thought they should be — he wrote about life as he observed it." Altman's work is similarly even-handed, and you'll never catch him wagging a moralizing finger at his audience. As I left that day I mentioned how much I loved the soundtrack to Nashville, which was out of print at the time and a very difficult record to get. A few weeks later he sent me a copy in the mail.

Our paths crossed again in December of 2001 when we met for breakfast at a Century City hotel to discuss his 32nd film, Gosford Park. He'd clearly grown more physically frail since I'd last seen him, and rumors of health problems had been circulating for months. That said, he still came across as a man of extraordinary vigor, and he had a recklessly high cholesterol breakfast while he fumed at length about various idiots in the film business. Since then he has released a 33rd film, The Company, and is in pre-production on the 34th, Paint.

Gosford Park *looks at the British class system as it was in 1932. Is the class system we see in the picture still operating?*

Servitude is no longer indentured, but the class system persists in England. There's a class system everywhere and it's usually defined by color and by how you speak. The one time there was a concerted effort to abolish the class system was communism, but that failed because equality and sharing are tough things to sell. There's always gonna be somebody who wants more.

One could make the case that movie people are America's reigning upper class.

I suppose that may be true of celebrities, but people aren't aware of much beyond who is or is not a movie star, and they don't spend much time thinking about actors. There's a big difference between being an actor and being a movie star, and once the movie star thing hits you're no longer allowed to be an actor. There are a few who've coped with it reasonably well – Paul Newman's probably handled it better than anybody else – but it's very tough. Still, I don't know many actors who'd turn down the chance to be a movie star because we get such mixed messages about what the goal is. Do you want to be a journeyman actor or a rich Hollywood celebrity? Everybody seems to think the latter is preferable.

Gosford Park *has a great deal in common with a film you made in 1978 called* A Wedding. *Were you aware of the similarities while you were shooting* Gosford Park?

Oh sure. The films are very much alike. In fact, there's one little bit in *Gosford Park* that I lifted directly from *A Wedding* – I think of it as my little homage to myself. By the way, *A Wedding* has been transformed into an opera and was to be staged by the Lyric Opera of Chicago in 2002.

You've commented that, "Acting is like any art. When you get too good at it you become facile and the art disappears." Precisely what is the art?

It's when an actor focuses his entire persona on the struggle to express something. Film is an actors medium, and once a film is cast all that's left for me to do is to create a framework that allows audiences to see the actors work.

With Mash *and* Nashville *you established yourself as a prescient observer of the American zeitgeist. What's the most significant change you've observed in this country over the course of your life?*

It certainly hasn't become less racist, and a mean-ness has developed in American business that's unnecessary for what the goals are. People get pushed out of business, nobody's kind to anybody any more, and we applaud this behavior and regard it as smart. America isn't any worse than any other culture – I think there's little difference from one to the next – but we are nonetheless a solipsistic people. Why didn't we know that the women of Afghanistan were forced to wear sacks over their heads for years? People are selfish when life allows them to be, and we didn't know because we didn't need to know. I didn't know and I'm embarrassed about that, and now that I do know, that knowledge affects my thinking about everything.

The events of September 11th were terrible, but basically it's the same money game in this country. In the months following the attack the studios felt obliged to scrap a few Arnold Schwarzenegger films so some pollution was kept out of the river, but that traumatic event didn't really change the country. My feelings about America have changed, however. I was in England in 2000 when the presidential election was taking place, and I said to my mates, "this will be O.K. because it's going to the

Supreme Court." It did go to the Supreme Court and we know what happened there. I felt like such a fool. I'm 76 years old and I still believed in America up to that minute, and at my age I should've known better. Now I don't feel any emotional or patriotic ties to this country at all.

Why are the idiots always in charge?
Because most people wouldn't take those jobs, and those jobs turn people into panderers. We used to have better leaders and the entire enterprise was more dignified, but now a guy can't hold public office if he ever fucked a woman other than his wife. The last good president we had was Roosevelt.

You're known for tackling movies of a really sprawling scale; are there stories that are too big to tell?
No. I equate what I do with painting rather than literature, and the first thing I want to know is; what's the size of the wall you're gonna give me? The bigger the wall, the more content somebody's gonna impose on me. You say O.K., you can have this 70-foot wall but you'll have to have horses in it, and I say O.K., I can do that, I like horses. Not all of my films are big in that way, however – a film like *Secret Honor* is a miniature painting. They're all different, but there are no limits in terms of scale.

You once commented, "When I get a stack of material that will become a film it's not important to me that the pages be numbered," and you've often expressed your disdain for conventional narrative structure. Still, audiences continue to demand it. Why? Is it a failure of imagination on the audience's part?
I wouldn't put it that way. The persistence of structured narrative has to do with habit and education, but it's also like the bullfighter's cape. You need something to get their attention and get them hooked, and the idea of a story is an effective way to do that. When people encounter art they don't immediately understand they tend to respond with hostility, so the audience has to be made comfortable. They have to feel confident they're gonna get it, and conventional narrative structure is good for that, too. When you look deeply into a work of art, however, you don't get a definitive answer or statement; rather, you get a view of this world that only one person could've created. There are no literate answers; there are only feelings. That's what art is.

Your filmmaking style pivots on closely observed episodes of human behavior. After decades of study what conclusions have you drawn about human nature?
It's essentially benign in that we all want to get along and be loved, but it's also unpredictable. There was recently a story in the news about a woman who drowned her five kids. How can you begin to draw conclusions about something like that? I believe it's in all of us to commit such acts when pushed to certain extremes, too, because everything is true, all things are possible, and we're all in a moving river. We can gauge the distance and the speed at which we're traveling, but we forget that everything around us is moving, too. As for this illusion called time that we live by, or where the river is going – it's simply moving in its direction and we have no say in the matter.

When was the last time a work of art – a painting, a piece of music, literature, a film – moved you to tears?
That happens all the time. You have to give up something of yourself in order to be vulnerable enough to experience that kind of pain and joy, but if we can't experience art that deeply then what are we doing here?

Little Edie

straw sunhat & grey sweater

green knee socks & green pumps

white lace tablecloth

bread for the raccoons

red wool dirndl skirt worn upside-down

Edie Beale

Grey Gardens is a 28-room mansion in East Hampton, New York that began life in 1913 as the summer cottage of Mr. And Mrs. Robert C. Hill. Sixty years later the house served as the location for Grey Gardens, a documentary film by the Maysles Brothers chronicling the relationship between Edie Bouvier Beale and her daughter, Little Edie, who occupied the house for more than half a century. Anyone who sees the film, which was released in 1976, comes away from it wondering what brought the Beales to the state in which the Maysles found them. The information I was able to dig up is as follows.

In 1923 the original owners of Grey Gardens sold the house to Phelan Beale Sr., who moved his wife and three children in. Phelan Beale's wife, Edie Bouvier Beale was born in 1893 and she had two brothers: "Black" Jack Bouvier, who made a fortune on Wall Street and fathered Jackie Kennedy in 1929; and Bud Bouvier, who made his money in oil and drank himself to death before he was 40. An aspiring singer, Edie Bouvier made a few records prior to her 1916 marriage to Phelan Beale, an Atlanta-born aristocrat whose grandfather was pals with Jefferson Davis. The couple had three children. The eldest, Little Edie Beale, was born in 1910. Next came Phelan Beale Jr., who went into business in Oklahoma. Bouvier Beale, the third child, became a lawyer. In 1933 Phelan Beale abandoned his wife and family, married another woman, and moved to Florida. Following his death in 1956, the bulk of his estate went to his second wife.

In the years after the divorce, Edie and her children continued to live in high style. In 1936 Little Edie had a lavish coming out party at the Pierre Hotel in New York, and she spent the next 16 years in Manhattan attempting to establish a career as a dancer. Back at Grey Gardens, however, things grew increasingly difficult for Big Edie, who was forced to rely on her family for funds to raise her children. In 1952 Little Edie returned to Grey Gardens, and she remained there with her mother until Big Edie died in 1977. Whether she returned because she was unable to make a life for herself in New York, or because she felt her mother needed looking after, is the subject of endless debate between them in the film.

Left to their own devices and with few demands made on them, the Edies drifted into an unsanitary state of enchantment. Both of them were bright, cultured women, and they were certainly familiar with the sorts of lives most people live, but they chose to turn their backs on all that and live exactly as they pleased. Cleanliness wasn't high on their list of priorities, so cats, raccoons and assorted rodents had the run of the house. Meanwhile, the Edies whiled the days away eating ice cream in bed at odd hours, popping favorite records on the turntable and singing along, performing impromptu dance routines, and playing dress-up.

The outside world intruded on the Beales' sanctuary in 1971, when the Suffolk County Health Department inspected Grey Gardens and cited it for several violations. When that failed to elicit a response, the East Hampton city fathers raided the house on the grounds that the Beales were harboring diseased cats. Tabloid headlines about "Jackie's aunt" followed, as did a third inspection, in December of 1971, that resulted in a threat of eviction that was never carried out. The Maysles brothers' movie took root two years after that ruckus when Lee Radziwill approached them about making a film portrait of her family that would include the Beales. When the filmmakers met the Edies the Radziwill project fell by the wayside, and the Maysles began working on Grey Gardens in 1973. In 1979, two years after Big Edie died at the age of 84, Little Edie sold Grey Gardens to Ben Bradlee and Sally Quinn.

When Grey Gardens was re-released in 1998, Little Edie agreed to speak with me about the film by phone from her home in Florida. As is apparent in the following conversation, Little Edie was obsessed with family lore, the feuds, rivalries, trust funds and betrayals. As she wistfully points out in a scene from the film that depicts her mother boiling corn on a hotplate next to her bed, "It's very difficult to keep the line between the past and the present." Little Edie obviously had her problems, but she had a fantastic spirit, and the life force in her was very strong. She died in 2002 at the age of 85.

Why did you and your mother allow the Maysles to come into your home and film you?

Why? Because we had no money for food and they paid us to come in and film. It all started when the Bouvier girls decided to make a movie about their childhood lives in East Hampton, and they sent the Maysles over to take pictures of mother and I. Suddenly these strange men came in the house with cameras, they marched upstairs to my mother's bedroom and began filming her in bed. I happen to read *The New York Times*, the theatrical section, so I recognized them and I said, "My god, you're the Maysles!" These poor Maysles didn't know me from Adam, they didn't know who I was or what I did, and they didn't know anything about my mother either, but they met us and dreamed up this movie. I guess they're happy with it, but I don't like it because I find documentaries depressing. They're difficult, don't you think? I liked the photography and mother's fine in the film, although they wouldn't let her sing. They wouldn't let me dance, and made me into something I'm not. The real Edith Beale is a Spanish dancer. I know 5,000 songs, all of which my mother taught me. She wasn't an opera singer – her field was operetta and popular music. Anyhow, after the movie came out we got a letter from the Maysles that said, "We spent a million dollars on the movie and we don't have any money now and there will never be any money because nobody liked the film and it wasn't a hit."

But people love Grey Gardens. Surely you must know that by now.

No, I never found that out. But I will tell you this, Miss McKenna, the Maysles made that movie on a shoestring. They had no money, they shot it in five weeks, and it took them three years to get it to the point where they could show it in theaters. Mother and I had our money problems too, of course, and they were a result of the fact that we had terrible trouble with our relatives. The family never cared for me and they hated my mother. She was a dancer and a singer with a terrific voice she'd inherited from her mother, and the relatives hated her because she was magnificent. My mother was a professional and I respected her for that. She had no interest in the social clubs and bridge games her family was involved with. They're all social climbers, and social climbing seemed horrible to me – I couldn't stand what you had to go through in America! American girls are crazy. I'm not talking about girls who work at a market or are trying to get into the movies; I'm talking about American girls brought up with money. They have all these terrible ideas.

Anyhow, my mother was singing, writing music and leading her own life, and her father gave her a lot of trouble for that. He arranged a marriage for her, and I don't think she ever wanted marriage and children. She was forced into it. I was nuts about my mother and I gave her my life.

You must miss her now that she's gone.

Oh my god, my heart is absolutely broken. After she died I thought about settling in San Francisco, so last summer I went to California, which is the most terrific state. My god, what is Los Angeles like? Very dangerous? My youngest nephew wanted me to live with him in this beautiful house he'd bought in Oakland, and I spent three months there. I was crazy about Oakland, and went absolutely nuts for San Francisco, but then there were two small earthquakes north of San Francisco and I got very nervous. My mother always said, "I never want you to go to California because they're going to have a terrible earthquake, and I don't want you out there." Aren't you afraid of living in California because of the earthquakes? Because, Miss McKenna, you don't know when the building you're in will fall on top of you, do you? Anyhow, my nephew was really nice. He's the youngest one and I'd been to his wedding eight years earlier, but it didn't work out because it brought back all this family stuff. I don't know who was the unhappiest about it all, whether it was them or me, but I decided to return to Florida, so here I am.

Why did you sell Grey Gardens?

It wasn't my idea, and I only sold it because I got into a frightful jam with Jacqueline Onassis. After mother died Jackie told me she'd hired all these people to renovate the house, but I didn't want Jackie and Lee to grab the house, so I sold it quickly for mere pennies. The people who bought the house, Ben Bradlee and Sally Quinn, were perfectly wonderful, sweet and kind – there are some nice people in the world, you know, I just don't happen to be related to any of them. Jackie was twelve years younger than I, and although I was never jealous of her, I never liked her. You know what Jackie wanted? She wanted the house. Yes darling, that's the truth, and she did everything she could to get it. Mother and I were doing fine. We had a lawyer of our own, we'd always been together and we were a team. Then, suddenly, the gardener disappeared and the grass grew high all around the house, and after that they took the plumber away. Then they raided the house and photographed everything. Because we were raided without a search warrant we decided to go to court, and even though we didn't have much money to pay our lawyer he decided to help us anyway. Jackie then got a Kennedy lawyer named Bill vanden Heuvel to say I was crazy and should be put away. I asked them who mother would live with if they put me away, and they decided not to put me away. I definitely am not crazy. I've always been terribly solid. Then Jackie sent her sister Lee, who I've always been absolutely terrified of – I think she's a big criminal. Lee and her boyfriend came around and started to tear the house down with axes. Don't go near any of those people for god's sake, they're all insane. And my god, the village of East Hampton! They put me through holy hell. I'm telling you the truth, but you can't tell Americans the truth. But listen, Miss McKenna, I will never be anything but an American. I think it's a fabulous country and I'm crazy about Bill Clinton.

How did you feel about his sexual indiscretions in the White House?

I was kind of shocked by it. At first I thought it wasn't true and that it was some campaign thing dreamed up by the Republicans, but I've come to believe that he did have a love affair with that girl. But my god, it's his own business! What does it matter? Mrs. Clinton doesn't want to divorce him, and he didn't give that girl a baby. I mean my god, he's so brilliant, when will we ever get another person like him? I've always been a Democrat, and I used to take politics very seriously, but I don't like politics any more because life is very different now. American life has changed a great deal.

Changed for better or worse?
Darling, I really don't know. They say it's gone downhill morally and ethically, and there are no standards of right and wrong any more. Everybody just lives together now because divorce is so expensive, but people go ahead and get divorced anyway.

Why didn't you ever marry?
I had the nicest people in the world want to marry me. I should've married Jack Hearst but mother didn't like him because he was divorced and had a child. Howard Hughes also wanted to marry me. He told me I looked exactly like his wife who'd divorced him. She was a beautiful girl named Rice, of the Rice family out in Texas, and she insisted on divorcing him because he was mean to her. It left him with a terrible broken heart that he never got over. He told me I looked exactly like this ex-wife, but I refused to go out with him because I was terrified of him. He was an aeronautical engineer who was always working on a new invention, and he was always covered with grease.

Have you been to Grey Gardens since the new tenants moved in?
Somebody from South Hampton took me by it, so I saw it from the outside, and I'll tell you something I don't like. In America they won't leave the old stuff like they do in England. Grey Gardens looks just like everything else now, and it used to have something that was quite terrific.

It had you.
Oh, you're so cute.

What prompted you to move to Florida?
I first got that idea when I was little. I was born and raised in New York City and the only thing I ever wanted to do from the beginning of my life was to live in Miami. I don't know, Florida's part of me, that's all I can tell you. I didn't care about Europe. It was Miami that interested me, and I think that was because of my father. He created a house there that was comparable to Hearst's Castle in San Simeon. All the materials for the house were imported from Spain and Italy, and my father created this whole thing in Miami. I guess that's where I got this terrible hunger for Florida.

You were 14 years old when your father left your mother; were you upset with him for leaving the family?
They said I was illegitimate, you know, and that I wasn't actually the daughter of Phelan Beale. My early life was very formal and lonely, and when my parents separated they didn't know what to do with my brothers and I, so we were all sent to boarding school. I was sent to Farmington where I got into the glee club and began singing. I was trained to perform and I went to the Spence School, where they said I had a marvelous future. Unfortunately we didn't have any money, despite the fact that my father was a very famous lawyer, because of what mother's brother did. Her brother, Jack Bouvier, took our $65,000 trust fund, invested it all for Jackie Kennedy, would only give mother $300 a month to live on, and he wouldn't fix the house.

Cats were such an important part of your life at Grey Gardens. Do you have cats at your home in Florida?

No, darling, the last cat died after my brother died. Both of my brothers are dead and I went to the FBI about the death of my youngest brother because I think he was murdered. He settled out west but we were very close. He called me every week and I wrote him letters. He was found dead in his house laying face down, and my last three talks with him made me very nervous. I wanted to go out there right away because I felt that he was in great danger, but my relatives wouldn't discuss it. Both of my brothers married while they were still in their teens, and one of my brothers had three sons, and the other brother had a daughter. The war did it, that's when we lost my brothers. Hitler ruined the whole world. My brothers went off to war and that was the last we saw of them. They became war heroes, you know. One was shot at Okinawa, but he killed several Japanese before he was wounded, so he was honored as a hero.

How do you entertain yourself down there in Florida?

I'm absolutely crazy about golf tournaments and I enjoy watching golf on television. Mother was a marvelous golfer, and I like to play, so we used to play golf at the Maidstone Club in East Hampton. It's a very beautiful place, although it's a corrupt organization – I guess the whole world is corrupt. Anyhow, I live in a suburb of Miami and don't go into Miami too often because it's dangerous. I'm in a darling place called Surf Side that's like a little French village. It's completely tiny and right on the beach. I hope we don't have another tornado. I went through a tornado one night this winter and I was scared to death. Darling, I'm always alone. I'm just an old maid who never married or lived with a man. If I'd had the time I think I might've gotten married, but I never had a minute because I had terrible problems all the time. I had a very difficult life, and I feel more free now that I'm getting to the end of it. I'm planning my funeral and have a few things to finish, but I'm not gonna kill anybody.

Who's your best friend now that your mother is gone?

Darling, there are five or six people I write to, but that's all I have. Over the past few years I've gone through eight deaths, and it was almost more than I could take. I wasn't surprised by Jackie's death because she'd had such a terrible existence. She was pregnant six times and had several children cut out of her. She was always pregnant and had a terrible life. She was grabbed by the Kennedys. Before she married Jack she was engaged to a darling man named John Husted who went to Yale and had a house in Bedford Village, but Jack Kennedy had more money than John Husted, so Jackie gave him up and said yes to Mr. Kennedy. Jackie had a beautiful face and she became famous, but her life was awful. And poor Lee was sick every minute and was constantly running off to sanitariums in Switzerland. Lee looks just about dead and gone. My mother really was the most extraordinary member of the family. She was always singing, and she had a wonderful accompanist she wrote music with. I was happy to be alone with mother because we created the sort of life we liked, and it was very private and beautiful.

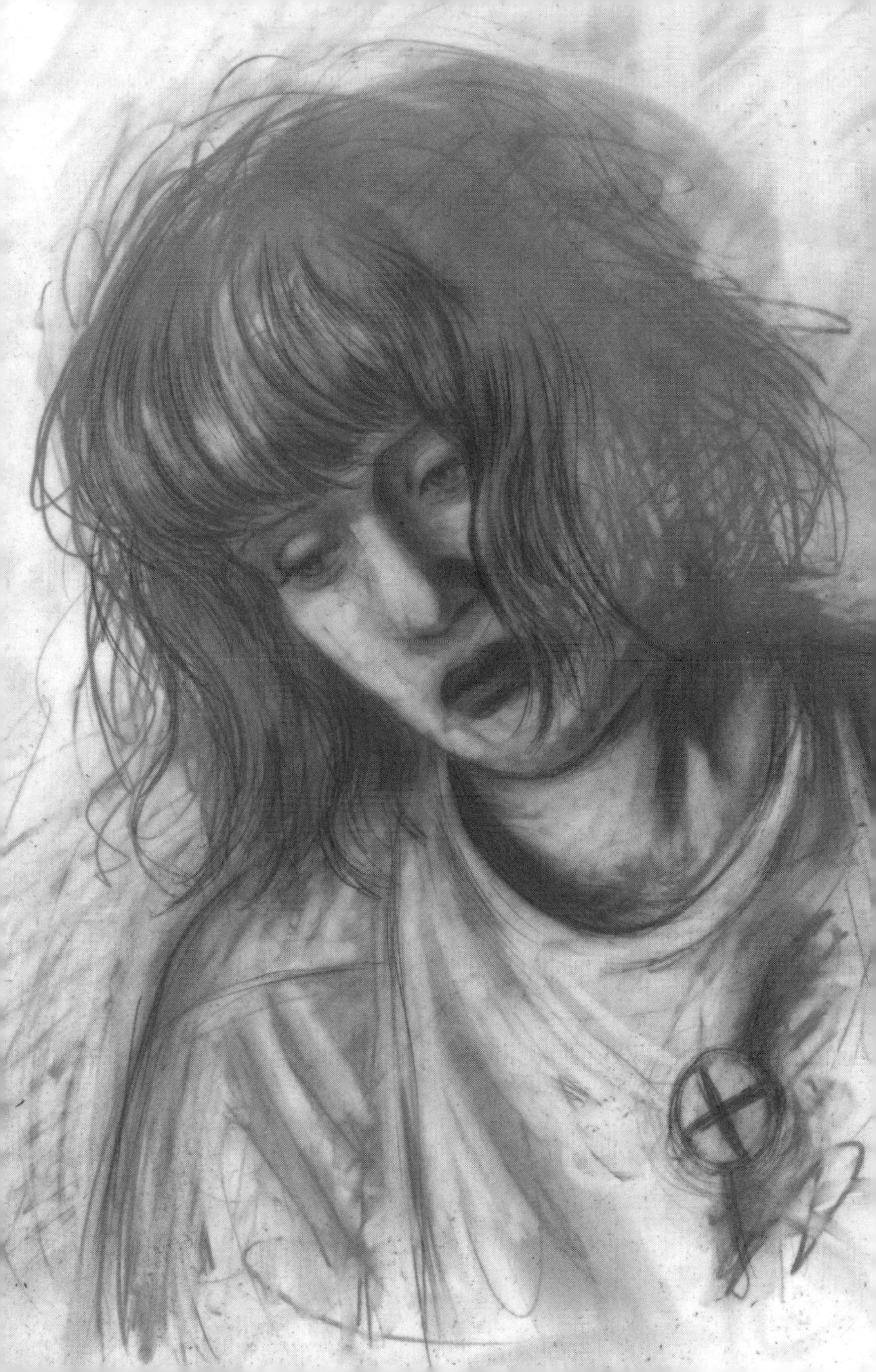

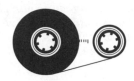

Exene Cervenka

Exene Cervenka was born in Chicago in 1956, the second child in a family of four daughters. Her mother, Mary Healy, was the child of Irish immigrants, and her father, Lewis Cervenka, was of Bohemian extraction. When Exene was three months old, she and her family moved to a small Illinois town where they lived until 1970, when they relocated to Florida. Exene quit school when she was sixteen, and following the death of her mother in 1974, she devoted the next two years of her life to looking after her two younger sisters. When her father remarried in 1976, she was free to hit the road and make her own life, and in August of 1976 she moved to Los Angeles. Shortly after her arrival she met musician John Doe at a poetry workshop in Venice; early in 1977 the two of them formed X, the most important L.A. band to emerge from the first generation of American punk. It's significant that John and Exene met at a poetry workshop; their eloquent lyrics played a central role in setting them apart from the hundreds of punk bands that sprung up in the '70s.

I met Exene during the first year X was gigging in Los Angeles and was immediately impressed by her. She was still so young, and she'd clearly been wounded by life, but she was such a dignified girl. Scruffy and fierce, she was defiantly true to herself always, and nobody else dressed like her or behaved the way she did. Exene patented her own brand of beauty, and she was brave. I'd watch her onstage and wonder how she got the nerve to be so original, so much herself. She's a powerful performer, and has been since the first time she walked onto a stage. This is remarkable, given that her childhood wasn't a very fertile one in terms of fostering creativity, tenderness, or courage. She developed those qualities in herself entirely through the force of her own character and will, and that is no small thing.

X released its debut album, Los Angeles, in 1980 and during the spring of that year Exene and John were married. A week after their wedding Exene's older sister, Muriel Cervenka, was killed in an automobile accident in L.A. This was a huge loss for Exene, but it didn't slow her down, and over the next six years X released five more critically acclaimed albums. 1982 saw the publication of Adulterer's Anonymous, a collaboration with Lydia Lunch that was the first of four books Exene has published, and her practice as a visual artist continued to deepen. A gifted collagist, she's created dozens of finely detailed journals that have the exquisite density of Faberge eggs.

In 1986 Exene's marriage to John Doe ended, and the following year she married actor Viggo Mortensen, with whom she had a son in 1988. In 1991 that marriage also ended. During the late '80s, Exene completed two solo albums, published her second volume of verse, Virtual Unreality, and continued to perform with X. In 1992 she collaborated with photographer Kenneth Jarecke on Just Another War, a book of images and verse concerning the 1991 war in Iraq, and in 2001 she published A Beer on Every Page. That same year she formed the Original Sinners, whose debut album was released in 2002. In August of that year she married musician Jason Edge, guitarist with the Original Sinners, and they share a cozy house in L.A. full of wonderful things; souvenirs of their lives on the road as traveling musicians, pieces of Americana and folk art, political propaganda, and funny things that caught Exene's eye. Her house embodies one of the things I like best about her, which is how unmistakably American she is. The child of poor immigrants, Exene is a Horatio Alger figure who rose from the prairies of the Midwest.

What's your earliest memory?

Stepping on a tack. I was coming downstairs and my grandfather was talking with my father downstairs in the kitchen. It was so early in the morning that it was still dark, and as I walked down stairs I stepped on a tack and started crying. They just told me to stop blubbering – the people in my family were all pretty belligerent. My mother's mother lived with us until I was in third grade, and she was a severe alcoholic who became wildly unpredictable when she drank. My mother also drank and did some self-medicating towards the end of her life, but my parents weren't wild partiers or pill heads.

My mother was Irish and although she was born in the United States, most of her brothers and sisters were born in Ireland, and her father was in the I.R.A. Supposedly he came to the United States because he had to get out of Ireland. I don't know what sort of crimes he committed, but he was heavy into the I.R.A. and was an extremely violent person. He and my grandmother were both raging alcoholics.

I went to the town in Ireland where my mother's family was from, and it was listed in the guidebook as the most forlorn place in all of Ireland, which is saying a lot. It's at the most extreme western point in Ireland, and it was shockingly bare – you look at this place and can't imagine how anyone could scratch out a living there. There was a stone school building, and some white houses with thatched roofs, but basically it was just rocky ground descending down to the sea. I guess that explains how my grandfather wound up in the I.R.A. He came from a line of hard people who beat their kids to keep them in line. I had a cousin in prison for murder, and most of my mother's brothers and sisters are dead.

My mother was only sixteen and my father was forty when they met. My father's still alive – he's 91 now. My mother's parents were living in Chicago and they ran a tavern where my father was a regular. He saw my mother there and they wound up getting married. My mother was seventeen when she married, and eighteen when she had my sister, Muriel. I was born a year and a half later, in 1956. They were sharing a basement apartment with another couple at the time, then a few months after I was born, we moved to a house my father built in a small Illinois town called Mokena that was just springing up out of the wheat fields and farm lands. The area is now part of an extended suburban network, but back then it had a population of 1,000 people, and it was in the prairie. The fields there had gone to seed because they hadn't been cultivated in years, but there were still rotting old wooden fence posts with rusting wire, and wild grass growing everywhere. You could see farms in the distance. It was the beginning of the suburbs.

I was the second child in a family of four girls, and when I was in third grade my first younger sister was born, then my second younger sister came when I was thirteen. They're really different from me and I don't have much contact with my family. I don't know what they think about what I do. My sisters and my father are close, but I've never felt like I could penetrate that little group and I finally just gave up. It's that weird family dynamic. You know how families often have one kid that just doesn't seem to belong?

When I was growing up my father was always off working as a carpenter, and my mother was a cocktail waitress until I was six. My mother was an emotionally tortured, introverted agoraphobic, and we never went anywhere. We never took a vacation except for one time when I was really little, and we went to a hillbilly place in the Ozarks where you could go on boats and go square dancing. There were no movie theaters in the town where we lived, so I went to the movies twice when I was growing up. I didn't know it at the time because we always had food, but we were really poor and my father did lots of trading to help us get by. He'd build an addition onto somebody's house in exchange for new tires for our car, or somebody would fix our plumbing and he'd go lay a floor in exchange.

In Illinois I attended a private Catholic school where I got a good education, then when I was fourteen my family moved to Florida so my father could get seasonal work doing carpentry, and I switched to a public school. It was still the era of segregation, and I'd never been around people of color. My mother had an unnaturally phobic reaction to black people – I have no idea why, but she was literally terrified of black people – and we were living in a county that was a bastion of segregation. There were race riots all the time, and it was horrifying. The white kids and the black kids hated each other for no reason other than that they'd grown up being tutored to hate each other for the same stupid reasons people have their little factional disputes today. I was regarded as a freak because I'd just moved down from Illinois and I was already wearing thrift store clothes. In Florida, people would stop in the streets or in the hallways at school and stare at me.

What gave you the courage to develop your own sense of style at such a young age?

My sister gave me the courage to wear unusual things. There was a thrift store in the farm town where we lived, and one day she said we should go there and we did. These were early days for thrift store shopping, plus we were in a small town, so it was full of great, really old stuff. So we started going to thrift stores and weird markets, and we'd ride our bikes to other little towns in the area and find overalls from the '30s, old hand-tooled leather cowboy belts – incredible things for five cents.

How do you explain that unlike most kids, you didn't want to look like everybody else?

Because there was absolutely no way for me to do that. There was a big price to pay if you wanted to look different back then, though, and I don't know what gave me the courage to do it because I really hated the abuse I got. If you looked different you could practically get lynched. But by the time I got to Florida I was already so into that look that there was no turning back. Finding some beautiful, unique old thing for a nickel, as opposed to trying to get on the train into Joliet to look for the latest, cutest thing, and then shop-lifting it – which is what I spent most of my early teenage years doing, because I had no other way to get stuff – it was a freedom thing. I just decided I could wear a beaded gown from the '20s if I wanted to.

What were you like when you were fourteen?

For most of my childhood I was pretty good, in a Catholic school sense, and I went to church seven days a week, partly because there was absolutely nothing else to do. There were only three television stations and two radio stations available in our area, there was no movie theater, and no place to go dance. We didn't go swimming or to the beach or hiking or to Chicago or to museums or shopping. We didn't have any books. I didn't hunger for anything though, because I didn't know there were other things. I played on the volleyball team and played a few games, but I didn't do very well at that because my temper was kind of bad. I listened to the radio, then when I was 14 I became interested in boys, and had a serious boyfriend from the time I was 15 until I was 18.

When you were attending church regularly did you feel that God was a real presence in your life?

As soon as I reached what I guess you'd call the age of reason all of that just evaporated for me, and I went from being a total believer to doubting every word of it. It was the '60s and a spirit of liberation was in the air, so I just shook all of that off. There was something about that time that made for individuals. Regardless of whether you were a woman, a man, a kid, religious or not, there was this sense of "I don't have to do this any more, it's just bullshit."

That was one of many things that changed for me when we moved to Florida. After we'd been there two years I quit school, got an apartment by myself, and got a job at Webb City, which was "the world's most unusual drug store." It was owned by this guy Doc Webb, and Webb City had everything – mile-high ice cream cones, a shoe shine stand and barbershop, groceries, toys, a talking mermaid exhibit, lingerie – it was amazing.

While I was working there my mother died of lung cancer, and after she died I had to give up my job and my apartment and move with my family to San Antonio, which was a small town in central Florida with a population of 300. My older sister Muriel made it clear she wasn't going to help raise my younger sisters so it was assumed I'd do it, but my father resented me for taking my mother's place. It was a nightmare, and was the hardest period of my life. That went on for a year and half, and then my father married this woman who was a good mother to my sisters, and I have a lot of gratitude and respect for her. At that point I moved to Tallahassee by myself.

How did your mother's death affect you?

It was just devastating, although she was really absent in a lot of ways. In my childhood memories, she's usually not in the picture. I think Muriel got the first-baby treatment – the "You're cute, you're pretty, oh look, she's laughing" – then when I came along it was like, "Oh look, there's another one." I've always felt like I was completely on my own, but I did love my mother a lot. Just before she died she got involved in politics, and it was interesting that she went through this cathartic period at the end of her life. She'd always been a chronic depressive who had no exterior life at all, but during the last few years of her life she suddenly started doing volunteer work for the Democratic Party and painting. Then she got sick and died.

Do you think depression is a medical condition?

Absolutely, but it can also be self-induced. People are just starting to realize how delicate the brain and nervous system are, and that drinking a little bit when you're 14, taking drugs, smoking pot or eating weird food are all capable of throwing it out of balance. And, if you do any of those things in excess at a young age you definitely alter the ability of the brain to perform. The brain's not even formed at the age of 14.

Does every generation carry the weight of its ancestors?

I think they do, and I think that's particularly true of children of first-generation immigrants. If they're lucky, that generation is able to deal with some of the psychological damage and hopefully they don't pass it along to their kids. I had many years of therapy and I think it helped me, but some things are never resolved. I no longer get involved with people who belittle me or men who dominate me. When I met Jason we were together immediately, and he could've easily turned out to be the wrong person for me. If he had been, however, it would've taken me about three months to figure it out and I would've broken up with him because I don't need to do that again. But I discovered things in him that I hadn't seen in other people, and that made it worth pursuing. I've been searching my whole life to find a relationship like the one I have now.

How many times have you been in love?

I don't know because I don't know what the definition of that is. Have I imagined I'd met the perfect person and together we were gonna fill all those holes? Yes, millions of times. There are people I've never even met who I imagined would be that person. But you have to fill those holes yourself with other parts of yourself, and I believe it's possible to do that. You really have to work at it though, physically, emotionally and mentally. And some days you just have to say to yourself, "Look, you live in a house that you own, and that's enough right there, so shut up and stop worrying."

So, it's total fiction, this notion that there's someone out there for each of us who's a perfect fit and can heal those deepest wounds?

Yes, it's total fiction and I think most people know that. Anecdotal evidence suggests that if you tell a roomful of people to select the people they feel most comfortable with, all the alcoholics will congregate, and all the other specific personality types with their specific problems will gravitate towards each other. The weird thing is that the traits you find most attractive in a person eventually become the things that tear you apart, because those are the things you're trying to fix in your mother, your father or yourself. And once you realize you can't fix those traits that drew you to this person, those traits become intolerable. People fall in love with alcoholics over and over again, and then can't accept that the person won't stop drinking.

Are people capable of changing?

Oh yeah, people change all the time. I've changed. I don't hate myself any more, and I'm no longer absolutely terrified every waking moment that something bad is about to happen. I no longer believe I'm the worst person alive and that I'm going to hell, which are things the church taught me. One thing I'll probably never get over, because it's constantly being reinforced, is that women are responsible for the downfall of the world because Eve gave Adam the apple. In my school we were taught that women are responsible for mankind's fall from grace, and that's why we suffer horrible labor and will always be worthless.

Has the feminist movement achieved anything in terms of changing that?

Feminism has split into two divergent camps: one is the Camille Paglia sex worker, porno, stripper thing, and the other is the Andrea Dworkin no make-up thing. A generation of women are confused about what liberation actually is. Women think if they strut around with no clothes on they're liberated, but they're conforming to stereotypes created by men for men. It's like we've regressed back to the '50s in that women would rather be '50s-style helpmates than be the person out in front. After 35 years of fighting the feminist battle I guess they concluded it just wasn't rewarding to be like L7, or be in an all chick band.

Guys who look up to women in bands generally have a Madonna/whore thing going, although there are a few exceptions. Kim Gordon is considered a goddess among a small faction of the intelligentsia, and some men appreciate me as an original punk rocker warrior chick. But that's a small group of fans that have accumulated over 25 years. In all the years I've been performing, I've rarely been approached by guys because men don't want to be in some girl's shadow, and they aren't into one night stands with a powerful woman. A lot of guys respected me and found me attractive, but they don't run backstage wanting to have sex with you.

What made you move to Los Angeles in 1976?
My sister's ex-boyfriend called and said he was moving to L.A. and he wanted to know if I knew anybody who might want a ride there because he needed someone to share gas. So I sold my car for $300, paid my back rent, which was $150, and left.

What was your first day in L.A. like?
I'd gotten a ride from Florida to Concord, California, and I took a bus from there to a Greyhound station that no longer exists in Santa Monica. It was pouring rain and there was thunder and lightning, all of which seemed normal to me, having just arrived from Florida. Of course, it was years before I saw weather like that in L.A. again. It was real early in the morning, and I got to my friend Faye's apartment in Ocean Park, and there were two girls she'd just met from Texas living there with her and her boyfriend in this one-room studio apartment. It was an idyllic little spot, and she'd gone to a thrift store and bought a kid's bed with a wagon wheel for a headboard, and I slept on that bed in the kitchen. It felt good to be out of the car because it was a long drive from Florida in a Pinto.

How long did it take for the city to feel like home?
I make it a point to feel like I'm home as quickly as possible whenever I arrive anywhere, even if it's a motel room. You embrace the concept of "this is my place, I'm lucky to be here, and isn't this a strange place to be?"

How has L.A. changed over the years you've been here?
The main change is that it's become much more crowded. I'm a tolerant person, but I must admit I do have an immigrant problem. It's not with any specific race – I just feel the whole world has been mismanaged as far as where people are and where they're going, and just how wrong everything is. I just get mad at the amount of people there are. The architecture and historical aspect of the city have also been almost completely wiped out due to the uncontrolled growth of the Reagan years. Mike Woo and all those people just ruined L.A.

So, do you think the world is going to hell in a hand basket?
Not really. Some of the alarmist rhetoric of the last fifty years was productive, but a lot of it was overdone. The world isn't as bad as we think it is when we're having a bad day, but the environment definitely is suffering, and the unspoiled places in nature are rapidly disappearing. At some point people will have to realize we do all live on the same planet. The thing that worries me is the death of ideas, and the horrifying possibility that people are going to run out of substance and creativity and we'll be left with an endless recycling of things. For instance, think about Glenn Miller for a second. Think about big bands just for a second. Think about a 30-piece orchestra playing flawlessly live, and being super creative, and everyone being a virtuoso, and then think about trying to find something like that now.

The mainstream degradation of women is the worst part of what's going on – that, and the dumbing down, selfishness and stupidity. It's a real Sodom & Gomorrah now, and this is becoming the norm. Once the hyper-sexualization of the culture has been exhausted, what comes next? Live slaughter? It's a vicious cycle where people get used to something, so they push it further. It's like a roller coaster – it takes more and more to excite people, so they push it until the 'g' force is painful.

What was the first punk rock you heard?

The Ramones, Patti Smith's *Horses*, the Velvet Underground, Iggy, the New York Dolls – I heard all that stuff around the same time while I was living in Florida. It's all mixed up in my mind how punk rock started, but I think the Ramones were the purest launching point into punk.

How did punk affect you as an ideology?

We all know that when you're younger your politics are more idealistic, and I was way more idealistic twenty years ago. I was insanely idealistic up until very recently, actually, but I've come to realize that there can be an element of false hope in idealism. Some parts of the punk rock mentality don't mean much to me any more, but other parts of it were valuable, and I still believe in those things.

Was there a moment when you gave yourself permission to be a singer?

I always wrestled with my legitimacy as a singer because of the way the press wrote about my singing, and the way women have traditionally sung. Generally speaking, women are considered singers if they have incredibly great voices. Men, on the other hand, are considered singers if they have a story to tell. I think I was able to sing because punk rock made that do-it-yourself thing acceptable, and you didn't have to be a great player or singer to be in a band. Punk valued substance over form, and that was a new thing. The Beatles, Elvis, and Brenda Lee were all great singers – it wasn't as if any of the people in rock'n'roll couldn't sing. But with punk, what you had to say was more important than having a polished voice. I was young, everyone around me was doing interesting things, and revolution was in the air. Because I grew up during the '60s I grasped what was going on, and I saw there was an opportunity to be a poet – and a different kind of poet from the ones I saw. I had respect for those poets – my favorite poet is Anna Akhmatova – but I wasn't an academic, I didn't want to become stuck in the small world of poets, and I didn't fit into any literary scene. So, when John Doe wanted to use my words for songs I said yes.

During the early years of X, did you feel you were working out the anger you felt over the difficulty of your childhood in your performances?

I didn't know I'd had a difficult childhood, but I definitely hated society and everyone in it, and there was never a second that I wasn't just incredulous at how wrong everything was. Yeah, I was pretty much mad about everything.

Was John Doe a crucial person for you in terms of valuing your sensibility?

He definitely was, but I was also determined not to let go of my stuff. I didn't want this guy I hardly knew to make songs out of my words and have that be the end of it.

Did he encourage you to sing?

The whole band did because they believed the dynamic between the two voices was going to work eventually. John's voice was almost too good for the kind of music we were playing and the times we were living in, and the music needed this crazy, chaotic element to make it stand out. But all of this is an intellectual reflection on something that happened without a lot of thought – which isn't to suggest we didn't work incredibly hard. X rehearsed three times a week, and John and I worked every day writing songs, and practicing endless rounds of choruses of songs. I hated him for it and didn't want to rehearse after dinner every night, but we were trying to get to the point that the notes and melody were so second nature that we didn't have to think about them when we were performing. We could just go.

Do you still have reservations about your voice?

No. You make progress over time, you do some things you're proud of, other things you think you could've done better, and say fuck it to the mistakes. I'm not the kind of singer who never hits a bad note, but I make up for it with believing in the song. I took voice lessons for ten years and I have pretty good pitch nowadays, but that's something I had to work on. It's a weird instrument, the human voice, a really strange instrument.

You and John married in 1980: did you enjoy being married?

It's hard to be married when you're young because you're so romantic and idealistic. There are good things about being married to someone you're in a band with, because you travel together and you're working towards a goal, but 23 is a little young to be married. That was the choice I made, so I don't regret it.

As a young girl did you look forward to being a bride?

No. I think in life you hook up with people because of what they do. Lets say you're immigrants, for instance. Why go to the new country alone? Why not go together and make a life? Or you're in a band, and you need somebody you can trust and don't want to go out every night and be with a different person. You want some kind of sanity in your life somewhere. I think we kept each other fairly sane, and John was really supportive when my sister died. On a weird level I think we were more soul mates than lovers.

Do you still feel that bond with him?

You're asking me on the wrong day [laughing]. I sometimes think of us as being like brother and sister. We don't even have to say anything to each other and we both know there's this seething resentment going on for no reason. But we still do our work together, and you know what? Nobody's perfect.

When you fell into the L.A. punk community of the '70s did you feel as though you'd finally found your tribe?

I really did feel a kinship with those people, at least as much as I'm capable. I'm pretty much an outsider, so it's always hard for me to feel like I belong, and the people in that scene were so disparate. It was like every kind of person. But there were wonderful moments. You could hardly know a person, then one night you'd spend several incredibly meaningful hours with that person, and for the next two years you'd just say hi when you saw them. Drugs and alcohol had a lot to do with the social climate then, but that community was also full of people who were seeking out incredible moments.

What was the common ground people met on?

Common ground and motivation are two different things. Common ground is when people's motivations synch up, so common ground can be tied to things like the pursuit of fame, picking up lovers, or scoring drugs. We did share the bond of being underdogs and getting recognized for it, and we shared an appetite for being perpetually excited, and feeling like every minute of our lives was a statement against something we thought was false. I think most of those people were caught up in that feeling, and we all thought it was fun to play and go see bands. It was definitely more fun then to go see bands.

Can you mark the point when the spirit you're describing began to dissipate?

X began hooking up with bands from other cities after we started touring, so we got a perpetual party going on around the country and it was still fun for us, even if things weren't happening in L.A. But I'd say that original group of people began moving apart around the time grunge started in the early '80s, and places like Raji's began booking bands. I never stopped meeting people and having fun, but after the hardcore scene kicked in I couldn't go to certain shows any more, or play with certain bands. That didn't ruin our existence, though, because our career took off around that time.

When your marriage to John ended was that a difficult decision for you, or did you just feel it was time?

I didn't want to be in the band, I didn't want to be with John, and I wanted to be with someone else. I wish I'd just got in the car and driven away for six months somewhere and then come back. Yes, it was hard, and for a while I was the one who ruined X. However, the band didn't actually break up until John signed a solo deal with Geffen. What happened was, John wanted a solo career and everybody was hot on the idea at that point, which was around 1987. Elektra wanted him as a solo artist and they said they'd also sign X as part of the deal, but Geffen was only interested in John and wanted nothing to do with X. So, John signed with Geffen and that's when X first broke up. That's when I did my two solo records with Rhino. [Guitarist] Billy [Zoom] was already gone so he didn't care, and [drummer] DJ [Bonebrake] is a musician 24 hours a day. From the day he was born to the day he dies he'll always play music with total integrity with whoever he feels is worth playing with. He has his ups and downs with what happens with X, like the rest of us.

How did you feel when people started relating to you as a hero?

I wasn't aware of that until recently. In fact, initially there was some resentment of me from punk girls, especially hardcore girls. I've always felt more a peer than a hero to people. The people who came to see us when we toured America were usually around the same age as us and it was like, "Hey, we're your age, we're doing it, you've got a band too, let's go have a drink." A few years ago people started telling me they were in love with me when they were 12 or something, but I had no idea young kids were into X, and never thought of myself as the person on the poster on someone's bedroom wall.

What do you think you represented to those boys who had a crush on you?

The dark side of the superhero woman, somebody who was the opposite of the girl next door and was wild. And I was wild when I was in my 20s and 30s – I had to be to overcome my fears. I had to be super-fierce, and it was almost like being a superhero. Talk about mild mannered, paranoid and scared. Then I'd walk out onstage with all my gear and just roar.

In retrospect, did the original punk community disappoint you?

No. What do you expect from a bunch of kids? It was a wonderful group of people who had an amazing youth. But then, everybody's youth is a nice experience, even if they're in college or something.

How much of that music holds up for you today?

All of it: F-Word, the Weirdos, the Zeros, all that stuff stands up – for what it is, of course. It stands up the way Love or the Doors or Laura Nyro stand up for me.

What's the most widely held misconception about the early punk scene?

That it was violent. The violence began in a different part of the state, with different bands and a different group of people, in an entirely different era.

Can you pinpoint the places in time where punk rock began and ended?
It hasn't ended, but neither has the beatnik era or the hippie movement. Punk
didn't die then come back; it just kept evolving and changing.

***How do you feel about the inaccuracies that are invariably built into
history? There's been a good deal of misinformation published about the
L.A. punk scene and it's regarded as fact by many people.***
Reality is subjective, and that says it all. It's relatively easy to illustrate the
discrepancies between fact and fiction in fields like math and science, but that's not
the case when it comes to life and art. People who kept diaries are the best sources
of information about the past, because they wrote things down as they happened, and
their memories aren't distorting things. The human memory does tend to distort things,
plus, I don't know how sane people are to begin with. Some people knowingly lie
about their own past in an attempt to make it seem more dramatic, and in doing that
they inadvertently reshape the pasts of others. You know – the parties were wilder,
they were friends with people they barely knew – this is how rumors get started, and
eventually they're treated as fact. All because one person decided something might
look good on their biography. Artists are notorious for misrepresenting themselves to
get more attention and seem more phenomenal, artistic and eccentric.

That suggests that most people feel that who they are isn't enough.
They wouldn't be onstage if they didn't feel that way. An element of narcissism
is required for a person to get onstage or in front of a camera, and narcissists are
incapable of seeing the world through anyone's eyes but their own. Consequently,
their sense of reality is often radically different from that of the people around them.

Does everybody feel outside?
I'm not sure. Girls who belong to sororities and guys who pal around with guys
and do guy things obviously feel a need to belong and share some kind of unified
vision. It's possible those conventional-looking people have the shakiest sense of self
of all, and that's why they need to congregate the way they do. Maybe rigidly conformist
people with no independent streak at all actually do feel freaky. I don't know.

How did losing your sister change you?
Because of the people she knew in New York, I think the projects I would've
ended up doing would've been more eclectic, and I probably would've spent more
time on experimental writing and visual art. I'm not a painter – I'm a drawer, an
illustrator and a collage person, and I like taking things that don't go together and
putting them next to each other. But that's just a guess. Initially, her death made me
a much more heavy-hearted person. It was really hard, but I don't think it altered the
path of X. I found refuge in touring, being with the band and with my little gang of
friends.

Who are your favorite artists?
I like Soutine a lot. He was a filthy Jewish guy who was poor and didn't fit in
anywhere, and that's part of the reason he isn't better known. I love all the great
artists, and love that experience of being in a museum, then you turn the corner and
there's that painting and you can't believe it's real. I love Toulouse de Lautrec – he's
my favorite illustrative artist – and I like Frida Kahlo, and Andy Warhol because he
was so ironic and over the top. He knew how to manipulate the press, and every artist
since has tried to do it, too. But I hate people who craft a life to bolster their artistic
credibility. I try to ignore those people.

How did getting money change your life?

When you're 21 you don't need money. What is there to buy? It wasn't like there was fashion or anything, and there was one color of red lipstick. Maybe you'd go hunt down some Mary Quant. But it wasn't a consumer society like it is now. We drank and ate and went to movies, tried to keep our cars running and paid our rent, and got everything we owned in thrift stores. It was the post-hippie days of three people sharing a house that cost $300 a month. Things didn't cost a lot, but the world has changed since then, and ever since the Reagan era America's been subjected to an ever-increasing fleecing of the public. Contrary to what some people seem to think, X never made money.

How did becoming a mother change you?

Having a baby is without a doubt the best and the worst thing you can go through in life. It's a physical upheaval from the time of conception to the end of breastfeeding and it's a constant challenge. You don't care about that, though, when the hormonal stuff takes over – the only thing you care about is you and your kid. This is hormonal stuff, ancient, protective stuff, and it's like "get out of my way, I have a baby inside of me." You're so profoundly in a state of awe of the human body, and the mind goes from one extreme to another in ways you can't conceive of unless you've experienced it. The miracle of conception and birth is beyond any other experience, and the idea that your baby could die at any second if you screw up is beyond any fear you could have. And, the love you feel for that baby is beyond any love you could feel for another person. The agony of day-to-day parenting can be so intense that some days you just want to kill yourself because, although you can walk away from anything else in life, you can't walk away from a crying baby or a child going through a difficult phase.

My son Henry is the best thing that ever happened to me and he's the thing in my life I'm most proud of. I never wanted to be a mother until I got pregnant with Henry. I met his father in New York in 1987 when we did a movie together called *Salvation*, and shortly after that we got married and had Henry. When he was six months old we moved to Sandpoint, Idaho, which is a small town in the extreme north of the state. I didn't want my kid to go to a public school in Hollywood and wanted him to grow up in a healthy environment, and Viggo was very into that too, so we moved to Idaho in 1988. Part of the time there was tough because we were very poor. Viggo's acting career was just getting started, and I had an infant. I did both of my solo records while I was living in Idaho, then I moved back to L.A. in 1991.

Why is there such terror around aging in this culture?

We live in a society that values youth and beauty to the exclusion of everything else, and doesn't recognize wisdom. And what do older people have that's of value other than their experience and wisdom? In fact, that seasoned perspective is seen as threatening because it suggests that the new thing isn't really new. Kids don't want some old person telling them their new thing isn't really new, and capitalism doesn't want people with memories or histories coming around fucking up the marketplace.

It's the shock of a lifetime when you hit your late 30s and realize you've become invisible. If I walk into a bar in L.A., I could stand around for two hours without one person saying one word to me. I know older women in New York who have a great sense of style and are oblivious to the cultural bias we live with here in Los Angeles, the superficiality of this town, and the selfishness of people. Nobody wants to talk to you here unless they think you can help them with their careers.

Where would you like to live?

I'd like to live in any small or medium-sized town somewhere in the South or the Midwest where these issues don't exist, and if you brought them up you'd be told that anybody who thinks that way is stupid. I love small town America, and the small towns are still there. The Wal-Mart is on the edge of town, and there's still a hardware store downtown. It's unfortunate that Wal-Mart put a lot of people out of business, but people can't afford to buy things that aren't made in China any more, and that's just the way it is. They can't afford hand-made things made in America by guys in coveralls, so that just doesn't exist any more.

What aspect of your personality has created the most problems for you in life?

The part of my personality that turns negative. I'll sometimes be walking down the street and I'll see someone laugh and I'll think, "What the hell are you laughing at? What's so funny?! God, people are sick."

What's the most significant historic event that's occurred over the course of your life?

This is an imprecise answer, but I'd have to say the '60s. Whatever that thing was, that incredibly all-encompassing political, musical, artistic, soul-altering vibe, it was unbelievable. It wasn't a single event, like somebody being shot or a war erupting. It was a worldwide upheaval that triggered a spontaneous change in the spiritual life of the world, and we're still experiencing repercussions from it. You can see it in things like holistic medicine, and the fact that people feel they have the right to question their own lives and to change them, to quit their job or move their family to an island. I was in a small town during the '60s, and I became aware of it through Life Magazine, FM radio, and television, and I could see the effects of it in every single person I encountered when I stepped outside that small town. It filtered into our town, too, and made people question the war that was going on. It was in the air in a way nothing else probably ever will be. Punk was a direct result of it too, and was simultaneously a positive and a negative reaction against it.

Not everyone was galvanized into action by the '60s. What gave you the courage to strike out and invent a new life for yourself?

I don't really know. I just made decisions as they came to me. I'd think of something and I'd do it – and in retrospect, I realize I did lots of stupid things that could've killed me. I can't believe I'm still alive, really. You never do know what's going to happen next, and I question every day why I'm here. But if you stop for one second and think about all the good things you've seen and experienced, and the people you've known, life makes a little sense. Sometimes I feel as if I've been directed in my life, which is weird, because I have no clue why I feel that way. Maybe everybody feels that. But when I make decisions, I always feel as if someone else is actually making the choice, and I'm just there going along with it.

What does it mean to you to play X's music now?

Unless I'm tired I still like the songs emotionally, and I still like playing them. It makes me really, really happy to play.

Have your goals changed as a creative person? Do you want to accomplish different things with your work now than you did 20 years ago?

Not really. I still want to create something that's such a perfect expression of what I felt that whoever comes across it will feel the exact same emotion and intensity, get it completely, and say, "Yeah, me too."

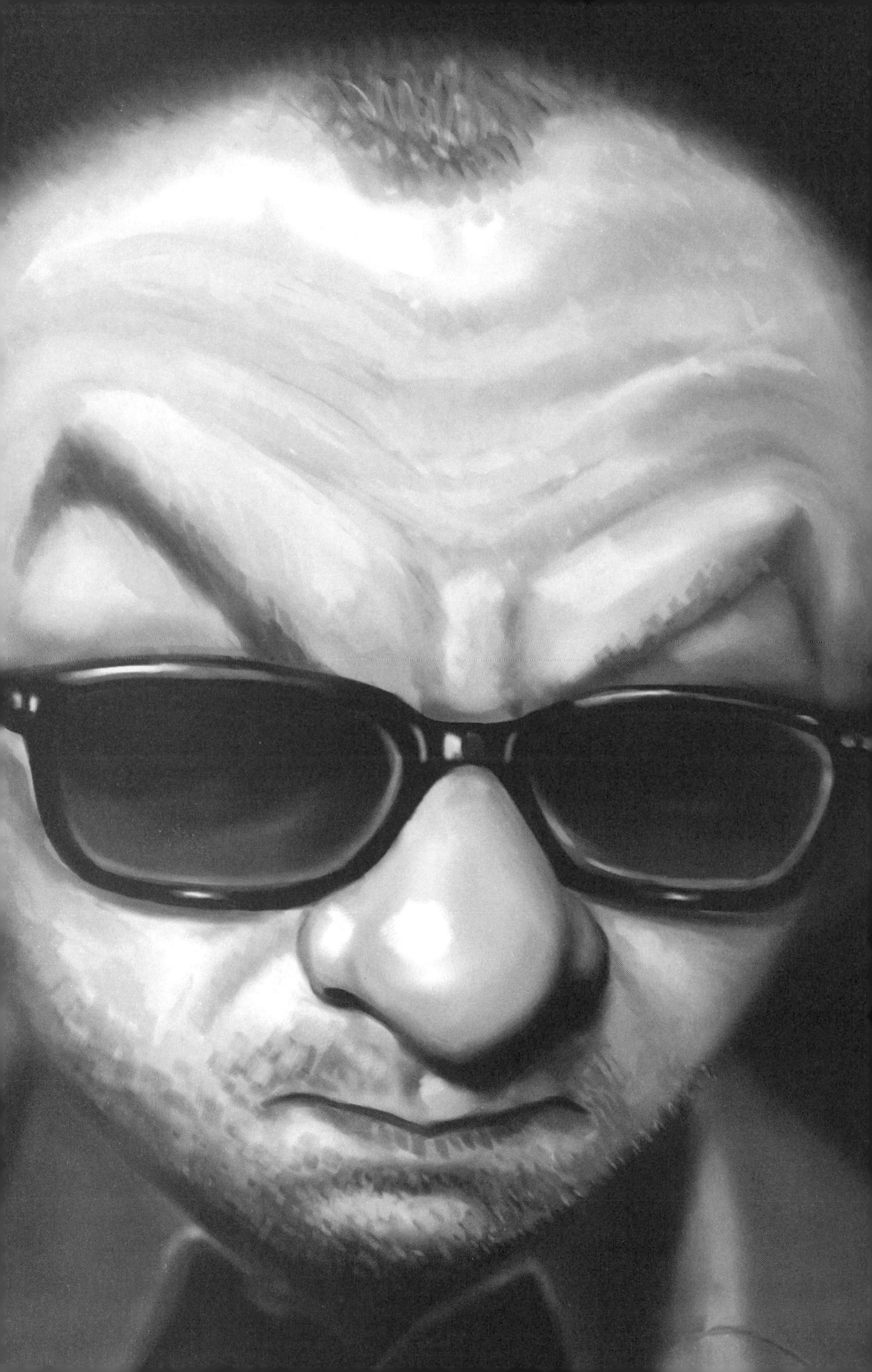

Elvis Costello

....

During my tenure as music editor at Wet Magazine in the late '70s, we published an interview with Elvis Costello in which he made the observation that "most journalists lack the imagination to grasp anything beyond the most obvious aspects of your personality, and then they exploit it as a kind of image." Costello never made any secret of his contempt for the press, so I shouldn't have been surprised by the experiences I had interviewing him. What that experience amounted to was the overwhelming sense that he was watching the clock and couldn't wait for me to be gone. He gamely answered every question I asked, but I could tell he didn't enjoy it.

My first interview with Costello took place in February of 1986 at a posh hotel on Central Park. The album under discussion was King of America, and Costello was a newlywed at the time, having just married Cait O'Riordan, the former bassist with the Pogues. We spoke again three years later in a conference room at Warner Brothers Records in Burbank. Costello was accompanied by his wife (he and O'Riordan parted in 2002 after sixteen years of marriage), a stern presence who didn't utter a word for the entire 90 minutes we sat together.

Costello was born Declan Patrick Aloysius MacManus in 1954, in a working-class section of London. He was an only child, his father was a musician, and his parents divorced while he was growing up. In 1977 he made the cheeky move of changing his name to Elvis and released his first album, My Aim Is True, which established him as one of the great songwriting talents of his generation. He's a staggeringly prolific artist as well, and as of 2003, he's written hundreds of memorable songs and released 34 albums.

–1986–

What's the most insidious idea currently being peddled by popular culture?
That things will be all right and we'll all be very cozy if we just allow ourselves to be sucked back into the comfy fireside embrace of Mr. Eisenhower's sitting room. I do a version of an old song called "Eisenhower Blues" that addresses this.

Are you an easily enchanted person or do you resist allowing your emotions to be manipulated?
I've certainly been easily led in the past but I'm not easily led at all now. I think that's a change for the good.

Is vanity a vice, an affliction, or a hobby?

That depends on who you are. If you're Joan Collins then vanity is a career. If vanity holds you back from doing your best then I suppose it's an affliction. And, if your vanity is somehow detrimental to other people, then it would be a vice.

Why is originality so highly valued in art?

Is it valued? Who by? Critics are the only people who care about that. Go to the Museum of Modern Art and look at Pablo Picasso's work and tell me that he valued originality. The Dadaists and the Surrealists parodied previous forms and used them for their own ends with ruthless abandon – all those people stole loads of stuff. I don't think they cared a damn about originality. Perhaps they realized they couldn't help but be original, and that's part of what made them great.

Do you enjoy being famous?

I'm not really a pop star, I'm just a singer, and though you get a degree of celebrity out of that, I don't think I'm particularly famous. There was a time around 1979 when I could've been railroaded into pop stardom, but then my career fell apart due to my being an idiot and an obnoxious drunk. People didn't want to be associated with me. People do sometimes recognize me on the street now, but it's not a trial to me. Occasionally I get an overly anxious person who gets a little too excited, and I get some funny mail and the odd strange phone call, but it's not a tremendous tribulation.

How important is a larger-than-life image in making an audience receptive to your work?

It's true that music is easier to sell with an exaggerated image, but so what? I was considered a more marketable commodity when I first appeared and they had five pictures of me and five opinions of me, but I refused to be a monkey on a stick or be bound by rock 'n' roll ritual. As far as what my image is now, the writer David Fricke recently made the comment that I'd been "consigned to genius purgatory," which I thought was great. There seems to be this attitude of "oh yeah, we know he's good, but who cares. He's not pretty or anything, so let's watch this other band instead."

Ideally, how should the press function in relation to music?

It should shut up and listen. Additionally, the press should be more than just an information channel because there's such a lot of terrible stuff put out that shouldn't go un-criticized. The press tends to imagine itself as being much more important than it actually is, and occasionally it behaves in an outrageously presumptuous way. An album of mine was recently reviewed by a guy in England who clearly hated the record, but he wouldn't just leave it at that. He went on to worry about my troubled mental state, my artistic block, and my love life. I haven't got any trouble in my love life. Over the past couple of years my first marriage reached an unhappy level. I failed in keeping that relationship going, but hopefully she and I will be stronger apart than we were together. And I love the woman I'm married to now very much, so I'm not unhappy and I'm not an alcoholic. I can drink a lot when I want to. I don't take any drugs. That London critic didn't just imply these things – he stated them as if they were fact.

The case has been made that the creative drive and an impulse towards self-destruction are intertwined; do you think there's any truth to that?

No. That's just a romantic myth perpetuated by artists lacking in self-discipline.

But that's not to say there isn't an element of creativity to be found in the pursuit of self-destruction. The two things are not mutually exclusive.

How do you explain the fact that two people can have a comparably painful experience, and one will come away embittered by it, while the other comes away having gained some wisdom?

I don't think it's that black and white – a number of other changes could be in play as well. You could be wiser and more bitter, or you could just be stupid. And of course, some people are more masochistic than others and enjoy the pain of, say, unrequited love. They come away neither wiser nor more bitter, but with something they can build a life style or a career out of. Many people do that you know.

What's the most important thing you get from your work?

I get it out of my head and therefore am a bit less neurotic. I can be very neurotic, a terrible hypochondriac, all those sorts of things. I'm a human being and have all the usual vanities and frailties. But I'm not going to make them into a career.

In Ernest Becker's book, The Denial of Death, *he presents the theory that what sets artists apart from other people is that artists tend to see the world as a problem – a problem they must address – whereas other people simply don't perceive life that way. Do you think there's any truth to that?*

No, I don't agree with that – I think that artists are the problem. They're the thorn in the side of the world and the ones with a problem. The world carries on as it would.

What's the biggest obstacle you've overcome in your life?

My own stupidity and selfishness – and I definitely haven't overcome either of those obstacles permanently.

How did getting money change your life?

Having money meant that I didn't have to rely on dishonest people to pay me the money they owed me. Consequently, I was less prone towards the physical violence I'd felt driven to when I'd been cheated.

You're knowledgeable about a wide variety of music, much of which is quite obscure. How have you educated yourself musically?

My dad was a singer with a band that did covers of the hits of the day, so when I was a kid I fell heir to many more records than the average kid. I spent all my money on music when I was a teenager, and when I first came to America I plundered all the secondhand shops for records that aren't available in England. These days, I might mention someone I admire in an interview and people will quite generously give me rare records and tapes of artists I like.

How do you explain the current trend of social conscience in popular music? [Ed. Note: This interview was conducted during the heyday of Band Aid, and Rock the Vote.]

Because there's such an unwillingness on the part of the people who should be doing something about the ills of the world, a few altruistic people and a few self-serving people have conspired for their varying motives to try and do something about these ills. The only pity is that these benefits have largely been a horrible travesty of what we call music. The music has all been well-intentioned rubbish.

What do you see as being the dominant characteristics of America?

I could say something glib and cutting – that's probably what people anticipate from me – but I think you should try and be more compassionate with people. I'm not trying to write big songs about America, but one of the recurring themes on my album, *King of America*, is the idea of travel and exile. Someone once asked me what I thought of America and I replied that it was a brilliant mistake. There's no country on earth founded on more righteous and noble principles, and there's never been a country where those principles have been abused as horribly as they are here. I'm not saying it's a total failure because the thing isn't over yet, but for something that started out so well it's gone down an awful lot. But that's just human nature and I tried to keep the commentary on the songs on *King of America* to a minimum because we've got no perspective of history. And even if I did, it wouldn't be right to go around making wild generalizations. After all, this is only pop music I'm up to.

I get the impression you spend most of your time in airplanes, recording studios and hotel rooms; do you feel cut off from nature?
No. I only have to look in the mirror to see nature.

What sort of landscape do you find most compelling?
I don't like being on the side of a mountain and I'm not fond of heights. I like lakes and being by the sea, and I like being in bed. What I like best of all is the landscape of the warm body of the woman I love.

–1989–

How has being happily married affected your creative practice?
For the better: the idea that you have to suffer to write well is a load of nonsense. I've been unhappy and written some good songs, but if you have to put yourself in that condition to write then it's very unnatural, not to mention dishonest. It's like this romantic notion that artists are supposed to be poor. This French photographer I know recently asked me to write captions for a book of photographs of musicians he's doing, but I couldn't find anybody in the book that I knew well enough to write about without it being from the removed point of view of the fan. Then I found a picture of Chet Baker, who I have worked with, and it was a very sad picture. He looked in a very bad way. I then found a picture of Miles Davis sitting in the back of a limousine looking very scary and invulnerable. Jazz critics used to say Chet Baker lifted his style from Miles, so I wrote this thing that juxtaposed the fate of one man against the other. Chet had just died around the time I was writing this. At the end of it I wrote, "I've never met Miles Davis and I suppose I never will, but I admire him in my own way and hope they always send the big car for him." In other words, forget your romantic notions. Musicians like this shouldn't walk in the gutter because it's too dangerous.

What were the key factors that shaped your worldview as a child?
I grew up in a fairly creative environment. I had a religious upbringing, and I suppose that was important during a period of my life, although it wasn't traumatic when I grew away from it. I went to Catholic school and was an altar boy and a choirboy, but I don't have any difficulty singing secular songs. Catholicism no longer has any meaning for me personally in my everyday life, although I must admit that I still recognize aspects of it turning up now and then in my attitudes. I'll occasionally find myself thinking, well, that went deeper than I thought it did! But my religious life hasn't been nearly as traumatic as those I know some people have experienced.

What's the first piece of music that made an impression on you?

My mother says it was Frank Sinatra's *Songs For Swinging Lovers*, and I do remember hearing that music. She claims I used to want to hear it before I could properly talk. She also says I could work the record player before I could walk.

How do you see your interests evolving? Are there themes you found compelling early in your career that no longer seem so intriguing to you?

That's hard to pinpoint because methods change along with interests, and the way you write can influence the things you're interested in writing about. You might be working in familiar territory, but the writing technique you employ can lead you to emphasize a different aspect of the subject.

What do you see as the recurring themes in your music?

I don't look for links or connections; I look for contrasts. I'm not a particularly introspective writer, and I don't think my songs are about philosophical issues. Most of the songs are emotional reactions to things, often current events, and because of that some people call them political songs. I deny that definition because I don't see politics as separate from life. We're all part of one thing, although we do respond in different ways. I respond differently from the man who beats his children because something has driven him to the point that he can't tolerate it any more. My response is a song, which is perhaps as much of an empty gesture as kicking the cat. It might be empty, or it might give somebody some satisfaction to hear a mean thing said about somebody they don't like, like hissing at a witch at a pantomime.

What's currently inspiring you?

You're asking conceptual questions, and I don't think like that, so I'm stretching to accommodate your thought processes. I don't think in terms of, "What's my inspiration?" or, "How do I see myself?" But, to answer your question, I'm reading a book called *Testimony*, which are the memoirs of Dimitri Shostakovich. It's a very interesting book and I recommend it to anybody involved in any sort of business because it makes you realize that any tribulations you think you might be suffering are really rather dull. Shostakovich had a very tormented life. He wrote a symphony when he was 19 and was a celebrated hero through the revolutionary period in Russia, then because he'd been influenced by things Stalin considered Western, he fell out of favor. Stalin feared anything complicated because he was basically quite stupid and a crazy tyrant, so during the course of Shostakovich's life he went from being the most acclaimed writer in Russia to being declared an enemy of the people. He spent decades fearing for his life because artists in Russia were often killed for causing offense. Compare that with what we see today, little bands crying because the record company didn't send the limo…

Do you find there to be an inordinate amount of whining in the record business?

Oh yeah. It's hardly grueling compared with going down a mine, is it? It's an awful lot harder to do just about anything compared with being in a band. The most difficult thing about doing something creative is the monotony and the boredom, a lot of which is self-inflicted. Of course, nobody asks you to be an artist, but one of the reasons I keep writing songs is because I'd rather do this than have to work for somebody performing a task I found totally meaningless. I used to work in a cosmetics firm as a computer operator, and I worked in a bank. This was many years ago when I was 19 or 20, and when the money was delivered to the bank I was instructed to blow this little whistle if there was a robbery. Who do you think they'd shoot first if there was a robbery? And that was a cushy job! It was very easy but it was also incredibly boring. The one thing about being a musician is that although there are moments of boredom, and I have to go up in airplanes which I absolutely loathe, and you sometimes meet people who don't know one end of a song from the other, and I occasionally get impatient with people who want everything laid on a plate for them and want to measure everything by something else they already know – other than these things, which are irritating, this job is a snap compared with what someone like Shostakovich went through. He never knew whether his next creative impulse might be the one to send him to his death. Then there's the kind of job my grandfather did. He was a gas-main layer before the Second World War, and when the bombs started going down over Liverpool there were millions of open gas mains. Somebody had to go down and fix them, and if a mine decided to explode, you had about 30 seconds to get out of the way or you were dead. I could've been doing that job.

Why have musicians been elevated to such an exalted position in society?

Are you aware of the fact that that's only true in America? This is a peculiarly American phenomenon, and there's much less of it in England. It's not a particularly healthy development, but I don't think it's the worst thing you could have either. I think it has to do with the fact that this is still a very young country, and therefore the culture you've created entirely on your own is important to you. Older people like rock 'n' roll in America much more than they do in Europe. I'm not saying people aren't wild about Michael Jackson and Bono in Europe, but beyond a certain age they're embarrassed to admit it. In America you can imagine your state legislator coming home and putting on his Allman Brothers album, whereas that's almost inconceivable in England. Over there, they're more likely to go to the opera, which is perceived as intellectual and elegant. I would add that although many people do regard musicians with an unhealthy degree of reverence, the public loves failure as much as it loves success. They like to see people taken down a peg and they like to see Elizabeth Taylor get fat. I wrote a song called "Suit of Lights" which is about this sort of morbid embrace of celebrity.

Does pop culture give people false expectations of life?

Absolutely, absolutely, absolutely! And, as far as what can be done about that, I suppose we could start with burning down Pepsi-Cola.

What percentage of your life is given over to music?

It doesn't consume my every waking moment, although during periods such as this it seems to. I'm always working on something, but that doesn't mean I don't have time to walk in the park or go for a swim. You still do the mundane things like cook your dinner, go to sleep – that takes up a fair amount of time everyday, just being asleep. I don't sing in my sleep. Yet.

What would you like to change about your life at this point?

I'd prefer to be in Dublin in our new house. We bought it last year and still haven't had time to move in. The house has a lot to do with what I'm doing right now; doing press will help my new record reach a wider audience, and that in turn will help pay for curtains for the house. See, I'm a professional musician. It's what I do for a living, but I'd usually rather be at home. In between touring this year I might get to visit the house and look at it wistfully in the rain.

When was the last time you surprised yourself?

The other day we went for walk in Muir Woods in Mill Valley. We were happily following these trails beneath a canopy of redwoods when suddenly I found myself walking along this very sheer cliff. I actually have vertigo so I'm afraid of heights, and I was surprised that I was able to get to the end of that trail. For me it was a very precarious thing and I didn't enjoy the rest of the walk because heights make me nervous.

What aspect of your personality has created the most problems for you in life?
My selfishness – I'm intensely selfish.

Some people consider selfishness a virtue and think it a necessity in order to do creative work.
Single-mindedness is a virtue, but there's a false assumption built into your question. I don't think that one specific aspect of one's personality is apt to consistently prove more or less problematic. At one time, jealousy might create problems; another time it might be selfishness. People are too complicated to be discussed in such black and white terms because they're constantly changing and responding to the circumstances and stimuli around them. You might see a film with a beautiful woman in it and lust for her, then you see that same woman with your best friend and you wouldn't covet her. The way we define our emotions shifts in relation to what's happening around us.

Do you find it pointless to discuss human nature in psychoanalytic terms?
I don't believe in psychology and don't see any value in it. I agree with what James Thurber said: leave your mind alone.

Do you feel you've successfully shaken the image of the misanthropic young man that seemed to dog you for several years after the debut of your first album?
Yes. Personally, I felt free of that image about ten minutes after I got stuck with it, but I did spend years explaining myself to people – and I still have to, to some extent, because people are dumb. With some people no amount of explaining is going to make the slightest difference to them because they refuse to hear anything that challenges what they already think. There are, of course, many people who understood my work from the start and always saw the humor in it. And, I should also say that I was sometimes self-defeating in the methods I employed.

Do you feel it's been a disadvantage that you came into prominence as part of the punk movement? Have you been taken less seriously because of that association?
Only in so far as people expect you to represent some clique that I never saw as really existing. And if it did, I certainly wasn't part of it.

What do you think you represent to people?
I have no idea. You'd have to ask people. I don't have any conception of an audience and never have. I occasionally meet people who buy my records or come to the shows, but I can't make generalizations about them. Sometimes people are slightly more earnest than I think is good for them and put too much store in what I say. In a sense they're asking me to do their thinking for them. Yesterday I was on the radio in San Francisco with this guy who was like a character out of a frat party movie. He was a big, goofy party animal and was really funny. So I joined in and started talking

the way he was talking, like, "Yeah! Awesome, let's rock!" Some girl rang up complaining that this guy was insulting me; that I was a serious artist and should be treated with more respect. I had to gently explain that we were having fun and there was nothing wrong with this game we were playing. We were on the radio and I don't expect to reveal my inner soul on the air or in this interview. Bits of yourself may be revealed because of the intelligence of the interviewer, or perhaps because you're relaxed and having fun. Personally I think a damn sight more is revealed in just fooling about. It's like seeing home movies of Stravinsky playing tennis. Those things can really give you a new perspective on a person.

What do you regard as your central strength as an artist?

I never consider if there's a flaw or fallacy in the way I work, rather, I consider if there's a flaw or fallacy in what I'm saying. I'm more interested in content than in mechanics. For instance, I wrote a song called "Satellite" that's about a difficult subject – a chain of pornography. I was aware of the fact when I was weighing up how to write the song that it required a lot of cunning to get such a large subject within the confines of a song. So, while I don't worry about technique, I do consider whether or not I have the strength to take on a subject. Or, take a song like "Tramp the Dirt Down," which is very much an outpouring of bitterness. After I initially spewed it out – and it was almost like a vomiting out of emotion – then the craft part of it came into play. The strength of the song is its intensity, while the craft makes the emotion comprehensible. The two things are either in or out of balance. Sometimes you put them out of balance intentionally, but one isn't more important than the other.

Do you have structured work habits?

No. They vary every time I make a record or even write a song. "Tramp the Dirt Down" literally came out in one ten-minute burst. With other songs, a tune might suggest certain things and then a story will start to unfold itself. Often I'll realize that I need more tune because the story is bigger than I'd originally thought it was, and I need to accommodate this very long story – to build up some drama to reach a peak, then bring it down and reach another peak. I'm aware of using technique, but I don't favor any one technique in particular. That's irrelevant to me.

What was the central idea you had in mind when you went in to record your last record, Spike?

In the time that elapsed between *Spike* and the record that preceded it, *King of America*, I traveled quite a bit, did a few small tours, and collaborated with quite a few people, all of whom taught me one thing or another. In accommodating all these people's points of view about music and subject matter, I learned a lot about my own writing. But actually, the most instructive thing I did incidental to pursuing my next record was the soundtrack to a film called *The Courier*. I asked T-Bone Burnett to produce *Spike* with me, and in playing him the demo tapes I'd put together I happened to play him some instrumental music I'd written for the film. That instrumental music allowed me to mess around with sound without the usual constraints. I wasn't dealing with issues like song structure or lyric, and was basically just coming up with lengths of music. It was very liberating for me and T-Bone immediately said that was the method I should employ for *Spike*.

That comment suggests that as a rule, when you go in to make a record you don't feel a sense of complete creative freedom. What sorts of things do you feel constrained by?

Songs often insist on moving in a particular direction, and you can often recognize the direction a song favors from the first time you play it on an acoustic guitar. Beyond that, there's a deeply ingrained, ritualistic aspect of rock 'n' roll or country music that demands that you follow certain patterns. The challenge is to get a new fix on the pattern, or occasionally, to throw the blueprint out the window altogether. Most often you use a part of the blueprint. Perhaps you'll cut out a section of it and move it over to a side of the page, then juxtapose it with something surprising.

Does the freedom you felt working on the instrumental film score have to do with a fundamental difference between songwriting and composing?

I suppose, although I wouldn't presume to say that I know how to compose. For *The Courier* I basically just juxtaposed a few sounds and melody lines, then conveyed my ideas in a very simplistic way to an arranger, who then scored my ideas for strings. It was a process that taught me a tremendous amount, and I'm quite pleased with some of the juxtapositions I came up with – like a swing brass section combined with a drum machine, and string drones with discordant vibes. There are so many interesting musical ideas you can never incorporate into songs unless you're making art songs, and of course, then they're impenetrable to people for other reasons. One of the great things about film music is that people expect it to almost have the quality of sound effects. For instance, if you listen to the film music of someone like Max Steiner [a film composer of the '30s and '40s] it literally mirrors every action that occurs on screen. That's also true of cartoon music, which is often absolutely brilliant in the way it illuminates every action of the cartoon in sound.

Is songwriting a form of storytelling?

I consider these songs a form of storytelling but that hasn't always been true of my songs. Quite a lot of the records I've done have been like taking pictures, and a few were like moving pictures. *Imperial Bedroom* was like an out-of-focus camera. When I was making that record I was aware that was what I was doing in the way I laid the words out, but I never explained it then because it sounds sort of pretentious, and there's no point in giving the game away. It's better for people to sort things out for themselves. Some people look at the lyrics and say, "This is incomprehensible to me." Others say, "Yeah, this is a series of images that go together to form a montage." If you start making demands as to how your records are listened to it defeats the purpose of using those more obscure techniques. My recent record has songs that are told very directly with no irony, and there are other songs built around a sense of mystery and mood. But, with all songs, there's very little ambiguity about the point of my songs, or my position in relation to it. Even when I speak in the third person those things are easy to see. On the other hand, a lot of the time when it says "I" in the song it isn't me at all. See, I would be quite happy to make records that didn't have my picture on them, but people seem to need to identify you with the person in the song. They want you to feel bad like you feel, and good like you feel. So, while I don't want to disillusion anyone, I have to confess that I don't feel remotely like many of the people in my songs. The characters in "God's Comic," "Chewing Gum," and "This Town," for instance, are very unlovely and I wouldn't want to be them. Actually, I don't think I'm any of the characters on my recent record, although in my least optimistic moments I suppose I identify with "Tramp the Dirt Down." In that song it's me speaking directly, whereas in a song like "God's Comic" I'm speaking through characters – God and a comic. Then there's a song like "Satellite," and I really do believe the little prayer that the song contains: "the satellite looks down right now and forever/what it has pulled apart let no man tether his own body to his dream/ his dream to someone else." I do believe that, so I suppose I identify with that song.

A few of your recent songs are based on real life incidents; how much freedom do you grant yourself to interpret or fictionalize those events?

As far as I know I didn't fictionalize anything people could check. The song most clearly drawn from real life is "Let Him Dangle," which is based on an actual case. I drew the details in the song from one interview with the central character's sister, and didn't research the story exhaustively – I'm not Norman Mailer. If you become obsessed with double-checking everything and are more concerned with accuracy than your emotional responses then it isn't songwriting.

What did you learn in working with Paul McCartney?

To explain myself a bit more clearly. I also learned all kinds of rather dull things about technique.

Were you a big Beatles fan?

Yes, but I wasn't intimidated by him. He wouldn't have called me up if he didn't think I could do the job, and the only person I have to let down is myself. Paul's just a human being who plays the guitar, sings well and writes great songs.

You recently commented: "my morbid dread is getting lumbered with that crass track that becomes popular and you have to play it forever more." Why do artists buckle to the commercial pressure to rerun the hit?

What I meant was that in a weak moment you might decide to make the lowest common denominator kind of record – and of course, there is no pressure to do that. The only pressure is your own greed to finally get the reward for all this righteous work you've done over the years. So, in a weak moment you decide yes, I'll do the record with Mutt Lange or whoever it might be that month – I don't even know their names any more. And suddenly you have a big mainstream hit and you have to find some way of integrating it with the rest of your music. The closest I've come to having a hit was "Everyday I Write the Book," and "The Only Flame in Town," neither of which fit in with the rest of my music. I don't play those rhythms naturally, and those songs were artificial efforts to make radio records. It was the only time I'd done that and I was sort of happy when the plan failed.

You also recently commented that "In recent years, rock's become an amazingly conservative music." In your view, what's led to this state of affairs?

For starters, there's this thing called rock. How interesting is a damn rock? Rock 'n' roll was an exciting euphemism for a very basic thing – sex, and the rhythm mirrored that. Rock, on the other hand, is a thing you dig up from the ground. A rock is not a very interesting thing to stare at, yet we've put it up on a big, bloody plinth. And the further up the plinth you put it the more boring it gets. Then there's all this measuring that goes on, all these awards and halls of fame – it's all a big mausoleum. Originally rock 'n' roll was a celebration of life, it was beautiful, disgusting, exciting, thrilling and dangerous, but it's been calcified with greed and the unwillingness to take risks. No one seems to have any faith that if they jump off, something will bear them up, so now people just want to keep turning it out. It's like, once they perfected the Model T they stopped making Model V and W; people bought the Model T so that's the one they made. Things have been extremely narrow for a long time – since Elvis went into the army really. From time to time somebody breaks out and things get less narrow for a while, but most people perceive any sort of breaking out as an ugly boil on a smooth, porcelain face.

Are we about due for an explosion in music now?
I don't think it will ever happen in music again.

Would you agree that it happened in 1977 with punk, which launched your career?
Yes, it happened then, but for how long? It had about three good weeks, which is about the length of time it took for business to step back, take a deep breath, and then clone a load of people that looked, smelled, and tasted the same, but were basically nothing. Then there are the individuals like myself that kind of cling to the underside of it like barnacles. I kind of think of myself as a rock 'n' roll wombat.

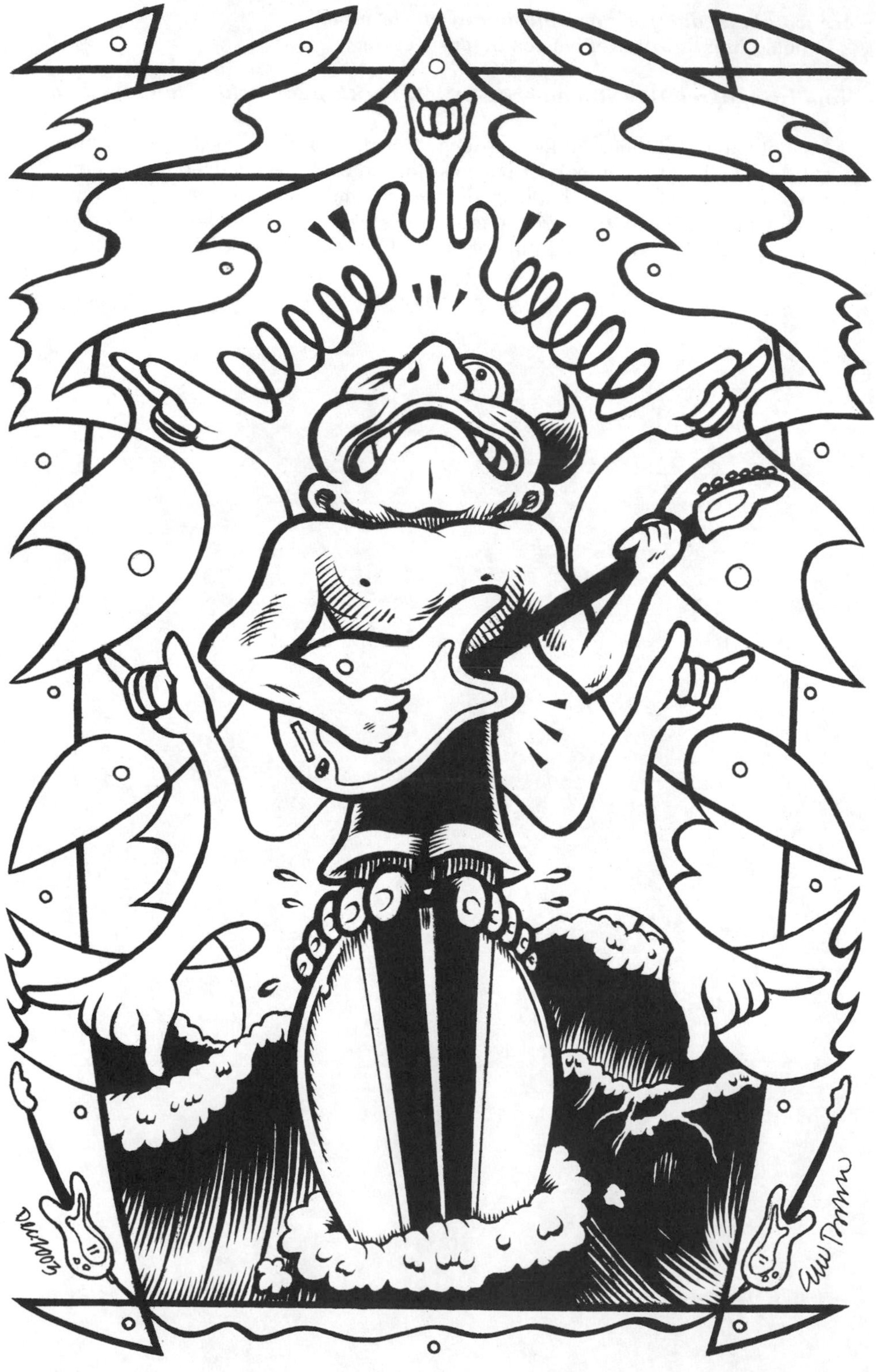
Dec 2003

Dick Dale

....

Dick Dale was born in Boston, Massachusetts in 1937. In the mid-'50s he moved to California, formed a group called the Deltones, and devised a reverb-heavy guitar style that led to his being crowned "the king of the surf guitar." Dale developed a huge and devoted following in the beach communities of Southern California, and he was a regular fixture on a circuit of dance halls where surfers congregated. In 1962 he released his first album – Surfer's Choice – and it included an instrumental track called "Miserlou" that became an international hit. Things were looking good for Dale at that point, and over the next three years he put out five more albums, all of which sold well. That upward trajectory came to an abrupt halt in 1965, when Dale was diagnosed with cancer and dropped out of sight. He didn't record or perform for more than a decade.

In 1980 I tracked him down. He was living in Balboa Beach, California, in a sprawling mansion built in the '30s by the Gillette family, who made their fortune in razor blades. At the time Dale was living with a Tahitian dancer named Jeannie, a leopard, a jaguar, and a bunch of tropical birds, and he seemed to have made a full recovery from his cancer. An intensely energetic man in his mid-'40s, he was involved in several projects, including renovating his house, taking photographs, running the nightclub he owned, performing occasionally, getting his pilot's license, studying martial arts, and surfing. Music, however, was at a pretty low idle for him at that point.

By the end of the '90s things had changed for Dale. His career was given a huge boost by Quentin Tarantino, who featured Dale's song "Miserlou" in his 1994 film, Pulp Fiction; Dale released two new albums shortly after that film introduced him to a new audience. He also got married, to a woman named Jill, and they have a son named Jimmy. Jill plays bass, Jimmy plays drums, and they sometimes join Dale onstage.

–1980–

COUNTRY MUSIC

I'm from Boston, Massachusetts. That's where I grew up, and I came out to California in 1954 during my senior year of high school and got a job as a heat-treater. After that I joined the National Guard and was in their crash group for six years. I didn't really choose to be in show business, but I've always had a talent for learning instruments. I can play every instrument there is and sound like I've been playing it for years – not because I'm especially learned, but because of the feeling I put across. My dad saw that, so he encouraged me in that direction. I'm left-handed so I had to teach myself because essentially I play backwards. I started out playing country music, which I still love, because it has a very personal feeling. It's crying music, and that's why it never goes out of style.

IN THE BEGINNING

When I started out there were no places for groups to perform because anybody who played the guitar was considered evil. This was around 1955, and I guess I was 19 at the time. I was living in Los Angeles and I used to ride my motorcycle down to Balboa on the weekends. Then I got a beach house down there, formed a trio, and we started out playing at the Rinky Dink Ice Cream Parlor for seven dollars a night. I asked for a raise and got fired instead so I went next door, to the Rendezvous Ballroom, where Stan Kenton was playing. Up until then he'd been about the hottest thing going, but the support for the big jazz shows was starting to fall off. Those old jazz groups like Kenton were a thousand times better than me musically, but I'd hit that primitive beat and people would go crazy because they could feel the rhythm I got from surfing. We started working the Rendezvous for free, playing in our bare feet, then the city officials started giving us a hard time, saying our music was a bad influence. We needed to spread the word before we got buried, so we started going to high schools. In fact, I created the first assemblies in California – they'd never had assemblies before us. For most of the assembly we'd play the tame stuff – "Sugar Blues," and "Begin the Beguine" – then, just before we closed the show I'd say "here's what we're doing at a place called the Rendezvous" and we'd totally cut loose. The school bosses would be screaming, "Shut the curtain!" and the kids would be going ape. We'd get kicked out of every school, but not until I'd made my point. After four months of traveling around to schools we were drawing 4,000 kids a night at the Rendezvous.

LOVE AND MONEY

In the early part of my career I made a million dollars a year, and each year I lost it. It went to managers, agents, the government – people who were just sticking me. I was just a little surfer kid who loved to do all kinds of things, and I was so busy creating I could've cared less about money. I started the Righteous Brothers, Jan & Dean – a lot of people. Glen Campbell played backup on my albums, and the Beach Boys were little kids who'd come around and watch me and try and figure out what I was doing. The kids used to say, "The bandstand is his pulpit." I used to have meetings at my house in Costa Mesa. I'd have kids from nine years old to 25, kids who'd been in reform school, hanging out at my house, swimming and playing pool. We formed a cult called Michella, which means "God is with you." It got to where there were about 1,500 members, with kids as far away as Nevada. The reason I did that was because I had 18 stitches in my head from one time when I surfed down south at a place called Wind'n'Sea. I was a new person, an outcast, so the locals gave me a hard time and made me wipe out. I wanted to form some kind of brotherhood so that when you went somewhere you weren't known you'd be greeted as family. I wanted to achieve that, and it was beginning to happen when I became seriously ill.

HEART ATTACKS

At one time I had four minor heart attacks, then the fifth one dropped me and I found out I had a cystolic heart. They gave me these pills to take, but I said, "Screw this crap." The last time I felt a spasm coming on I thought, "Well, if you're gonna take me, you're gonna take me swearing at the world." I went out to my backyard, grabbed all the weights I could, lay down on my diving board and started pumping weights like crazy, in the middle of a heart attack. And let me tell you, it worked.

ED SULLIVAN

I was the first person onstage who was actually made by the people. When the big shots came up to me and said, "Okay son, we're gonna take 75%," and all that bullshit, I said get lost. I had the top five singles on the charts at one time. I had no promotion at all, but Time and Newsweek came around, Life magazine did a big spread on me, and then I got a call from Ed Sullivan. I was the first rock-type group to appear on his stage. I played an instrumental and he got so excited that he walked over and shook my hand, and he'd never shaken anyone's hand before that because he was always in pain from the war. That was a first, and it was told to me by his people. From then on he started shaking everybody's hand.

DICK GOES NATIVE

I was named "King of the Surf Guitar" because I created the sound of surf music – I was the first. It's a sound that's in my head and it's always been there. When I moved to Balboa in 1954 all the guys I was hanging out with were surfers, so I started surfing. I could feel the rumbling out there, and I wanted that in my music, that sort of primitive feel that goes all the way back to the natives. When the natives had their sex orgies, they would hit a beat and keep that rhythm going until their bodies started pumping, and before you know it they'd become totally sexually activated. Whenever I do anything I do it with my whole body. I'm always behind my band pushing them to feel pain when they play, to get into the son-of-a-bitch.

ELVIS

The first time I met Elvis, we sat up until five in the morning with him showing me his favorite scriptures. Things written before time almost, before Napoleon, saying there would be long-haired groups that would infiltrate and undermine kids through music, telling them to use drugs and kill their mothers and fathers in their sleep.

CANCER

Thirteen years ago I was given three months to live. I had rectal cancer, and two weeks before I went into the hospital my uncle died of the same thing. They cut 14 inches out of my rectal tract, and removed six tumors and seven cysts. How did I survive? I quit smoking, went to a psychiatrist, studied hypnosis, went to Hawaii to recuperate, and prayed a lot. You gotta believe in something, whether it's a stone, yourself – whatever. But as far as I'm concerned, everything comes from the Maker.

JIMI HENDRIX

Jimi Hendrix said he patterned his style after Dick Dale. When he died he wrote it down: "I patterned my style after Dick Dale."

BLIND FAITH

I was raised in the church but I drifted away from it for a while. I disbelieved there was a Maker and studied a lot of different religions trying to find an answer, because I had to live in blind faith. And that's what I learned – that when you come right down to it, you have to live on blind faith, because anything can be disproved. I feel the Maker gave me the tremendous strength I have. I sleep only three hours a night. I've never had marijuana or anything artificial in my body in my life, and that's hard to believe coming from an entertainer. But when I get onstage I can go like a son-of-a-bitch. I loosen the teeth in my gums when I play. I've actually snapped microphone stands right in half and never even felt it. I've always wanted to be a preacher because I get great satisfaction out of sharing what I've learned. I've had people come to my dances in wheelchairs, kids who've never moved in their lives, and they sense this rhythm I put out and they start moving. Music is the greatest way on earth to reach people – it's a teleportation out to the people in front of you. You can make them laugh, cry, anything you want, as long as it's real, because they can always sense it if it's not from the heart. In 26 years I've never once planned a show. It's always off the top of my head. I say a little prayer: "Lord, you're pulling the strings, now let's go." And bam! I'm flying!

THE RAMONES

The Ramones came and played a club I own in Garden Grove, California, and when I saw the kind of people they drew, it just blew me away. I wanted to put them all in a cage and gas them! Or at least shove ''em up against a wall and show them what discipline really is, because you've got to have discipline within yourself, and discipline means going against the grain. Anybody can mellow out and float down the river – look at a leaf. But we're like those damn fish that die trying to swim up the river. Living is never an easy job but the rewards are phenomenal.

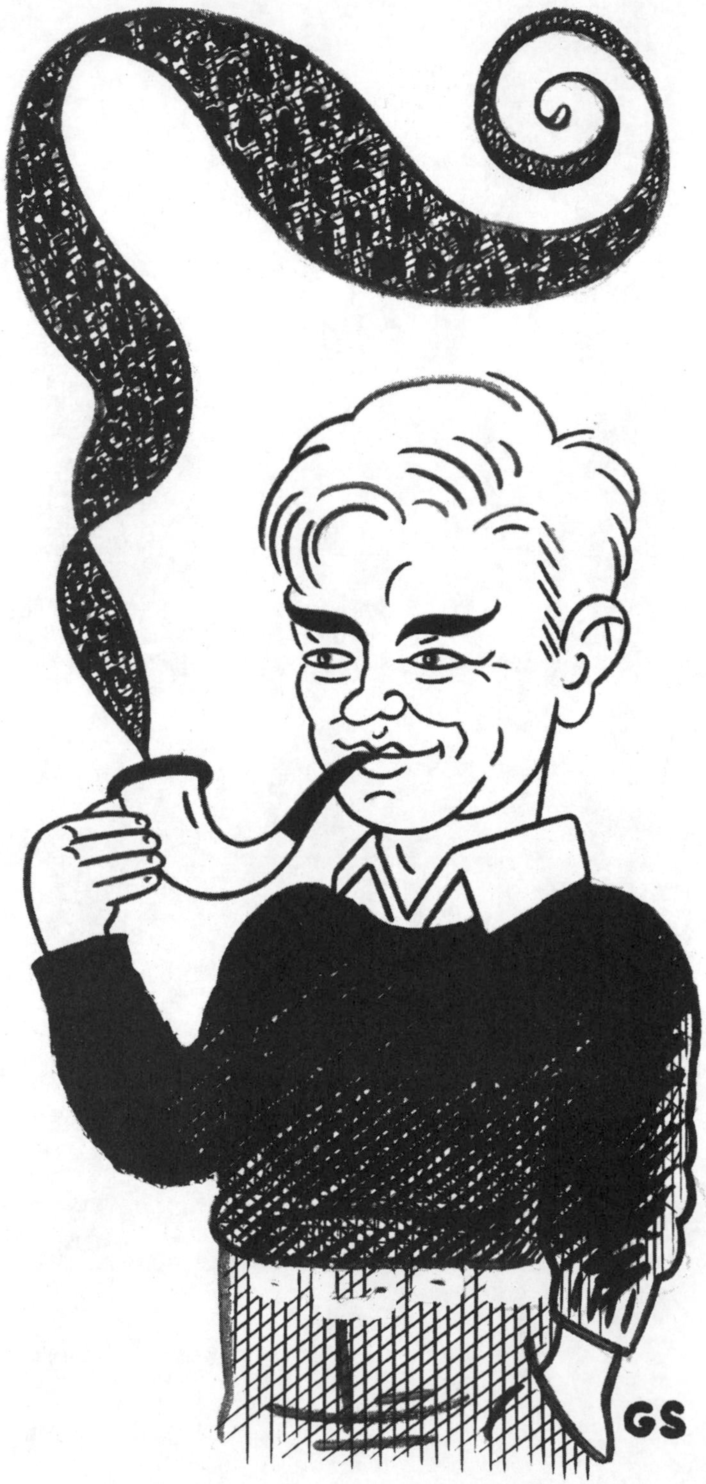
GS

Jacques Derrida

When people talk about crazy French intellectuals and esoteric superstars, when they stumble over the word deconstructionism in Entertainment Weekly and wonder what it could possibly mean, when college kids around the world are forced to figure out what it means, as they have been for the past 20 years, it all goes back to Jacques Derrida. One of the reigning figures of intellectual life of the last 35 years, Derrida is the father of Deconstructionism, a controversial system of analysis designed to dismantle language and reveal the biases and false assumptions embedded within it. Rooted in the belief that language is freighted with things we're either unable or unwilling to bring to full consciousness, Deconstructionism is a flexible methodology that can be applied to any and all texts – and indeed, the impact it's had on literary criticism is equal to, if not greater than, the mark it's left on philosophical discourse. Routinely dismissed as an infernal machine by those unwilling to take the time to follow its logic, Deconstructionism nonetheless appears to be here to stay. Derrida has published 45 books that have been translated into 22 languages, and they've secured him a permanent place in the pantheon of world philosophy.

Born in 1930 to a family of assimilated Sephardic Jews in what was then French Algeria, Derrida began questioning intellectual prejudice at the age of ten, when Algeria was overrun by France's collaborationist Vichy regime. At that point Derrida was expelled from school after being informed by a teacher that "French culture is not made for little Jews," and he went on to a career as a disruptive, inarguably gifted student. At the age of nineteen he moved to Paris to study philosophy at the Ecole Normale Supérieure, and it was there he met Marguerite Aucoutourier, a psychoanalyst whom he married in 1957. Attending the school from 1952 through 1956, Derrida focused primarily on the works of the German philosophers Edmund Husserl and Martin Heidegger, and his writings on their work led to a scholarship to Yale in 1956.

Derrida returned to Paris in 1960 to teach philosophy at the Sorbonne, and two years later he declared his independence as a philosopher with a translation of Husserl's Origin of Geometry, appended with a book-length introduction that dwarfed Husserl's essay. In 1967 he laid out his central ideas with the publication of three seminal books – Speech and Phenomena, Writing and Difference, and Of Grammatology – that catapulted him to the center of the philosophical discourse. In 1972 he took a teaching post at Johns Hopkins University, and since then he's divided his teaching between Paris and the U.S.

I interviewed Derrida in April of 2002 in his office on the campus of the University of California at Irvine. He's been a visiting professor there since 1986, and, in a major coup for the school, Irvine acquired the Derrida archive in 1990. U.C. Irvine is a sterile complex of wide, empty boulevards leading to bland buildings seemingly devoid of human life, and Derrida's digs there are modest, to say the least. His office is housed in a structure organized around long, narrow, absolutely silent hallways with identical doors running down both sides. It's straight out of Jacque Tati's Playtime. There's one chair at the end of each hallway, and I sit on one of them while I wait for the great man to appear. He does, precisely on time, and we enter a tiny, airless room with zero décor and no window. Surely a man of his stature deserves a window! Piled on the desk is a copy of Thomas Hobbes' Leviathan, along with texts by Montaigne, Aristotle, and Deleuze & Guattari. I don't think he does much frivolous reading.

Given the fearlessness and ambition of his work, Derrida is surprisingly humble and approachable in person. He's a self-effacing, soft-spoken man with beautiful manners, and I've never met anyone who took language more seriously, or weighed his words with greater care. He's an extremely earnest conversationalist, and he listens as intently as he speaks.

Can you recall the moment when you first realized that god, as the word is conventionally understood, was a notion you could never embrace?

To discuss this we must insist on that definition of god – as the word is conventionally understood. But yes, I can recall it. While I was growing up I was regularly taken to a synagogue in Algiers, and there were aspects of Judaism I loved – the music, for instance. Nonetheless, I started resisting religion as a young adolescent, not in the name of atheism or anything negative, but because I thought the way religion was practiced within my own family was fraught with misunderstanding. I was shocked by the meaningless way my family observed religious rituals – I found it thoughtless, just blind repetitions. And there was one thing in particular I found and still find unacceptable, and that was the way honors were dispersed. The privilege of holding, carrying and reading the Torah was auctioned off in the synagogue, and I found that terrible. Then when I was thirteen, I read [Friedrich] Nietzsche for the first time, and though of course I didn't understand him completely, he made a big impression on me. The diary I kept then was filled with quotations from Nietzsche and [Jean Jacques] Rousseau, who was my other god at the time. Nietzsche objected violently to Rousseau, but I loved them both and wondered, how can I reconcile them both in me? I've never been able to, of course, but they're still both very present in my work and teaching. I never left them.

In an interview he gave shortly after World War II but ordered withheld from publication until after his death in 1976, Heidegger said, "Philosophy after Nietzsche could offer neither help nor hope for mankind's future. All we can do is wait for a god to reappear. Only a god can save us now." Do you agree?

I wouldn't use the term 'a god,' of course, but what's interesting to me in this statement is that Heidegger was anti-religious. He was raised a Catholic but he vehemently rejected Christianity, so the god he refers to is not the Jewish, Muslim, or Christian god we know. He refers to a god who not only hasn't come yet, but perhaps doesn't exist. He gives the name of god to the one who is hoped for, and implies that the one who'd come and save us will have the name of god. Of course I don't agree with this if it encourages hope for salvation, but if the statement means that we're waiting for the arrival of an unpredictable one, and that we must be hospitable to the coming of this one, then I've got no objection. This is a form of what I'd describe as messianicity without messianism, and we are by nature messianic. We cannot not be, because we exist in a state of expecting something to happen, awaiting the arrival of someone whom we hadn't anticipated.

Do we set ourselves up for unhappiness living that way? There are many lives in which the arrival never occurs.

Even if we're in a state of hopelessness and despair, a sense of expectation is an integral part of our relationship to time. Hopelessness is possible only because we do hope that some good, loving someone could come, and that's undeniable. If that's what Heidegger meant then I agree with him.

Did you fear for your life as a child growing up during the second World War?

No. My experience during the war was difficult, but it couldn't be compared with what happened to the Jews in Europe. There was terrible anti-Semitism in Algeria and all the Jews there were expelled from school, but there were no Germans in the country, no concentration camps, no massive deportation of Jews. But the traumas occurred nonetheless. When you are expelled from school without understanding why, it marks you.

In Ron Rosenbaum's book of 1998, Explaining Hitler, *he suggests that meaning itself was Hitler's final and ultimate victim, because coherent meaning simply cannot be found in the Holocaust. Do you agree?*

I'll go very slowly here. I know there are philosophers, some of whom are my friends, who think that what was absolutely new in the genocide of the Holocaust was that it had no sacrificial structure. It was cold, rational, industrial, and it was given no sacrificial meaning. I'm not sure that's true. I'm not prepared to answer that question without giving it a good deal more thought.

What are the central questions philosophy came into existence to answer?

First of all, how to handle one's life and live well together – which is also politics. This is what was addressed in Greek philosophy, and from the beginning philosophy and politics were deeply intertwined. We are living beings who believe we have the capacity to change life, and we place ourselves above other animals. I'm critical of the question of the animal and how it's treated in philosophy, by the way, but that's another issue. Still, we think we're not animals, and that we have the ability to make decisions and organize our lives. Philosophy poses the question: what should we do to have the best possible lives? I'm afraid we haven't made much progress in arriving at an answer to this question.

In philosopher Peter Singer's controversial book of 1975, Animal Liberation, *he made the case that animals and humans should exist on an equal moral plane: Do you agree?*

I'm very much in favor of a massive change in our relationship with animals, but I don't believe in what's referred to as the rights of the animal. This concept of rights has its roots in the philosophy of [Rene] Descartes, which is precisely responsible for the repression of the animal. So while I'm full of sympathy for the plight of the animal, I wouldn't subscribe to a charter outlining the rights of the animal.

Are you a vegetarian?

I'm not a strict vegetarian, but I'm more and more inclined not to eat meat.

One could make the case that philosophy and theology are much alike in that both are systems of thought that have what could be described as tenuous ties to the physical world. What's the most significant difference between the two?

This is a huge problem. I used to think – and this is rather Heideggerian, and though I don't always agree with Heidegger, in this respect I do – that philosophy cannot be disassociated from ontology and theology. That's why Heidegger coined the expression ontotheology. This refers to the area where the ontological question of being merges with the theological question of the most important being. It's very difficult to separate these two strands of thought.

What's the difference between knowledge and wisdom?

They aren't heterogeneous, and you can know lots of things and have no wisdom at all. Between knowledge and action there is an abyss, but the fact that there is an abyss shouldn't prevent us from trying to know as much as possible before making a decision. Philosophy is the love of wisdom. Philia is love and sophia is wisdom – that's the way it defined itself at the beginning, so the duty to be wise is what philosophy is. Nonetheless, decisions don't depend exclusively on knowledge. I try to know as much as possible before making a decision, but I accept the fact that at the moment of the decision I'll make a leap beyond knowledge.

In a piece on Sir Karl Popper published in The New Yorker, Adam Gopnik commented that, "Popper believed that competing hypotheses fought each other off nobly while we watched; the reality is that competing hypotheses are mauled, and then one creeps away to die in peace. No one ever really changes his mind about anything; there are just more minds that think the new way. Behaviorism, Freudianism – no one refuted them, really. They just passed away out of loneliness." Do you agree?

No, I don't agree with that idea. I met Karl Popper in Sicily one year when we both received the Nietzsche Prize, and he made very little impression on me.

Did arriving at the set of understandings that you presented in your three books of 1967 enhance the quality of your life and bring you greater happiness?

I wouldn't say it made me happier, but it gave me the strength and motivation to continue. I lead a very active, exhausting life, and I'm sure I derive much of the energy required to maintain this schedule from the reception my work is given. People are generous with me and my work, and I'm sure I would collapse without that generosity. If someone had told me when I was twenty that I'd be doing what I do now at the age of 72, I wouldn't have believed it. I was more physically fragile then and I would've collapsed from doing a fraction of what I do now. The reception of the work gives me this energy.

Why aren't there any female philosophers?

Because the philosophical discourse is organized in a manner that marginalizes, suppresses and silences women, children, animals, and slaves. This is the structure – it's a fact, it would be stupid and unfair to deny it, and consequently there have been no great women philosophers. There have been great women thinkers, but philosophy is one very particular mode of thinking among other modes of thinking. But we're in a historical phase when things like this are changing.

Would you describe yourself as a feminist?

This is a huge problem, but in a certain way, yes. Much of my work has dealt with the deconstruction of phallocentrism, and if I may say this myself, I'm one of the first to put this question at the center of the philosophical discourse. Of course I'm in favor of ending the repression of women, particularly as it's perpetuated in the philosophical groundings of phallocentrism, so in that regard I'm an ally of feminine culture. But that doesn't prevent me from having reservations about some manifestations of feminism. To simply invert the hierarchy, or for women to appropriate the most negative aspects of what's conventionally viewed as masculine behavior benefits no one.

What's the most widely held misconception about you and your work?
That I'm a skeptical nihilist who doesn't believe in anything, who thinks nothing has meaning, and text has no meaning. That's stupid and utterly wrong, and only the people who haven't read me say this. This misreading of my work began 35 years ago and it's very difficult to destroy. I never said everything is linguistic and we're enclosed in language. In fact, I say the opposite, and the deconstruction of logo-centrism was conceived to dismantle precisely this philosophy for which everything is language. Anyone who reads my work with attention understands that I insist on affirmation and faith, and that I'm full of respect for the texts I read.

Your book of 1997, Cosmopolitanism and Forgiveness, makes the point that forgiveness that seeks any kind of response is not forgiveness at all, but is in fact a negotiation. This idea is very Buddhist in nature, as is the rejection of dualistic thinking that runs through your work. You've often made the point that life can't be reduced to either/or dichotomies, but rather, life is the vast, immeasurable territory that stretches between two opposing positions. Are you aware of the parallels your work has with Eastern philosophy?
Many people have commented on the relationship between my work and Buddhism, and Zen Buddhism in particular, but I must confess to having only a superficial knowledge of Buddhism. If Buddhism is a way of transcending binary oppositions, I would say yes.

With sufficient understanding of the Other, could the impulse to kill be erased?
The drive to kill will never be erased because it's part of the human animal. The human animal has a capacity for cruelty, and to make the Other suffer can be a source of pleasure. That isn't eradicable, but it doesn't mean we have the right to kill – and, one of the crucial functions of philosophy and thinking is to learn to handle and negotiate this irreducible drive. Cruelty is always there and we must do our best to control it and transform it into something good – and it can be transformed into things that are beautiful and sublime. When I write and teach there's an element of aggression in these activities, but I attempt to transform that aggression into something useful. Aggressive energy can be transformed into something more interesting than killing, and of course, you can kill without killing. I can kill the Other without putting an end to his or her life, and can be aggressive in a way that's not despicable.

Concepts of territory and ownership seem to be at the root of much human conflict; where did these ideas originate, and why do we cling to them?
These concepts have become quite destructive and while they needn't be abolished, they must be changed dramatically. The need for that change was central to politics throughout the 20th century. For many centuries the city was a crucially important center of activity and commerce, but with new technology that's no longer the case, and the politics of owning a place are different. Nevertheless, the place remains important. A friend of mine recently said there are two things today that can't be de-territorialized or virtualized: they are Jerusalem – nobody wants virtual

Jerusalem, they want to own the actual soil – and the other thing is oil. The capitalistic nation states live on oil, and although that could be changed, the whole society would collapse if it did. That's why oil is a problem. It's more of a problem inAmerica than it is in Europe, but we share the same concerns. Everything is always more in America, for obvious reasons.

What's the most significant historical event that's occurred over the course of your life?

Because it's relatively fresh in the collective memory, many people would probably say nothing comparable to September 11th has happened for centuries, but I wouldn't agree. This isn't to diminish the significance of that event. I was in New York just after it happened and was deeply wounded by it. I'm in love with New York, and although I never found the Twin Towers beautiful, I had a sentimental attachment to them and I'd taken many friends there over the years. I was staying in an apartment ten minutes from the site a few weeks after the attack occurred, and it took me a week before I had the courage to go there. Then, when I finally did go, my reaction was emotional beyond any political consideration. Since then, I've felt compelled to acknowledge this event every time I've spoken publicly. I can't avoid opening my lecture with a reference to it, and I'm very interested in how people perceive it, and why it's viewed as a monumental event. Is it a major event? I'm not sure what the answer is.

You've been with the same woman for fifty years; to what do you attribute the strength and longevity of your marriage?

Is it so exceptional? Neither my wife nor I have any special skills for marriage. What we have is love, so it's thanks to that, and to our children. For a long time I was against family and I lived for several years with the person who became my wife with no intention of marrying. It took quite a while for me to accept the notion of marriage.

Why does love die for many people?

Love doesn't die; rather, it becomes buried by other things. Sometimes it's buried alive, or it's buried by another love. There are periods when a love can be shared and be inscribed into a life, then that period ends. People take divergent paths and the love must then remain secret. It's buried, but not forgotten. I never stop loving the people I love. We're not speaking of sexual love here, but when I love someone, it may happen that I stop declaring it or making it manifest, but I'm faithful to love. I cannot not be faithful to love because I have a passion for memory and faithfulness.

Is the past more apt to be a source of pain or pleasure for people?

This differs from one person to the next, but I'm fortunate in that I have a happy relationship with the past. I even keep happy memories of difficult parts of my life that I know were terrible. I'd like to repeat my life, and would accept that everything be repeated endlessly, exactly as it happened: the eternal return.

How did becoming a father change you?

I wouldn't say it changed me, but it's been a major event in my life. My two sons are the most important things in my life, not only because I love them, but because both of them are extraordinary, exceptionally intelligent people. I'm intimidated by them and I'm always shy and anxious about their judgment. Both of them are philosophers, and they write – one is a poet who makes film. Their judgment counts for me more than anyone else's.

In 1997 you gave the filmmakers Amy Ziering Kofman and Kirby Dick permission to follow you around and film you for the documentary, Derrida, which was released in 2002. Why did you agree to be filmed?

I didn't do it out of a narcissistic desire, nor did I immediately agree to it. In fact, when Amy initially contacted me about doing the film I sent her a postcard telling her no, this won't be possible, but because my handwriting is impossible to decipher she misinterpreted the postcard as my saying yes! She finally did convince me, but I proceeded with deep reservations that had to do with the discomfort I've always felt about my image in photographs. I succeeded in publishing for almost twenty years without a single image of myself appearing in connection with my books, and there were two reasons for that. First, I had what you might describe as ideological objections to the conventional author photograph – a head shot, or a picture of the writer at his desk – because it struck me as a concession to selling and to media. The second reason was that I've always had a difficult relationship with my own body and image. It's hard for me to look at myself in photographs, so for twenty years I gave myself permission to erase my image on political grounds. Over the last decade, that became increasingly difficult because I was constantly appearing in public spaces at conferences attended by journalists, many of whom took pictures. It finally became impossible to control, and as I felt it was time to overcome this resistance I finally let it go.

Why are you uncomfortable with your image? You're often described as being quite handsome.

I'm happy to hear that, but it's not the relationship I have with my own image. I saw the film on the big screen the other day and there were moments that were terrible and I was horrified when I saw myself. I don't know if this warrants being printed, but when I'm filmed in profile it's more or less okay, however, some of the frontal shots of my face are ghastly. Nonetheless, I was pleasantly surprised by how successfully the film intertwines the private everyday life of family, with things less private – a trip I took to South Africa during the filming, for instance – and reflections on big subjects. The film has a consistent through line in that it continually questions the biography of authors. Should a philosopher have a biography?

How could a philosopher not have a biography?

Of course he has a biography, but the question I raise is whether we should publish it. Should he himself narrate his own biography? Should he let his own life be public and be interpreted?

How can you separate a philosopher's writing from his life?

I don't know if you can, but most classical philosophers did try to separate them, and some of them succeeded. If you read philosophical texts of the tradition, you'll notice they almost never said "I," and didn't speak in the first person. Philosophy is something empirical and outside, something else.

You don't think the philosophy is shaped by the life?

It is, but the private empirical life is considered an accident that isn't necessarily or essentially linked to the philosophical activity or system. From Aristotle to Heidegger, they try to consider their own lives as something marginal or accidental. What was essential was their teaching and their thinking.

There's a scene in the film in which you're asked, if you could hear the philosophers who've been important to you talk about anything, what you'd like to hear them talk about. You reply, "their sexual lives, because it's the thing they don't talk about," but when the interviewer then asks you about your own sexual life, you decline to answer. Why is this territory off limits?

I declined to answer not because I think these things must be hidden, but because I don't want to disclose the most personal aspects of my life while improvising in front of a camera in a foreign language. If I'm to discuss such things I prefer to sharpen my own tools – my writing. If you read me you'll find there are many texts where I address these questions in my way. I don't want to disclose everything, but I don't hide, and certain texts – *The Post Card: From Socrates to Freud and Beyond*, [published in 1980], *Glas* [1974] – are autobiographical. My own life, my desires and loves are inscribed in all of my writing – in a certain way, of course. They're not confessions, but I do take the risk of making my life part of what I write.

What's important to you today?

How can I answer such a question? Many things private, public and political are important to me. Today I'm concerned with what's happening in the Middle East and in France. As you probably know, the far right candidate Jean-Marie Le Pen came in second in the first round of the French presidential elections on April 21st, and this reveals something in my country that disturbs me deeply. But I think of all these things with a constant awareness that I'm aging, I'm going to die, and life is short. I'm constantly attentive to the time left to me, and although I've been inclined this way since I was young, it becomes more serious when you reach 72.

Have you made your peace with the inevitability of death?

So far I haven't and I doubt I ever will, and this awareness permeates everything I think. It's terrible what's going on in the world and all these things are on my mind, but they exist alongside this terror of my own death. And it's not just death – one struggles with aging as well, because it forces you to make decisions about the future. Yesterday I had lunch with the librarian at Irvine; then I had dinner with the dean, so we could discuss the future. I left my archive here, so during this lunch we had to consider events referred to as "beyond my lifetime," in terms of my papers. And with the dean, I plan to return next year, but the following year I'll be 74, and it would probably be wise to reduce my schedule at that point. These decisions must be made now.

At what point did you become an adult?

This is an intriguing question. I've always believed everyone has more than one age, and I carry three ages within myself. When I was twenty, I felt old and wise and full of experience but now I feel like a child. There's an element of melancholy to this, because although I feel young in my heart, I know objectively that I'm not young. The second age I carry is my real age of 72, and everyday I'm confronted with signs that remind me of it. The third age I carry – and this is something I only feel in France – is the age I was when I began to publish, which for me was 35. It's as if I stopped at the age of 35 in the academy and the cultural world where I work. Of course that's not true, because in many circles I'm considered an old, well-known professor who's published a lot. Nonetheless, I feel as though I'm a young writer who just started publishing, and people are saying, "Well, he's promising."

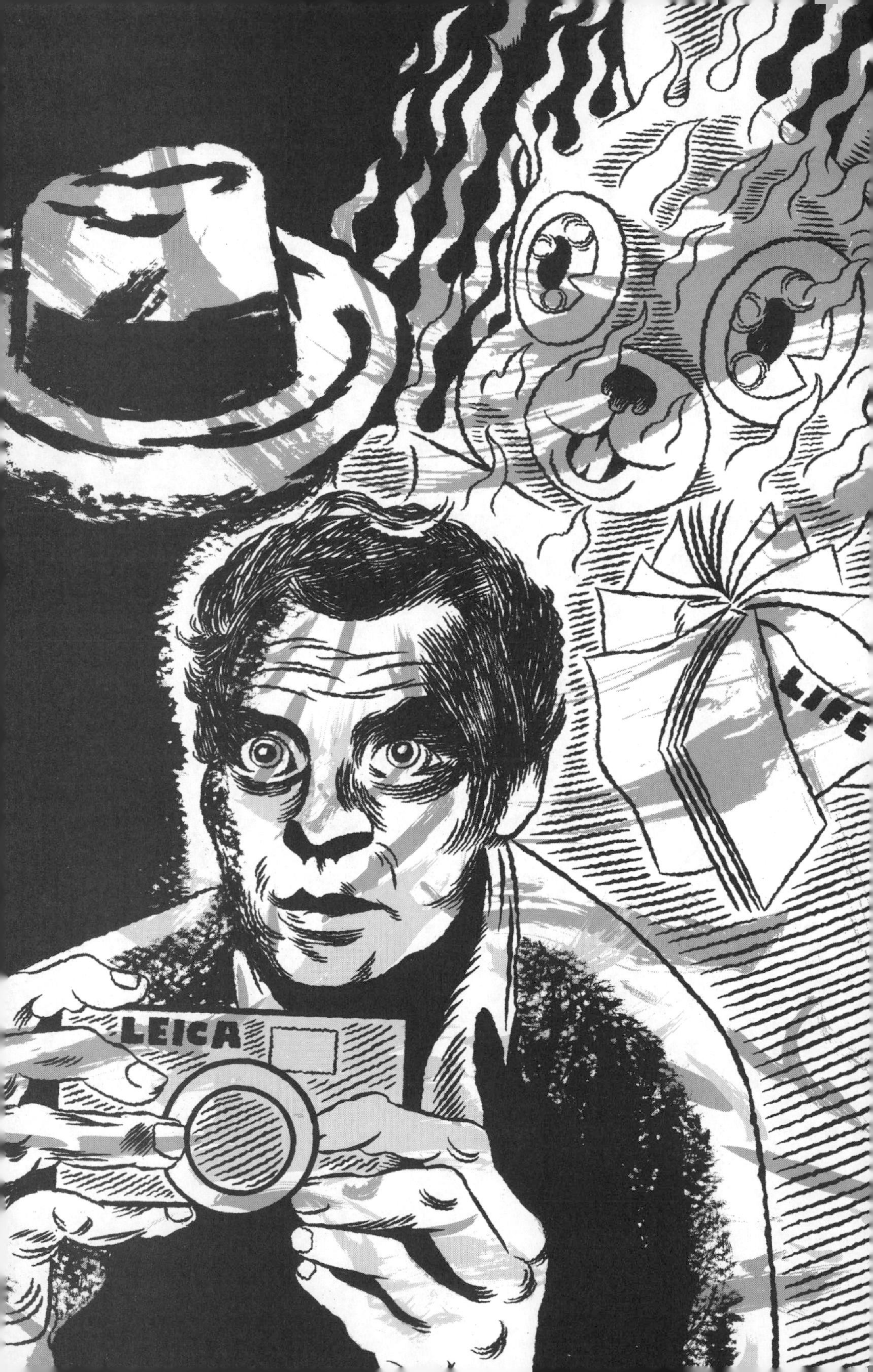
LIFE
LEICA

Ralph Gibson

....

Street-photography was one of the great art forms of the 20th Century. It was the form that gave us Henri-Cartier Bresson, Diane Arbus Robert Frank, and Walker Evans, among many others, and it was the starting point for artist Ralph Gibson. Born in Los Angeles in 1939, Gibson was a complicated boy who flunked out of high school and wound up in the Navy, which proved to be a lucky break for him. The Navy sent him to photography school, and by the time he left the service in 1959 he was a crack technician.

Because Gibson had the soul of a poet, he took all he'd learned and set out to become an artist; his first step in that direction was shooting photographs of San Francisco, where he was living at the time. Gibson's pictures from this period reflect central themes of classic street photography; the ephemeral loveliness of the city street with its unrelenting river of faces; the loneliness of the solitary individual and the comfort of the crowd; the workers solemnly bent to their tasks; the ever-changing light capable of transforming the mood with a single passing cloud. The hand of the artist is muted in these pictures, and Gibson continued working that way when he moved to L.A. in 1962. He remained there for four years and created an indelible portrait of a specific time and place with pictures of soldiers, the groovy nightlife of the Sunset Strip, hippies, strippers, girls in bikinis, and convertibles.

Gibson's learning curve ramped up considerably in 1966 when he moved to New York and landed a gig as assistant to photographer Robert Frank. It was then that Gibson began moving toward his signature style. The composition of his pictures became more graphic and dramatic, the subject matter grew increasingly surreal, and the objects and forms in his pictures took on a quality of mystery and portentousness; these stylistic advances culminated in his first book, The Somnambulist, published in 1970.

By that point Gibson had completely moved away from street photography in favor of impeccably composed images of people, places and things distilled to their essence. Over the past 33 years he's published 21 books, and created photographic portraits of Berlin, Manhattan, San Francisco, Egypt, France, Italy and Japan. He's taken hundreds of luminous pictures of women, many of which feature his adored companion of 25 years, Mary Jane Marcasiano. He's also amassed an incredibly large circle of accomplished friends. Gibson seems to have known or hung out with every significant photographer of the past 50 years, and he knows lots of painters and musicians, too. All it takes is one encounter with Gibson to understand how he's accumulated so many friends. A warm and open man, he's a nimble and knowledgeable conversationalist with a great sense of humor.

What's your earliest memory?

Seeing the incredible shock and awe on my parents' faces as they stared at an old gothic shaped radio broadcasting the news of the bombing of Pearl Harbor. I was around two at the time.

Where were your parents from?

My father was from Philadelphia, and my mother was from Costa Rica. Her brother was a classical pianist, and when she was very young she went with him to New York where she met a classical conductor who went to Hollywood to score films. I suspect he took her along as a kind of family friend/au pair.

Your father was employed by Warner Brothers and worked for a time as assistant director to Alfred Hitchcock, so you spent lots of time on movie sets as a child. Were you enraptured with movies then?

Yes. I liked the magical quality of movies sets, those high contrast carbon arc lights, and the incredible mystique of the camera. I worked as an extra as a child; then when I was around 12 I began getting bit parts. I finally got a decent part with three or four pages of dialogue in a film called *The Eddie Cantor Story*, then one day my father came home with a roll of film of my performance he'd found on the cutting room floor. That was a huge shock to me. The rejection, the idea that it was cut out – I started hating Hollywood at that moment.

Before turning your back on Hollywood you worked in films by Nicholas Ray and Alfred Hitchcock; what do you remember of those men?

If they needed a kid on the spur of the moment they'd call me at school and send a car, and in 1952 I was summoned to play a little Mexican boy in a Nicholas Ray western called *The Lusty Men*. I arrived on the set of this Western town, and off camera was a posse of horses that was supposed to gallop into town. I remember Ray pinning me with those eyes – that eye – and telling me that if I stood perfectly still the horses would gallop past me and wouldn't hurt me. I believed him, too – in those days I had faith in people like doctors and directors. Hitchcock I mostly spoke with on the phone when he'd call my dad, then in 1951 I worked as an extra in the carnival scene in *Strangers on a Train*. It was a great job because we got to ride all the rides and eat all the popcorn.

What sort of art or culture were you exposed to as a child?

Primarily literature. My mother was an avid reader – she was the cultured one in the family. But more important, I was really formed by *Life Magazine*. On Friday afternoon I'd get out of school and I wouldn't walk, I'd run the mile or so from school to get to that new issue of *Life*. In those days it was largely black and white, and I know that from a purely subliminal point of view that's where I formed my proclivities. I don't know why I responded so intensely to photographs – in fact, I didn't even know I was responding at that point. It wasn't until I decided to be a photographer while I was in art school that some of those earlier childhood feelings coalesced into a clarified definition.

The photographs in Life Magazine *during the '40s were considered* photojournalism *at the time they were published, then in the mid-'50s, with the publication of works like Robert Frank's landmark book,* The Americans, *that kind of work came to be regarded as fine art. Is there a difference for you?

The Americans wasn't considered fine art when it first came out. If you look at some of the early reviews, it's clear that it was seen as a hugely subversive, anti-McCarthy statement, and was basically seen as a failure except for students of my generation, who were utterly galvanized by it.

It sounds as if you had a fairly idyllic childhood; did you?

Up to a point. My parents divorced in 1954 when I was 15, and I was living with my father. Then my dad remarried, I flunked out of school, and I enlisted in the Navy when I was 17.

While you were in the Navy you trained as a photographer at a school in Pensacola, Florida; what's the most valuable thing you got out of that experience?

There was an enlightened aspect to Naval photography at the time because Naval photography was founded by Edward Steichen, who was a four stripe captain during World War II. I had a chief who'd taken a workshop with Minor White. I didn't know I was an artist yet, but I was starting to really want to be one, and the most valuable thing I got out of that Naval training was something one of the chiefs told me. He said, "Gibson, you have to learn it all and then you can forget what you don't need. But you have to learn it first." That's what Robert Frank did. As a student he was making view camera shots of gears floating in space, but by the time he got to *The Americans* it was all one-handed, out of focus and funky. But that was a deliberate formal choice. It's the same thing as playing jazz. Ornette has years of theory beneath his harmolodics.

Can you recall the first time you responded to a work of art?

During the late '50s I was in the Navy and my ship was berthed in Brooklyn, so I used to go into Manhattan in my little sailor suit and hang out at the Cedar Bar and the Five Spot Tavern. I just wanted to know about that stuff and was magnetically drawn to it. During that period Abstract Expressionism was the lingua franca, and I met a German painter named Walter Gaudneck who let me crash in his loft on Tenth Street in exchange for me taking photographs of his paintings. So, I got on the Tenth Street scene and looked at lots of Abstract Expressionism, I listened to Sonny Rollins premiere *Wagon Wheels* in a little club, and I heard Kerouac and Corso in the Village all the time. I went to the Museum of Modern Art a lot, too, and I remember standing in front of Matisse's *The Piano Lesson*, which has a tiny area of raw, unpainted canvas. This is a very vivid memory because it's the first time I really perceived a work of art. I understood his intention – I just got it – and it was such a powerful recognition of two-dimensional art that I was able to apply that one perception to lots of subsequent looking. I have a vocabulary of shapes, and lots of the shapes that recur in my work are shapes I've seen in paintings.

Who are your favorite painters?

I'm good friends with Eric Fischl and I love his work. I like David Salle and I've always loved early Jasper [Johns]. If I had to pick one painter it would be Matisse because he answers so many of my questions. I was at the Matisse chapel a few weeks ago and it's incredible. Stained glass and ceramic tiles painted black and white to form the stations of the cross – it's really a triumph. He did this at the very end of his life so he was probably a religious man at that point.

You were still in the Navy when The Americans *was published; did you see it shortly after it came out?*

I didn't see it until 1960 when I was in art school, and seeing that book was like being hit at the back of the knees with a baseball bat. I couldn't believe the power of it – it's probably the most powerful photography book of all time. And the source of its power is Frank's venom. Because Robert is a poet there's also great tenderness in the book, but ultimately Robert is the direct lineal descendant of Céline in that he works from the void and wants his work to take him further into it.

Robert's had a difficult life, but he would've anyway, regardless of whether he was making art. He helped me a tremendous amount when I was struggling, but the minute I had some success our friendship effectively came to an end. I knew him very well, though – I lived in his home and traveled with him, and he gave me the enlarger he used to make *The Americans*. I'm still using it, in fact. But we were polar opposites. I'm an optimist and I'm just not an existential artist and he is. He's probably America's greatest existential artist.

You were discharged from the Navy in 1959 and settled in San Francisco, where you enrolled at the Art Institute. Who were your important teachers there?

I only went to the Art Institute for a semester and a half because I couldn't afford tuition. But I did have a teacher named Paul Hassel who was important because he loaned me his Leica, and a cultural anthropologist named John Collier Jr. who taught me how to read photographs. When I left the Navy my goal was to work for Magnum and do fashion photography because I didn't know that wasn't art. That realization came after I got into Magnum, did a little fashion, and started working with Robert Frank. By the time I was 28 I'd fully exhausted any interest in the commercial world.

In the early '60s you spent 18 months working for Dorothea Lange, who's said to have been an extremely difficult woman. Was she?

Yes. I was this crackerjack technician from the Navy so I worked in her darkroom. She knew nothing about technique, but she wanted passionately to change social conditions, and the sheer force of her will made the materials obey. She was a messianic personality who wanted to change things, and she did. It often happens that work infused with the degree of passion Dorothea had is called art, but I don't think she ever set out to make art.

What did you learn from her?

I showed her my work once and she said, "Your problem is that you have no point of departure. If you're going to the drugstore to buy toothpaste, the chances of encountering an event are greater than if you just stand on a street corner waiting for something to happen." It wasn't until I started working on *The Somnambulist* that I really understood the importance of a point of departure, and to this minute I always have one when I pick up a camera.

In 1962 you returned to Los Angeles where you remained for four years; how did the city shape you as an artist?

It really didn't. I was fortunate in that I got to know a group of artists that included Wallace Berman and Dean Stockwell, and that crowd was the best part of L.A. for me. Wallace was an incredible man, just amazing, and he was a great influence on all of us who came into his orbit. But basically, L.A. was synonymous with failure for me for a long time. When I got to L.A. in the early '60s I had a portfolio and I started freelancing, but with the exception of one or two graphic designers, people didn't get my work. My family had failed in L.A., it's where I failed out of high school, and there I was starting my career and failing. I was fighting a very difficult battle in L.A. because my cameras were usually pawned, I was driving $100 cars with three flat tires, and I was always getting evicted. L.A. was a real *Mein Kampf* for me, and I was extremely fortunate that I left when I did. I went to New York with $200 in my pocket and I immediately got work, I got into Magnum, and I met Robert Frank. I found myself.

You were living in L.A. in 1965 when your mother died; were you in touch with her?

Yes. She died in a hotel fire in downtown L.A. I remember walking through the ashes of the hotel and seeing a little stuffed rabbit I'd made for my mother in kindergarten smoldering away, and thinking should I pick it up? I decided to just leave it. My mother had been lost to me for many years by the time she died.

You've describe yourself as an optimist, yet your early life was very difficult; how were you able to transform that?

When I was in my 20s I was very unhappy. I was living in Beverly Glen in Los Angeles, and in 1964 I met a guru who'll remain nameless who turned me around. I left Beverly Glen to live with him for three years, and it was an extremely difficult Gurdjieffian kind of program, but it did wonders for me. There were ten or twelve of us, we lived in a mansion together, and it was all day and all night long for a couple of years. It was the best break I ever got.

In the fall of 1966 you moved to New York, and early the following year you met Robert Frank and worked with him on two of his films, Me and My Brother, *and* Conversations in Vermont. *Which of his films do you think are most successful?*

I haven't seen all of them. Robert is very candid about the variable quality of his films, and I remember him saying when he started *Me and My Brother*, "I might fall flat on my face with this one, but you have to be original." I think his films are very original, too. *Conversations in Vermont* was a total success in terms of what he set out to do, and although I haven't seen all of *Cocksucker Blues*, I imagine it's pretty good.

On arriving in New York you checked into the Chelsea Hotel, where you lived for two years. What was going on at the Chelsea then?

Harry Smith was living there and I got to know him, and Leonard Cohen was there too, and we hung out a lot. Robert Mapplethorpe was living there but I didn't get to know him until the mid-'70s when he was living on Bond Street. I used to go to his studio and he'd have these ring binders under the coffee table with all his S & M stuff, which was unbelievable. But he became a salon photographer.

Warhol's Factory was in its heyday when you arrived in New York. Was that of interest to you?

Yeah, but I never wanted to be in Warhol's entourage and I didn't want to get involved with the drug scene. I used to like booze and cigarettes but drugs were never my thing. Anyhow, I had an artist friend I'd met in San Francisco named Frosty Meyers, and Frosty was big at the Factory and he knew everybody. Max's Kansas City was going so Frosty got me a cabaret card to Max's, and Warhol was always there. I had total entree into that world but I didn't go after it.

During your first year in New York you befriended Mary Ellen Mark and Larry Clark; how did you meet them?

Bruce Davidson had recommended Mary Ellen, Danny Lyon and me to Magnum, and I was the one they picked. Mary Ellen went on to become a great photojournalist, of course, and she and I were very close for a long time. We're still good friends. I also knew Diane Arbus and Louis Faure, who came over to my loft one day and dropped my camera, then gave me a lecture on how to drop a Leica. In those days if you went up Fifth Avenue you'd probably run into Diane or Garry Winnogrand, and Lee Friedlander was on the street, too. Larry Clark had just arrived in town from Viet Nam and the minute Larry showed up he and I just bonded. We had a lot to say to one another.

Garry Winnogrand once told you, "It's guys like you that are the problem with photography." What did he mean by that?

He was expressing the fact that he hated my guts. First of all, I was Robert Frank's assistant and there was always something between the two of them. It's a very interesting story, what happened with those two. In the 1950s, a bunch of photographers that included Louis Faure, Robert Frank, Sid Grossman and Garry Winnogrand were around, and strangely enough, Louis Faure was the one the art world chose to back as the great talent. Louis loved girls, though, and he went off to Paris to shoot fashion so he could score models. He basically walked on a huge career, at which point Robert came through the door. Steichen became a mentor to Robert, who was also the protégé of Walker Evans, and Evans and Steichen got Robert the Guggenheim that allowed him to do *The Americans*, which is a masterpiece. Robert then quit. Winnogrand was doing really sensitive early work and the art world wanted somebody from that generation, so it fell to Winnogrand by default.

Do you think Winnogrand was a great artist?

No. He was a very difficult man and not a nice guy. In my opinion he was more of a paparazzo and should've been working for *The Daily News*.

Much of your work has a strong graphic quality evocative of Walker Evans. Was he important for you when you were finding your voice as an artist?

I like Evans' point blank frontality, but I've never subscribed to the modernist philosophy of which he is the major exponent. For quite a long time the world of photography was engaged in a holy war that started with Walker Evans and MOMA curator John Sarkowski, and continued with Lee Friedlander and Garry Winnogrand. They espoused the modernist ethic, which decreed that you don't make subjective, personal images – you make ice-cold pictures of purity and precision. That modernist ethic continues to operate to this day in work by German photographers like Thomas Ruff, Andreas Gursky and Thomas Struth, who all use the objectivity of the lens to produce their version of the modernist idea. My work has always been solipsistic, subjective and introspective – the complete opposite.

Photojournalism was in its heyday when you were coming of age as a photographer; what's happened to that form?

The power of photojournalism was based on its ability to show you things you couldn't see otherwise, and the photojournalism that works today is still somewhat predicated on that ability. But that's not where photography is at now, because the visual I.Q. of society has gone way up since the '50s.

During your early years in New York you were enraptured with the writing of Jorge Luis Borges, Marguerite Duras and Alain Robbe-Grillet. What appealed to you about that work?

Reading those novelists felt like the way I feel when I look at something. It's that over-wide, solipsistic stare, and that aura that objects take on – that low frequency hum that can emanate from things.

In 1969 you founded Lustrum Press, and the following year you published your first book, **The Somnambulist,** *which was a turning point in your career. In 1971 Lustrum published Larry Clark's legendary photo essay on a gang of Oklahoma speed freaks,* **Tulsa.** *Did you have any idea at the time of the impact that book would have?*
I knew it was a very good book, so I said to Larry, "Let's do it," and Robert Frank went to Danny Seymour who gave us $5,000.00 to publish it.

In 1975 you began exhibiting with the Leo Castelli Gallery. How did that relationship begin?
In 1975 Lewis Baltz suggested to Leo's then wife, Toiny, that she have a look at my work and I wound up becoming good friends with the family. Leo was really my best friend for a number of years. Leo changed the course of art history because he perceived pop art long before anyone else did. He knew it was important and what its impact would be, and he was directly responsible for the discovery and development of some great American masters.

Were you excited about Pop art?
I like anything done well and I'm very interested in contemporary masterpieces. What I'm not interested in are things like Damien Hirst and 'Cremaster.' That kind of spectacle doesn't interest me because I think of it as entertainment.

In 1976 you began incorporating bits of color in your work, and in 1990 you published your first book of color photographs, **L'Histoire de France.** *What prompted you to begin using color?*
One reason is that I could finally afford it – in fact, it's become cheaper to do color than to work in black and white. Color has less drama than black and white, and for that reason it's an incredible challenge. Eventually I hope to achieve the same level of satisfaction I get from some of my black and white pictures, but that hasn't happened yet. There are, of course, some real masters working with color, and William Eggleston is the most interesting one of all. His form/content thing is completely worked out, he makes great use of perspective and focal length, and he understands color totally. All those elements conspire to produce that antebellum Dixie thing – his work just oozes that feeling.

When did you first fall in love?
The first big relationship was with a neurotic woman in the late '60s. I was taken by this woman's beauty, and she was very much like Sylvia Plath in that everything she touched turned to art. She was enchanted and hugely disturbed, and the last time I saw her was in the mid-'70s and she was heading towards becoming a born-again Christian. Then I was with a woman named Sheila who left me to be a Zen nun. I've had a great love life.

Why does love die?
Because it's finite. It's fixed in the stars that there are a certain number of kisses to every love story and not one more. Love stories that seem to go on forever simply haven't exhausted that final kiss. Putting people on the couch because they're having trouble in love is ridiculous. Nobody's asked to sign a contract saying, "I agree to be

successful," or "I agree to be healthy." But you're supposed to sign a contract that says I agree to be happy in love. It doesn't work that way.

You've said one thing you've always wanted to do that's eluded you is make a book of genuinely erotic photographs. Why is erotic experience so difficult to capture in a picture?
Because sex doesn't always look the way it feels. And I don't think any artist has captured the way it feels successfully enough to create a libidinal response in both men and women.

What's the difference between art and pornography?
It probably has to do with staying power and how long the work is good for.

Why is photography the appropriate vehicle for what you want to express as an artist?
An anthropologist once told me that I was "over-wide," which was her way of saying that I don't blink enough. I like to stare at things and always have.

Who's currently making work that excites you?
I've been doing a series of portraits of jazz guitarists, and what's exciting me now is avant garde jazz guitarists likes Mark Ribot, Derek Bailey, Andy Summers and Bill Frisell. I recently came to a conclusion – which I shared with Brian Eno, who agreed with me – that melody is to music as reality is to photography.

What's the most significant historical event that's occurred during your life?
I used to think it was the collapse of the Communist empire because that completely changed the economics of the world, but it might've been 9/11. The world was totally changed by the event and the America of the 20th Century is no longer. There's another demographic now, the third world is expanding, and all these races and countries are gonna blur into one uno mundo. I was in my studio in Tribeca on 9/11 and all my friends were urging me to get out of the city and come to the country, but I was determined to go down with the ship and refused to leave the studio. Maybe it was my Navy training, but I had no desire to be anywhere but here.

What's important to you today?
My next photograph. And I'll know what it is when I see it.

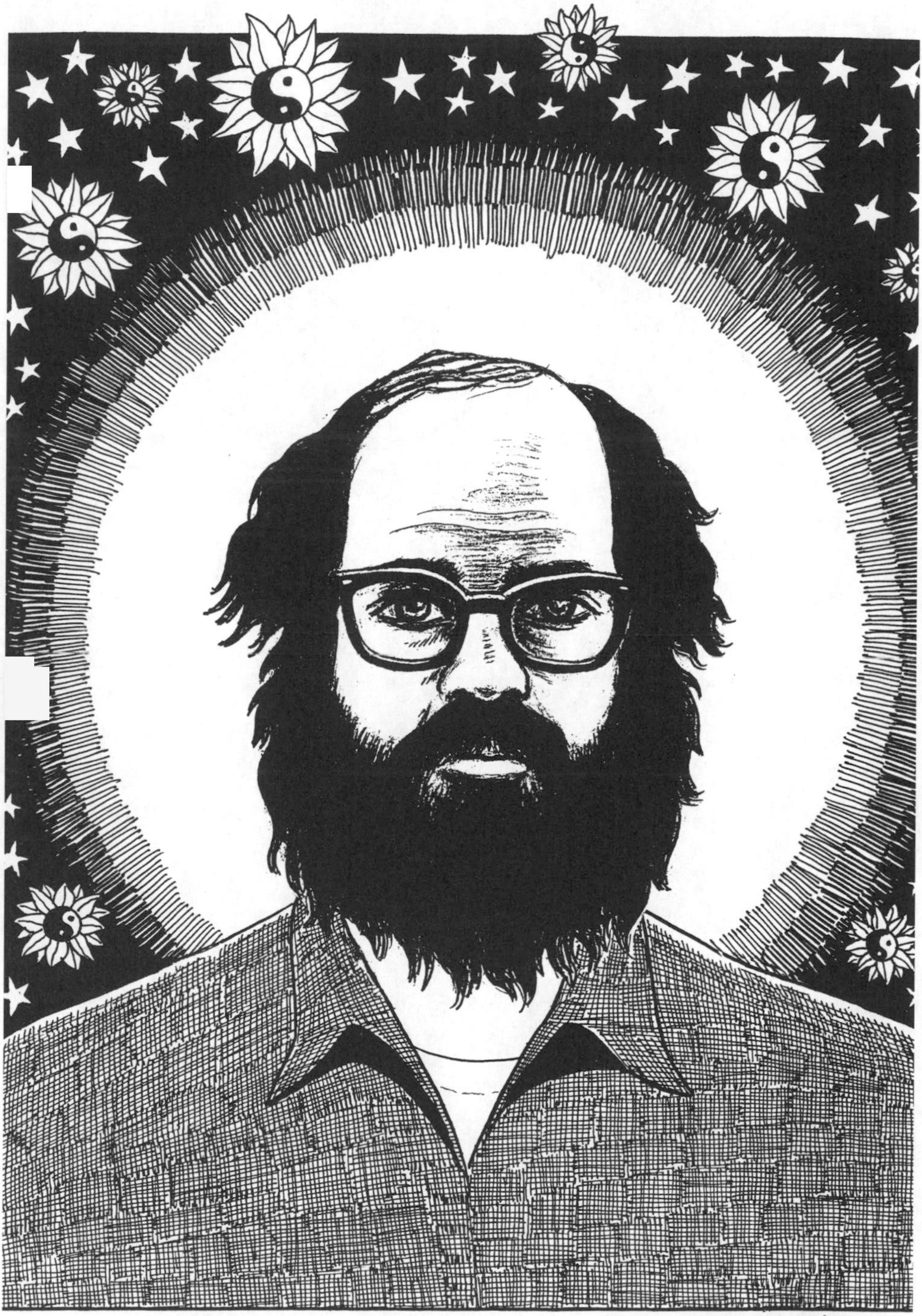

Mack White

Allen Ginsberg

"Howl" is the Allen Ginsberg poem everybody knows, but I'm partial to another poem he wrote during the same year, 1956, called "America." It's a shamelessly charming poem that speaks in a saucy, flirtatious voice, and it finds Ginsberg beseeching the country he loves to please get on the right track before something really bad happens. He wraps the poem up with the wonderful line, "America I'm putting my queer shoulder to the wheel," and anyone who paid attention to culture in the 20th Century can tell you that's exactly what Ginsberg did. He was a singularly game citizen who embraced every social revolution that occurred during his lifetime, revered his poet ancestors as much as he loved the eternal parade of brash upstarts determined to unseat them, and remained astonishingly present up to his dying day. "Mentally, Allen is never uptight," said poet Kenneth Rexroth in a 1971 interview included in David Meltzer's 2001 volume of interviews, San Francisco Beat: Talking With the Poets. "He is always available and he is always connected with people." What a tremendous achievement.

Born in Newark, New Jersey, on June 3, 1926, Ginsberg had a difficult childhood that was largely shaped by his mother's descent into madness. Ginsberg's father was a poet who taught high school, and his mother was a Russian immigrant and devout Marxist who suffered a series of nervous breakdowns that led to her being lobotomized in 1948. Jack Kerouac came into Ginsberg's life in 1944, shortly after Ginsberg began his freshman year at Columbia, planning to become a labor lawyer; with that fortuitous encounter the seeds of the Beat Generation were sown. In 1948 Ginsberg experienced a vision of William Blake that prompted him to formally dedicate himself to becoming a poet, and with the encouragement of his friends Kerouac and William Burroughs, he began to refine the approach to poetry that defines his work. Synthesizing the language of the American streets, the fractured, hallucinatory vocabulary of Surrealism, and mystical incantation, Ginsberg hammered out a populist style of poetry that liberated it from the stuffy halls of academia and returned it to the people.

Ginsberg proved to have a good deal more stamina than the rest of the Beats, and by the time of his death of liver cancer, on April 5, 1997, he'd published hundreds of poems, been arrested repeatedly for various acts of political protest, and founded the Jack Kerouac School of Disembodied Poetics of the Naropa Institute in Boulder, Colorado, a Buddhist university where he taught poetry and meditation.

I interviewed Ginsberg on February 9, 1994 on the eve of the release of The Life and Times of Allen Ginsberg, a documentary film directed by Jerry Aronson. The ostensible point of our conversation was to promote the film, but much to his credit, Ginsberg didn't care much about marketing and was happy to discuss other things.

You were raised in a Jewish home. How did Judaism mark you?

The monotheism of Judaism was always troubling to me, and I was more drawn to the cultural identity – you know, the delicatessen intellectual tradition of Kurt Weill, Freud, Marx, Einstein and Bertolt Brecht. I worked with Rabbi Zalman Schachter a few times, and the rituals are very exotic, but Judeo-Christian monotheism has always struck me as a mind trap and a semantic mistake, among other things.

What was the most valuable thing you gained from witnessing your mother's life?

A tolerance for chaos and irrationality, but it also made me thick-skinned. The tolerance I developed for insanity and eccentricity is accompanied by an ability to distance myself from it emotionally, so it's a plus and a minus.

As a poet, you use words as the raw material for your art; what is language good for?

It unites heaven and earth. The heaven of the mind – the impalpable and the infinite – wants to communicate with the physical body and the earth, and language can be a vehicle for that.

How does language trip us up?

It trips us up when we confuse words with things – take the word Macedonia, for instance. The Greeks and the Yugoslav Macedonians are arguing about who owns the word Macedonia, and seem to believe that the word has an intrinsic essence that must be monopolized by one side or the other. Historically, the word god has always functioned in a similar way. People are willing to kill for their word image of god, and they use the word as an excuse for mass murder.

What does the word mean to you?

Old No-Bo Daddy on high – nobody's daddy on high. That's William Blake's phrase. He said that for centuries man has been asleep under the guidance of old No-Bo Daddy, trying to substitute some abstract concept of a god who's outside everything, rather than taking the initiative and making the effort to develop his own awareness. Man refuses responsibility for his own creation of the nuclear bomb and acts as if it was something given from above. "I didn't do it, I swear. It crawled into my hand." One thing that has changed in this particular area, however, is that the fantasy of the government as a protective father figure has disintegrated. Everybody realizes now, as they didn't in the '50s, that the government is not to be trusted, that they lie, it's a snake pit in there, and nobody knows how to clean it out.

Was there ever a period when you felt daunted by the impact "Howl" made?

No. I sort of felt sorry for people who got stuck there, but I never was. When I first read "Howl" at the Six Gallery it felt like a good poetry reading, but I had as good a night last week when I did a benefit for a Buddhist group preparing for a visit from the Dali Lama. And I've certainly written other poems I felt were as good as "Howl." "Witcheta Vortex Sutra," "Father Death Blues," "September on Jessor Road," "Plutonium Ode," and "White Shroud" are a few that come to mind.

You're currently teaching poetry at Brooklyn College; how do you approach that task?

Poetry is of the soul and you don't teach that. I teach the craft of poetry, and I try to inspire the soul through behavior, body language, the poems I pick, and the way I read them. I try to expose the students to language as expressed by Ma Rainey,

Robert Johnson, Charlie Patton, Skip James, and Bessie Smith, wonderful works of African American culture like the signifying monkey and the dozens, Aborigines with long sticks – all of these things are manifestations of the contest of the bards. My Buddhist practice is identical to my poetic practice in that aspects of mindfulness and awareness are central to both of them, and I encourage my students to learn to meditate because the breath is central to poetry and meditation. Certain kinds of poetry that could be described as spiritual – Shelley's "Ode to the West Wind," the Moloch section of "Howl," or Hart Crane's "Atlantis," for example – have a quality of exaltation and unobstructed breath. Breath is, in fact, one of the subjects of Shelley's "Ode to the West Wind," which describes the body as being like a hollow reed through which breath and ideas flow without obstruction.

The essential subject of all your poetry has been the theme of love. Why does love die?

I don't think love dies. It just gets buried under bad experience and incommunicability, or people go mad, suffer money woes – many difficult things can happen to people in the course of a life. But if you look to your dreams you'll find the original love tears, throbs and grief remain completely intact. The emotions remain in the body, the mind and the heart, and they often come out in dreams.

Why can't we live those dreams more fully?

Fear of the rejection that might come if we show our sensitivity, vulnerability and funkiness. Walt Whitman addressed this when he said, "I celebrate myself and sing myself" – that's a song of self-acceptance, and there aren't many models of self-acceptance around these days. So, it's fear of rejection, and that you'll get involved with something beyond your depth that will drag you down and you'll lose. We live in terror of what might be asked of us. People walk pass the homeless and avoid having eye contact with them for fear that if they have any kind of sympathetic connection with that person they'll wind up having to give them everything. Rather than acknowledge the suffering, they just look the other way. To subject people to these moments of no communication and total helplessness, to not even see when they wave or speak, diminishes us all. If you can't give them money, at least nod to them and wish them a good day. Cheer them on and be friendly instead of behaving like a guard in a concentration camp refusing to notice the people starving in rags on the ground. If I don't have anything to give, or I don't want to give, I at least look at them and wish them well.

What's the most widely held misconception about the Beat generation?

That we weren't literate. We were more educated than most of the academic critics who dismissed our interest in Eastern thought as irrationality simply because it was non-linear. It was a different kind of thinking, but it was thinking, and it required cultivation and a good deal more discipline than western logical simplifications. Still, they dismissed us as unruly beatniks with wiggy hair, bongo drums and cockroaches on the floor. That was the common stereotype image produced by the Luce magazines during the '50s and '60s – which isn't to suggest that Henry Luce didn't drop acid, by the way.

During the '90s there was a reappraisal of the literary value of the Beats, and people began to realize that we weren't just a star that exploded long ago. Most of us continued to write, and with the exception of Kerouac and Cassady, very few of us fell by the wayside. We have a good longevity record compared with most of the academic poets who killed themselves by drinking. We just smoked a little grass instead of totally knocking out our livers with booze, and the ones of us who died young were the alcoholics. The notorious dope fiend business tuned out to be a better bet than all-American suicide on alcohol.

Other than not killing you, what did drugs do for you?

They're a good educational tool. I'm more of a workaholic so I never got hooked on anything, but they reinforced certain individualistic and visionary tendencies I had that have been useful to me as a citizen and a poet. I once asked Dr. Hoffman, who invented LSD, what philosophic principle he derived from it and he answered that it showed there are many different universes possible. I'd already seen a few, but I hadn't seen as many as I saw on acid. Everybody knows there are many realties beyond those that are easily labeled, but to experience it is something else. I had some interesting experiences on LSD, and more recently with Ecstasy, which I think is misnamed – it should be called empathy. I got high on Ecstasy and began empathizing with some people I thought I didn't like politically. I've had some sacred, totemic enemies in my life, and I had to thank them for being there for me to bounce my head against. I still smoke pot when I feel like it, and although that doesn't happen too often, I still like to check out supreme reality every once in a while. The last time I did that was with mushrooms.

What's been the great achievement of the American counterculture of the 20th Century?

It altered mainstream culture completely, and introduced several bodies of thought that have never lost their relevance. Beginning in the '40s, Kerouac, Burroughs, and myself became interested in the operation of consciousness and began experimenting with psychotherapy, psychedelics, Eastern philosophy, art, and ideas about the alchemy of the word that were first introduced by Rimbaud. We were looking for a way of using language that would actually alter consciousness, and that led to a change in literature and art; people began to model painting, poetry and music on the way the mind actually functions. Surrealism fed into this change, of course, because the Surrealists became interested in Freud, dreams and the nature of consciousness in the '20s. One of the best of the San Francisco Beat poets, Philip Lamantia, was in direct contact with André Breton, and over the years I met many of the Surrealist painters and poets. The Beats developed this train of thought that began with the Surrealists, and now we're comfortable with art that speaks through montage, collage, discontinuity and jump cut. The great monuments of writing – Pound's "Cantos," Kerouac's "Mexico City Blues," William Carlos Williams' "Patterson" – all have that quality of montage. It was a revolution in art that led to the form becoming more open, and to a vernacular poetry that could be understood by people. I remember Bob Dylan telling me that "Mexico City Blues" inspired him to become a poet and when I asked him why, he said it was because it was the first book by a poet that spoke to him in his own language – American.

The Beats also played a crucial role in bringing Eastern thought to the West. By 1950 Kerouac had become very involved with Buddhist beliefs about the nature of reality, the human mind, and subjectivity. Buddhism is rooted in the understanding that we create the world in our minds, everything is transitory, and existence is painful because if you're born in a body you must die; in America, during the '50s, these were radically new ideas. In 1955 we encountered the great Buddhist poet Gary Snyder, who was studying Chinese and Japanese, and was preparing to move to a monastery in the Far East to perfect his Zen practice. This all laid the groundwork for Kerouac's "Dharma Bums," which was published in 1957 and set off a rucksack revolution of meditation, long hair, and an increased reverence for nature. Buddhism became increasingly important for me personally because I went to India in the early

'60s with Gary and Peter Orlovsky, and I formed alliances there that bore fruit many years later. In 1972 I began working with Trungpa, and two years later I founded the Naropa Institute of Disembodied Poetics in Boulder, Colorado.

Then there was the strand of political pacifism and social activism. In their willingness to speak openly and publicly in exactly the same way they spoke in private, the counterculture advocated an end to political schizophrenia. This position is in dramatic contrast to that of politicians and the media, who accept the difference between what reporters know to be true, and what their publishers will allow them to say in print. For instance, the so-called war on drugs is phony and everybody knows that. The legalization of marijuana obviously makes sense, but this country might fall apart before that comes to pass. One of the causes of its falling apart will be that we filled up the jail cells rather than dealing with the subject in an open and honest way. The counterculture spoke out against hypocrisy of this sort.

The counterculture also led the world in terms of drawing attention to the ecological crisis currently gripping the planet. As Kerouac said in *On the Road*, "the earth is an Indian thing," and fears about the destruction of the planet were central to the Beat poetry of Gary Snyder and Michael McClure in the '50s. We have maybe 100 more years before we've completely wrecked the planet, because I see no evidence that we're slowing down the destruction – in fact, it's worse than ever. Our awareness of the problem is greater, partly because the counterculture began sounding the alarm forty years ago. At the time, of course, we were accused of being un-American doomsayers for suggesting we should stop eating so much gasoline, and bombing to get gasoline.

And there was the sexual liberation aspect, which led to gay liberation, and the women's movement of the '60s. People are at least aware of sex now.

Did the sexual revolution drain sex of any of its power by making it less mysterious and forbidden?

Nah, no way. Sex is as mysterious, urgent, and tender as it's ever been. That idea sounds like it was cooked up by the CIA, the fundamentalists, the Catholic church, or someone who doesn't like sex. The rest of us are just sad that sex isn't safe any more.

You say the counterculture fostered a revolution in form that shifted poetry's position from the academy to the street; have efforts been made to return it to the academy?

Yeah, they're always doing that. You know, the new formalism, bla, bla, bla. Actually, it's still mostly in the academy if the anthologies edited by professors for use in high schools and colleges are any indication. Kerouac's poetry is never included in those books, and Gregory Corso is rarely included either, despite the fact that he's one of the most popular poets around. Those books are filled with poets who are still working out of the tradition of Robert Lowell. My work is included in most of them, but that of my teacher, Kerouac, is not.

What was the great failure of the counterculture?

Once when Kerouac was high on psychedelics with Timothy Leary, he looked out the window and said, "Walking on water wasn't built in a day." Our goal was to save the planet and alter human consciousness, to be more aware of what we were doing, more playful and free and less neurotic. That will take a long time, if it happens at all.

Looking back on Kerouac's life, do you regard it as a tragic one?

No. [Poet] Philip Whalen once pointed out to me that it's hardly a tragedy, in that he did more in one lifetime than most people do in ten. And remember, he had alcoholism, which is an illness, and it contributed to the sadness that came at the end of his life. I think everybody gets unhappy in the final ten years of their life, though, and the unhappiness runs deep because you realize you're gonna die and the body begins to fail. I have diabetes and high blood pressure, I have to monitor my blood, I can't eat meat and can hardly get it up.

What aspect of your personality has created the most problems for you in life?

My aversion to physical work. Earlier in my life I tried to overcome it by getting jobs in factories and on ships and as a welder, but I still don't know how to catch a ball. I'm four-eyed and physically inept. I've had computers around for years and I still don't know how to work them.

What's the great privilege of growing old?

You get funnier, smarter, and you acquire the ability to take a long view of things. And despite the physical prowess you lose, erotic desire never fades. Having crushes, seeing some brilliant face in the crowd, your heart melting – that's always there. As William Blake said, "Your youth and your day are wasted in play / and your winter and night in disguise."

What was desperately important to you when you were young that no longer seems quite so pressing?

Getting laid. Erotic desire never fades but it can be transmuted, and since I have difficulty getting it up anyway, it isn't so urgent that I get my cock out with somebody. More important now is to have friendliness, someone to help me get things up the staircase, and to provide affection, maybe naked affection.

How would you explain the concept of reality to someone unfamiliar with the idea?

If you stub your toe against the desk, it hurts – that's reality. At the same time, the hurt is impermanent. In 100 years your body and the desk will be gone, and ultimately it's all a dream, so reality has no hell to pay, nor heaven to reward. Therefore, you're completely free, as in a dream. That's the score about reality.

How do you explain the fact that you've always had the courage to speak out publicly about controversial things?

I had no courage at all. I was just following my nose and was as confused as everybody else. I did know what I was thinking, though, and I knew that my job was to write down what I was thinking. If everybody wrote down what they were really thinking, then everybody would be out front. People lie to themselves quite a bit because they think they might be safer that way. It's horrible to face the fact that you've lived your life based on some wrong idea, and I've felt that a number of times in almost every area of my life. But I keep trying to update those realizations and acknowledge them in my poetry. I believe in letting your neurosis be your style, which is a Buddhist notion of turning waste into treasure. Walt Whitman said, "I sound my barbaric yawp over the roof of the world," and there's an absence of ego in that because ego is identifying with the vastness of space.

What aspect of the American character do you find most endearing?

The handsome, youthful, punk, impudent tenderness that was there in River Phoenix, the comradery among workers celebrated by Whitman, the naked feeling you find in jazz and black culture.

If you could own any single artwork what would you choose to have?

Brueghel's "The Triumph of Death," because it's so big and ingenious, and is such a masterpiece of black humor. It depicts thousands of skeletons bowing before a group of terrified living people who are pulling out their swords and struggling to battle down the skeletons. That was the first painting I saw when I was traveling through Europe in 1957. I went from Tangiers up into Madrid and to the Prado Museum, and bam, I saw that painting and it opened my eyes. Bosch's "Garden of Delights" is next to it, and both paintings are really terrific.

What's the most significant change you've observed in yourself over the course of your life?

My hair's fallen out and my teeth aren't in good shape any more, but my essential nature is, and always has been, empty, and that doesn't change.

How do you reconcile this concept of emptiness with the fears and desires we're all gripped by? Are we empty of these things?

No, but the things themselves are empty. It's comparable to having a nightmare. While you're having the nightmare your body is filled with fear, but after you wake up you realize it wasn't real. Our existence is transitory and nothing is permanent. Pleasure isn't permanent, but pain isn't either, so with impermanence you always have an out. This is the wisdom of the East that we've lost out on in the West, where there's a permanent god who has the power to damn you to hell or bring you up to heaven. So you have to work hard your whole life to make sure you're not eternally damned, because you only have this one chance. That's a lot of pressure.

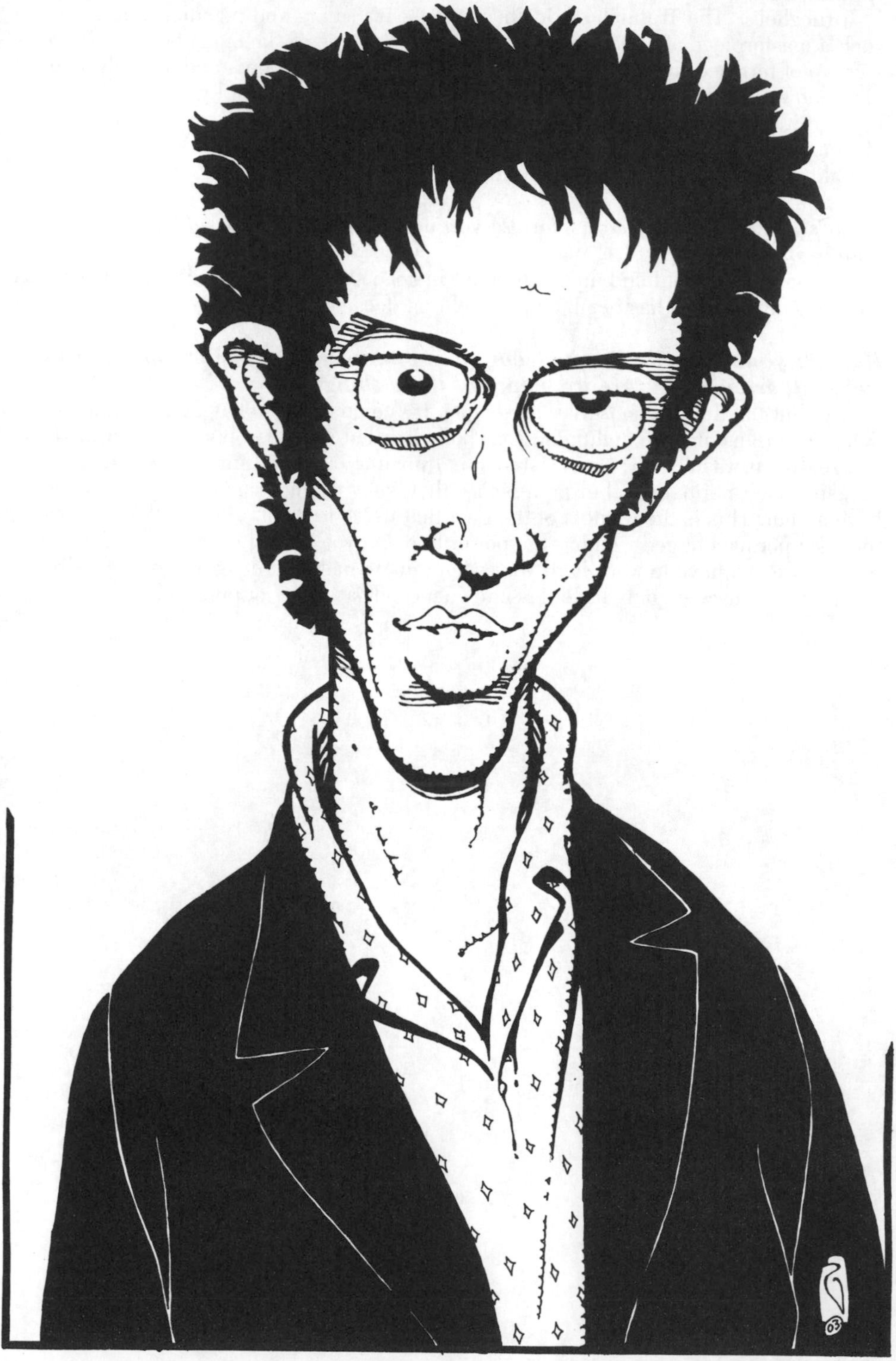

Richard Hell

I knew I loved Richard Hell when I heard his definition of his chosen profession: "rock 'n' roll is trying to convince girls to pay money to be near you." Too hilariously true! If Hell had never written a note of music he'd still rate high in my book as a humorist. Lauded by Elvis Costello in 1978 as "the most brilliant guy in American rock 'n' roll," Hell coined the phrase "blank generation," pioneered that punk essential, the shredded T-shirt, and helped lay the foundations for the New York punk of the '70s. A devilishly handsome man with a beautiful mouth and a bad attitude, he was one of the most charismatic figures to emerge from that scene, and that he's not better known can only be attributed to the haphazard methodology by which history is written.

Born Richard Myers in Lexington, Kentucky in 1949, Hell dropped out of school when he was 16 and took a bus to New York City to become a poet. He spent the next few years working in bookstores and publishing in small literary magazines, then in 1972 an old high school pal named Tom Miller blew into town, and together they formed a band called the Neon Boys. Miller changed his name to Verlaine, Myers took the name Hell, and the race was on. The Neon Boys morphed into the hugely influential band, Television, but conflicts between Verlaine and Hell prompted Hell to strike out on his own two years before Television released its first album in 1975. Whereas Verlaine was a musician to the bone, Hell was a performer who happened to use music; that annoyed Verlaine no end, and their childhood friendship ended on a very sour note. Hell then hooked up with notorious junkies Johnny Thunders and Jerry Nolan, who'd just left the New York Dolls, to form the Heartbreakers, but he left that group after a year without having recorded anything. In 1976 he formed the Voidoids and finally made it into a studio to record his debut album, of 1977, Blank Generation. Featuring tunes of major genius such as "Love Comes in Spurts," the album was hailed by no less an authority than Lester Bangs as "some of the most fitfully dangerous rock 'n' roll I've heard this decade." There was a lot of momentum behind Hell at that point, but his business instincts were never the greatest, and it took him five years to record his second album Destiny Street. Two years later he quit the music game altogether following the release of the aptly titled R.I.P., a collection of outtakes and unreleased material spanning the previous ten years.

During the '80s Hell appeared in several independent films, including Susan Seidelman's first film, Smithereens, and its follow-up, Desperately Seeking Susan. What he really focused on after putting music on the backburner, however, was getting back to the work he'd initially moved to New York to do, and over the past twenty years he's published two novels and three collections of poetry. In 1998 he helped launch Cuz Editions, an offbeat publishing house that's produced nine books thus far, including one by Hell titled Weather. That same year he exhibited his drawings at Rupert Goldsworthy Gallery in New York. In 2000, Hell returned to the studio with the original Voidoids to record the song, "Oh," and the following year Powerhouse Books published Hot and Cold, *a glossy, best-of collection of Hell's writings and visual art. All the things that made Hell such a great rock 'n' roller are operating in full in his writing, which is smart, irreverent, ruthlessly honest, and very funny.*

-1983-

How do you account for the success of some of the first generation New York punk bands – Blondie, Talking Heads – and the failure of others that were acknowledged to be just as worthy – The Ramones, Television, and Richard Hell & The Voidoids?

I can guess why the Ramones didn't make it, I don't know why Television didn't, and I know exactly why I didn't. Commercial success was never my main priority and my music was cryptic enough that the only way to make it popular would've been to tour all year long for three years – which is what Blondie and Talking Heads did. I was never willing to do that, and I don't regret the decision at all because I'm real happy with the position I'm in now. One of the biggest problems I've had to deal with in my career is the fact that I go into deep, dark depressions that are hard to overcome. That's taken up about half my time in the past, but I've learned that the busier I am the better I feel. I've finally found a good manager and I'm excited about the band I've got now, and I'm working up new material for my third album, which will be on a major label. I'm also working on a book – a compilation of things I've written over the past ten years. I'm scheduled to make another film this spring where I'll be playing a Las Vegas type, a real vulgar saloon singer who's supposed to be in his 40s. So, I'm doing a lot and I feel real good right now.

When Susan Seidelman's first film Smithereens was released in 1982, your performance in it garnered quite a bit of attention; did that have a noticeable effect in your life?

The film had a much larger effect on everyone involved than we'd imagined it would. It drew a diverse audience because it's like a film about the White House, in that it shows a closed world people are curious about and wouldn't get exposed to otherwise. And it shows them a funny, slightly glossy, homogenized version of that world, so the film made me palatable to a class of culture lovers I've never had any appeal to before. Not that the movie's dishonest, but it was reviewed as "exposing the nitty-gritty of the cruddy fringes of the rock scene" by critics who had no way of knowing how accurate it is. In fact, that scene is much grittier than *Smithereens* shows, but the movie does give an accurate picture of one particular class of kids. These are kids who live in a world of mutual manipulation and just take it for granted that that's how people behave with each other. They're likeable, and although they're not the sort of people I'd want to have to trust, they're not sophisticated enough to be corrupt. They're young and don't see much future for themselves because they don't fit into conventional society, so they're just trying to get as much as they can. The kids – and *Smithereens* – are post-punk in that they reflect an attitude of careerism and ambition that now dominates the rock scene, and that didn't exist ten years ago. When I started out rock 'n' roll was thought to be more a religious thing, and it wasn't something every high school kid considered as a future career possibility.

Has the music suffered because of the climate of careerism that surrounds it at present?

That's always been part of popular music, and maybe there is more room for people to take chances than there was in 1973, so perhaps things have changed for the better. But it's an illusion to believe that the stuff that gets into the charts isn't just as much a preconceived product designed for listeners as it's ever been.

What are you presently listening to?

My favorite new wave group is Flipper – I really dig Flipper, but I don't listen to them. I listen to great singers – Sly Stone, Marvin Gaye, Aretha, Smokey Robinson.

Aren't there any great white singers?

There are but I can't think of any offhand. I tend to listen to stuff that's as far as possible from what I'm capable of doing, maybe in the hope that I can absorb a little bit of it.

In Smithereens you play a smirking, opportunistic rogue who's bad in such a charming way, that girls hand over their wallets even as you laugh at them for doing it. Several critics have made the observation that you're basically playing yourself; how much of a hand did you take in defining the character?

My performance is autobiographical only in that I wasn't confident enough in my skills as an actor to try to invent a new style of behavior, so I had to draw on my own experiences and ways of expressing myself in real life. I was fairly tight and self-conscious in the scenes that were shot towards the beginning of the schedule, but I think my performance improved as the film progressed. I was given a lot of freedom to improvise while we were shooting, and little things like putting beer in my hair and putting the pizza in the toaster were my idea. I didn't contribute much as far as dialogue because they'd somewhat rewritten the script with me in mind after I was cast in the part and I thought the script was well written.

Does acting call for skills similar to those involved in performing rock 'n' roll?

The best rock 'n' rollers – Dylan, Jagger, Bowie, The Beatles – have all the skills an actor has, but the reverse of that certainly isn't true. You can't assume that a good actor could also perform rock 'n' roll.

If your career as an actor took off would you be content to leave music in the past?

No, but I have always wanted to write and direct movies because film involves practically every other medium – music, writing, acting. I haven't had the opportunity to direct movies, and though I'm no way certain that I have what it takes, I really hope I get a chance to try. The thing about directing is that you have to really be a diplomat in order to keep a diverse crew of people not just content, but excited and inspired.

I've read that Elvis Costello's former manager, Jake Riviera, bankrolled you in a film project in the mid '70s. Did he?

No. He commissioned me and [photographer] Roberta Bayley to do a book based on this wild idea he had. Jake had this vintage 1959 Cadillac and we were supposed to drive it across America and do a book based on the trip. I was looking forward to the southern leg of the journey as being the most fertile territory, but the car gave out on us in St. Louis. It was a very unprofessional automobile.

What do you consider to be your greatest strength as an artist?

Writing, probably. When I first came to New York I bought a printing press for 100 dollars and I was publishing books, pamphlets and magazines out of my house. I was collaborating on a lot of stuff with Tom Verlaine. We were living together then and hanging out all the time, and it was right before we started playing. We'd stay up all night writing stuff. I always considered our writing projects the literary equivalent of what Television was musically – at least when I was a member – but with me and Tom's roles reversed. With the writing projects I ran everything and made all the decisions. In Television, Tom had all the power, because at that time he was the musician and I was really dependent on him for everything except extra-musical ideas, aside from the fact that I sang and wrote the words to half the songs.

It seems that you and Verlaine had an exceptional, creatively stimulating relationship. Do you regret that the relationship is over?

I hated him for years after I left Television because we really were each other's best friends. But even at its best, it was always a volatile friendship where we sort of hated each other as much as we liked each other. Basically, we were the only people that could appreciate and respond to certain things in each other, so we were forced to be friends because no one else understood the way we thought! But we both always felt we were being taken for granted by the other, so it was impossible. But I really did hate him for a long time, because I thought Television could've been the most important group to come along in years. But because Tom was the musician – even though I wrote half the lyrics and was learning how to write music – he felt, probably justifiably, that he was the group and I was tagging along and lucky to have fallen into the situation.

Do you really believe he felt that way?

He sure did insist on doing all the interviews and being the spokesman for the group to everyone who got interested – which was a lot of people, fast. And half of what got the group the immediate attention it received in New York were contributions I made that Tom sneered at as being superficial, non-musical and extraneous. I thought of Television as being more than just a rock 'n' roll group, and I wanted it to be a cultural force and really have an impact. So I conceived of a way of dressing and presenting ourselves onstage and to the press, themes and ideas for the lyrics and music, that were crucial to what made the group what it was at the time. But Tom had never had any power in his life and he'd always had this real strong resentment towards the world for ignoring him, because he always thought of himself as being some kind of genius or something. And the moment he started getting some kind of attention he just went totally berserk and started trying to squeeze me out of the group. He said he wanted a better bass player – that's how he explained why the group would be better off without me. I used to go really wild onstage, and the first thing that indicated I was on the way out was when he told me to stop moving onstage. He said he didn't want people to be distracted when he was singing. When that happened I knew it was over. When we formed the band we were co-leaders and things were democratic, but the moment we got some attention everything changed. And because the group could survive without me, but it couldn't survive without him, he had the power to insist that I leave. Last year Verlaine and I had to go into the studio together to remix some things for a compilation EP and we were perfectly civil to each other. I don't have any hard feelings towards him any more, and it's conceivable he might play guitar on a song of mine or something, but there's no way we'd ever really try to work together again.

Were you able to realize some of the ideas you had for Television with the Voidoids?

Yes, but I got that part out of my system pretty quickly once I had an outlet for it. The Sex Pistols picked it up and carried it out so completely that it was unnecessary for me to pursue some of the ideas I'd begun with.

How do you see your music evolving?

Destiny Street was sort of a transitional album. Now I have a clear idea of what I want to do and a band that's capable of doing it, and the next album will sound completely different. It's gonna surprise people. The guitar players are of the same caliber of the ones I've always worked with, but the record will have a much stronger rhythm section.

One thing I've always disliked about the first two albums was that songs were recorded within a month or two of when I wrote them, and they always sounded far better a year later after we'd been playing them a long time. So now we're evolving the material with extensive rehearsal and squeezing out everything the songs have to offer before we record them.

Did your family encourage you to pursue a career in show business?

Are you kidding? I was the high school drop out kid of a college teacher. My father died when I was seven and I was raised by my mother until I was 17, when I quit school and ran away from Lexington, Kentucky and went to New York. My mother's in Romania right now on a Fulbright Scholarship so she hasn't seen *Smithereens*, but it's nice when on that rare occasion, something happens in my life that I know she'll get a kick out of. Like, last year, a teacher at New York's School for the Visual Arts wrote to tell me she included my records along with T.S. Eliot and Allen Ginsberg in her literature class. That's the kind of thing my mother likes to hear. But generally speaking, my material isn't exactly up her alley. Basically, I think she's relieved that I didn't just overdose on drugs or become a fully-fledged petty criminal.

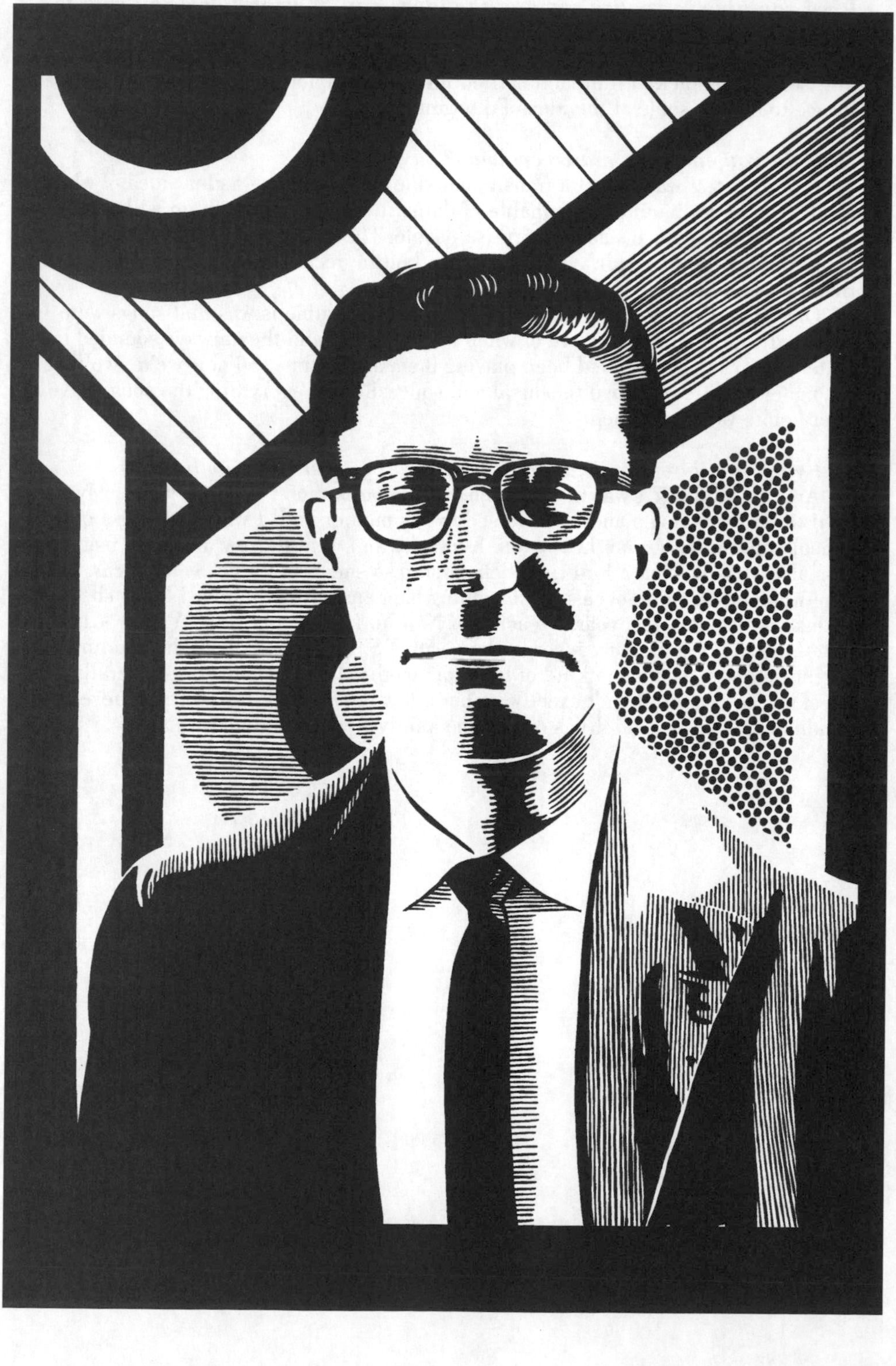

Walter Hopps

....

Walter Hopps isn't known outside of the art world, but within its cloistered confines he's a legend. Born in 1932 to a middle-class family in Eagle Rock, California, he was in high school when he befriended Walter and Louise Arensberg, who had amassed a world-class collection of Surrealist art. The primary patrons of Marcel Duchamp, the Arensbergs owned all of his key pieces, and seeing that revolutionary work set Hopps' course in life. There were, however, many fascinating detours along way.

In 1951 he teamed up with Jim Newman to form Concert Hall Workshop, an agency devoted to the booking and promotion of jazz, which Hopps loved. By 1955, however, he'd put music aside and opened his first gallery, Syndell Studios, in Brentwood, California. In 1957 he partnered with artist Ed Kienholz to open the Ferus Gallery, which is acknowledged as the first significant Los Angeles gallery to showcase the work of young artists. Among those who received support from Ferus early in their careers are Ed Ruscha, Ed Kienholz, Bruce Conner, Robert Irwin, Jay Defeo, Andy Warhol, Roy Lichtenstein, Ken Price, Peter Voulkos, Wallace Berman, Jasper Johns, and Frank Stella. Hopps bought out Kienholz's share of the gallery shortly after Ferus opened, and not long after that he began organizing exhibitions for the Pasadena Museum of Art. In 1962 Hopps was hired as a full-time curator at Pasadena, and he gave his share of Ferus to dealer Irving Blum. In 1963 Hopps was made director at Pasadena, and he mounted several historically significant shows during his tenure there, the most noteworthy of them being the first retrospective of Marcel Duchamp.

By that point Hopps had earned a reputation as a dazzlingly brilliant man who was mercurial in the extreme. The museum world is a starched and stodgy institutional milieu, and Hopps carried himself like a rock star. He took drugs, showed up late or not at all, led a complicated romantic life, and had no trouble telling people he found stupid that they were stupid. Artists loved him, museum board members tended not to, and just about everyone who hired him wound up firing him eventually. Exasperating though Hopps could be, most of the people who had run-ins with him wound up forgiving him, for the simple reason that he's so much more fun than most people in the art world.

Hopps' first firing took place in 1966 at the Pasadena Museum, which let him go after he suffered a psychological breakdown that required several weeks of hospitalization. After he got back on his feet, a fellowship at the Institute for Policy Studies took him to Washington, D.C., where he landed a job as director of the Corcoran in 1967. He remained there until he was fired in 1971, and the following year he became a curator for the Smithsonian's National Museum of Art. In 1980 he began a long and fruitful partnership with the great art patron, Dominique de Menil, who made him founding director of the Menil Collection when it opened in Houston in 1987. By 1989 it was clear to all involved that Hopps' gifts are as a curator rather than a museum director, and he was made consulting curator for the Menil, a title that allowed him a great deal of flexibility. During the '90s he worked for various museums organizing traveling exhibitions of work by Ed Kienholz, Robert Rauschenberg, Joseph Cornell, and Marcel Duchamp, among others. In 2001 he was made an adjunct curator for the Guggenheim, which invited him to organize a retrospective exhibition of work by James Rosenquist. It opened in 2003 at the Menil in Houston, where Hopps lives with his third wife, Caroline Huber.

The following interview, which was conducted in 1993, draws on a tiny fraction of Hopps' frame of reference. In the interest of brevity I tried to restrict the conversation to art, but Hopps is capable of speaking knowledgeably about music, movies, California history, poetry, racism in America, literature, fashion, photography, cars, comic books, advertising, class and anti-Semitism in America, shamanism, the Mexican revolution, the theories of Freud and Jung, the C.I.A., theoretical physics – he knows about lots of things. During the '90s Hopps was plagued with a series of health problems that slowed him down considerably, but he's still the fastest draw in the West when it comes to supplying information about any artist you care to name. His remarkable memory is a central component of his talent, and his visual memory is particularly acute – he seems able to recall in detail every artwork he's ever laid eyes on. The second crucial component of Hopp's gift is his enthusiasm; he has a lust for life that's a beautiful thing to behold.

Why do you love art?
Because it's the most beautiful secret language we have.

What's the first artwork you recall seeing?
A landscape by Conrad Buff. There were paintings of his in the house where I grew up, and I liked them very much. During the '20s and '30s Buff developed a kind of transcendental landscape painting rooted in Wordsworth's notion of the sublime – you know, "god is in every blade of grass" – and at its best, Buff's work articulates a reverence for the frontier and nature that was all over my family. A lot of what was in my family had to do with getting away from big cities, and many of my relatives lived lives close to what I'd see in movie westerns. I grew up reading all the western hard-boiled people, too, and there was lots of Steinbeck in the house. My father loved Steinbeck because of his anti-cleric, rational transcendentalism. One of Steinbeck's great fictional creations was the character Ed Ricketts, who was a biologist and a wise man, and I was raised to have a deep trust in natural history that's colored my attitude towards the profession I'm in. I don't like aesthetics but I love ethnology, and whatever work I do has to stand up as reasonable ethnology.

I later learned that Buff was Swiss born, and was part of a Teutonic tradition of idealized nature associated with the Swiss-German artist Ferdinand Hodler. Buff was given a bland retrospective at the Los Angeles County Museum of Art several years ago, but he's a fascinating painter and is one of the great missing links in the culture of Los Angeles. There was a great polarity between 19th century realist painting and plein air modernism during the years Buff was active, and his great nemesis was Stanton McDonald Wright.

Southern California has a grand tradition of lyrical abstraction that I refer to as Los Lyricos, and Wright is a key figure in this school. In 1905 he went to Paris and immersed himself in the great Cubist and abstract innovations that took place there in the teens, and by the late '40s he was doing extraordinary work in the fluid end of lyric abstraction. Helen Frankenthaler works out of this territory too, but her work has gone limp. She was always a little mushy, and the smeary side of anima was there at the very beginning for her, but there's an early painting called "Mountains and Sea" that's very strong. Her work was never gritty, but it had a crazy daring early on, and she was doing splashy stuff that she pulled off. Then the work went flat. Lorser Feitelson is another artist who warrants mentioning here. During the '40s, Jules Langsner was the only sophisticated critic in Southern California, nervous, neurotic and depressed though he was, and he grasped the significance of that work, coined the term hard edge, and was an early champion of the work of Feitelson. It was a blind spot that Arensberg didn't go near people like Feitelson and Wright.

It sounds as if you were exposed to art and culture at a young age; would you describe your childhood as idyllic?

No, I would not. When I was in third grade I contracted a severe case of rheumatic fever, which is a bacterial infection of the heart muscle. There were no antibiotics then, and I had to drop out of school and spend months in bed. I was hit with another bout of it five years later, which meant I spent puberty and part of my adolescence confined to the second floor of the family house. By the end of the ninth grade the illness was essentially over, but I'd endured years of what I considered confinement, and I think I've spent the rest of my life making up for that.

I was left to teach myself, and I spent lots of time with my paternal grandparents who lived with us during World War II. They were elderly, especially my grandfather, Walter Hopps I, who was born around the time of the Civil War in the region we now call Oakland. He was a rancher and self-taught inventor who ran away from home to pan gold when he was 13, and in 1880 he ran away to Mexico to seek his fortune. My father was born there, in Tampico, Mexico, early in the 20th Century. To have someone around who could remember that far back affected me a lot. My grandfather worked with ranchers in the Owens Valley to help blow up the Mulholland aqueduct, so water rights were something I grew up hearing about. I guess you could say I'm on a certain side of Chinatown.

My family were boat builders, gold miners, adventurers, and crafts people, and beginning with my great-grandmother, they were doctors. There were doctors in my family going way back, and my maternal grandfather, Doctor Finney, studied in Vienna and maintained a wonderful library I had access to. I spent a lot of time with books when I was young and I read everything: Dashiell Hammett as it was just coming out, Havelock Ellis, medical books, *The Encyclopedia Britannica* – all sorts of things.

I had books but it was a lonely existence, and one thing that got me through that period was developing the skill of remembering what I'd seen and where I'd been. It's a skill I still use when I'm on planes or have an idle moment – I'll just walk through places I've been and look at everything in my imagination, reconstructing things and doping it out from bits of remembered or printed matter.

One of the tragedies of the illnesses I suffered as a child was that my father practiced on the family. He was so confident of his skills that he refused to trust another doctor to care for my mother, brother, or I, and although he knew the ethical prohibitions about this, he took my tonsils and appendix out. He had no psychological insight into the effects of his actions, and after removing my appendix he presented it to me in a bottle.

You grew up in Eagle Rock, which was considered the wrong side of the tracks to the wealthy, neighboring community of Pasadena during the '20s and '30s. Were you aware of that as a child?

Absolutely. I went to a high society nursery school in Pasadena called Broad Oaks, and I knew that the reason I was able to attend that school was because my mother served as the school doctor. Eagle Rock was largely founded by working class Irish entrepreneurs and my mother's side of the family, which had roots in Eagle Rock, were shanty Irish. The difference between Eagle Rock and Pasadena was something I was always aware of, and the poignancy of that difference sank in when I returned to Pasadena after missing most of grammar school, as a scholarship student at the Polytechnic School, which was a day prep school attached to Cal-Tech. It was a fancy school that put you on a fast track, and there were four of us there who were the nerds in class. Within days we all knew who we were, on what basis we were in that school, and that we were different from the Chandler and the Irvine children who were there. At Polytechnic everyone had to address the morning assembly, but my fear of standing up in front of the class was so intense that I'd throw up. I was 14, I was terribly shy, and gym class was physically terrifying. My mother was sensitive to the problems I was having and she did an amazing thing, which was to bring in an older foster brother to live with us. She knew that when it came to cars and girls my father wouldn't be any help to me because he and I were growing increasingly alienated. So she got this charming, sociopathic guy from Syria to live with us named Abbott Dugally. He was a year older than me and he'd had delinquency problems, but she sized him up as right for our family. She knew I wasn't much of a pal to my hunter-fisherman father – who, of course, raised all kinds of hell at this guy suddenly being brought in. But she stood her ground, he became a real buddy to my father – which took the pressure off of me – and he looked out for me. He was a street-smart guy who gave me my first condoms, and he was a fantastic gymnast. He told me, "Look I'm gonna be on the gym team and I'm gonna be a star, but you can make the team too, and you should, because the fastest girls at school like gymnasts. There are a few things you'd probably be good at and I'll train you." That's all it took, and he was right. I worked on the side horse and made the team in rope climb.

At what point did you begin the transformation from shy geek to art world mover and shaker?

I dropped out of the Polytechnic in fairly short order and demanded that I be allowed to attend public high school, and that's where things changed for me. I became entrepreneurial, and beginning in high school I was active in the art world in my own way, but I kept that from my parents. I was never asked whether I wanted to be a doctor – it was assumed I would be – and after my grandfather died I was given his laboratory equipment. My father coached me how to kill birds and dissect them, and I remember him chiding me for the way I got the respiratory system out of a blue jay. I felt terrible about having to shoot the birds in the first place, and I'm thinking about beautiful doves and wonderful blue jays, while my father's saying, "Isn't it interesting – the blue jay has a larger brain."

Even as your family was pressing a career in medicine on you, your interest in art was developing in the form of a photographic practice. How did that start?

In 1943 my father gave me an enlarger and everything I needed to make pictures, and I had a darkroom all across the '40s – that was the only physical activity I had during the months of confinement. I tried to do sophisticated things with Brownie pictures – still lives and so forth – then when I ran out of things to photograph I started re-photographing pictures in books. That's why I have a sort of special fondness for the likes of Richard Prince. Some of my early photographs were published in *Semina* [a limited edition, hand-made magazine created by the artist Wallace Berman], but I've only had one exhibition, which was at the Coronet Theater on La Cienega Boulevard in 1953. Certain people know about my work, but I've said no exhibitions while I'm alive. I've told a few people they could do a 50-year retrospective after I'm gone. I stopped taking pictures in the mid-'70s, but now I've got all sorts of curious objects I want to photograph.

As a child you had experiences in which you were close to death; how did that affect you?
Several relatives died in the family compound in Eagle Rock, and as a result of that, I think I'm a bit more fatalistic about these things than other people. I was very close to my grandfather Finney, and I was with him when he died in 1938. I was six at the time, and the thing I remember about his death is that during his final days he wanted me to be with him and he wanted to listen to the radio – he wanted to go out knowing what was going on. His death induced a curious hallucinatory state in me, and he later appeared to me twice and spoke to me as I walked by myself in the hills of Eagle Rock. It was more vivid than an acid trip and was so compelling – it was a heavy experience, this thing. I dealt with it years later working with a Jungian analyst who helped me to understand that we create these things.

Having been raised an atheist, how did you reconcile this experience with the beliefs you'd been taught?
That wasn't a problem because there was lots of lore in the family and discussion of paranormal things. My grandfather Hopps and my father had lived in Mexico where they witnessed amazing stuff with the magic people known as the Brujos. When Carlos Castaneda's books came out my father read them and chuckled and said, "It's funny someone's finally writing about these things I grew up with."

You were a young teenager during the years that the Holocaust was unfolding. How did that affect you?
It's astounding how little sense we had of that during the '40s. In the popular literature of the time goddamned little information about that came through, and it wasn't until I was in high school that I began encountering literature on the left. After 1950 it became an enraging issue for me, but prior to that, the world was irrevocably changed for me with the atomic tests in New Mexico and the bombing of Hiroshima. That was mega for me, and was comparable to Martians landing. It was a very big deal in my mind, I still think about it, and for me it's the greatest story of the century.

During the same period all the left baiting and persecution at the hands of Joe McCarthy was going on. It was terrible, and it had a hellacious effect on the art world in Southern California. The first curator for modern art at the County Museum, Jim Byrnes, was derided because he bought a Pollock for $250, which was the first Pollock to enter public domain in Southern California. Eugene Delacourt was head of the entire complex at the time, and he was ordered to take "Communistic work" out of the collection, so a wonderful Picasso from around the time of "Guernica" had to come off the wall. A Magritte had to come down too, for god's sake! No one's more apolitical in modern art than Magritte, unless it's Balthus.

In the early '50s you were booking and promoting jazz concerts. How did that begin?
Music was hugely important to me when I was young. I went to the Hollywood Bowl a lot in the '40s, and I remember seeing Stan Kenton there before I left for college. One of the strangest musicians in his band was an alto sax player named Boots Mussulli who was a pure id Italian honker who didn't belong in the world of cool jazz. His showcase number with Kenton was a nuts version of "Come Back to Sorrento," with Boots doing a big, slavering solo. It was considered quite radical for

Stan Kenton to be at the Bowl, and the audience was a strange collection of young white hipsters. There were practically no black people, probably because Kenton's band was too Weber's Bread white. Shelly Manne was the big, over-the-top drummer, and there was an incredible guitar player in the band named Laurindo Almeida. Before there was Carlos Jobim with that wonderful Brazilian music — some of the best pop music ever made came out of Brazil — there was Almeida, who was right at the edge of being a classical guitar player. He was the most sophisticated Hispanic anywhere near jazz at the time, except for Chano Pozo, and the extraordinary Afro-Cuban people who played with Dizzy Gillespie. Guitar, singing and drums seem to be how south of the border got into popular music and jazz.

While I was in high school I used to see the Ellington Band all the time at the Million Dollar Theater downtown on Main Street. On weekends the Million Dollar would have a double bill of crummy movies, then you'd get these fantastic matinee or early evening concerts. The second bill on the show was usually the Will Mastin Trio starring Sammy Davis Jr., and that's where I first met Sammy. Music is one of the greatest integrating forces in America. Whites could go into the black world in those days if they were cool and looking for the music down on Central Avenue, or at Norman Granz's concerts at the Philharmonic, which were big sweaty deals. Living out on the edge of Pasadena I was in a damned lilywhite area, and, since Eagle Rock was less classy than Pasadena, you didn't even have black servants.

I harbored the illusion that the great Afro-American music was going to be recognized and make a fortune for everyone, and figured that if I was part of that booking and recording world I could support my interest in contemporary art, where there was no money to be had. I had it totally backwards, but at the time I never dreamed that work by Pollock or De Kooning would be worth a fortune. Many of my artist friends during the '50s and '60s were deeply involved with jazz, too. I knew Frank Stella just as his career was beginning to take off, and we shared an interest in Ornette Coleman. Before we'd seen the great brilliance of John Coltrane and understood how extraordinary he was, there was Ornette, who was amazingly ambitious in those years. I figured that when Frank was money ahead he'd sponsor Ornette, much as [Robert] Rauschenberg and [Jasper] Johns sponsored John Cage when it was tough going. Frank didn't step up to the plate, though, and then one day he told me he'd bought a racehorse and it put a real strain on our friendship. I just couldn't believe it. I asked, "Did you name him Ornette," and Frank gave me one of the black Sicilian looks he's capable of. He knew what I felt but never said a word.

A friendship with Frank Stella is really heavy maintenance and I don't like getting boxed in by artist friends who have severe notions of who I should spend time with, or who is or isn't worth knowing. Frank's a brilliant artist but there's a streak in him that's not so nice. You can feel a buried away humanity in a [Piet] Mondrian that you never quite feel with Stella. Towards the end of his life Mondrian became a kind of social activist working with prisoners, and you sense in his art that he felt he owed something more to life than just his art.

When you first began running galleries, many of the artists you promoted — Sonia Gechtoff, Jay DeFeo, Frank Lobdell, Hassel Smith — lived in San Francisco. How was that connection established?

During the late '40s and into the '50s, the real action in art was in the Bay area, and an awful lot of what I was interested I had to import from San Francisco. I thought my first museum job would be at the San Francisco Modern, and although it turned out to be at Pasadena, I kept thinking one day I'd get a job up north. Then, as it got deeper into the '50s and the '60s, it became increasingly intractable to do anything in the Bay area.

I'd like to talk a bit about some of the artists associated with the Ferus Gallery, and thought we might start with Wallace Berman. How did he come into your life?

You're in a room where everybody is affecting the posture of being cool, and then Mr. Really Cool walks into the place. That was Wallace. Wallace had it in him to be a killer but he chose not to be, and people were conscious of that power in him. He was an extraordinarily generous, gentle man, and was a Jew who believed in Christ, very much so.

The first time I saw him was in 1951 at a jazz club on Central Avenue, but we didn't talk until the first time I visited him at the house in Beverly Glen where he lived with his wife, Shirley, and their son Tosh. I was impressed by Wallace and we hit it off, so I'd often go there for the evening after spending a day at UCLA. It was a simple environment you entered through the kitchen, and the bedroom was basically a kind of nest off to the side of this all-purpose sitting room where people ate, sat around, listened to music, smoked dope or whatever, through the night. An amazing range of people passed through that house. It wasn't as if there was a sign somewhere announcing, "Come one, come all," but people learned of it by word of mouth. It was similar to the situation with William Burroughs. Why did people knock themselves out and go all the hell over to Tangiers to see Burroughs? Because it was an important thing to do to go see Bill, and in the same way it was important to see Wallace. When I was making photographs, the person I most wanted to like what I was doing was Berman, so I was really proud that two of my things were in the first issue of *Semina*.

Berman had a distinctly different persona from most of the artists associated with Ferus. Was that a source of conflict at the time?

It's been said that the Ferus Gallery had two crews, the mystics and the lumberjacks, and that's kind of true. The lumberjacks were also known as the studs and they didn't relate well to Berman. At that point Berman and Kienholz were the leaders in these two contingents, and there was a great distance between them. Kienholz finally couldn't stand it any more and he challenged Berman to a game of pool, and because Berman liked Kienholz he said, "Okay," and the word went out. There was a pool hall on Santa Monica Boulevard where the game was to take place and everybody showed up there on the appointed night. They decided to play snooker, which is a very hard game compared to pocket pool, and Berman walked over to the blackboard for keeping score, and wrote "Kienholz," at the top of one column, and "Winner" at the top of the other column. Ed was a good player, but "Winner" cleaned his pipes. Kienholz didn't want to have any truck with Berman personally, but he absolutely backed Berman showing at Ferus because he knew he was a good artist. It's a testament to how interested all of us were in Berman's art that Kienholz was delighted to have the show there.

That Berman show has become the stuff of legend in that it was shut down by the L.A. vice squad, and Berman had to stand trial for exhibiting pornographic material. What are your recollections of that episode?

Wallace knew there were things floating around in the culture that were much more raw and offensive than anything he had in that exhibit, and he was very upset when they raided his show. When he appeared in court he told the judge that an angel appeared to him and told him to marry a good woman and devote himself to God. That was his defense in court, and it didn't hold any water for the damn judge, who figured he had a nut case on the stand, who was involved with pornography. After the show Wallace gave me the one small section of the show that might've been deemed pornographic by some people – a small wooden box with an erotic photograph in it that hung from a cross. The rest of the Cross, along with the Temple, were burned up as best I know in his friend Bob Alexander's back yard.

Who do you think brought the show to the attention of the authorities? There are those who contend that it was Kienholz who contacted the vice squad in an attempt to generate publicity for the gallery.

I think that it came from the general public, and had absolutely no sense that Kienholz or anyone else known to us staged it. By that point, Ferus had enough of a reputation that a wide range of people came in, and I think someone wandered in and said, "Holy shit, you can't have this image hanging on the cross!" The dumb vice cops who showed up to raid the show were pretty clueless, and after walking around the gallery they finally said, "We got a report there were some pornographic images in this show." They hadn't noticed the image on the cross, so they walked over to the piece titled "Temple," which included an erotic drawing made by the artist Cameron while she was on peyote, and that's what they arrested him for.

Berman made many different kinds of art; which of his works do you feel is the most representative and crucial?

To me, it's all of a piece, with the possible exception of the bebop surrealist drawings he made in the late '40s, which represent a period of his life he turned away from. He became absolutely opposed to hard drugs, but there was a period in his life when he was involved with all of that, and was a brilliant gambler and a hustler. Those drawings are a product of that period and they're part of an imagist tradition that extends back to Edgar Allan Poe. When I first met him, that drawing period was just winding up. Among that body of work is a drawing that's one of the toughest things I've ever seen. It's a rendering of a guy with a giant dick that he's jammed in the face of a woman whose head has been torn off. The body's there on its knees with the damned head just ripped off! It's like an S. Clay Wilson drawing, and obviously there's a lot of hostility towards women in it. For a period, some of his art evinced hostility toward women many of us might've been feeling in that place and time. Somehow Wallace got through all that, and I think he adored women. He certainly became something else when he began his life with Shirley. Her gentle instincts and the centering force of the family they created together brought tremendous contentment and peace to Wallace, and he moved through the world very differently after he married her. He used a few fragments of that earlier art in some collage paintings he made, which were handsome, somber things that were simultaneously contemporary and archaic looking. They sort of jumped outside of time, and were an important part of his show at Ferus. There were the sculptural tableaux – primarily "The Cross," "The Temple," and "The Panel," which comprised the core of that exhibition – and he did posters for film festivals that were wonderful. Wallace loved film, and he made a film called *Semina*. There's a singular sculptural piece titled "Homage to Hesse" that wound up in Dean Stockwell's collection, and he made box assemblages out of wood, rock, glass and chain. And of course, there was *Semina*, which was a strange mix of rough, secular stuff and bits of ethereal transcendence. Berman was the first artist I knew to create a literary and visual arts portfolio that included beautiful things from the past. Taken together, it points to a world beyond.

Did you remain in touch with Berman up until his death in 1976?

I moved to Washington, D.C. in 1968, so there was a period of eight years when I'd only see him when I visited L.A. I observed a change in him over those years, and noticed that he became much more quiet and inward. One of the things that resulted from Berman's Ferus exhibition being raided by the cops was that he refused to show his work in galleries and would only display his art in his own private little shows. Over the years I periodically asked him if he'd consider letting me arrange for a showing of his work, and shortly before he died he expressed some interest – albeit, interest of a very specific kind. Berman loved William Blake, who's an example of a great artist who was totally at odds with the tide of art history. Blake had a real belief in God and Christian mythology at precisely the point when we were supposed to be free of all that, and today his retarded work looks infinitely better than that of most of his English contemporaries. In 1967 Berman went to London for an exhibition at the Robert Frazer Gallery, and after he returned he said, "I loved seeing the William Blakes at the Tate in London. Could you get me a little show near the Blakes? That would be cool."

What's your most vivid memory of Wallace?

Watching him look at art when he felt that he was unobserved. He'd sit at attention, shoulders a little extended, leaning forward, staring hard into a piece of art. He had a visibly acute way of looking at things.

On to Ed Kienholz.

Ed's early life was complicated and was mostly on the road. He grew up on a hardworking farm outside of Spokane that was fairly successful, and the affluence of his family is a little more than people realize. Ed strikes an aggressive, country boy, anti-intellectual stance, but he had brushes with art school, and his knowledge of what was going on in art is more than he allows. He's similar in that way to Rauschenberg, who tends to downplay what a good art education he got.

One of the things I wanted to foreground in the Kienholz retrospective I organized in 1996 was his grounding in abstract expressionism. Kienholz set up his first serious studio in a storefront in El Paso, Texas in 1953, and there was very little work from 1953-57 in the Kienholz survey Maurice Tuchman mounted at LACMA in 1966. Kienholz always had a bent towards painted relief, but he comes out of a milieu of expressionist painters in the Pacific Northwest. He had tangential knowledge of Kenneth Callahan, C.S. Price, and Gilda and Walter Morris, and Mark Tobey, and Callahan and the Morrises intrigued him and pointed him in a direction.

A better known influence on Ed is Nancy Kienholz, who had a very real effect on his work. Nancy was Ed's fifth wife, and it was such a natural mating that Ed went back and put her name on everything he made from the moment he met her as a gesture of his regard for their union. He encouraged Nancy to participate and she became deeply involved with the gathering of materials, the exchange of ideas, and the actual painting of the works. Ed watched and guided her as she worked, and if he liked it, it flew. If he didn't like it she stopped. There was a number one and a number two hierarchy there, and she was perfectly realistic about it.

Jumping back to the 19th Century for a second, there are two great stances in American high culture, both of which are highly cultivated and are clearly apparent in the literary world. On one hand you have someone like Henry James, and on the other hand you have Mark Twain. Both of them are brilliant, but their stance, style and the things they address in their image and mythology are totally opposite. Those two poles operate in 20th Century art, too, but the Twain model is dominant. If Twain were to invent an American artist around the time of World War II, he would've come up with Kienholz or Rauschenberg. That marks a huge shift in American art history because in the 19th Century artists were of the salon and were groomed for the upper echelons of high society. John Singer Sargent was the prototype, and you couldn't be an artist without adjusting your life and your work to the rules of proper society. That crowd took curious exception to artists like [Albert Pinkham] Ryder – which is, of course, one of the reasons he appealed so much to mid-century modernists. A wonderful artist who showed at Ferus and came out of the Twain tradition was John Altoon. Southern California lost one of its most important artists in Altoon, who died much too soon. Altoon was at home in the world of Berman, who admired him and included his work in Semina. And, whether they admit it or not, he put the fear of God in artists like [Billy Al] Bengston, [Craig] Kauffman and [Ed] Moses with his beautifully lyric painting. Altoon earned a living as an illustrator, and he drove people at the ad agencies nuts. He'd come prancing in there – he was a real dancer-prancer – and do his illustrations like a man signing a check for Bank of America. Another Ferus artist who died prematurely was Arthur Richer, who was an interesting expressionist painter who unfortunately didn't live long enough to develop as fully as he might have. When I was running Syndell Studios Wallace Berman convinced me to show Richer, who was one of the most irascible wild men I've ever met. He was a good artist but a difficult character, and he took his own life eventually by overdosing on drugs. I was driving a car once with Richer and the actor John Saxon riding with me, when Artie suddenly stabbed John in the knee with a fork for no reason at all. He did things like that all the time.

Is it fair to say that Bob Irwin – whose work is extremely cool and calculated – represented the opposite end of the emotional spectrum at Ferus?

Bob has a maniacal drive that can be terrifying, so, no, I wouldn't say that. Bob used painting as a springboard into a vision as broad as the earth itself, and his art is fairly humorless – there aren't a lot of laughs in Irwin's work. He has the capacity to narrow his focus so sharply that he can't bear the existence of anything other than the object of his obsession, and this caused a few quarrels between us. He once got furious with me when I expressed my admiration for Dick Diebenkorn's work. Speaking with awesome intensity, he demanded to know how I could care about Diebenkorn and also profess to support what he was doing. Obviously Bob's an extraordinarily selfish person, but he has to be to be the kind of artist he is. He can be generous in all the nominal ways, but ultimately the kind of focus he's capable of is selfish. I use the word selfish in the best sense – Irwin's selfishness is similar to that of [Wassily] Kandinsky or Mondrian. These are incredibly directed people. I saw Bob not long ago and he seemed more at peace than he was when I first met him, but I don't know whether he really is at peace, or he's simply learned how to behave at peace. With Irwin one never knows.

One of the first Ferus artists you befriended was Craig Kauffman; how did that relationship begin?

Kauffman and I went to the same grammar school, and by the time we met he was already making art. He was the first artist I championed, and part of what turned me on about Craig was that although he was extremely skilled, he was also a dysfunctional blunderer socially and emotionally. From the start he could get with anything I was seeing in terms of understanding it, and I find it tragic the way his career has unfolded. He has the admiration, openly and sometimes grudgingly, of every lyric abstractionist I know, but he's had bouts of real insanity, the blame for which goes to his monstrous parents. Craig's father was a judge who took pride in having sent teenagers to the gas chamber, and there was violence and craziness in his family of a Faulknerian dimension. Kauffman was a kind of sex maniac and early on he went through horrible machinations with downtown whores just to get laid. He was a voyeur, an uncontrollable exhibitionist, and a dandy, but then, most lyric abstractionists are dandies. Hard edge abstractionists don't tend to be, but dandyism runs in the world of the fluid ones.

In high school Kauffman had a spellbinding genius for mechanical drafting, and his instinct for architecture was uncanny. He was always winning prizes for his art at the state fair, so I encouraged him to enter a competition that offered the prize of a scholarship to USC's School of Architecture, and was to be judged by Richard Neutra. USC had an extremely sophisticated library, and many important books came into my life that way. Kauffman was seeing them too – things like Moholy-Nagy's Vision and Motion and so on – so he decided to enter. He submitted an architectural rendering that included a sling chair, which had just become fashionable at the time, with a beautiful nude girl curled up in it. This was 1949 and people didn't do that then! Neutra saw Craig's work and declared him a genius, but when it was revealed that Craig was still in high school they decided he had to take second prize. Neutra kicked up a fuss and insisted he get first place, so in 1950, as I head off to Stanford for my freshman year, Craig goes to USC architecture school. By the fall of the following year I'd transferred to UCLA, and Craig started hanging around because he felt cramped at USC. Architecture school is highly constricting, and Craig didn't have the emotional machinery to be an architect, although he probably could've been a genius one. A career in architecture meant that you end up working for wealthy people if you're lucky, and none of us yet grasped the fact that the great world of art, architecture, and patronage, the Case Study houses and all that, was beginning to die out. Tragic: a beautiful blossoming that had to die.

So Craig arrives at UCLA as a sophomore, looks around at the faculty and sees their work and says, "I can't go through a year of this Mickey Mouse mechanical rendering – I know all that." The official academic vanguard in Los Angeles then was the romantic Cubist stuff associated with Rico Lebrun, who was considered the distinguished artist on campus at UCLA. In 1950-51 LACMA mounted this grand retrospective of Lebrun's work based on the Crucifixion, and though it was regarded as scary and awesome by the general public, the beginnings of my gang went to the show to scoff and raise trouble. We thought it was overblown bullshit. So Kauffman sees Lebrun's work, files a petition that he immediately be placed in graduate school, and tops it off by saying to the faculty, "What do you want me to draw? Do you want a Cezanné? Do you want me to work up a Picasso? What am I supposed to be studying here? Let me draw you a Matisse." Then he grabbed a pencil and from invention and memory whipped out Matisse forgeries like they couldn't believe. So Craig roars into student life at UCLA and there's this older guy in there working, just sweating like crazy, Rico Lebrun. What an asshole. Craig was just twenty years old and he was scaring the shit out of the other students in a way I heard Sam Francis scared people when he was a student at Berkeley; very interesting, the occasional student who blows the classroom right off the map.

An expressionist painter who started exhibiting at Ferus at the same time as Kauffman was Ed Moses; any thoughts on Moses?

Ed was born in Long Beach to a Mexican-American mother and a runaway naval officer, so he's got an absent father and kind of lower-class mother. He's nobody from nowhere. Some fear of appearing pansy compelled Ed to lie about his age when he was still 16 and get into the damned Marines, where he wound up in one of the invasions in the South Pacific where the entire platoon was wiped out. Ed said it was just hellacious chaos – guys shooting each other, puking, shitting in their pants, crying for mommy. The medical officer was killed, and because Moses was one of the few men left alive, he did everything he could to help people stay alive. He was stuffing intestines back in bodies and the experience affected him profoundly. He's a war hero, in shell shock, miraculously alive, then they find out his age and he's honorably discharged from the service. He wanted to be in! I never heard him say, "God, I was glad to be out."

The idea of willfully putting yourself in a situation with an unpredictable outcome, and it proves to be way beyond what you could've imagined, and more horrific, and through some miracle and/or luck you survive, and the visceral bloodiness of what it was and what it looked like – it was the informing experience of Ed's life, and it's there in all of his best work. There is no wonderful Moses without blood, excrement, mucous membranes and all of his delights and terrors. Only viscera can offer any kind of bliss and allow one to transcend the terrors of this world, so we turn to bodily orifices, vagina, mouth, asshole, depending on one's orientation and taste. It's no coincidence that his hero, the Buddhist teacher Trungpa, lived without rules and without knowing what came next. He was a man who would prevail in what Ed experienced, who would already know and respect that.

In 1963 you become director of the Pasadena Museum, where, at the suggestion of outgoing director Tom Leavitt, you mounted the first full retrospective of work by Marcel Duchamp. Why Duchamp?

The philosophical and scientific core of the Enlightenment of the late 17th and 18th Centuries were pervasive for artists like Picasso and Matisse, and they represent the final flowering of the 19th Century. Contrary to popular opinion, they aren't the foundation of what we think of as the art of our time. What was lacking for them was that they couldn't see the endgame of what had been evolving for hundreds of years, and couldn't grasp all the possible morphological permutations that go beyond just what you could do. By the second decade of the 20th Century what was unique to the art of that century was under way, and the artists who laid the foundations for it include the likes of Alfred Stieglitz, Gertrude Stein – I'll say more about them in a moment – and, of course, Duchamp. Duchamp realized that nothing in the world of Matisse and Picasso was cognizant of the radically changing aspect of materials, let alone the conceptual universe that was opening up, and he was able to imagine the kinds of issues and materials that subsequently unfolded throughout the century. Duchamp spent a crucial period of his life as the librarian for the mathematics division of the Bibliothéque Nationale. Being there, immersed in the everyday implications of relativity, time, space, and conceptual dimensions beyond what we assume surround us, led him to question all he might be doing.

Specifically, what new territory did Duchamp shift his gaze to? Science and mathematics?

You can't put it that simply because Marcel had the longest view and he covered so much. He was polymorphic, schematic and very economical. Duchamp had a Cartesian asceticism and he would make the thing no more than once – the model, the prototype, and the example of it is quite enough. Beyond that, he'd rather read, take walks, think or sleep.

In his New Yorker *review of the 1993 Venice Biennial, Adam Gopnik was bemoaning the poor quality of the work in the show, and commented that, "The man to blame for the descent of art is Duchamp, who made arbitrariness in art respectable." Is there any truth to that?*

Adam Gopnik is well educated, he writes well, he's a charming man and in many respects I like him, but he's totally full of hooey. He's an idea flipper and he's very limited in his capacity to really look at art and see what's going on. He did have a great insight working with Kirk Varnedoe on "High and Low," a show conceived to explore the impact of cartooning on high art. Unfortunately, this very important idea was lost in a mess of a show that was gracelessly installed at the Modern.

Getting back to Stieglitz and Stein for a moment, the blueprint for the 20th Century was partly laid out in New York between 1904 and 1924. A kind of bohemia existed in Europe all across the 19th Century, but America's first bohemia didn't appear until early in the 20th Century in New York and San Francisco, and it incorporated the early insights of proletarian literature. The spirit of the masses and radical politics – go back and read William Dean Howells or Willa Cather and you'll see what I'm talking about. The conviction that ordinary folk were going to be part of serious literature in America appeared for the first time with Twain, of course, and he was a giant. What he began took hold powerfully in the 20th Century, and it was part of the new politics and the kind of societies that were coming. The idea that powerful culture could come from outside the world of the socio-economic elite is a theme that runs throughout the century, whether it's Walter Lippman, Eugene Debs drifting through the Arensbergs' salon, or some gobbledygook we've got to deal with in *October Magazine*.

Stieglitz was there, too, and he is the father figure in my life, in the sense that he is where it begins. Elitist that he was – and he was a rather harsh elitist – he was still an extraordinary man, a great artist, and a crucial interpreter who brought so much new art by others into prominence. As Stieglitz is the father, the mother I adore is Gertrude Stein. I love her so much that when I got stuck in the army for six months and twelve days I wrote imaginary love letters to Ms. Stein. Here's this great lump of a pear-shaped lesbian, and I decided I love her. It drove Shirley [Nielsen, Hopps' first wife] nuts. We weren't married yet, and I used to send her my love letters to Ms. Stein and ask her to forward them. Gertrude Stein's mind, her thought, her rock solid determination to just be who she was and not another thing were enormously impressive. She seemed one of the most wonderfully uncompromising people that I'd ever heard of in American culture.

Stein raises an interesting question; how do you explain the fact that art history is almost exclusively dominated by men?

I'd begin my answer by saying that's changing. A guy my age coming from the class I come from, sexist conditioning has been bred into me, but I'm conscious of it and intellectually it's something I abhor. Nineteen-Seventy-One was a very politically radical year, and I did an American painting biennial at the Corcoran that year. I invited 11 artists to participate, then asked each of them to choose another artist for the show. I chose a mixed bag of eleven men that included Sam Francis, Richard Estes, Roy Lichtenstein, Peter Saul, and Ed Ruscha, and the male artists I chose all chose male artists. The Women's Art Caucus was just getting rolling at that point and they picketed the show, but there was no getting around the fact that there simply wasn't a woman artist I wanted to choose. There are lots of good women artists but I chose exactly the 11 artists I wanted. Anyway, they picketed, and the museum trustees told me to get rid of those damn women. Talk about sexist and racist! The Corcoran board was notorious. They called black people niggers. We're talking 1968-69, Martin Luther King's already been shot, and they're saying nigger at meetings in the boardroom of the nation's capital's oldest art museum. I told them no, I don't want to get rid of the damn women, and what I did instead was invite the women to set up tables in our atrium and told them I was happy to hear anything they might have to say to me. I took a lot of shit for that, and although this generally doesn't get published, I encouraged them to schedule their first national meeting the following year in the Corcoran auditorium, which they were pleased to do.

The politics of that period wound up costing me my job at the Corcoran because I refused to fink on a unionizing campaign. I knew who was involved and when my trustees found out I had that kind of information and wouldn't finger anyone they fired me. The idiot who was head of the art school at the Corcoran at the time, Roy

Slade, was only too happy to fink and later he was made director of the museum. Typically. Wonderfully. Slade is a lousy, miserable person and a total betrayer. The Corcoran was justified in throwing me out because directors are supposed to support management and I wasn't doing that. I have no shame in that firing, but unfortunately Hal Glicksman was forced out too and I had to let him go.

Glicksman was also your assistant at the Pasadena Museum, where you were fired following a psychological breakdown. What led to that?

I've struggled with depression during my life, and at that point it had become exacerbated by years of a hyper-charged existence on speed. Basically, I crashed. I was around a lot of dope via the musicians I knew in the beat world, and when I was trying to go to school, keep the gallery running, plus find extra ways to make money, I was always up late and needed to be at work at eight in the morning. So I'd set the alarm for 6:30, drop a black beauty, go back to sleep, then within half an hour I was chomping like a pony. Believe me, you're there and you're never late. Tranquilizers weren't easily available at that point, so me and my partner at the lab where I was working, Bioscience Lab, would inject oranges with ethanol, and our mid-afternoon snack would be orange slices full of 200 proof grain alcohol that would calm us down. That double life went on through my college years, and there were moments when I realized the craziness of how I was living, but it was exciting because I was running galleries.

A key part of the permanent collection at the Pasadena Museum is the Galka Scheyer Collection of works by the Blue Four, which includes Paul Klee. You've cited Klee on several occasions as an unfairly overlooked artist. What was his great contribution?

I'll edge into the answer to that question. Let's start by looking at Marc Chagall. Structurally, Chagal had nothing to work from to make his paintings other than what was clearly given by Picasso and Matisse – use wild colors, do anything you want with them, and look to the Cubist model as to how to put a picture together. Technically, Chagall had less chops than a third-rate Dadaist, but the self-conscious primitivism and childishness of his work came out of the intellectual world of Prague, Munich and Vienna that crystallized with Paul Klee. Before there was Dada or Surrealism, Klee understood the power of crudity and innocence in work by mad people and children.

The idea that there was such a thing as innocent power begins in Germany's curious Post-Romantic movement, and two fascinating things come out of that: the first is something we take for granted, which is that art should please us and show us some meaningful aspect of humanity; second is that there's a wonderful power of humanity in works created by the unskilled. Klee should be credited with pushing this understanding into the foreground. A blind spot in art history has been its failure to explore what went on at the turn of the century in Prague and Vienna. The artists active there are generally perceived as decadent 19th Century romantics, but some very sub-consciously new stuff came out of that place and time. Most of what we call new initially penetrates the culture in a very self-conscious way and by the time that happens it's really not new any more. All newness is inherently highly self-conscious.

Is an artist apt to make better work if he can transcend his own self-consciousness?

Part of what artists like Ed Moses and Francis Bacon struggle with is surrendering control and letting the picture take over. That idea is very deep, and the first inkling that this could be a viable way of working surfaced in 19th Century art. It didn't become prominent until artists like Max Ernst positioned it in the foreground of their work, and it became one of the great insights of 20th Century art. However, it wasn't a major issue with every artist of the period – it certainly didn't mean much to Andy Warhol, for instance. Andy's like our Edouard Manet. Like Manet, he made paintings and drawings, and in many ways he was a very conventional artist. At the same time, the conceptual weight of Warhol far outweighs anything achieved by any of his Pop art colleagues, and he's too complex to be explained in terms of content or historical moment.

I would add, in regard to innocent power, that too much emphasis has been placed on Pollock's so-called awkward early work, which serves to set up the theory of innocent, miraculous sudden invention. In fact, there was a great deal going on in Pollock's work prior to the drip paintings, but people love the myth of the magical creature and the eureka moment because it's like the lottery, in that it could happen to their children. There's an element of disrespect for artists in that theory as well, because it fails to acknowledge the daily drudgery that goes into the life of an artist.

Do you ever doubt your aesthetic judgments?

When I think I've made a mistake I love to get it clarified, and I've certainly done shows that were less than what I'd hoped they'd be. I did a show at the Museum of Contemporary Art in Los Angeles in 1984 called "The Automobile and Culture" that was fraught with problems largely a result of the fact that I never had total control of it. That whole show was like a movie gone sour, and it was Sammy Glick, a.k.a. Richard Koshalek [the former director of MOCA], who wrecked it. When *The Los Angeles Times'* arrogant art critic Christopher Knight reviewed it he said, "This is not what we expect from Walter Hopps. We're sorely disappointed!" I wanted to write him back and say "Dear Chris: So was I." The show was originally conceived for the Pompidou in Paris, and was to have been a complicated three-ring circus that chronicled the course of modern art as it filtered through car design, and was supposed to include a large section devoted to the fetishistic world of customized cars. Pontus Hulten was the director of MOCA at the time, and he and I had done a terrific themed show called "The Machine Seen at the End of the Industrial Age," for the Museum of Modern Art in the late '60s, so I was excited to work with him. I was busy in the early '80s with the Menil, which was in its formative stages then, so it was hard, but Pontus and I persevered. Pontus' assistant director, Koshalek, had no interest in the project, and Julie Brown [who left MOCA to marry artist James Turrell, whom she subsequently divorced] was there, but Richard discouraged her from having the least interest. Richard loves the world of design and he brought in the Cambridge Seven design group. I'm like Hermann Göring when it comes to designers unless they're geniuses, and even then I like to look at them from a distance. I reach for my guns when designers are brought in on any curatorial project, but Koschalek was determined to put a heavy overlay of Cambridge Seven on the show, and I had to fight that. Then Hulten got so many knives in his back and was so gas-lighted, that he became disgusted and quit. Once Hulten was gone, the museum deflected budget for the show into other areas, and I was left mid-stream to try and salvage it working with much less money than I'd anticipated and design people I thought were terrible.

What's the major error that's consistently made in the way shows are hung?

The person in charge doesn't know enough about the art being dealt with. Let's look at the craft of conducting for an analogy. Great conductors not only really know the composer and the work, but more importantly, they've arrived at a position on the work. They're only able to do that if they know more than just the piece at hand, and hanging a show is a similar situation. Whether you're doing the early work, the final culmination, or a single facet of an artist's work, you must have an overreaching view of how it all went together in order to know how to place the emphasis. You can shape visual emphasis in a show in a way that's akin to timing and dynamics in the performance of a complicated piece of music. These may be subtle distinctions to an audience at large, but they're very real distinctions. For instance, in Bob Irwin's 1993 retrospective at MOCA, which was curated by Richard Koshalek, it was obvious the artist felt ambivalent about how his work from the '50s up through 1961 – mostly small, abstract expressionist pieces – was going to be treated. I'm referring to the work he made that preceded the line paintings that mark the beginnings of his signature style. The installation expressed ambivalence about how seriously that early work should be treated in that it was hung on a darkly lit wall in a remote part of the museum. The paintings were practically thrown away.

Do your aesthetic judgments tend to be based more on facts or intuition?

Intuition is a pretty vague word. What I can see counts for a lot, and those are facts. I accept as fact that Bill de Kooning can draw like an angel. I know what kind of command of drawing he has, and I think I understand how he's translated that command into an almost automatist mode of intuitive mark making. De Kooning's automatic, gestural moves are comparable to some kind of unbelievable fusion of Fred Astaire and Ornette Coleman. De Kooning is steady and knowing, he has skill at his disposal in the same way Astaire can move across a floor, and he knows how to extend the structure in a way evocative of a great jazz musician. If I'm looking at a younger artist who may be working in the lyric end of abstraction – someone like Terry Winters, for instance – I may notice certain strained or labored passages that bring to mind a dancer like Gene Kelly, who would finesse or disguise shortcomings in his technical command as being part of a butch aesthetic, as opposed to the effortlessness of Astaire. Terry Winters is an excellent painter, but he doesn't have the moves at this stage of his life that de Kooning had, and I can see those finessed passages in Terry's work in places where I suspect he maybe wishes they weren't there.

In a lecture on a 1972 performance that involved having himself shut into a foot locker for three days, Chris Burden commented that he didn't like the way the photographs documenting the performance looked, so he tried to re-shoot the pictures of the foot locker, without him in it, but the pictures simply didn't work. What does this suggest to you?

It points towards the preciousness of a real document. The picture you take from the top of Everest after you've climbed it is different from the picture you take when you fly in by chopper. The documentary photographs of Chris' performance are more than just pictures of a locker, even if we can't see him in there, because what we know about a photograph carries as much weight as what we see when we look at it. Regardless of whether one is a casual or an educated viewer, we can't shut our minds down and suddenly be knowledge free. Most of us approach everything with an attitude of some sort. Say, we don't know who Chris Burden is and we see a picture of a locker, we'll think, what is that supposed to be? That's a pretty boring photo. What can I connect it with? I can't shut my mind down and not think of Walker Evans' wonderful photographs of doors, or of cathedral doors created in the 19th Century, or tomb doors down in Egypt. I look at a photograph of a door and I can't stop thinking about every damned photograph of a door I've ever seen. If I have no authorship, that's what I'm left with. If I know it's a Chris Burden photograph, the next question is: where's Chris? Most people who bother to look seriously at a photograph of a Chris Burden performance will assume that Chris is somewhere in the picture and deduce that he probably stuffed himself in that locker. So, looking at the picture with no information other than what's already stored in my head, I've filled in a good deal of what it's about.

So we ignite the image, the image doesn't ignite us?
Of course, Duchamp explained that very well. We're in total participation with anything we look at by virtue of what we bring to it.

It's been said that to read a book, the reader should be prepared to work as hard as the person who wrote it. Does that same idea apply to looking at art?
It shouldn't be painless to enter a work of art, but it shouldn't be work either. I find looking at paintings by Cézanne nerve wracking, and when I hear someone say, "That's a beautiful Cézanne," I want to hit them because they are nerve wracking almost to the edge of psychosis. If I'm doing the work I think Cézanne put into those pictures, it's enough to give me a headache.

What is your central creative gift?
Being able to maintain attention for long periods of time. I've got a Bruce Nauman print by my desk that says, "Pay Attention Motherfucker."

You have a reputation for being a very restless person. Would you say that you're easily bored?
No, just the opposite. I drove a girlfriend nuts one afternoon when we were in Barney's Beanery and she was getting bored. "What the fuck are you talking about!" I said to her, "There's no possibility of being bored!" Then I dragged her out onto the street and said, "I'll show you how exciting it can be with nothing – we're going to look at cracks in this sidewalk for a while!" I really started getting off on that, too, and that was not a drug induced experience. The world is absolutely, unbelievably enchanting. It's just amazing, and it's all happening all the time.

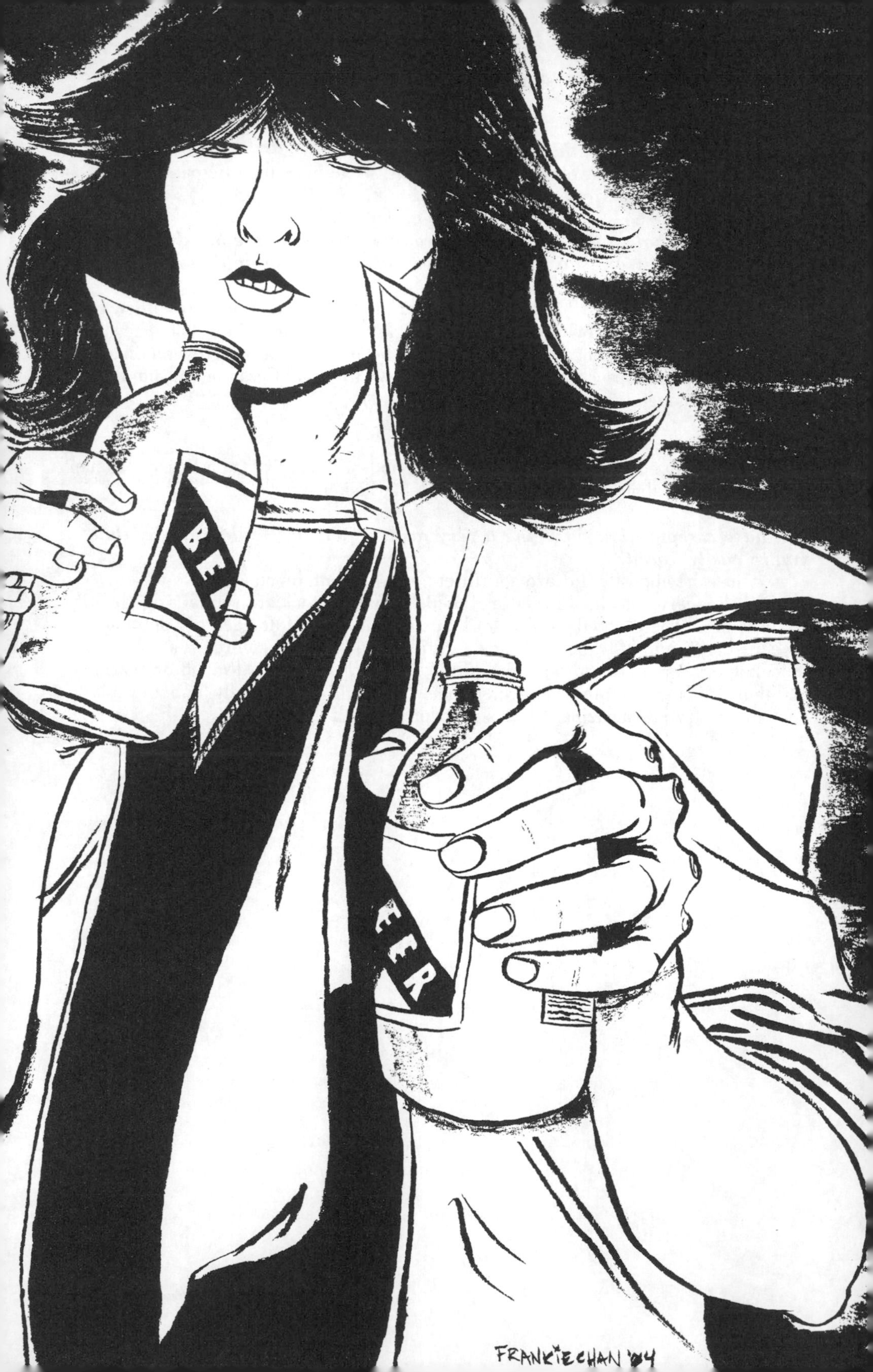

BEE
EER
FRANKIECHAN '04

Chrissie Hynde

Chrissie Hynde was born in Akron, Ohio in 1951. In 1973 she moved to London where she began writing about music for New Musical Express, *and fell in with the gang of iconoclastic misfits who were about to launch the British punk movement. She knocked around that scene for five years, lived in Paris for a while, and was in and out of a series of quickly aborted bands. In 1978, she finally unveiled her own group, the Pretenders. It was immediately apparent that Hynde had a lot more going for her than most of her fellow punks. For starters, she had a huge amount of range as a writer, and seemed to have no trouble turning out a credible punk rave-up, followed by a melodically beautiful ballad worthy of Burt Bacharach. She's a distinctive singer, too – the phrasing and timbre of her voice are immediately recognizable – and she's really sexy. She's tough, too. Over a period of ten months in the early '80s, two of the founding members of the Pretenders (James Honeyman-Scott and Pete Farndon), died of drug overdoses, but she soldiered on, reconstructed her band, and kept making hit records. She's released nine albums thus far and there's not a clinker in the bunch.*

Hynde is a disarmingly modest woman who leaves it to others to praise and dissect her music. When we spoke in 1990 shortly after the release of the Pretenders' album, Packed, *she wasn't interested in discussing the record and tended to dismiss her musical skills as merely adequate. "I'm capable of giving a song a credible rock 'n' roll delivery," was about all the credit she'd give herself. The mother of two daughters (one by the Kinks' Ray Davies, one by ex-husband Jim Kerr of Simple Minds), Hynde lives in London with her husband, Lucha Brieva.*

Why have pop musicians been elevated to such a lofty position in the culture? In many ways they're regarded as gods.

That's true and that's a mistake – although I was certainly guilty of thinking my heroes were gods when I was growing up. They're treated as gods because we live in a sick society and they represent things that push everybody's buttons. It's primarily sex appeal – when you become famous you're automatically endowed with sex appeal. They get to wear the coolest clothes and seem to have the freedom to do what they want, and because they're so privileged, people seem to look up to them – as if privilege were a virtue. This relates to a phenomenon I find very peculiar: People who manage to make and multiply money successfully are regarded with great respect right now. Personally, I find nothing interesting or admirable about the multiplication of money, because if you market something properly you can sell almost anything. Yet the people who do the selling are considered very worthy people. I find that odd.

Feeling ambivalent about commerce as you obviously do, how do you feel about being part of it? Your records put plenty of coin in corporate coffers.

It's never been a moral dilemma for me that I live in a world with a moral dilemma. I think money will lose its value in about ten years and that's going to be a very interesting period in history. I have no idea what will replace it either, but it seems like all systems are going to break down because there's an incredible escalation on at the moment.

You say you used to perceive your heroes as gods; how did you get over seeing them in that light?

I met them. Superficial charisma comes with fame, but real charisma comes from intelligence, and I discovered you don't have to be deeply intelligent to be famous. All it requires are drive and ambition. Lots of successful people are actually quite dull when you meet them. They've learned how to work the system to get to the top, but that isn't necessarily connected to artistic talent. But basically the thing that changed my attitude was getting older. I've been around a bit and I know now that rock 'n' roll is not a religion. That doesn't mean I like it any less – I'm still a great fan. But I've learned to separate my feeling of appreciation for someone's artistry from my own personal life.

Do pop culture and mass media shape the culture or merely reflect it as it already exists?

The media shape the culture in a very negative way. Most people are permanently plugged into their TV sets and their consciousness is constantly being fed with information, most of which is worthless. The media confuse people and distract them and make all issues – some of which are very important – seem equally disposable because there's just too much information all the time. Instead of informing people about things that are relevant to their lives, the media draw them into a false reality of movie stars and meaningless scandals.

Why is pop music obsessed with the theme of romantic love?

It's not just popular music – literature and theater have been obsessed with it for centuries. It's always been that way because romantic love revolves around sex, which is the strongest drive we have.

What gave you the drive to invent a life for yourself so drastically different from the one you were born into?

The fact that I read was probably the biggest factor. I was into Kerouac and all those writers who romanticized the idea of the nomadic life, plus there was a freight train that passed by my school and that put ideas in my head. I was also deeply affected by the music of the '60s, and freedom was the central theme in the music of that period.

You once described yourself as being "mired in the '60s"; are the ideals of that period still a guiding thing in your life?

Yes they are. The '60s were a period of introspection and self-realization, but by the time we got to the '80s the culture had degenerated into "me generation" thinking – which is a peculiarly American thing. I thought that really sucked, this self-involved, "you have to satisfy yourself" nonsense, and now that the '90s are here, the bill for that thinking has arrived. We have to look at the global picture now and there's no time left to be concerned with personal gratification because we're on the threshold of an environmental crisis like nothing we've ever imagined. The ideals of the '60s are more relevant than ever now.

Although you were born in Akron, Ohio, you've always been an outspoken critic of America, and you emigrated to England in 1973; do you feel any bond at all with the United States?

I do still feel like an American, but it's not something I'm proud of, nor am I proud of being an English resident. I'm not a proud person and I have an aversion to patriotism. It's wonderful to love your place of birth, but this idea of "We're the best country in the world" – well, that's clearly not the case with America. We're living in a media dictatorship, and this is particularly true of America, where the media is completely all encompassing. And this oppression by media is very much in keeping with the history of the country. America was built on a foundation of genocide and you can't expect a whole lot out of that. The karmic reaction to murder is always murder. We killed the people who lived in North America and stole their land and we've got a lot to answer for taking more than we deserved or needed. Obviously, I still find much about the country deeply troubling.

You've always perceived yourself as an outsider and taken pride in that identity, but you're now a highly successful woman; how have you reconciled those two things?

But I am still an outsider. You're an outsider when you're concerned with philosophy and religion – that automatically puts you in a different bag, because most people are happy to get by on self-gratification. I wasn't one of the popular kids in high school and I've always been on the side of the misfits, and that's where I want to have a place.

In order to maintain a sense of yourself as an outsider, have you made a conscious effort to keep your career from getting too big?

Definitely. I don't want to be a huge star playing mega-arenas. I don't want to put my audience through that experience because I hate going to those places myself. All I can think is, "Where's the toilets? Am I gonna get in a traffic jam? And why am I standing in billows of hamburger smoke?" Plus, I hate the fuss that surrounds extreme fame and don't ever want bodyguards or any of that nonsense. Before I started making records, I hated the feeling of being an invisible face in the crowd, so I wanted to carve out some kind of identity – I think everyone wants that – but as far as being a recognizable celebrity, that's an uncomfortable feeling.

I'm an adequate musician, but I'm certainly not in a league with the people I really admire – people like Bob Dylan, Van Morrison or Lou Reed. They're real artists and I don't put myself in their league because I'm not too productive. But that doesn't make me lose sleep, because I don't think the world needs another Pretenders album – it's no great shakes if I have a record out or not. But I do enjoy making them, so thank you for letting me carry on and do my thing. I'm just a hayseed from Ohio who got lucky.

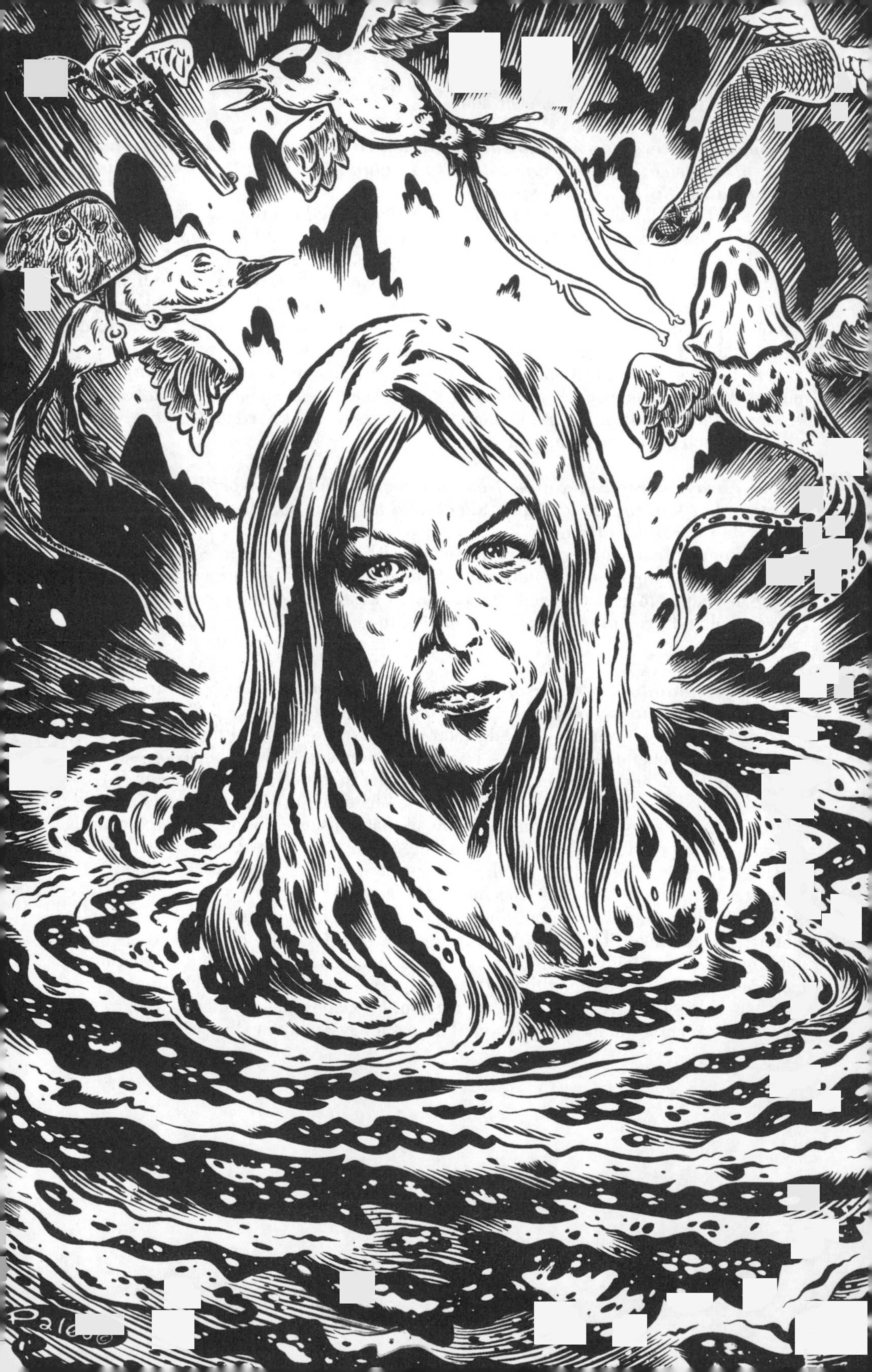

Rickie Lee Jones

....

Rickie Lee Jones was born in Chicago in 1954. Her father was an aspiring actor, her mother was a waitress, and her grandfather was a one-legged vaudevillian and carny dancer who went by the name of Peg Leg Jones. The second of four children in a family she once described as "lower-middle-class-hillbilly-hipsters," Jones began running away from home when she was 14 years old; she moved to Los Angeles in 1973 when she was 19. She wrote her first song, "Easy Money," in 1976, began performing in 1977, and two years later she was on the cover of Rolling Stone *when she had a hit record with her song "Chuck E.'s in Love."*

Like Tom Waits, who was Jones' pal during the lean years in the '70s before their careers took off, Jones has a gift for concisely drawn characters studies, and an abiding love for misfits, eccentrics and outsiders. Incorporating elements of rhythm & blues, pop, Tin Pan Alley, country, and Broadway, her music is deeply American, and the canvas she works on is as expansive as the open prairie. Onstage she seems more like a poet than a musician, and there's a lot of theater in her live shows. There's a good deal of jazz in her music, too, but ultimately, she's such a singular artist that she doesn't fit into any one genre of music. As is true of Billie Holiday, Laura Nyro, and Nina Simone, there's a tremendous amount of pain in Jones' art, and her range – both emotionally and musically – is immense.

I've interviewed Jones twice, and the first time was in 1984, in her manager's office on the Sunset Strip. She was wearing shorts, running shoes, and a T-shirt that day, and I remember being struck at the time by how fragile she seemed. She came across as guileless and childlike, and hardly seemed equipped to handle the huge career that had grown up around her ethereal music. She had a hard time adjusting to the notoriety that descended on her in the late '70s, too. She changed cities six times between 1979 and 1987, married and divorced, and went into deep funks that made it difficult for her to work; that she battled her demons with great valor is evident in the fact that she's released nine brilliant records over the past 24 years. In 1989 I interviewed Jones a second time, and on that occasion we spoke in her room at the Chateau Marmont Hotel in Hollywood. Her daughter, Charlotte Rose, was with her that day, and motherhood seemed to have had a stabilizing affect on her. She looked healthy and good, and we laughed a lot.

Do you consider yourself a lucky person, or have you had to struggle for all you've achieved?

I think I'm very, very lucky, if that's the word – blessed would be the word I'd use. I'm here where I want to be, and whether the blessing is my ability to recognize that fact or my ability to get here doesn't matter. Both those things are necessary. You have to allow yourself to be somewhere you wanted to be, realize that you're there, and be able to say to yourself, "Good, I'm happy here." Because there's always more to do and other happiness to find, we're always struggling to get to the next place, to the point that we don't allow ourselves to ever be happy. People sometimes drive themselves because they're afraid that if they stop and be happy they won't move any more. But you shouldn't gauge yourself in other people's eyes.

It sounds as if you have a pretty good perspective; has that always been the case?

No. There was a time when I was completely consumed by my persona and this is something I've had to work very hard on. My rational mind is constantly being challenged by this business, and I'm trying to keep my eyes open because this is real life. Sometimes one regards this sort of thing – doing interviews or going on TV – as a fantasy, but it's real life. So I've learned to go slowly and to ask myself: Do I want to talk to this person? Do I want to talk about this? I've learned to be delicate and think a little more about what I say and do.

What's the chief disadvantage of fame?

I don't like fame at all and think it's very evil. A little bit of fame is nice I guess, like if you're on the school football team, but fame where millions of people think they know you is disturbing. It's disturbing because they see you different and bigger than real life, and almost every time you'll start to perceive yourself that way. It's hard to keep your vision of yourself clear when you're being assaulted by that. When people begin to behave differently towards you, how can you move through your environment and remain untouched by it? Eventually you must accept that things have changed, then try to put that into perspective. You tell yourself, this is part of my job, I'm a famous singer and they're recognizing a famous singer, but I'm still this size when I go home. I never change this size.

How has fame been of use to you?

It will be of use to me now because I've finally accepted that I want it. I wanted people to hear me and they have and that's good. Many people seem to hunger for fame just for the sake of being famous. I don't know, maybe it gives them a sense of immortality, a feeling that after they've died, people will still know they were here. As an artist, you like to think that fame is an acknowledgement of your art, but the thing I like best about being famous is the wonderful letters I get from people. I get letters that are so deep and personal that sometimes I read them and say, "Oh, you got it!" You know, records are not just a seal of music, but of everything you are at a particular point in time, and sometimes people pick that up. Perhaps you do press out parts of your living soul into music and when that sound comes out it sprinkles out all that living soul. Sometimes you listen to somebody's record and I swear to God you can feel them.

Why do you think millions of people are so willing to subjugate their own ego to celebrities?

Media. Because we have television and hundreds of pictures and movies, you get to know people not in real physical blood, but only in terms of what they represent to you.

What's your media intake?

I have my TV in a little room off to the side, so it's not something I can have on casually, and I don't like to hear things I didn't ask to hear. The only records I play tend to be classical music or my own. Once in a while I'll play Marvin Gaye if I feel like dancing, but playing those records is like going to visit someone – in fact, it's more than that. It's like going to visit family! It's packed with emotion, information and gyration, and I don't subject myself to that unless I'm really in the mood. I rarely go to see live music either. I do read.

How did getting money change your life?

It changed my value system about money in a very good way and a very bad way as well. There was a period when I had real disregard for money because I got too much too fast. I was very poor then got very rich, so I squandered a great deal of money, and I didn't enjoy doing that. I bought nothing and just spent it. Money's a powerful thing, and although it doesn't have to be horrible, it's generally very evil because it evokes feelings of greed, and greed is a killer. One of the things I went through with money was, all my life I felt that I didn't have any friends, and I started measuring friendship on the basis of my money. A woman who already didn't trust people now seriously mistrusted people in a much deeper way. These people want to fuck me because I have money. You wouldn't disrespect yourself enough to admit that to yourself but it's in there, and it's a bad double bind. I've had to do some serious work about this and it's a hard one. There was a period where I either wouldn't give anybody a dime, or I'd give anyone everything I had, and that would change day to day. I recently decided to give away most of my clothes, and I think it's good to do that periodically, to give it all away and begin again.

Have you always been a compulsive shedder of things?

In a sense: yes. I used to run away from home and leave everything behind, but I never had a lot so it didn't really matter. We always moved around so much that I never got attached to articles the way people who live in one place seem to. I learned to see possessions as boxes that you carry around. And my stuff got stolen so much!

When I was 13 we went to Chicago and all of our things were in the car. We went in the hotel and slept, then when we came out in the morning our car had been stolen and I lost everything I had. Four years ago my landlord in New York, who was a complete manic- depressive cocaine addict lunatic, went into my apartment in some drug fit and threw every thing I owned into the street. I had about $25,000-worth of stuff in there – clothes, guitars, amplifiers, books, records – and of course, none of it was still in the street by the time I returned home. That was a time of real deep evil in my life. This guy wasn't my boyfriend but he was relating to me in that way. "How come you didn't call me," he screamed – people do that you know. They have sudden fits of jealousy, or whatever ego involvement he had about the fact that I was living above him. He was a nut!

It's a popular theory that an artist must be in some sort of turmoil in order to create. Do you think there's any truth in that?

Creation does come out of struggle, either physical or emotional, but struggle doesn't have to be self-destructive, and people confuse this issue. For whatever reason – fame, guilt – they manifest their own hell in order to keep themselves perpetually creative. I think you have to keep yourself healthy, observing and smart, and when it's ready to be born it will come out. And you will have a struggle; you needn't doubt that. I've stored up enough blues throughout the course of my life that I never need to have the blues again – I have a big well of it I can draw on for the rest of my life, and I don't have to make that up. It's not necessary to live a miserable life and you don't have to live in hell to be an artist – in fact, the artists who do, generally die.

What's the chief pitfall an artist need be on guard against?

It's never any one thing. It's a real dance and you gotta watch where you're going. One simple thing you must remain aware of is that you mustn't try and anticipate what your audience will like because you're afraid you'll no longer be able to make a living if you don't please them. If you do it to please them you'll be unhappy anyway, so either way you lose. You must do what you love and hope you'll be able to make a living, and you probably will if you continue to grow. Your audience, status, position – whatever, all that's about may change. Hopefully it will! I'd hate to have a career like Led Zeppelin. They appeal to exactly the same people they appealed to 15 years ago, so they must behave as they did then, regardless of how they've grown – if in fact they have. Maybe they're not very creative and haven't grown. How lucky to not move for 15 years and continue to make millions! I should be so lucky.

Can you think of an artist whose career has unfolded in a way you admire?

Yes, Katharine Hepburn. She played aggressive parts and yet she was very feminine, and brought a wonderful dignity to women. She was able to be strong and beautiful. She was wonderful and I love her.

You recently returned to Los Angeles after having lived in Paris for four months. How did Paris affect you?

Very well, I think. I don't speak any French and I went there on the run at the very end of the dark side of the moon, knowing I was about to get very well. But when and how I was gonna do it I didn't know. Because I didn't speak French I learned to be humble because in order to communicate with people I had to calm down and really make an effort to connect with people. How am I gonna get this bread from this little jerk behind the counter who wants to make fun of me? Shopping was a major trauma. How am I gonna buy groceries from people who're so mean to me? It was a wonderful lesson and I did a lot of growing in the time I was there. It's a different culture. Maybe they're mean, maybe they're not. Whichever, move through it smoothly and don't take it all so personally. In three minutes that snotty clerk will be gone and she'll have forgotten you completely.

How do you see your music evolving?

It's difficult for me to compare my records in a linear way because they're like children to me and I don't see one as being an extension of another. Comparing my recent record with the first one that I made, I'd have to say that the first one was older. I wasn't a lesser writer when I started out, but I was writing different things. I wasn't as good a singer then, but because I was nervous and had to push harder for the notes, I did things I'm unable to do now. Now I'm able to sing with real ease.

Are there things you'd like to do with your voice that you're technically incapable of?

When I speak, perhaps, but not when I sing. There's always something you're working on, but everything I set out to do I can do. When I made my first record, I had close to a four-octave range, and now I can feel in the upper part of my throat that I don't have that any more. But the idea of having a greater range just for the sake of it isn't very interesting to me because emotionally, it's hard to put all that range to use.

How do you compose? Do you have structured writing habits?

Each time I write a song I seem to go about it differently, though I usually keep a lot of notes. I might have a notebook filled with thoughts on a specific theme for a song, but by the time I reach the end of the notebook there might be only three lines directly connected to the idea I began with — and they might end up as the bridge of another song. For instance, "Living It Up" started with the line "Eddie's got one crazy eye and he sits and watches Baretta all day." The initial idea for the song is a portrait of somebody who's unhappy, and then I find whatever images will tell more about him.

What percentage of your ideas do you discard?

Oh man! I start a lot of things and write many songs that just aren't good enough. And I'll know they're not good enough early on, but I'll continue to work on them because I know they'll lead to something else. I also discard a lot of good ideas simply because I'm not ready to do them.

How do the arrangements of your songs come about? Are they developed in the studio?

The songs are pretty intact when I go in to record them. Some of the horn lines I might make up on the spot, but my sense of what the song is is already there. More than in the past, I made up the horns and stuff on the spot this time.

Do you think you hear differently than other people do?

I do, because part of the hearing mechanism never formed in me. But I think everyone has a personalized way of hearing.

What are your favorite non-musical sounds?

Water, vacuum cleaners, washing machines... Those machines create a kind of circular drone and have a note that's like a mantra. Bagpipes do that too, and they also get me. All their melodies spring off of a constant drone. When I was a little girl and my mother would vacuum, it would knock me out. If she wanted me to go to sleep all she had to do was vacuum.

Do you have any interest in working in theater or film?

I am moving into theater. People stick you in these little houses, but there's a lot of space between all these types of art to be explored. There's a bit of Broadway in my writing, in the way I paint, turn and speak to the audience, and I suppose I'd like to see a Broadway production of my music if I wrote it. I'd like to write a show and be in it as well, and I think I'd feel at ease on Broadway. But I don't want to be a rock 'n' roll star acting, so I'm not real gung ho about getting in the movies.

What's the most widely held misconception about you?

Because I write about certain types of people, I'm thought to be a big party girl or some kind of tough street girl, and I'm not that at all. That might have been true a few years ago, but it's not true now. Dominant or forceful personalities in women are generally perceived as toughness because it's hard for people to accept women in a dominant role without making them whores. In movies, feminine heroes with any guts or vitality are cast as whores, and I don't see that changing at all. The women's movement seems to be for women of about 40, who married and followed a social dictate, and are now following another social dictate that's telling them not to follow the old one. It's not individuals saying, "I'm gonna do this." Part of me thinks fine, I hope the women's movement helps them, but I don't like social orders of any kind and don't see that it's any different than the life they lived before. They don't know how to be women and be strong, so they emulate the behavior of men, they dress like men, they go see male strippers, and they're promiscuous. They've picked up the worst attributes of masculinity and I don't think that's the way to do it. You must be who you are. Be a woman.

How would you describe the American Dream?

It's a capitalistic dream based on the individual succeeding without any social barriers. It likes that word "individual," and has to do with the idea that each person can be President. They don't have that idea in Europe. I don't think one system is better than the other, but the American dream has caused incredible personal chaos in people's lives because their place in society has no definition. It's a beautiful dream but it causes a lot of agony because it tells every person, you could be and if you're not, there's something wrong with you. And that's a lie, because we do have a social order here and there is real class suppression. The men who wrote the Constitution – and you notice it was only men – were so bourgeois that it didn't occur to them that some little peon might seriously believe it was his Constitution too. They were aristocratic and didn't consider that ten million niggers and five million China-men would believe they had a right to be President too. So it's a bad dream here because a little black child hears that he can be President, that it's his right, when in fact we're living under a specialized constitution for white men.

What's your idea of an important achievement?

There are many kinds. Living on a farm and teaching our kids something they're gonna carry with them always, or to be a doctor and teach people about nutrition. I'm pretty careful about what I eat, and nutrition is my personal love in medicine because I know what it's done for me. I fasted for a few months on a liquid food, and that made me realize that people rarely eat for nutrition. They eat out of nervous tension, for sexual gratification, because they're lonely, because they're too nervous to be able to share with people without eating. You go out with somebody and instead of saying, Gee, I like you, I'd like to sit with you and be with you, you say, Let's go eat, let's go drink, let's go do something so we can pretend the reason we're together is not because we like each other.

What would you like to change about your life at this point?

Nothing. I'm real pleased at how it's growing. I do wish I had more furniture in my house and that I had somebody to clean it up, but other than that, whatever's wrong, whatever's right, it's such a beautiful picture I wouldn't want to change or correct anything. It will correct itself and move where it's going. Whether or not it's the picture I would've drawn as a little child doesn't matter. I like it. What I'm trying to do is find out what's good about things. It's too easy to concentrate on what is wrong.

What's the biggest obstacle you've had to overcome in your life?

As with everyone, I've been my own biggest obstacle. I don't know how to talk about what I'm learning, but I think I'm learning to love, and part of that is learning to give. I don't think I used to know how to give, and what it is you give, you cannot say. There's no way to say what that is, but I never did this before. I'm less prideful and stubborn than I used to be and that's a lot to learn. It's a lot to learn not to walk out of a room, not to say, "Alright, you're gonna pay for that." It's a lot to be able to say you don't have to pay.

Beyond the obvious essentials, what things must you have in order to live?

I have to have love; when I see myself without love I see myself angry again. I can always endure without it and get lots of work done, but I don't know how much I like my life without love now. I think it was always that way and I simply refused to acknowledge it, but I don't have anything to prove any more by saying I don't need anything.

Why do people cling to the past?

It's true that very few people are able to live in present time. Obviously the past is safer because it's already gone by and we know how it ends. It's a constant exercise to exist here, to find a reason to exist here, and the soul is always looking for a reason to be. People say things like, "I'm bored." Bored? You cannot be bored! There are too many things to see and feel and hear, so obviously they're blocking that out because they don't want to be here, probably because they find it too hard to be here. That's a pretty serious question, and I think it requires more thought than we have time for here.

Is memory a source of pain or pleasure?

It's obviously both depending on what you're remembering, but I'd say it's more a source of pleasure. We only do that which we want to do, whether it's feeling pain or feeling good. Pleasure may be the wrong word, but many people find great satisfaction in feeling bad. As for memories, whatever you've taken with you from the past is something you've chosen to carry with you.

What's the earliest memory fixed in your mind?

Riding on my brother's back in some water and there were poles coming out of the water ahead of us. The main thing I remember is the sound of the water and the laughter. I'm holding onto his back and we're going down a stream and there are crabs biting his ankles and I'm strangling his neck and he dumps me off his back because these crabs are biting him. And my mother's standing on the side of the bank. It's a beautiful memory. When I was little, whenever I took a bath, I'd put the washcloth on the side of the tub and listen to the inside of the bathtub because it sounded exactly like that stream. The sound of the water was the salt of that memory.

–1989–

Early in your career you seemed highly ambivalent about the prospect of life as a recording star. Do you still feel that way?

I feel less ambivalent, but I still have sleepless nights. This line of work puts a strange light on the way you live your life – for instance, it's part of my job to talk to you. Journalists visit me and I ask them what they want to talk about, and that feels similar to being a whore. Some journalists don't really care about you and you're aware of that, yet you know your conversation with them will appear in the paper anyhow. Under normal circumstances you'd get up and walk away from a situation like that, but in my line of work you don't have that option. You have to go through a long journey to come to terms with your career, and fame can be quite devastating and corrupting – and at one point it was the destroyer for me. When you start out you're sheltered and you don't have a career – you have your art. Art and career are two separate things and I don't think they can merge. I'm just beginning to sort these issues out, but I've made some good progress in the past few years.

One of the things that plagued you early in your career was a lack of faith in your talent. What do you attribute that to?

I could tell you about episodes at school but it must have started before that. When I first started school I was really confident and I was the boss, but then we kept moving and I kept changing schools and I completely lost my self-esteem. I think that's mostly what did it. I remember one year when we'd just moved to a new town and suddenly there was a lot of trouble at home. There were terrible scenes, my dad disappeared for a few months, and we had no money for Thanksgiving. My sister ran away and got pregnant and the police came to our door looking for her, and I was sent to the door to get rid of them. I told them in a really mean voice "nobody's here," and just as I said that I saw my sister running across the lawn behind them. They turned around and saw her and tackled her, and I ran out and started kicking them. That kind of stuff went on all the time. It wasn't till a couple years later that I realized I had a fairly rotten life, because I spent most of my childhood in an imaginary world. I think that's why I have such an intense imagination – I needed an escape. I think that's one of the reasons people have imaginations – because they can't maintain existence here. Now, as an adult, I need to surround myself with people who give me lots of reinforcement because left to my own devices I revert back into thinking negatively about myself. As a kid I was also obsessive about my teeth because they were real jaggedy and I hated the way I looked in my school pictures. I'm sure there were other kids with jaggedy teeth who felt fine about themselves but mine made me hate myself.

Are you happy with your appearance now?

Yes. I'm very happy with my weight now and because I'm happy with the way I look I'm losing weight really easily. I don't eat obsessively any more. I always wished I had stickup size C boobs – the perfect boobs you see on TV – but I finally decided hey, I have great boobs.

How did marriage change you?

One of the great things I learned from my husband is patience and how to give up myself a little bit. When I married him I was still a pretty angry person but I learned a lot about how to cooperate and make things work out the way I want them to. In a sense, I left one person behind and a new one came. For a while I hated the old one and didn't want any part of her, but now I'm able to remember how much I love her and what good stuff she did – and how much a part of me she still is. Marriage helped me integrate more aspects of my personality than I was able to a few years ago.

Have your ideas about love changed substantially in recent years?

Possibly. I think of romance as temporary and painful, and I didn't do much growing in the love affairs I had in my 20s and early 30s. On the contrary, love tended to polarize my position and I became even more rigid. But after my last bad love affair I finally decided I just wasn't gonna do that any more.

As is the case with many people you had a turbulent relationship with your father, yet he was a central figure in your life. How did his recent death affect you?

I made peace with my father before he died. He had cancer and had a bunch of his throat cut out, but he was still smoking right up to the end. He was an alcoholic all my life, and seeing him the way I am now – off drugs, on a strict diet and trying to maintain control of myself – made me removed enough to realize that he'd spent his life killing himself, and that I'd grown up watching his slow suicide. Somehow, that realization really set me free. Still, I was really angry that he wouldn't stay around to be a grandpa. I wanted my daughter to know him because he was a very kind fellow. He was a good songwriter, and I learned to sing from him – in fact, I have his phrasing. He had a thick, warm, Mills Brothers kind of voice, and we sang together all the time. He understood my music very well – and he was always telling me how to do it better. Towards the end of his life he grew into a much less violent man. He'd always been a kind of racist drinking guy, and he lost all that rage, gave his guns away and quit going hunting. He told me, "I don't hunt any more because I shot a bunny once and saw it die. After that I threw my guns away." The real man in there wasn't a killer at all, and when he found out he was gonna die he decided to be who he really was for the last year of his life.

In recent years you've spent a lot of time in Paris; what's the attraction of France?

I don't know, because when I'm over there I don't like them at all – although I do like the way everything's on the table with the French. France used to represent a very romantic world to me, but I don't have that feeling about it any more. I learned a lot about America while I was there, and one of the things I learned is that my attitude is distinctly American. We're a nation of dreamers, whereas Europe is pretty dead in that respect. People there don't have much of a chance or aspire to greatness because they live in societies that grew out of monarchies. No matter what they do they can't escape the structure of peasant vs. ruling class. I'm not talking about the very poor people in America, because they are helpless, but the other classes here feel like it's their baseball, their music, and they could to that if they wanted. People still feel involved – not in government, don't get me wrong. Everybody feels pretty helpless in that sense. But people feel hopeful in other ways. The French are still under a Napoleonic code and they don't have rights. It's not their country, and different ethnic groups are still excluded from the French identity. I also learned how much Americans love each other and how connected they are.

What aspect of your personality has created the most problems for you?

My paranoia. I'd say my anger but the two are really joined together. I've been quite mistrustful and spent a lot of time thinking somebody was out to get me. You never can be sure what people are up to, but I don't think people are basically selfish. Nonetheless, when I get overly tired my view of humanity can get a little skewed. One of the reasons I get overly tired these days is because I don't have a nanny. Charlotte is very special to me, and I'm very careful about who she spends time with. I don't have a nanny because I'd have a very hard time letting someone else into our house. I've tried and I get really uptight. I wish I could have a male nanny because it's really hard for me to open up to another woman and include her in my family circle, especially someone I just met.

I notice you work exclusively with male musicians, and you prefer male nannies as well. Do you trust men more than women?

Yes, but that's only natural. Charlotte's just a baby and I can see that she feels more comfortable around men. It's an instinctual thing – men and women are attracted to each other. Relationships with women are more narrowly defined because they're not allowed to be sexual, so there's a built-in tension because anything doesn't go. With men anything's possible. Maybe, maybe not – we're gonna get to know each other and see. And of course, women are always competing for men and that creates additional tension. I sometimes meet women I like, but I never really feel comfortable with them. I was always the girl who hung with the guys when I was growing up.

Did you enjoy making your last record?

Not really, because I had to be away from the baby a lot. She was only six months when I went to work, and at that point I would've been happy to never work again and just stay home and be a mom. To be honest, the only reason I went back to work was because the people around me wanted me to. They said you've waited a long time and this is the time. I think I'd built up a block against it and they could see I was gonna have to be pushed. I was very resistant to the idea and felt quite cynical about the possibility of finding a good producer.

Why were you cynical about producers? I've always had the impression you had a good rapport with Lenny Waronker and Russ Titelman (the producers of Jones' first two albums).

I had a great relationship with Lenny and Russ, but my second album, *Pirates*, was so emotionally exhausting for all of us that Lenny quit producing altogether after we finished it, and Russ and I just burned out on each other. I have to admit, I was venturing out onto the western slopes when we were making that record, and I often left them waiting hours for me to come in. This was around 1980-81 and I was still reeling from the success of the first record. That was a dark time on Earth. It was around the time John Lennon died and it seemed like it was always nighttime in my life. A lot of people got strung out then.

Why did you select Walter Becker to produce Flying Cowboys?

The people at Geffen suggested him as a possible producer, and I have to say, from his pictures Walter looked like one of the meanest people I'd ever seen. Steely Dan's music wasn't too friendly either, so I was kind of scared. But I knew we'd gone through similar things so I agreed to meet with him, and I found him to be really nice and quite intelligent. Walter could destroy you if he wanted to with his scathing wit, but he never did that with me and he was really patient and gentle. The atmosphere with the musicians was great too, because every male that entered the room was incredibly respectful and excited to be there because of the legend of Steely Dan. Walter never pushed his point of view on me at all – in fact, I sat around for a while waiting for him to tell me what to do, because it was as if I couldn't remember how to work any more. We had many conversations before I got the picture, but finally he said, "Rickie, in talking to other people about how you work, they say you pretty much know exactly what you're gonna do and do it all yourself." After a few conversations like that I finally took back the imaginary power I'd given him and was able to work.

The central metaphor on that record was flying cowboys; what does that image mean to you?

Flying cowboys are kind of magical creatures, and when I first thought of them they were sitting in a wooden shack up in the sky, then a wind came and blew them down to the earth. They were all connected but they didn't know it, and some of them died, some of them got corrupted, and some of them found their way back to this circus.

Have you always had such a vivid imagination?

Yes, although there have been periods when it shut down. In 1986 – around the time my father died and I left America for France – the world looked very dark to me, and my imagination was pretty exhausted. It was the first time in my adult life that I didn't write and I didn't have any ideas. Usually my imagination is just humming away, and my job is to pay attention and write down all the clues that come to me. I'll often find that an image or a line from three years ago is the missing piece to something I'm working on.

How would you describe your working methods?

It's hard for me to say what I do because I tend to block out the memories of the making of my records because it's usually a fairly painful process. Each time I experience deep despair and feel like I'm never gonna write again, and there's a tremendous feeling of excitement and fear when I go in to record. It's so overwhelming that often I'll sit down at the piano and play for a minute then I'll have to get up and walk away. Creativity is more about magic than a set of techniques and tools, and it's still a complete leap of faith for me. When my career first got rolling everything about music seemed so terribly important. It's lost that importance, so I think it's gonna be easier to do. I can sit around and play and make up songs in front of people now – Charlotte for instance – and I never used to be able to do that. If anybody else was in the room I froze up.

What was the toughest track on Flying Cowboys?

"Atlas' Marker," which is the cornerstone of the album for me. That was the first song I wrote and it was a very simple, good song. Then I played it for someone and they said to me "but Rickie, what's somebody in Illinois gonna think about this song?" That was a terrible thing for me to hear because I'd just started writing and I was already feeling kind of on the outs. That comment caused the song to splinter into 12 different directions – I just couldn't stop writing it, trying to find the guy in Illinois! I'm very easily shaken in the early stages of writing. You can say the wrong thing to me and I'll throw the song away.

What was the hardest part of making that record?

Being away from my baby. I'm sure it changed our relationship. There were many days I would've spent with her in my arms, but I think the separation made us really strong. She's a very confident, grown-up little baby, but I know that now she really doesn't want to be away from her mom.

There's a song on the record called "Ghetto of My Mind" that proposes the idea that we each invent our own reality. Have you been able to invent a good one for yourself?

I have. I'm reluctant to say this because I'm a bit superstitious, but I'm much more solid and grown up now, and I have a good idea of how far to let myself go. Having a family takes a lot of the weight and importance off show business, and doing things like interviews can be fun now because I have a life and a home and this isn't my life. When I was single my career was my life, and that wasn't a good reality.

Fans tend to be reluctant to allow the artists they love to change too drastically. Your persona thus far has been that of a troubled, self-destructive rebel; do you expect your audience will accept you in this new, happier incarnation?

I think what people liked about me – if I can say something like this – is that even with all the self-destruction, there was a light and a smile and a great reaching out. And that hasn't changed. The only thing I've lost is all the drama and ambivalence about whether or not I should be here.

What aspect of your work brings you the most pleasure?

The fact that people are nice to me now: I notice when I go places and people don't know who I am that they're not very nice – and I think people generally aren't very nice to each other. I don't care if they're being nice to me because I'm famous – whatever the reason, it takes the weight off another horrible interaction. I've had people in the same breath be rude, find out who I was, then completely change their attitude. I never confront them because they have to live with it, not me. And, I used to be that way too. I didn't think about how I spoke to people because I was so involved with my own problems. What changed me were a couple of interactions when I said something to somebody and saw their reaction clearly. I thought Oh, I did that, and I began to realize that the things I say and do affect people around me. People seem to feel that being nice is giving something away and that it's important not to give anything away, but I've learned that the nicer you are, the more niceness comes back. It just is that way, and when people are mean they're uncomfortable, they get headaches and they live a life of meanness.

What's been the high point of your life thus far?

Having Charlotte. She's given me definition, confidence and lots of happiness.

What's a typical day like for you?

I spend most of my time cleaning and taking care of the baby. I have a studio in the house but I never get to it because I've gotta watch the toddler all the time. I don't have a manager so our days are completely filled with the telephone. Sometimes I'll have a phone in each hand! I don't have a manager because I don't like them. Managers supposedly save you money but I haven't met any who did. I've tried with managers and it never works and it's not my fault. So why hire one when you know it will bring trouble? I'm due to get a big speech about this from my record company.

What sort of music are you currently listening to?

I like this group called The Blue Nile quite a lot and I also like the Sugarcubes. I love that girl singer, Björk – she's from fairyland. Fine Young Cannibals are pretty good and I still listen to a lot of Van Morrison, who I'll always love. We're going through a fairly cold-hearted era in popular music and there's not much emotional stuff at all now. It's mostly just sexual posturing, and people seem to prefer the posturing to the real thing when given the choice. But the pendulum is always swinging back and forth so maybe this new record of mine will be welcomed.

Who are your heroes?

When things go wrong I refer to certain people who have a place in my heart – Katharine Hepburn, Van Morrison and Frank Sinatra are a few of them.

What do you hope to have communicated in this conversation?

What I hope I haven't communicated is a saga of rebirth. I get weary of reading about rebirths because we're all growing all the time and somehow it diminishes the life you've lived to say, "I'm a new person." I'm not a new person, but I am always changing my mind. It's still me, but I have a lot of fresh air and fresh ideas.

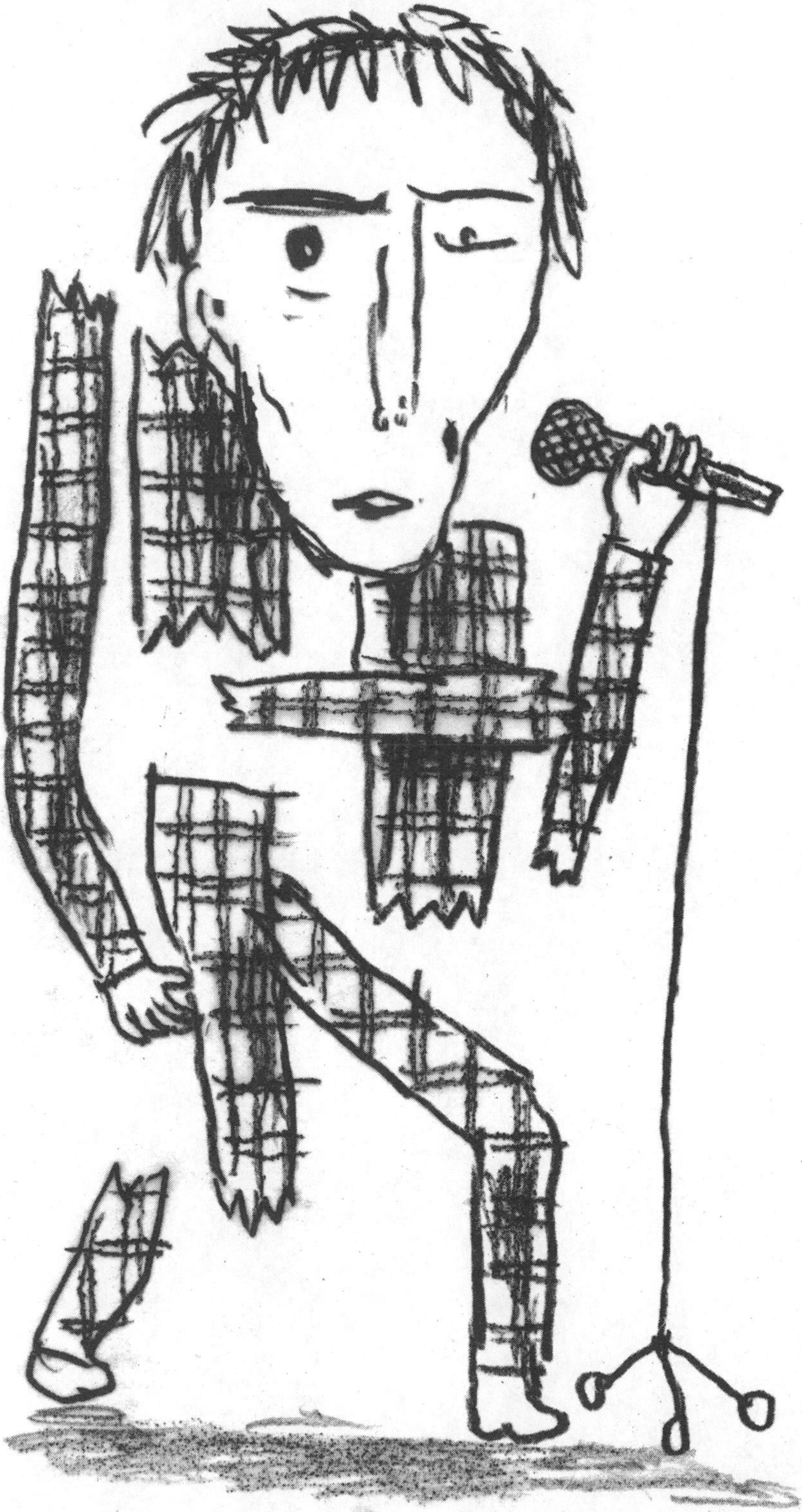

John Lydon

....

The reason the Sex Pistols are the most famous punk band is that they were the greatest punk band. They were incredible. And the thing that made them incredible was John Lydon. I had the good fortune to see the Pistols' final performance at Winterland in San Francisco on January 14, 1978, and he was an extraordinary stage presence. Everything about him was original – the way he moved on stage, the way he sang, the way he interacted with the audience – and he was indescribably beautiful, too. He had a delicate, aristocratic face that was ghostly pale, a long, elegant nose, and a piercing gaze that could stop you in your tracks. I felt enormous compassion for him watching him onstage that night, because he was clearly too smart for the situation he'd found himself in. Punk was never meant to be about hooliganism but it degenerated into that in fairly short order, and it was Lydon's bad luck to become the symbol of a movement that was misunderstood and co-opted by the press and the music business from the moment it began. To his great annoyance, he was forced to spend several years explaining himself following the demise of the Sex Pistols.

He was no quitter, though, and a few months after the Sex Pistols went down in flames, Lydon rose from the ashes with Public Image Ltd., a fluid organization conceived to revolutionize the way pop groups operate. By the time Lydon's two years as a Sex Pistol came to an end he'd had his fill of record companies, and this time he planned to do things differently. PIL was a band, but it was also a multi-media outfit, and they intended to maintain full control of all their output, make their own videos, and oversee their own marketing. It was a lot to take on, and PIL never really achieved all it set out to do. Band members came and went, a few of them had serious drug problems, PIL records suffered inadequate distribution, and their music was too challenging for mainstream audiences. Today there's a long list of hip young bands that cite PIL as a source of inspiration, but when PIL's music was initially released it was a tough sell. Despite that, Lydon still refused to just roll over and be a well-behaved famous person, and he continues to this day to do his best to provoke people. For proof of that, check out his cable television show of the late '90s, Rotten Television.

The first time I interviewed Lydon was in Manhattan in 1981, and we spoke in a vast loft space in the meatpacking district that PIL had leased for two years. The loft was to serve as world headquarters for their communications company, and I visited John there on a hot August afternoon and found him busy setting up housekeeping. The previous tenants had hastily vacated the place and left it littered with children's toys and assorted debris, and John was bustling about with a can of Pledge. We spoke again the following year at a recording studio in upper Manhattan where he was working with PIL guitarist Keith Levene, with whom he subsequently had a serious falling out. The third interview took place in 1989, in a posh Beverly Hills restaurant. Lydon was 33 at the time, he'd been happily married for several years, and he clearly had no interest in leading anybody's revolution.

Contrary to what one might assume, Lydon is reasonably well mannered – he's rather shy, in fact – and he's a fiercely loyal man. I realized that after reading his autobiography, No Irish, No Dogs, No Blacks, *which was published in 1994. As is made clear in the book, he adores his family, and his best friends today are the same people who were his best friends when he was a teenager; in fact, he's presently managed by his high school pal, John Rambo. Lydon moved to California in the mid-'80s, and he continues to live there in a modest home in Marina del Rey with his wife of 24 years, Nora Forster.*

–1981–

Why do you think people are so interested in you?
It must be because I'm great. (Laughing). I don't know. That's a silly question. Maybe it's because I'm actually doing what others talk about doing.

Do people tend to regard you with suspicion?
Yes, even intelligent people – in fact, intelligent people can be your worst enemies because they become clouded with how lackluster they are. I'm often credited with this amazing fucking intelligence and to behave the way I'm expected to behave I'd have to be such an almighty, devious genius I'd need to have begun planning on the day I was born! And that just ain't so.

Is anger a productive emotion?
Of course; you need to be angry when you're insulted.

I would imagine it's been quite a while since you've been insulted. It seems you're treated quite reverently these days.
Oh haw, haw! You're bound to get some of that from silly cunts, but you get that no matter what you do. (In a sing song voice), "You're really a bank manager? Oh, how wonderful. What's it like to be a lawyer?" My particular curse is I'm constantly forced to deal with people who are trying to out-rotten Rotten. I'm still gettin' it – "Why'd you leave the Sex Pistols, you sold out." Well I've said my bit on it, and if people want to create a fantasy then they will.

Why do you think the public seems compelled to turn people such as yourself into fantasy figures?
I can't speak for the entire human race, but a lot of them are just very lazy and prefer to have others dictate the rules. They like to fit into patterns because that's what they're trained for from their first day of school. Sit at your desk and be told by teacher. People come to depend on such formats.

What gives some people the strength to rise about that sort of programmed behavior?
Maybe it's genetic. I look at some people and their activity level is fucking phenomenal, while I'm a lazy cunt and come from a long line of lazy cunts. But by being lazy I achieve more than most.

Why has PIL relocated to New York?

It was a matter of common sense. England doesn't have the facilities we want to use, and there's no access to things like video there.

If those things aren't made available to artists how does it happen that England seems to lead the world in the field of music?
Because music is the only thing you can get into without being part of a union, and even there, you're forced to deal with the M.U. You can't get on telly unless you've paid your contribution. I hate being dictated to and I'd had enough of that bollocks.

Beyond the fact that it's a more efficient work environment, are you attracted to American culture in other ways?
No, I don't want to become an American. You've given the impression everything can be achieved easily in America, that a farm boy or a lousy "B" movie actor can become President, but that isn't really the situation. Everybody puts on an air of super-confidence, "Oh, I know everything," but so many people here have analysts and need to discuss their marital problems with a psychiatrist. People are lost – it really is quite sad. Psychiatry is a joke yet it seems to be an instinctual thing in America, and an analyst seems to be part of the lifestyle here. People take it for granted they're supposed to be neurotic once they achieve a certain income.

Do Americans perceive you differently than the English do?
Yeah, there's not as much mistrust here as there is in England. Americans are more resistant than the English are to something new, but in England there's a feeling of "how dare you be different! What are you up to? Are you conning us? Is PIL just a big joke?" What an expensive joke! If that was the case, the joke would be on me. The only way to wake people up is with an out and out assault, not a physical, but a mental one.

Do you think the work you've done over the past five years warrants the acclaim it's been accorded?
Of course... I wouldn't do it if I thought it was worthless.

What do you think your primary talent is?
Being stubborn, and having the attitude of "I will stick to what I said and that's that." And I really don't know what to attribute my willfulness to.

Do you see yourself as having a puritanical moral code?
No, I'm flexible. I've never tried to inflict my views on other people or demanded that theirs be the same as mine. I'd have no trouble hanging out with a born-again Christian – why wouldn't I? That would be his kettle of fish. You don't choose a friend according to his religious beliefs, nor do you reject someone because of them. I know a number of very religious people whose views are quite different from mine, but they mean well. The Moonies I'm not so sure about.

Do strong religious beliefs tend to make a person intolerant?
The Protestant scheme of things is certainly all about intolerance. I happened to have been raised Catholic but that's not particularly significant – it could've been anything. All kids get religion inflicted on them one way or another.

Is media a form of religion?
It's a form of government control. It dictates.

Does PIL plan to do more live performances this year?

We plan to begin what we set out to do this year, which is to get into film totally seriously. Until now we haven't had a place to do that. I prefer to call what we do film because the word video has become fucking boring and I'm sick of reading it. Video is just a nice, flexible way of filming without having to pay millions of pounds, and I'm more interested in the content of what we film than how great the equipment we use is. We will not make "rock videos" because I don't like the whole idea of that. It's not good enough just to sing songs, especially since there are three of us. I'm not going to tell you exactly what we have in mind because we've done that before and found it used by other people two weeks later. You know how bastards operate – take out the best aspects of an idea and absorb it into their dullness. Let's just say we'll deal with specific subjects but in a spontaneous way.

I hear you had a few offers to do movies, including one from Martin Scorsese. Why did you turn them down?

The offers just weren't good enough – they just wanted Johnny Rotten. Scorsese didn't offer me anything, he just wanted to observe me – you'll notice that in his movies he always makes observations on set trends. Well I'm not definite enough for his scheme of things. I like his movies, though. They show you what you already know, slightly glamorized, with a huge dose of paranoia added.

What are your thoughts on the current situation in England? [When this interview was conducted, in 1981, unemployment was at an all time high in England, several of the unions were threatening to strike, and there was rioting in the streets].

Well, I'm not surprised. There's always chaos when a conservative government gets in and Thatcher has triggered something that's been brewing for years. I saw this coming in 1977, and at the time I was disgusted by the apathy of people. It was obvious that it was going to have to happen because the country needed to clean itself out. People have been told to accept a kick in the face from any quarter that deemed it necessary, and they're finally fighting back. "We will not take it any more! Why should we pay taxes for fuck all!" It's insulting! You're told you're working class from the day you're born, and you're meant to stay that way. If you manage to escape the working class you move into the middle class, where you're hated if you refuse to follow their set social trends. You must change your accent and your surroundings, and you mustn't deal with people from your past. Just after the war the working class was a proud thing to be, but Thatcher has destroyed that. Her attitude is, "If you don't have a job it's because you don't deserve one." She's not up for re-election until 1984, and if she doesn't come to her senses, which she obviously won't, there's going to be a civil war.

How do you explain the fact that despite the economy being so bad, the British education system seems so superior to America's?

That's the problem exactly. The British people are educated enough to hate the way they're forced to live, but they're given no way out of the situation. You have to save for years and years just to buy a guitar.

Do you still have contact with the people you grew up with?

Of course, they're my friends – on that I've been very stubborn. Just because I moved into a different scheme of things, I've never allowed myself to be cut off from what I was dealing with before. That's my sanity. I'm always judging things against where I came from because it helps me to understand things. Otherwise you become impressionable and you get lost.

You don't seem like an impressionable person. Have you gone through periods where you felt you were getting off track?
Of course, that's natural. I'm not totally imperfect – there's a lot wrong with me in fact.

What other cultures intrigue you?
I wouldn't mind trying Japan for a bit. The Japanese aren't part of the human race in that they're almost ant-like and they work for the system. For them the system is all-important, yet they like for Westerners to come there so they can observe then imitate them down to the last strand of hair.

Why do you think Asia has such a different attitude towards work?
Well, they didn't just invent it last week – it's something that's been handed down through the ages. China is so fuckin' sensible I can't believe it. As a race they seem to have more respect for each other there than anywhere in the world. They remain communist but aren't trying to hide the fact that another way of life exists. They're taking some of the better aspects of the Western world and absorbing them into their culture, and aren't accepting anything wholesale. Unfortunately, there isn't any interesting art or music coming out of that part of the world because they seem determined to run away from their own culture.

How do you keep abreast of the times? Do you read newspapers?
Newspapers are such rubbish. I read them intensely for a long period until I understood the format and how each paper works. If you grasp the approach of a paper it's possible to get valuable information from it because you understand why they have the opinions they have and you're no longer influenced by them; newspapers are a very powerful instrument of control largely because most people are too damn lazy to even question what they read in the paper.

What was the last thing you learned on television?
That American advertisements are very badly done – the quality in England is much higher. People here pay thousands of dollars for thirty seconds of absolute amateur hour bollocks, but then, I imagine that's the effect they want because it does seem to reap rewards. In England there was a series of Schweppes adverts that were really fuckin' good, but they drew attention away from the product. People were interested in the presentation rather than the product, so they discontinued the ads because they want the ads to be pure product.

It's a popular theory that one has to be in some sort of turmoil to do creative work. Is that a false belief?
Of course it's false, but it's easier not to question those myths – to question them threatens the whole bullshit rock 'n' roll dream. We're real rebels – rebels limited to a verse-chorus-verse format, the same guitar lines, and the same stage antics. The only things that change from one band to the next are the fucking clothes and hairdos.

How is music different from noise?
Noise isn't deliberate. If you deliberately want to create something from noise then that's music. As far as I'm concerned, music isn't notes played perfectly – it's

the right rhythm. I don't believe in A-D-E or any of that, and contrary to popular belief, you cannot dance to rock 'n' roll. Everything – bass, drums and guitar – plays the same pattern, the louder and more distorted the better, until it becomes a wash whose sole purpose is to induce stupidity.

Did the Sex Pistols play rock 'n' roll?
As I've told the world, that was the last rock 'n' roll band. Every single aspect of rock 'n' roll was dealt with in one glorious swoop.

How conscious of that were you at the time?
I knew what I was doing, but I doubt that the rest of the band did.

Who's currently making music that interests you?
No one. The only people I've seen lately are Grace Jones and some disgusting hippie, this terrible pox, a boil of the backside of the universe, this jazz twat with long curly black hair named Pat Metheny. You should've seen the looks when I walked into Town Hall to see him. All he did was cover all the popular themes and melodies you hear in advertisements, bullshitted up with loads of twaddly bits on guitar. All the people in the audience sat there feeling so superior, but they might as well have gone home and listened to the commercials on telly and had more fuckin' fun. One of his songs was based entirely on that commercial jingle "Red Lobster for the seafood lover in you." My friend Nora started singing along and I started laughing so loud I had to leave. I cracked up!

What is the most overrated trend that is currently winning cheers from the masses?
Talking Heads. Like all those types of bands, they're obviously out of ideas and can't come up with anything of their own so they're slavishly imitating somebody else's fuckin' efforts. They're so preoccupied with keeping up the Joneses that they have no understanding whatsoever of their own culture. The only way they can justify themselves is to hang around with the other people like them, also out of ideas and busy looking over the garden fence to see what the other is doing.

Why are the ideas of newness and innovation so valued in art?
That's a cheap and shoddy way to evaluate the worth of something, and one of the great falsehoods of rock 'n' roll. It's not new to be new, and if you do things just to be new, weird and arty then you really are a cunt.

Do you listen to ethnic music?
I don't go out of my way to hear those things. People described [PIL's fourth album] *The Flowers of Romance* as tribal and primitive, but I deal with English culture, folk music, church music from the Eighth Century, and the English Renaissance. It's English culture but nobody wants to acknowledge it. Like England's stately mansions, classical music is not English culture – it's merely a collection of imported styles.

What's the most effective way to draw attention to oneself?
It's no good just being noticed – and why is being noticed so bloody important to people? God doesn't look funny or odd or different. What's important is the value of what one is doing and what can be learned from it. I can't learn from the romantic scheme of things. That isn't romance – it's bullshit.

How would you describe your sense of fashion?

I don't have one. I know what I like and don't feel the need to wear clothing espousing a message. If you need to hide behind a whole jamboree of clothes you may as well be put away into the ground.

What's your idea of an important achievement?

Having a hit record certainly isn't important, particularly since the charts are rigged anyway. It's very odd how in America you continually hear this music that all sounds the same. You go into record shops and you don't look for specific music – you merely pick record covers.

Do you think man is becoming more violent as time goes by, or is the media simply amplifying that side of his nature more dramatically than in the past?

I'd say he's becoming less violent, wouldn't you? We're no longer in the Middle Ages of kill or be killed, and violence has taken the form of mental activity now. There are factions of the British working class who wear their ignorance like a medal, and are proud to be thick and know nothing. I don't know where the human race will progress to, but this stupid worshipping of ignorance has got to stop.

Is there such a thing as a "natural life?" Contemporary life seems to involve irresolvable stress that may have to do with the technological direction the culture has taken.

Irresolvable stress is the human condition, and evolution will sort that out.

Did a serf working in a field 200 years ago have more manageable problems since his world was smaller and simpler?

They knew nothing beyond their immediate world, but you can't say they were happy because of that. There've been peasant revolts throughout history, and although it's fashionable to romanticize the peasant's life of 200 years ago, nobody really spoke from a peasant's point of view so there's nothing to be used as evidence. It's merely hearsay.

Would you agree that human beings have basic needs – for community, a family structure, meaningful work, and a religious ideology that deals with the subject of death?

I'd say bullshit. That sounds like government manipulation to me. What you need is respect for yourself and your ambitions.

–1982–

Do you feel you've successfully shaken the image of Jesus of punk?

Oh my god, is that my image? I don't think people have forgotten the Sex Pistols, and I don't think they should, but they shouldn't expect me to be the same either. The whole idea of doing anything is progression.

Does it annoy you that your music is often given less attention than the sociological baggage that surrounds you?

Yes, I find that bloody irritating, but that's the avant garde for you. I'm accused of taking the piss out of people and dismissed as a prankster, and the press generates a lot of that. They don't understand what I'm doing either.

Does having the critics on your side work for or against you?

Critics can be good sometimes because they can point out where you've made certain mistakes and that's very useful. Where they go wrong is when they become opinionated to the point of total domination. That I find offensive. Generally, though, I don't read the music press – I've given up on it. New Musical Express was really good for a while, but the writers there no longer have any interest in anything and they should be sacked. They refuse to see any hope because they like being miserable, but the misery British rock writers contribute to the world is definitely not wanted. Right now they've latched onto African music for the simple reason that they need a new trend. Pathetic. Next month they'll probably go Arab. England's always been that way. It's so small in comparison to America, it's like a village, and trends can come and go there overnight. I never realized how spitefully snobbish they all are until I left and lived in America for a year. I like the way the American press writes. It's very open and you can understand what's being said.

What are the qualities in Keith Levene that led you to form a group with him?

He has no fear of trying the unknown and that's a rare quality in a musician. Our music is mostly developed spontaneously in the studio, and there are no patterns to how we work – we try to leave things completely open. If you limit yourself to tried and true methods you eliminate new possibilities and that's what we're interested in. Memorizing plans and words or knowing how to play an instrument isn't the important thing – it's the guts and energy.

Do you strive to be impersonal and non-autobiographical in your writing?

No. Practically everything I write is about my life and what goes on around me, so I'm definitely not removing myself from the songs. It's my opinion, so obviously it's personal.

Do you rehearse prior to laying down vocal tracks?

Yeah, I howl away to myself. I've been known to sing in the bathroom, although I don't use the bath – haven't got one.

What effect do you hope your music might have?

You must do what you think best, and that's all. If you get into any other ideas you just get too conceited. All that, "Let's make what the people will like and what they need" nonsense doesn't work.

Have the original idea PIL was founded on proven to be workable?

Yes, that's bleedin' obvious – it's exactly what we're doing. It's true we couldn't manage to get it together in England because trying to accomplish anything there is like shouting at a brick wall. It has taken time, but it's getting there. Warner Brothers were, of course, no use to us whatsoever – they were counterproductive, in fact. I definitely felt some kind of suppression there. We'd like as many people as possible be able to hear our records, and they weren't exactly well distributed in America.

1989

THE CLASS OF '77

Very few of the first punk generation have gone on to do anything worthwhile. This might sound odd coming from me, but Ariana, formerly with the Slits—and my wife's daughter – moved to Jamaica and became a reggae star and her work is very good. It's the genuine article – it's not just some white girl getting trendy. I never liked Elvis Costello, and despite his punk image I put him in the same bag as Springsteen. They sing in the same silly way: "Oh, oh, woke up, headache, got in my Chevy and drove…"

RAP

Rap music was interesting when it began but it hasn't progressed and it's now very tired and boring. Early on I liked the occasional rap record – I thought Grandmaster Flash's "The Message" was excellent – but there's nothing with that lyrical content any more. They all use the same rhythms and rhymes now, and if I hear one more wicki-wicki scratch on a rap record I shall puke. A lot of people claim that rap is part of the tradition of black protest music, but I think it's more in the tradition of rock 'n' roll. It's too formalized to be genuinely rebellious and it's popular because it's easy to understand. The parameters of rap are clearly set and nobody challenges them.

ROCK 'N' ROLL FUNDRAISING

Once again, the elite gather together and refuse to share the stage with anyone less popular than they – you'll notice it's the same old motley crew at every one of these events. They've found a new way to make themselves feel important, which of course they're not. These are compulsively greedy people who hog every spotlight they can find. Who am I referring to here? Sting, Springsteen – that lot. And, I'm sorry to say it, but Peter Gabriel, who used to genuinely care, has gone completely showbiz. The relentless flag waving and charity sloganeering annoys me deeply because I consider charity a bit of an insult. I don't like free handouts. Beyond that, nobody really knows where all these charity funds go.

NATIONALISM

National pride is nothing more than a form of elitism and it must cease if this planet is going to survive. I used to think there was something particularly English about me, but I've been about a bit and come to realize that's not true. Human beings are the same the world over, and I consider myself a part of this planet rather than any particular county. People cling to nationalism for the same reasons they cling to religion – fear, and the fact that they're too lazy to think for themselves. They prefer to have politicians and priests make their decisions for them.

THE ABSTINENT '80s

If people don't want to drink any more that's well and fine, but they shouldn't do it out of fashion – and it is very much a fashion in America right now. It's just another trend for people to follow, the sheep-like mentality running rampant in a new way.

POP CULTURE

Pop culture gives people false expectations of life, it covers up the wrongs of society, and lulls people into a false sense of security. A Madonna record will not save you from anything. As long as you're aware of that then go ahead and enjoy it.

IDOL WORSHIP

Musicians have been elevated to an exalted place in society because they obviously fill a neurotic need. Perhaps it's a symptom of the religious crisis of the Western world, but something tells me it all comes down to financial clout. There's quite a bit of money being spent to convince people that they need to go out and purchase certain products. It's very hard to combat the constant drilling they subject us to, and the music business can sell literally anything they decide to get behind and sell.

JOHN'S ROTTEN IMAGE
The most widely held misconception about me is that I'm nasty. That image has been a protective device for me for years, but it can't work forever, and it's getting tedious both for me and the viewer. I can be as jovial as the next guy.

APOCALYPSE NOW
People have become more aware of the crisis with the ozone layer and things like that, but it might just be too late. I don't think anybody will be able to stop corporate greed and the recent oil spill in Alaska proves that. Who benefited from that disaster? The oil companies. They've raised the price on everything, including current stocks, since their little mishap up north, and nobody seems eager to punish them. There will be a few small fines and promises of a clean-up campaign and that will be it. Everybody – including myself – seems to be going on about the end of the world, but I don't see that as a bad thing. Good riddance to the bad rubbish known as the human race. And, if we've got to go we should go in style. Let's not be morbid about it.

AN OBSOLETE DREAM
I've given up trying to change the world. It's too grandiose a task and I'm really not capable of such a thing. No one individual is.

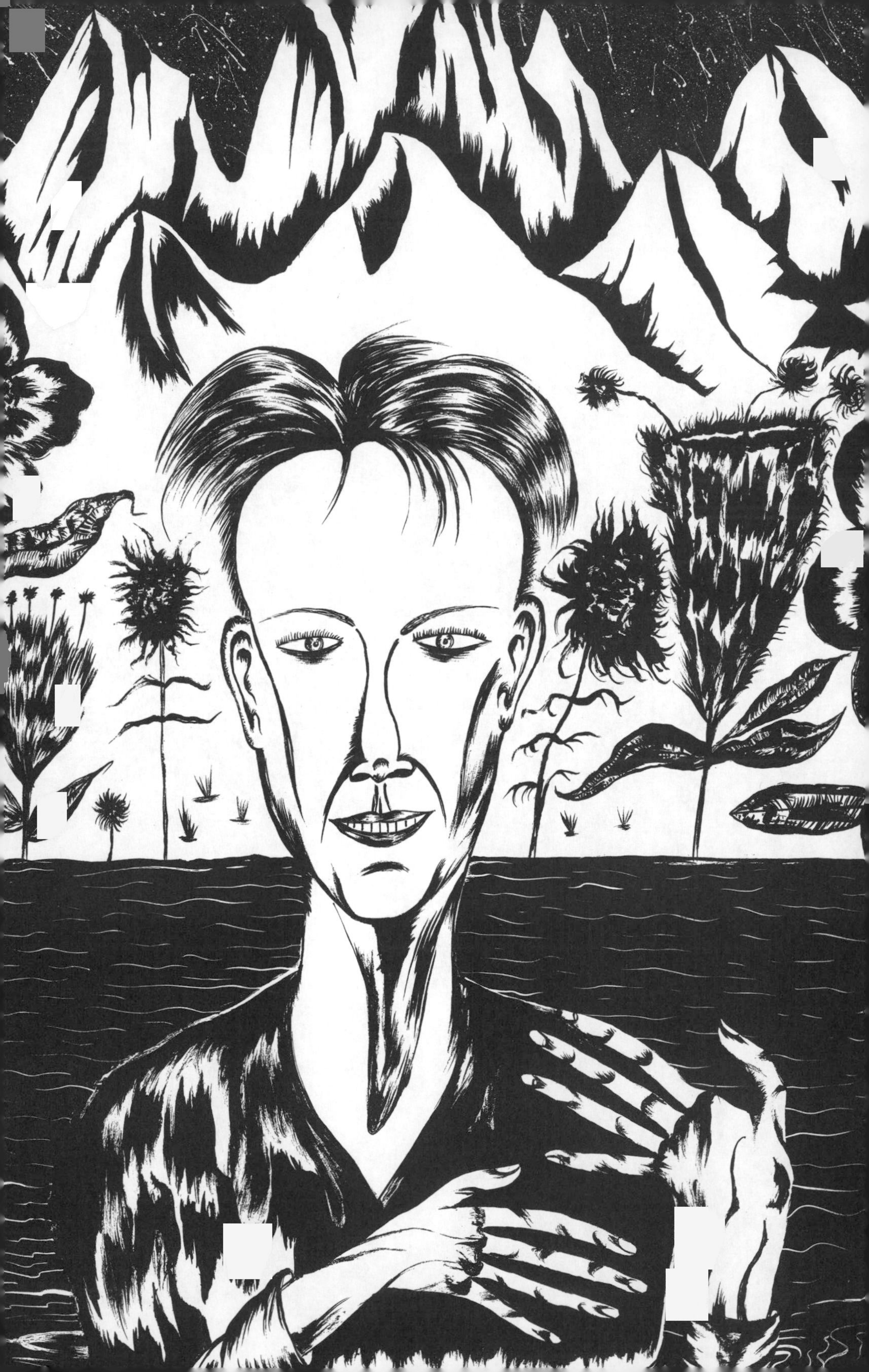

Guy Maddin

....

Guy Maddin was born in Winnipeg, Manitoba in 1956. He's of Icelandic descent, and his father was a prominent hockey coach who lost an eye as an infant when his mother pulled him to her breast and pierced his eye with the pin from an unfastened broach. Maddin's mother ran Lil's Beauty Shop, a salon she named after her beloved sister. As a child, Maddin received a piggyback ride from Bing Crosby. When he was seven years old his teenage brother committed suicide, and when he was fourteen his father died; these losses can be seen resonating in the films he's subsequently made.

After earning a degree in economics at the University of Winnipeg, Maddin became increasingly obsessed with film while working a series of crummy jobs that included house painting and bank telling. When he was 29 he played a character named Concerned Citizen Stan on the cable access television show, Survival!, and the following year he completed his first film, the 26 minute short, The Dead Father. A moving portrait of a young man whose dead father haunts him in daydreams and nightmares, the film contains all the seeds that would later blossom into Maddin's mature style.

Maddin has described digital effects as "grotesque artifacts of the present" and his predominantly black and white films operate on one level as homage to the silent cinema of the '20s. Artificially aged through the incorporation of jarring edits that suggest old, broken reels of film clumsily spliced back together, soundtracks riddled with cracks and pops, and a mannered, melodramatic performing style he coaxes from his actors, Maddin's films seem to call out from a remote, murky past. At the same time, they're clearly the work of a late 20th Century man well acquainted with the astonishing trauma of that bedeviled century. Fraught with anxiety and dread that often erupts into black humor, his films invariably circle back to a thematic point you'll never find in an old silent film; that point is the inevitable loss of that which we hold most dear.

In 1988 Maddin teamed up with the screenwriter (who would become a longtime collaborator) George Toles on the brilliant Tales from the Gimli Hospital, a wickedly funny study of male rivalry and romantic longing. Two years later he completed his second film, Archangel, after which he contracted an incurable neurological condition called Myoclonus, which causes him to feel as if he's constantly being touched. He soldiered on, nonetheless, and in 1992 he completed Careful, the story of an alpine village whose residents must forever speak in hushed tones, lest they trigger an avalanche. Twilight of the Ice Nymphs was released in 1997, and four years later he directed the filmed ballet, Dracula: Pages from a Virgin's Diary.

Maddin's sixth film, The Saddest Music in the World, was released in 2004. Based on an original screenplay by Kazuo Ishiguro, it's a Depression era melodrama set in Winnipeg, where a beer baroness (played by Isabella Rossellini) hosts a competition to determine which ethnicity produces the saddest music. Also out that year was Cowards Bend the Knee, a film installation Maddin premiered in 2003 in Rotterdam that was released as a single panel projection. Maddin has also completed 18 short films; they're difficult to find and they're all fantastic, so don't miss them if they come to your town.

What's your earliest memory?

My mother showing me her naked breast and telling me that's where milk came from. My mother is no naturist, so that's a strong memory. I also remember being stuck to the floor of the beauty salon where I grew up because everything there was coated in layer upon layer of ancient hairspray. I'd play on the floor and crawl around the nyloned ankles of all the women sitting in a row under the hairdryers, and whenever someone spilled a tray of curlers I'd gather them up and build little castles out of them. I was pretty young to be glued to a beauty salon floor.

Do memories enhance or impede our ability to enjoy the present?

You couldn't make anything of the present without memories so they make our enjoyment of the present possible. We're constantly building up our library of memories, but we're constantly losing memories, too, because we haven't revisited them enough and finally they fade away. It's as if you're building on a beach that's constantly eroding, so memories don't really provide much of a foundation.

To what degree do we unknowingly fictionalize our own past?

Most people have a small set of stories they tell repeatedly that take on the quality of tales told around a campfire by cavemen. Those stories do become more like cave paintings than an accurate recounting of something that happened, and they become more beautiful and useful as a result. I willfully fictionalize my own past as much as possible, but strangely enough, I find the more I attempt to mythologize my own past, the more raw and cathartically confessional I become. I recently made a movie called *Cowards Bend the Knee* in which the protagonist is a man named Guy Maddin who's a triple-murderer, hairdressing, hockey player – none of which I've ever been. But in the way that fairy tales can be incredibly true, despite the fact that they involve talking wolves, the character feels like an authentic version of me.

Is it true that in directing The Saddest Music in the World *you copied various descriptions of depression and synonyms for sadness onto index cards to create a deck of 52 cards, then had each actor draw a hand of cards every day and use the suggestions on them to shape their performance that day?*

Yes. I'm willing to try anything because I'd be revealed as a complete impostor if I tried directing my actors conventionally. So I had these beautiful little sentences from Burton's *Anatomy of Melancholy*, and synonyms from Roget's *Thesaurus*, and it was just a way of forcing the actors to channel their lines of dialogue and their gestures through the suggestions on the cards. It worked, too – I think it refreshed their approach every day.

What elements of Ishiguro's original script remain in your adaptation?

I had a real free hand in adapting his screenplay. In his version there was a contest, as there is in mine, but his took place in London on the eve of Perestroika. I switched the place and time to Winnipeg on the eve of the dissolution of prohibition. Ishiguro's main concern, which he made sure I included in every draft of the script, was the heartbreaking irony of Third World countries that are already suffering under immense privation, but are still compelled to exaggerate their privations because the competition for world charity is so stiff. So you get this grotesque sight of a starving populace pretending to be even hungrier than they are so they can be the sexiest charity of the season. Ishiguro wrote his script in the early

'80s when the Ethiopian drought sparked several all-star pop fundraisers, so his concerns were essentially political. I've never been a political filmmaker, though, and I wasn't interested in making a political satire.

Is it possible to make a film free of politics?

If you succeed in being honest about your characters a political reading will always be possible, but I think you can have a story that's more timelessly political and explores the way hegemonies invariably work out. Some countries have more power than others and it forces them into inevitable roles. That's apparent in everything from Euripides to Archie Comics.

Archangel includes a scene where a shower of bunnies rains down on a group of people huddled in a barn. You've described the scene as being so delightful that it's a portent of something bad, which suggests you feel that any high point of joy must inevitably be followed by a fall. Do you think that's true?

Yeah, I guess it's that feeling you get right after the first time you masturbate – everything is cute until you're on the far side of the parabola. Those white, fluffy bunnies seemed to fit so niftily into a phrase like, "The white fluffiness of forgetfulness." I wanted everything to look cozy because forgetfulness can be as comfy as getting tucked in beneath a giant, goose down duvet. In Henry Green's novel, *Back*, there's a man who loses a leg after being shot by a sniper hiding in a rose bush. There's not just a thorn in the rosebush, there's a bullet too – it's fun to combine things like that.

What's the difference between nostalgia, melancholy and grief?

Nostalgia and melancholy are relatively benign, but grief is something I'm terrified of. There've been times in my life when grief was called for and I just didn't have it – when my father, my brother, and my Aunt Lil died, for instance. Instead of grieving in one big payment, I think I grieve on the installment plan in my films and in my dreams, where I encounter all sorts of unfinished business. The bill collectors come around almost every night, and I engage in uninhibited grieving in my dreams, then I wake up refreshed.

What do you think happens after death?

I'm afraid it's nothing. It's funny, if you believed it was nothing it shouldn't be frightening at all. But then, no one understands what nothing really is.

You've said, "I don't need anything to happen to me any more. I have plenty of sadness in reserve. I can lie down with a fine, vintage memory and sip it all night long." This suggests that sadness is a source of comfort for you. Most people go to great lengths to avoid feeling sadness; how do you explain your ability to embrace it?

I avoid pain like a normal person, but I digest sad memories the way other people listen to CDs or watch movies. I don't do it so much any more, though, because I'm such a busy adult with this movie making, and melancholy takes time. You need big, white expanses in your daybook to enjoy it properly, and I've been a bit too busy. My girlfriend, who I've been with for four years, has sort of trained me not to talk about it so much, too, but it's always been a major pastime for George Toles and I. Don't get me wrong – we're not just sitting around reminiscing about funerals – but when we're screenwriting we're openly fabricating our past and transforming it into an exotic blend of melancholy and joy, much in the way people blend whiskey or tobacco.

When a sad song strikes someone at a point of the compass that's so completely personal and unique that they can't even explain why it's so deliciously sad, that song has been transformed into a fantastic commodity.

Name a song that always makes you cry?
This is really sick, but some songs actually make me cry tears of pride. It has to be a song that's not too good, because a really good song is beyond envy. But if it seems so simple and clumsy that I almost could've done it myself, I find myself sliding into a temporary reverie that I was, in fact, the author of this work. That's why I like basement bands, early rock, and any period of the Ramones. There are primitive films that affect me that way, too – Bunuel's *L'Age d'Or*, for instance, or Jean Vigo's *Zero For Conduct*.

What was the essence of Vigo's genius?
Some people have taste and aspire to make things, but they don't have the technical skill or the experience to do it, but Vigo's voice coincided perfectly with his talent. He was a primitive and he knew exactly what to do with that primitivity. He was probably aware he only had enough command over his actors to get stylized, blocked out performances, but he knew how to use that style of performance. And he gave his gifted cameraman and editor the same careless, open, free-for-all he allowed his actors. Every aspect of his work is so consistently primitive and out of control that it takes on a quality of control. Jonathan Rosenbaum made the observation that when some lost scenes were restored to L'Atalante it didn't make the movie any better or worse, and you do get the sense that you could remove or reorder the sequence of the scenes and it wouldn't affect this great movie at all. I'm not great at talking things out with actors, so my approach has always been to use broad narrative strokes then try to cover up with lots of baroque effects and film grain. So I'm always looking for people who work in analogous ways.

You once commented, "Sometimes it's liberating to be self-destructive." Could you elaborate?
I may've been referring to a foolish decision I made a few years ago to have my diaries [*From the Atelier Tovar*] published. I happened to have them with me on an occasion when I met a publisher, and it came up in conversation that I kept these diaries. He asked if I'd ever considered publishing them and I replied no, then he asked if he could take a look at them. I said, "Sure, take them – you can publish them as far as I'm concerned." I regretted that instantly because I knew as I handed them over that a lot of people would be mad at me – and they were. But it sort of cleared the air, and I found out who my friends were. I'm really not sure what's in the diaries because I've actually never even read them. The sound of my own voice, even written on a page, bothers me, so I don't like the sight of my own handwriting. I'm kind of phobic – I'm about two steps removed from late Howard Hughes right now.

You've also said, "You do the darnest, broad stroke, crazy things when you're in agony." When was the last time you were in agony, and what crazy things did you do?
There's nothing like mad love to force you into a surreal experience of your own life, and when I said that I was probably referring to the agony of unrequited love. The first time it happened to me I was about 20 and I didn't know how to deal with it at all so I made a jackass of myself. One of my favorite scenes in *L'Age d'Or* is when it's star, Gaston Modot, responds to getting jilted. He wanders around in an apartment, he tears open a pair of pillows and puts a handful of feathers on a windowsill, he

picks up a giant plow then he throws a burning Christmas tree out the window. It's pretty liberating being that irrational because you get to blast things to smithereens. The second time I got hit I was old enough to have some dignity, which I unfortunately didn't have. I was once at a party where this girl I loved was ignoring me, so I responded by phoning up a taxi for each person at the party – and there were about 50 people at the party. I remember pointing at people and saying, "This taxi is for you!" I finally realized I was making a fool of myself and got into one of the taxis myself.

What's the most destructive thing about romantic love?

There's all sorts of damage done, but it doesn't feel like damage at the time because it feels so good to surrender yourself to the other person. It feels like everything you've been waiting your whole life for, and you give up so much of yourself in those early days without any sort of negotiation. But you've actually just signed over huge parcels of land that you can never reclaim unless you want to start a war at a later date. And maybe it's just an excuse to have a war, because they feel pretty good too. It's no mystery why love can turn to hate because those two emotions are extremely close when the stakes are so high and two countries are sharing a border. I'm in love with romantic love, that's for sure, but there's always a price and you have to decide whether it's worth it. I've considered the alternative, which is being without my girlfriend, and that's not an idea I'm crazy about. It's not that I'm afraid of being alone – I can be alone standing on my head for fourteen years and I've done it in the past – but I'd miss her and always be thinking of her.

What's your definition of a bad decision?

Something that looks ludicrously irrational from the outside. But the thing about wild gestures and ill-conceived battle plans that cause massive collateral damage is that when the smoke clears, the desired result is often still attained somehow. Maybe the desired result was all the collateral damage, or to make a huge, imperialistic claim for your romantic self. There are many lessons to be learned from nature, so we're well advised to remember those marshland mating rituals, with giant animals making bizarre noises while opening themselves up to their natural enemy.

Jung says we're all archetypes playing out ancient, eternal fables. Freud says we're simply animals enslaved by biological drives. Which sounds more accurate to you?

I've never been a very good student of either of them, but I have groped out a murky, working theory for myself that embraces aspects of both those positions. I believe there are stories painted on the insides of our stony heads, there for reading and re-reading and palimpsest-ing our selves. But I also can't help but see us as selfish alimentary canals sort of bumping into one another.

How selfish? Are people incapable of truly putting the interests of someone else above their own?

Probably, but that's too reductive. If you love other people and are even willing to sacrifice your life for them, yet that somehow satisfies some need in you, are you selfish? I suppose you could call that selfish, but you'd be doing a disservice to the extremely complicated and inscrutable transistor-sized wiring of what's really going on in our heads. But human nature certainly feels selfish enough of the time without it having to be selfish 100% of the time.

Is evil contagious?

It can certainly spread like wildfire, and it probably has a very short incubation period. Unfortunately its symptoms usually aren't so apparent to the host organism, even when they're fully infected.

George Toles has described the impulses that swim up from the unconscious as "deliciously unsavory, unsightly and extreme." Is the unconscious basically a fetid swamp?

Yes. It's a bog filled with sperm and eggshells and old teabags and discarded statuary. There are lyrical things down there too, and every now and then, through an act of will and imagination, you can make something beautiful from those raw materials. But mostly it's a roiling, furious, unforgiving and stinking realm.

You've commented, "Most filmmakers don't have the nerve to be really cruel to their characters, to give them what they deserve and what the audience secretly wants, even if they don't know it." Do people enjoy witnessing the suffering of others?

Yes. A lot of it is just glee that it's not them, and a chance to vicariously wonder what it would be like if it was them. That's why people slow down around car wrecks. When I was a teenager I had this *Lord of the Flies* fantasy and I used to wander around the beach naked throwing stones at birds. In time I developed a really strong throwing arm, and one day I actually hit a sea bird in the head. It was surrounded by its flock and all these birds cried as this bird floated off. There was an off shore breeze that day, and the birds cried for hours as this bird slowly floated away. I've never thrown a stone since.

You've said that when you saw Eraserhead *you thought, "Wow, this is my biography. How did someone read my mind and project it onto the screen?" What aspects of that film resonated with you?*

The general state of delirium Henry Spencer films himself in. I'd been a father of an unplanned pregnancy – I assume David Lynch had as well – and I remember feeling plucked from a state of quasi-virginal youth and stuck into this domestic situation with me as the completely impotent paper mache patriarch of a family. The tenor of my life during that period coincided exactly with the tenor of *Eraserhead*, which evokes those middle of the night trips to the washroom where you don't quite have your balance and you're staggering and you have to brace yourself against a wall and you're scared you're not even peeing into the toilet. Then all of a sudden one of life's truths comes swinging out of the darkness at you and says, "You're 20 and you're married and you have a child and your father's dead and you'll never see him again." During waking hours when the sun is high all sorts of misty veils pile up and envelope you in a sort of amnesia, and your troubles seem somehow abstract or fictionalized. But in the middle of the night there are moments when there's an unavoidable, painful truth right at the center of everything, and that's what *Eraserhead* felt like to me.

How did you go about surfacing from that very deep lake?

I wasn't aware that I had to because I kind of embraced it in a way. Parenthood has tremendous rewards and I loved it, just as Henry does. Every now and then he gives a little admiring look down at the baby – although mostly, of course, he just stares into his radiator. When you have a child you love that child more than anything you will ever love, and my daughter is a wonderful person. She's a designer and someday I'd love for her to design a picture with me.

The actor Ross McMillan has said, "In every scene George Toles writes there's someone doing something to someone else." How would you describe Toles sensibility, and what makes him an appropriate co-writer for you?

George is always doing something to someone else, and he's never happier than when he's manipulating a situation to create conflict. He treats every room like a stage in which a short scene must be played out, and he's perfectly willing to fabricate misinformation or involve wives and lovers to get things going. George treats human beings like piñatas, and once you understand that about him it can be fun to be part of his ongoing theater improv involving real human stakes. I thought we would've broken up long ago, but we've only had one little bump in the road, and we both mourned each other's absence so much that we decided to repress what we found annoying in each other. It hurt too much to be alienated from each other.

Toles has described your third film, Careful, *as "a pro-incest movie"; do you see it that way?*

I don't think it converted many people to incest, but we did try to work under the banner of making a pro-incest movie. It's hard to control an ideology, even if you're a skilled propagandist, which I am not, and I think it ended up being a pro-repression movie that offers a patent lesson in what awaits you if you let yourself slip and do what you want to do. Everyone in the film ends up getting punished for letting slip.

A central theme in your films is male rivalry which you describe as a situation that's homosexual without the sexuality; what sort of territory does this theme open up for you?

I'm just trying to make sense of male rivalry. I know that when I've been intensely competitive with someone they become a point of principle for me, and I actually come to my rival's defense if someone else attacks them. There's a certain jailhouse logic operating there, and it's not much of a stretch to find some kind of sexual analogue in it.

You've described yourself as highly resentful and competitive. Who are you competing with now?

Right now I'm competing against the clock. I had a very elderly uncle, my Uncle Ron, who's been in most of my movies, and he recently passed away at the age of 95. He tricked the system because everything went right for him – he lived a great life and died painlessly. But somehow, his death finally brought it home to me that you die. I can't count on living to 95, so while I still have my health I'd like to make one masterpiece. That's my dream.

What are the qualities a work must have in order to be a masterpiece?

It must have the quality of something that was always there, but was waiting to be expressed, and now it has finally been said. It carries an element of surprise with it because it's obviously so right that it's startling its gone unexpressed for so long. It doesn't have to be big – in fact, my favorite writer, Bruno Schultz, is considered a minor writer because he didn't leave a huge body of work. His complete body of work is, nonetheless, a masterpiece.

Which of your films is most fully realized in your opinion?

With *Archangel* I thought I was on my way to saying everything there was to say about how we love, but I was kidding myself and I confused myself and my viewers a lot in its execution. I was pretty happy with [2000 short] *The Heart of the World,* but it's not trying to do as much as some of my longer films. I'm really proud of *The*

Saddest Music in the World because there are moments in the montage sequences where the music works the way music is supposed to – as a mnemonic device that drags up all sorts of cargo. And there are things I really like about my hugely autobiographical film, *Cowards Bend the Knee*, which is a very primitive, low-budget movie.

What historical period is most compelling to you?

Although it's true that all my films seem to exist in the past, I've never been much of a historian because I hate doing research. Every once in a while some historical episode does engage me, though, and at the moment I'm trying to learn everything there is to know about the Borgias. I'm drawn to them because they were bad and charismatic, they had cool, sexy names, and there were no small gestures in that family. There was fratricide and incest and it was all true – not that that should matter at all, because nothing's really true anyway. I'm always amazed when a film boasts, "Based on a true story!" Who cares? Whether it happened or not, it's how a story is told that's important.

You lost many of your ancestors to an 1876 Pox epidemic in a Canadian town called Gimli, and you now maintain a Winnipeg scrapbook of newspaper clippings that include stories of mad dogs dragging off children, hockey stick bludgeonings, and a father shooting his children during a fight over a snowmobile. This brings to mind Michael Lesy's book, Wisconsin Death Trip, *which in turn is evocative of the Bunuel film,* Land Without Bread, *the Brecht/Weill opera,* Mahagonney, *and your second film,* Archangel, *which is set in a region of Russia that experienced a collective amnesia following World War I. All these works deal with places that seem to have fallen under a sort of dreadful bewitching; do you think there are places that are cursed?*

Yes, and they're there for anyone who chooses to see them. There are invisible cities piled up all over the place, and if you occupy those spaces with just the right focal length on your spectacles you'll see the skyline in all its, horrific, lugubrious, glowering splendor. And all it takes is a population of humans to create one of these places. Artists have been trying to pinpoint our humanness for a long time, and we seem to be inexhaustibly cruel and compassionate by turns, but nobody's ever figured out why.

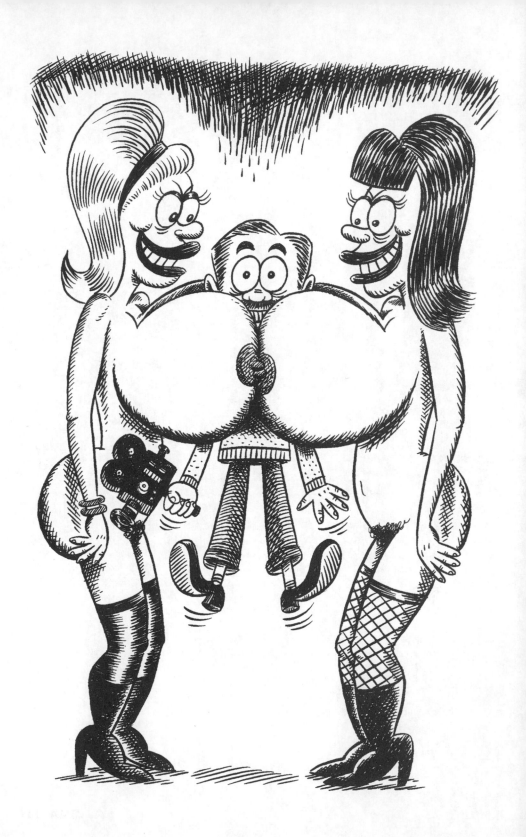

Russ Meyer

....

Russ Meyer is widely credited with the invention of the sexploitation film. The director of 25 trash classics, including Faster, Pussycat! Kill! Kill!, *and* Beneath the Valley of the Ultravixens, *Meyer perfected a style so ludicrously over the top that it manages to satirize sex even as it celebrates it. A frantically-edited mix of extravagant violence and big-breasted women, his movies are peopled with tough motorcycle mamas, buxom waitresses, wild, hitchhiking hippie chicks, voluptuous go-go girls, obliging handymen, horny truck drivers, sinister strippers, muscle-bound ranch hands, lascivious nurses, virginal farmer's daughters, and sex-starved preachers. It's a potent mix of archetypes that's the very essence of white trash America.*

Meyer was born in Oakland, California in 1922, and he began shooting home movies when he was a teenager. He honed his skills as a filmmaker as a combat cameraman during World War II, but almost two decades passed before he succeeded in making his first feature, The Immoral Mr. Teas, *which was released in 1959. He was nearly 40 by then, but he made up for lost time during the '60s; before that decade was over he'd released 17 films, every one of which turned a profit. This isn't surprising – who wouldn't be interested in seeing films with titles like* Skyscrapers and Brassieres, *or* Wild Gals of the Naked West?

I interviewed Meyer in 2000 at his home in the Hollywood Hills. He lives there on a tree-lined street, in a brown two-story house badly in need of a paint job. The fleet of automobiles parked in front of the house suggest that Meyer could easily afford to have his home painted if he cared to; there's a gold Mercedes, a Jaguar, several new compacts, and a weather beaten truck with a bumper sticker that says Hanoi Jane.

Divorced three times, Meyer is currently single, and he answered the door himself in cut-off jeans, a blue cotton shirt whose buttons pulled across his ample stomach, and bare feet. His staff of three was also on premises, as the Meyer empire is run entirely out of this house – it's no small empire, either. If you want something by Meyer you must order it directly from him, as he's retained the rights to every scrap of work he's done. He's a savvy businessman, and his goofy films have made him a rich man.

Meyer is one of those people who save everything, and his house is like a three-dimensional scrapbook of his life. There isn't a bare surface in the place, and the walls and ceilings are papered with photographs, posters from his films, and personal mementos. Sitting on a sofa littered with odds and ends is a box labeled "Don't Drop!" that contains the ashes of Meyer's beloved army buddy, Bill Teas, who starred in Meyer's first film. Meyers is a sentimental old guy who loved his mother, and he's a gracious host, too. He does have a wicked sense of humor, though. When I asked to use the restroom, he inquired if he might be allowed to watch. And, as is apparent in the following monologue, his sexual politics are impossible to classify.

Mother influence is extremely important, and I had a great one. My father was a cop, and my mother was a nurse who got married and divorced six times. When I was 12 years old she bought me my first movie camera, and she had to pawn her engagement ring to pay for it – she defended me to the teeth, and everything her son did was right. People have said my interest in breasts goes back to my mother, and that's possible, because she did have big breasts. I don't remember seeing them a lot as a child, but I must have.

I enlisted in the army in 1941 and was stationed in Europe as a combat cameraman through 1945, and that was the greatest experience of my life. My friends from the army mean a great deal to me and I'm still in touch with most of them – we're very close. I loved the excitement of the war, and the opportunities for relationships with women that it provided. After the war I went back to Oakland and started taking photographs for nudie magazines, and it was around that time that I met Tempest Storm. She was an exotic dancer and we moved to Los Angeles together in 1948. Tempest is with somebody now and that makes me mad because I lost a hell of a good lay. In 1952 I married my first wife, Eve, who was a *Playboy* centerfold. I knew I'd marry her the minute we met, and she was the greatest love of my life. We broke up in 1970 because I was a no good son of a bitch.

When I got to Los Angeles I worked for *Playboy*, which was in its early days then. I've known Hefner for years, but I don't like him any more. He's a little king, and he's doing fine, but sometimes I wonder if he's as fine as he thinks he is. In 1959 I released my first film, *The Immoral Mister Teas*, which was basically three naked women, 60 minutes. It cost me $24,000 to do that movie and it brought in more than a million dollars.

I didn't deal with censors – I dealt with the police. They'd arrest me at theaters where my films were playing on grounds of nudism, but I always had a good lawyer so I never had to spend time in jail. The people who had real trouble were the people making hard-core, which I didn't do. I've never cared for pornography. I'm more interested in putting on a show with women who are overbuilt.

When *Faster, Pussycat! Kill! Kill!* first came out in 1965 it flopped because people couldn't handle the idea of women being in charge and beating men up. It's not a man's picture, per se. It doesn't have enough bare knockers as far as I'm concerned, but it went on to be very successful, and three years after it came out I was offered a production deal at 20th Century Fox Studios. This was in 1968 when Dick Zanuck was running the studio, and I had the whole birthday cake when I was there. They gave me generous budgets, didn't ask me to change a thing, and marketed my movies as art movies. Loads of women came in wanting to work for me and I told them right off, "I can't promise you a role, you're gonna have to take your clothes off, and I may ask of your pleasures." I never had a girl leave when I said that, because the women who came in knew my reputation. Fox knew what I was doing, too, but they never said a word for the simple reason that I was making money for them. Most guys in the movie business are incredibly sleazy and they're always trying to get into women's pants, but they do it in a manner I find sickening. Studio executives are the most evil people in the world, and I'll take an independent guy any day. My last picture for Fox was an adaptation of an Irving Wallace novel called *The Seven Minutes*, and it flopped because it didn't have enough tits. Fox decided they'd had enough of me when that one came out. But I know there are people out there who still want to see my stuff because I'm making money all the time.

I intend my films to play as comedies, because sex is funny. People take sex much too seriously, and that's where Russ Meyer comes in handy. Members of the feminist community have complained about my movies, but women are always in control in my films. By and large, the men are the fools. It's true that there are scenes in *Finders Keepers, Lovers Weepers*, and *Beneath the Valley of the Ultravixens* where you see women getting the tar beaten out of them, but some of those women needed a good, round thumping. And yes, it's true that the star of *Supervixens* gets electrocuted in the bathtub, but she had to learn she could not just have her way.

There's no such thing as a breast that's too large – I will somehow fit it in. I start to get interested at about a D cup – anything smaller than that is just too small for me. You wanna get some really big numbers, and I've seen them as large as triple F. Men love women who are overbuilt – we love to grovel with them, to get them down and penetrate them. I've never been interested in working with mainstream actresses. I'm interested in working with women who are built from the ground up, and the women with the biggest breasts are the most important actresses as far as I'm concerned.

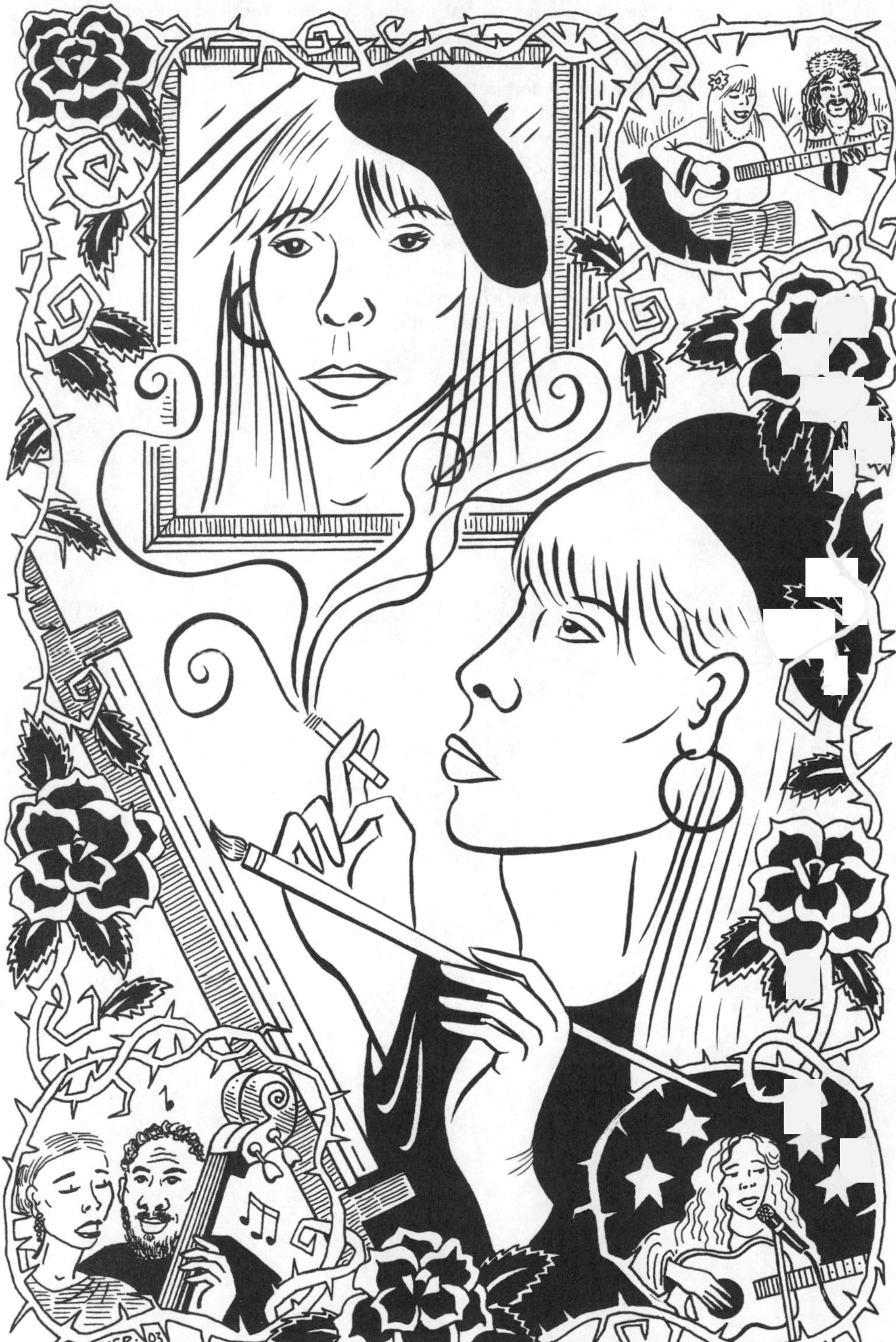
FLEENER·'03

Joni Mitchell

....

   Joni Mitchell has often cited Georgia O'Keeffe as an important source of inspiration, and the two of them are remarkably alike: both are wise, sensual iconoclasts with a penchant for speaking the truth. Both have been criticized, too, for being cranky. One of the most acclaimed singer-songwriters to emerge from the Woodstock era, Mitchell garnered some nasty press in 2002 for referring to the music industry as "a corrupt cesspool." People seem to forget that Mitchell didn't arrive feeling that way, and that her opinion is the result of 35 years in the trenches of the business. Moreover, it's hardly surprising that she feels this way, given the idealistic nature of her music – Mitchell was never cut out for the shuck and jive of selling.
   Born in Fort Macleod, Alberta, Canada in 1943, Roberta Joan Anderson had no brothers or sisters, and she suffered a series of illnesses that made for a lonely, isolated childhood. While attending art school in the early '60s she was honing her skills as a singer-songwriter, and she subsequently developed a following on the coffeehouse circuit, first in Calgary, then in Toronto, where she met and married folk singer Chuck Mitchell. Now called Joni Mitchell, she moved to Detroit with her husband in 1964, and her career continued to pick up steam. By 1967 she'd divorced Mitchell and was in the studio with David Crosby who was producing her debut album, which was released the following year. For the next six years she could do no wrong, and released five greatly loved records that are an essential part of the musical canon of the social revolution that began in the '60s.
   Her fans began to find her music a bit more challenging in 1975 when she released The Hissing of Summer Lawns, which marked the beginning of her transition from folk-pop to jazz. She completed that transition in 1979 when she made an album with Charles Mingus, and at that point some of her fans, and some members of the press, grew quite crabby with her. Why wouldn't she make another record like Blue, they demanded to know? Apparently it escaped their notice that Mitchell never signed on to be a hit machine, and that she'd always insisted her music be allowed to grow and change.
   The first time I interviewed Mitchell was in 1982, at her manager's office in West Hollywood, and I was pleasantly surprised by how much fun she was. There wasn't anything particularly light-hearted about most of her music of the '70s, which revolved around the themes of restlessness and the loneliness it engenders, romantic betrayal, and environmental apocalypse. Consequently, I wasn't expecting to have the rollicking good time with her that I wound up having. Mitchell's a down to earth woman with a bawdy sense of humor and a tough intelligence, and the only thing diva about her is her insistence on chain-smoking. A few days after my profile of her was published, I received a dozen roses with a note that read, "It was nice to recognize myself in your piece." I assure you, nobody else I've interviewed has ever sent me roses.

We spoke again in 1988, and at that point she'd settled comfortably into married life with bassist Larry Klein, whom she wed in 1983. We met at her record company that time, and she was beautifully dressed, as she always is – Mitchell is quite a clothes horse, and the things she wears are unusual and expensive. Her practice as a visual artist was becoming increasingly central to her life then, and she'd made her peace with the fact that the adoration she enjoyed early in her career had to be sacrificed if she wanted to evolve as an artist. Our last conversation took place in 1991, again at her record company office on Sunset Boulevard. She arrived on foot, having just completed a long walk that included a very steep hill, and she was only slightly winded. She was 47 then, and chief amongst the subjects we discussed was the relinquishing of the ingénue that middle age demands.

–1982–

You have a reputation for being reluctant to meet with the press. Why do you dislike being interviewed?

There are many reasons. First of all, the form doesn't bring out what I feel are the most interesting parts of me. I'm full of vignettes and stories, but it takes the associative process that's at work in a conversation to bring them out. In an interview you're fielding questions about ideas and feelings that you probably haven't thought through, and your initial responses aren't always accurate. Then you're held to these improvisational comments that are often very stupid. And the relationship between the interviewer and interviewee is sometimes kind of like a trial. I don't know what kind of peer group pressure journalists are subjected to, but it seems they often look on the celebrated person with animosity. You feel like you're going into enemy camp, as if it's a heavy competitive sport or something, and you've got to be on guard all the time – which obviously doesn't lead to a very good exchange. I've been in this business a long time and have noticed this recurring pattern that if nice things were said about you last year, then this year it's your turn to get attacked. I happen to be at the point in the cycle where I'm due for nice things.

As I recall, your last record, Mingus, got fairly good reviews.

They were mixed. There was a lot of controversy around the record, which is good. The European press and the jazz press seemed to have a fairly good understanding of it, although some jazz circles thought it was presumptuous for a white woman to work with Charles who had a reputation of being racist – which wasn't true at all. He was just outspoken about black problems. The pop press didn't know what to do with the record so they either ignored it, or treated it as some kind of breach of orthodoxy, as if I'd been a Catholic and suddenly become a Baptist. They called it pretentious and a lot of the kinds of adjectives that implied, "Don't you know what you are?!" It just seems to be human nature to typecast – friends even do it to one another, so it's not just the press or record buyers. For an artist, once your audience realizes that change is part of your style, they assume an attitude of, what will he do next? – and then you're home free. I think that finally, after 15 years of making records, people have adjusted to the fact that I change and my changes are more comfortable now.

Many people see your music as being very much intertwined with the myth of Los Angeles. Has L.A. played a prominent role in shaping your style?

No more than New York has. There's a lot of New York mythology in the songs, too. I was living in New York when I made my first albums and that environment inspired many of the songs, including "Chelsea Morning," and "Marcie." I hadn't quite gotten hold of that city's wavelength at that point, and it was a period of disenchantment for me. Plus, New York's self-esteem as a city was at a low ebb then.

Do you think there's any truth to the clichés about Los Angeles?
It's definitely true that the city suffers from a lack of community, but the geography doesn't allow for that. And yes, it is a rather indulged, spoiled place but there are good people in L.A. too.

What do you see as the recurring themes in your music?
Well, there's ecology, although I did throw cigarette butts out the window the other day so I have no right to talk. [Laughs.] Of course, the anatomy of the love crime is my favorite subject. There are many kinds of love and there doesn't have to be a victim for it to be love, but the big hurt and the big pay-off seem to be the most popular form of love. I think that's just a bad habit this culture has, because there are cultures where love doesn't work that way.

Your music is sometimes described as being introspective to the point of moroseness. Is that a fair assessment?
Most of my writing has dealt with the inner landscape and we're living in a time when a lot of people have become numbed-out adrenaline addicts. I write about personal, inner intricacies, and people who prefer not to deal with those things probably do see my music as depressing. I think depression is generally misunderstood, though. I hate to get poetic on you, but it's sort of like winter and is necessary for further blooming.

Must you be in a winter state of mind in order to write?
It helps, because if you're rolling along having a good time you're less likely to put yourself in the isolation that writing demands. I admit that I'm an overly sensitive person. I have a kind of loud antenna and sometimes I pick up too much, to the point that it becomes chaotic, but I don't see myself as a melancholy person. My wonder is still intact and I laugh a lot. There's certainly plenty in life to make us sad and pensive, though. There is kind of a weird anti-climax to the industrial revolution we're living in!

What aspect of your career have you found most difficult?
I love the behind the scenes processes and go willingly to a canvas or a recording studio, but it's hard for me to work up enthusiasm for touring and doing interviews. I guess I find the more public aspects hard.

Has fame forced you to lead an insulated life?
No, on the contrary — actually, that's kind of a hasty thing to say. Fame does cause you to get very unnatural responses from people. Somebody will call you an asshole in a public place, then someone tells that person who you are and they light up like a Christmas tree. I receive an inordinate amount of affection, which is a lovely thing, but sometimes, depending on your own undulating patterns of self-esteem, it can be terrifying. If your self-esteem is at a low ebb and you're being showered with affection it seems out of whack — it's like someone you feel nothing for telling you they love you. It's a weird feeling. I was very maladjusted to fame in the beginning, and it's taken me ten years to learn to deal with it. It was easily the biggest upheaval in my life, and when it first hit it was so extreme that when people looked at me I wanted to shrivel up. I just couldn't get used to people sucking in their breath when I walked by. But I insist on my right to move about the world and I go a lot of places by myself — as a

writer, you have to. Every few years I take off on a long car trip by myself and I encounter people in little restaurants in the boonies who know me, and I'm as capable of being comfortable with that as they are. My relationships really sort of depend on how comfortable the other person is with my career. If they're too impressed by me what usually happens is, the first time I show any signs of being human they're disappointed and they attack. One of the things that attracted me to the jazz world was the fact that a lot of jazz people didn't know who I was and there was no phenomenon surrounding me there. I found that delicious. I also like the fact that the jazz world allows you to grow old gracefully, whereas pop music is completely aligned with youth.

In reading past interviews you've done, I got the impression that you considered jazz to be the superior form compared with pop.

I have to admit that Miles Davis' *Nefertiti*, as well as some of Miles' romantic music is something I've always revered and looked to as the real shit. To me, it had incredible contours, depth, whimsy – it had everything. Miles had the full musical talent: a gift of composition, shading, emotion, everything was there. At the time when that music came into my life, pop was in a formularized, simplistic phase. It had fallen into the hands of producers and been packaged for commerce, and a lot of it was very sterile. Of course, that happens to every musical form at one time or another, and then a temporary messiah comes along and revitalizes it. The Beatles brought new blood to rock 'n' roll after a very bland period, and punk brought some new textures in as well. Punk interested me as an act of revolution, but its strength was in social rather than musical ideas. I keep hoping that something musical will flower out of it.

You once commented that Lambert, Hendricks and Ross' The Hottest New Group in Jazz was your Meet the Beatles, in that it was the first music that completely thrilled you. What was it about that music you found so appealing?

It just had a sassiness and dexterity that I loved. People talk about punk having an attitude but that music really had attitude! It was sophisticated, wry and it just really swung. The harmonies were so far out I'd sit here thinking, "Wow! How can they do that?"

Did you grow up in a liberal, bohemian atmosphere?

Not really. I recently went home to this sort of class reunion and met a man I didn't remember as a child, but who lived across the street from my friend Frankie. Frankie was a piano prodigy who could play the church organ when he was seven years old, and I thought he was just splendid. He and I were the only artists in what was basically a real jock community. The man I met never liked Frankie and wouldn't play with him when they were kids, and at this reunion he said to me, "You know, you and Frankie were the only creative people in a town where everyone threw balls and stones." So: liberal? No.

Have there been pivotal episodes in your life that shaped you as an artist?

Yes: I was an only child, I had a lot of childhood illnesses, and we moved a lot. You can see in early pictures of me that I started out as an extroverted, hammy kid. But a number of moves, the polio, scarlet fever, chicken pox bordering on smallpox, nearly dying with measles – all that isolated me a lot. Every summer all the kids that threw balls and stones would hang out at the lake, but my family would pile into the car and drive someplace like Minnesota.

What sort of rules and boundaries do you set for yourself when you work?

During the making of an album I become sort of musically narrow minded, yet open at the same time. I'm kind of hard to please because I'm looking for something fresh that I haven't heard before, but I can't ask for it because I don't know what it is – yet. I like to hear every musician play with a ripe, blooming personality, and the records are very much a collaboration between the musicians I work with and myself. A musical talent is a complex thing and there aren't many people who have all of its facets. There are players who have power, dexterity and technique, but perhaps aren't aware of subtleties in structure. Or maybe they don't listen to the lyrics and play licks instead of moods, and I'll have to lead them to shade the song in a particular way.

What sort of things do you keep in mind in laying down a vocal track?

Unless a song means something to you you're not gonna get any magic, and that's all there is to it. I have an acute sensitivity to false sexuality or false emotion in a voice. Moans and groans are OK if they're stylized to the point of parody, but if it's trying to pass itself off as real heart, it usually just seems like bad acting.

Do you think most people have a finely tuned enough ear that they're able to detect that kind of falsity?

Yes, I think people hear music more comprehensively than they know, but it varies how much a person will connect what he senses intuitively to his intellect. For example, there's a song I did called "Shadows and Light" that includes a spot where 26 voices are overdubbed and they're all tangled up together. One of the voices was really out of tune, but the way we'd worked up the piece made it impossible for us to correct it. David Geffen came to hear the song at a playback and when it hit that note he noticeably started, as if a doctor had hit his knee to check his reflexes. After the thing was over I asked him if he'd heard a sharp note and he said no. I told him maybe your mind didn't hear it, but your body did!

You've always managed to get by producing your own albums. Is producing an overrated skill?

I once tried working with a producer on a song for my second album and it nearly broke my heart. He was so fussy about his sound that if I closed my eyes and swayed off the microphone he had a fit. The guy was constantly hitting the button and he made me a nervous wreck. David Crosby did produce my first album, but he did it with the idea that he'd keep producers off me. For the most part, producers are spirit bruisers. They're formula people who usually only know what's been before. They hire a player for what he's played before and I don't want a musician who recycles old licks. It's not going to thrill me unless he comes up with something that surprises him too.

What step in the music-making process is most likely to prove the undoing of a record?

Cocaine! There are entire albums that would probably be different if that drug didn't exist. Cocaine seals off the heart and creates a very intellectual mood. It takes all your energy out of your spine and sends it right up to your brain.

Your records are sometimes described as being cinematic. Do you think that's an accurate description?

Yes, I think they do have that quality. I should preface this by saying that I think of the album as a modern form comparable to a symphony or sonata. Most of today's serious musicians aren't going into classical music, they're getting into the popular recording industry, so I think it has to be taken seriously. As far as the cinematic qualities in my music, there's one technique in particular that I use that's sort of like sticking clips of old newsreels in a film. For instance, in "Harry's House," a song on *The Hissing of Summer Lawns*, I inserted a passage of "Centerpiece," which is an old Lambert, Hendricks and Ross song. On the new album there's a song called "Chinese Café" that includes bits of "Unchained Melody" and "Will You Still Love Me Tomorrow."

Does the idea of having hit singles still interest you?

As I was working on my last album, I found myself saying, "Gee, that sounds like a single," but I really don't know what a single in 1982 is. I'm interested in musical trends so I listen to the radio a lot and most of what they play reminds me of that banal spell in the early '60s when music went through a very anti-intellectual phase. I really think that Bobby Dylan and that movement – we did our part in growing up the American pop song. But I don't find much deep thought in the music on the radio right now, and by deep I don't mean it has to be down. There isn't even much wit in current popular music.

You're very involved in your work as a visual artist; if your career as a painter took off would you be content to leave music in the past?

I'm there already. I've always considered myself a painter first and a musician second. My main drive is to paint and since I turned my last record in I've had no desire to pick up an instrument. When I made this album, I wanted it to be my swan song because in a way it summarizes everything I've got to say about love. It was to be my last record for Elektra, but as it turns out, it's the first of five records I'll do for Geffen Records – and there are days when I regret making that commitment. David's pretty good with me, though. We're friends – we lived together for a few years – and he knows I wanted to quit, so I don't think he'll pressure me. But I'm sort of like a good girl in that when I make a commitment I pressure myself, and I told him, "Look, if I sign up for five years I'll be back under the harness and I'll make myself do it."

Why did you make that commitment if your heart is in painting?

Out of some kind of obedience, I guess. There is some logic to the decision, though. The new album is good and has the potential of reaching a lot of people and I haven't made an album too many people could relate to in a long time. So the idea is to get a lot of mileage out of it and then I can afford to drop back.

Does it frustrate you that you're known as a musician rather than as a painter?

No, because I haven't come into my talent as a painter yet. I've been painting all my life, but I haven't reached my stride and the work is really just beginning to ripen.

Will your career in pop work against you in trying to break into the fine arts world?

Basically I've got two strikes against me: a woman has to be twice as good as a man to make it in the art world, and coming into the fine art world from the pop field, you've got dilettante written all over you. My friends in New York have told me that if I show my paintings in Los Angeles first I'll be categorized as a movie star painter like Henry Fonda, or Red Skelton, who paints clowns.

Are you looking forward to touring again?

I'm looking forward to touring, but I'm dreading the rehearsal. I don't remember anything! I don't even remember the titles of some of the songs on the new album. The past is the past. My manager, Elliot Roberts, gave me a pep talk the other day. Run, Joan! Swim, Joan! He says that when you're pushing 40 you have to run back and forth like Mick Jagger. I told him to just push me out in a wheel chair and I'd do the whole set sitting down. Maybe I'll just go out there and throw paint at a canvas and hum.

Who is your audience now?

Elliott tells me that most of my audience is dead already! (Laughing) I expect that kids who are unfamiliar with my music will make up the bulk of the audience for these concerts, because there seem to be large numbers of kids turning out right now to see the old guard perform before they croak!

You seem to be in a pretty good frame of mind about things in general.

Yeah, I think I'm learning to accept life. You just get up every day and try to make the most of it. Hopefully you'll see or feel something in the course of that day that makes it worthwhile. There have been times when I feared I might be done in by the conflict around me, but I think that the major crises of my life are behind me now. And every time I flirt with one of them again I get the dreaded feeling it's going to latch on and stick to me, but it never does. This isn't to imply that I've solved anything, because nothing is ever dealt with and done with, and human beings are always in conflict. And for an artist, to run away from conflict is the kiss of death.

–1988–

Are there themes you were preoccupied with in your early work that no longer seem so compelling to you?

I certainly don't have the attitude, "Oh, I know all about that," because you never know all about anything. In your 40s your life becomes epic, and things you experienced in your 20s come around again but the nuances are different. I can't think of any theme that's expired for me except the search for love, because I'm happily married now.

Your husband Larry Klein co-produced your last album, Dog Eat Dog. *Since you hired him again I assume you work well together.*

With the making of *Dog Eat Dog*, I was pressured for the first time in my career to make some kind of change. My manager at that time – I've since switched management – almost insisted that I be produced. I felt they were trying to laminate me to someone who was popular at the time and I found that insulting. I don't want to be interior decorated out of my music – I'm a composer, not a pop star who can be decorated into fashion. So we argued and argued and producers were paraded through, but my husband and I remained convinced we could do the job with the assistance of a good engineer and a keyboard man who could set up sounds for us. The keyboardist we chose was Thomas Dolby – and it was not a successful collaboration. Thomas accepted the job, fully aware that he was to set up sounds then relinquish the keyboards to me, and though he said that would be a pleasure, in the end he couldn't handle it.

Making that album was like being in a band because there were three heads – my husband, Thomas Dolby, and the engineer Mike Shipley – none of whom agreed with my approach to the studio. I feel that when you enter the studio you must allow ideas, even ideas that initially appear to be bad, to run until you recognize that it either succeeds or fails. You can't kill it off before you've even begun because that's the only way you discover anything. Working with them I had critics around at the beginning of an idea for the first time in my career, and that was very difficult for me.

What was the central idea you had when you went into the studio to make that record?

I don't work that way. I discover what I'm up to in the process of doing it and never know where I'm headed when I begin. To watch me work you'd be apt to think I don't know what I'm doing — and in a way I don't, but that's part of the process. Not knowing is an open-minded state that allows things to come to you.

How would you describe the mood of the record?

It's an emotionally complex record, and how dark you find it probably depends on what you bring to it when you hear it. For me, it's neither optimistic nor pessimistic, but rather, is a series of characters commenting on different times. The female narrator in "The Tea Leaf Prophecy" comments on life in the 1940s, after the bombing of Hiroshima. The central character in "The Beat of Black Wings" is a kid who's been to Vietnam and he talks about war. "Dancin' Clown" is a couple of guys standing on a corner watching a beautiful girl go by.

How did you go about selecting the guest players on the album?

Some of the recording was done at Peter Gabriel's studio, which I'd borrowed because it happened to be near a studio where my husband was working. Peter dropped by one day so I put him to work. My husband was working with Ben Orr, who has a rich baritone that he rarely uses, so I put him to work. Basically I make use of what's at hand; James Taylor and Crosby, Stills, Nash and Young were around when I was making my earlier records and I put them to work. What I did do on this record that I'd never done before was seek out singers I didn't know personally, because I thought they were suited to the song — Billy Idol and Willie Nelson fall into this category. I saw Billy at the Grammy Awards a few years ago and I thought he was a great rock 'n' roll singer, so I called him and he came down the next night. He was a delight to work with. I've always loved Willie Nelson's voice and met him at Farm Aid, but I didn't really know him when I invited him to sing on the album. Tom Petty sings a very small part, which I offered him with an apology because it is such a small part, but he came in and sang and was great about it. Prince had been inviting me to attend a lot of things and wrote a song for me called "(You Are My) Emotional Pump." I didn't cut it but I like his music and think he's the greatest performer I've ever seen. His timing is amazing. Anyhow, I met Wendy & Lisa through Prince. We'd seen each other socially — at dinners and so forth — and wound up working at the same studio. With Wendy & Lisa it was a case of meeting by the coffee machine and saying, "Hey, how'd you like to sing some backgrounds?"

The song "Number One" reflects on fame and the roller coaster of success and failure. How do you feel about the way your career has unfolded? It's widely assumed that one of the reasons you moved into jazz was to escape the pop rat race.

I moved into jazz because pop musicians didn't have the harmonic sophistication my music requires. They couldn't understand what they described as "Joni's weird chords," and it's true that my sense of harmony is somewhat unusual. Chaka Khan once told me my chords were like questions, and in fact, I've always thought of them as chords of inquiry. My emotional life is quite complex, and I try to reflect that in my music. For instance, a minor chord is pure tragedy; in order to infuse it with a thread of optimism you add an odd string to the chord to carry the voice of hope. Then perhaps you add a dissonant note because in the stressful society we live in dissonance is aggressing against us at every moment. So, there's an inquiry to the chords comparable to the unresolved quality of much poetry.

The song "The Recurring Dream" makes the point that material things are ultimately without value, and throughout your career your music has stressed the importance of spirituality over worldly goods. And yet, I get the impression that you live in a world of luxury and beautiful things.

Yes, this is a great paradox. When I first got the money to acquire things I firmly believed that luxury arrives as a guest and then becomes the master, and I think there's an element of truth to that. In the early '70s I bought a piece of undeveloped land in Northern British Columbia because at that point, the madness of both sides of my family was manifesting itself in me. We have a tendency to give up on people and become anti-social hermits. I spent a summer up there living in an older fisherman's shack with plastic in the windows, bats hanging from the roof, and no electricity or running water, and I got so I could walk through the bushes at night without any fear. I wasn't afraid of the wilderness the way I was of cities. Last year my husband and I went up there with fourteen years having elapsed since that earlier summer, and I found I couldn't swim in the ocean because it was so full of life and little things crawling around. We were planning to stay just two weeks but I told him I couldn't leave until I got over my fear. I was turning into a hothouse plant and losing my earthiness! So I stayed and scrubbed my copper pots squatting in the sun and got on friendly terms with nature again. We get into our vacuumed boxes and forget what it's like to lie down in dirt, that it's quite lovely.

You once commented that the three great stimulants are artifice, brutality and innocence. Can you elaborate on that?

That's an idea that I borrowed from Nietzsche but I agree with it. I rarely wear flamboyant makeup, but whenever I do I have to peel people off of me who are responding to the seduction of artifice. Face painting, hiking up the skirt – these are the flags of artifice. As for brutality, this culture is terrified of sex and thrives on decapitation. We're a culture of adrenalin addicts and need ever larger doses of horror to get off, so movies like *Halloween III* make millions. And innocence? A businessman wakes up in his mid-40s, jaded and thick-skinned from battling for financial opportunity, and he yearns for what he has lost – his innocence. One of the recognizable characteristics of a culture in decline is the seduction of innocence.

But wouldn't you agree that to yearn for innocence is to have it in a sense?

If you want it in yourself perhaps that's true. If you want it in your bed, that's something else entirely.

I get the impression you lead an extremely private life.

I do lead a private life and enjoy being able to move about with a degree of anonymity. The more high profile you are, the more lunatics you attract, and just having my house mentioned in connection with a recent storm in Malibu created problems. As soon as your name is on the news they come out of the woodwork. So no, I'm not out pounding the pavement. I'm a loner by nature and the kind of attention the Beatles received would be a nightmare for me. I never courted that kind of fame because I'm a back bush Canadian. I come from small towns and was raised to believe that if you stick your head above ground, it'll probably get knocked off.

Speaking of high profile versus low profile, do have any immediate plans for live performances?

There's some pressure being put on me to tour, but my last few performing experiences have been very unpleasant. I was doing benefits and I get eaten alive at benefits. At the Amnesty benefit I was asked to go on at the last minute, so we rehearsed backstage with borrowed equipment and went on and did three songs, for which I received my annual Worst Of award from *Rolling Stone* – for years, *Rolling Stone* has been giving me a Worst Of something-or-other award every year. Anyway, people were throwing things at me at the Amnesty benefit. Then I did the Leonard Peltier benefit where I was playing to Willie Nelson's audience. Everyone knows that audience comes to party, and I don't do well in that setting because my music is fragile and requires a more thoughtful setting. I don't make good-time boogie in the sun stuff and my music doesn't work in daylight. My audience is relatively small and when I do benefits I'm sandwiched between acts whose audiences are much bigger, so when I go on, they use the time to talk. It's left me feeling a bit shy about performing.

It sounds quite discouraging. How does this stuff affect your life on a daily basis? What's a typical day like for you?

There is no typical day. I may paint every day for a month, then not pick up a brush for weeks. Unfortunately, I'm not at all a creature of habit – I just sort of fall out of bed and into life.

What was the last album you bought?

Jimmy Cliff's *Bongo Man*. I love the title track. I spend a lot of time in the Caribbean – at least I used to. That area of the map always tries to kill me! When I go there I invariably come home on a stretcher with some weird ailment or another. Anyhow, I listen to reggae when I go there.

What are your thoughts on the popular music scene right now?

All I can talk about are the things I miss in popular music right now. We're living in an era of specialization created by middlemen, and I wish I could turn on the radio and hear an old Miles Davis cut followed by Edith Piaf then Chuck Berry then Mozart. No matter what station you turn on, you hear the first song and know that if you listen for six hours you'll only hear more of that one song.

Is there a slot for you in that scheme of things?

No, I don't fit in anywhere. People hated my last two albums, and ate me alive on the Mingus record. *The Hissing of Summer Lawns* was named the worst album of 1975 by *Rolling Stone*. My album of 13 years ago, *Court and Spark*, was probably the last time there was a consensus of good feeling, but I couldn't handle all the attention that record generated around me. And of course, after that, it was time for me to pay because once you've had your glory they're out to get you. I'd like people to hear this record, but I seem to be out of synch with the times in this decade. Am I early or am I late? I don't know. In 1982 I released *Wild Things Run Fast*, which was an album of love songs celebrating my marriage. It came out during the most anti-romantic period in pop music I can remember, ever. This was right when videos were first happening and the videos were not very tender – lots of women in spike heels grinding men's hands into the ground. The general response to my record was, "Yuuck, love songs." From that we segued into a period of rah-rah Reaganism, at which time I released *Dog Eat Dog*, which espouses an almost evangelical humanism. At that time people didn't seem to want to think about the things we were bringing down on ourselves, and although *Time* magazine eventually did in-depth discussions of almost every issue the album raised, people seemed to think I was immature to have this point of view when it came out. These things are frustrating to me, but I've come to accept that I must write what I feel when I feel it, and can't make my life unravel in a particular way. I can only do what is given me.

-1991-

What's the most valuable lesson you've learned in life thus far?

I don't know if I've learned anything yet! I did learn how to have a happy home, but I consider myself fortunate in that regard, because I could've rolled right by it. Everybody has a superficial side and a deep side, but this culture doesn't place much value on depth – we don't have shamans or soothsayers, and depth isn't encouraged or understood. Surrounded by this shallow, glossy society we develop a shallow side, too, and we become attracted to fluff. That's reflected in the fact that this culture sets up an addiction to romance based on insecurity – the uncertainty of whether or not you're truly united with the object of your obsession is the rush people get hooked on. I've seen this pattern so much in myself and my friends and some people never get off that line. But along with developing my superficial side, I always nurtured a deeper longing, so even when I was falling into the trap of that other kind of love, I was hip to what I was doing. I recently read an article in *Esquire* magazine called "The End of Sex" that said something that struck me as very true. It said: "If you want endless repetition, see a lot of different people. If you want infinite variety, stay with one." What happens when you date is you run all your best moves and tell all your best stories – and in a way, that routine is a method for falling in love with yourself over and over. You can't do that with a longtime mate because he knows all that old material. With a long relationship, things die then are rekindled, and that shared process of rebirth deepens the love. It's hard work, though, and a lot of people run at the first sign of trouble. You're with this person, and suddenly you look like an asshole to them or they look like an asshole to you – it's unpleasant, but if you can get through it you get closer and you learn a way of loving that's different from the neurotic love enshrined in movies. It's warmer and has more padding to it.

What did you have to surrender in order to have a happy home?

My husband has let me keep more of myself than most people I've been with. Even when he disapproves of me – and there's plenty to disapprove of – he has a very warm way of doing it. We're both monks, and I think that's one of the reasons we cohabitate so well.

Is the ability to be happy a skill one can cultivate in oneself?

Yes, although I'd add that I think this culture has an unnatural obsession with the idea of "happiness." There's nothing wrong with melancholy as long as you don't overindulge it. It's part of life and is necessary for growth. And let's face it, there's plenty to be sad about in this world, and in a healthy culture those things would be acknowledged and time for grief would be provided. If you're a nine-to-fiver, it's like, hey, what's wrong with you? What are you down in the dumps for? Lighten up!

Do you cry easily?

Not now, but I went through a period in my late 20s when I cried at the drop of a hat. At that point everything had been stripped away – people had no masks and I had no mask, and you can't go around in that state. Life just went transparent, and I could intuit what was going on behind the composed faces people present to the world, and I couldn't handle it. I'd lost all my illusions about myself and others and it took me several years to come back from that place. I made several albums when I was in that state – *Blue* was the first of them, and there's a purity to that album because I had no defenses at all when I made it. People say to me, "Why don't you make another album like *Blue*," but I can't, there'd be no point to it, and I'd never want to go back to such an undefended place.

How is your work evolving?

My voice is changing and I like it better now because it's rougher. My goal has always been to sing like Edith Piaf, not like Joan Baez, which is where I started from. I began with a very clear voice that was limited in terms of dramatic range – people forget this is a theatrical business, but what I'm basically doing is creating roles for myself to play. Take a song like "Cold Blue Steel and Sweet Fire" – that song has some really gritty imagery, and when I recorded it I couldn't bring out the grit. I sing it better now because I've learned how to really lay into a line and bring out the humor. I have a fuller palette in my voice.

What's the most significant change you've observed in yourself in recent years?

Other than the deterioration of the flesh? There is that, of course, but that's less terrifying to me than it once was. It's still scary, but I think one begins to get comfortable in one's skin during one's 40s.

Western culture does accord enormous importance to youth and beauty, particularly in women, and consequently women expend a lot of energy and money trying to fight the clock. How did you resolve this issue for yourself?

That's a difficult transition, and I'm beginning to discover it's what your 40s are about. Suddenly in your mid-40s you notice the heads don't turn any more. Nobody likes to have less than they had before, and if you've been a pretty woman you feel a sense of loss. And, the more attractiveness you've had, the greater the sense of loss you'll feel as it declines. If you're used to a certain kind of attention based on your appearance, then your transition is going to be that much more difficult. If you haven't set up that appetite for one reason or another – either through character or lack of beauty in the first place – perhaps the transition isn't so difficult. As a celebrity, if I don't look good and somebody my own age looks at me, they think they don't look good. They tend to get irritated with you if you look bad – it's as if it's part of your job to look better than your age for them. That's annoying for me, especially since I've had a hard life physically. I've had a lot of illness and led an experimental life – I lived through the drug era, and that took a toll on all of us. I have my weak moments, as any woman does, and the question of whether or not to fall beneath the blade tends to come up when a middle-aged woman is feeling bad about herself.

Have you ever hated anyone?

Yes, I have, and it's a very difficult thing to work through. In order to hate someone, you have to feel that something terrible has been done to you, that some affront has occurred, and that's a feeling that will poison your whole life. Krishnamurti says that the man who hates his boss hates his wife, and it's true that if you indulge in hate, it has a tendency to permeate everything. So how do you dissolve that poison? Judaism says, "An eye for an eye," but most revenge is as evil as the thing being revenged. The goal is to get rid of the poison, not to increase it, and for that it's best to turn to Christianity. One must struggle to forgive, and the best way to do that is to figure out what you gained from the wrong that was done you.

Do you have a structure of religious belief?

I believe in bits of a lot of different things, but I don't believe anything completely and have no formal meditation practice. I was given an amulet by Chogyam Trungpa Rinpoche, who's the bad boy of Zen but a great teacher nonetheless. I was dragged to see him by a disciple of his during a period of crisis in my life, and I said to him, "Look, I hate to come around asking for something, but I don't have anything to focus on. In a moment of travail I can't cross myself and I don't know what to do – I need some kind of amulet." I felt embarrassed asking for something like that, but he said, "I've got a really good one for you; it's a trinity of three H's: heart, humor and humility." When you think about it, one or all of those things are absent whenever you're in strife.

Several people I've interviewed have said their entire lives were shaped by a few pivotal childhood events. Is that true for you?

Definitely. Having polio as a child changed the course of my life completely. I probably would've been an athlete had I not gotten sick. I had a tremendous amount of childhood diseases – I was the first polio victim in our town – and it must've horrified my mother to have this sickly child because, until recently, she was never sick a day in her life. For a while I couldn't even stand up, and there were doubts I'd ever walk again. I developed my creative skills as part of my determination to get out of that polio ward. To speed my healing I sang and developed my imagination and an inner life.

What's the most significant difference between the masculine and feminine sensibility?

The masculine principle is angular, sharp-edged and geometric, while the feminine is more languid and fluid – it's sort of like the difference between art deco and art nouveau. You can't have a good piece of art without embracing both of them. I see both genders in all people, and with women entering the workplace I think that as a species we're moving towards a less drastic split between masculine and feminine. Speaking for myself, I don't think of myself as a woman – I think of myself as an artist, and artists are kind of androgynous because they have to combine a balance of strength and grace. Occasionally it's brought to my attention that I am a woman and that that's a handicap of sorts, but both sexes have an equal share of assets and liabilities. For instance, I think many men envy women for their natural ability to create in their capacity to bear children. On the other hand, when it comes to the realm of commerce, it is a man's world.

Are things improving for women in the music business?

We're in a visual era now. In the '40s, performers came to their public through movies. Bing Crosby, Frank Sinatra, Peggy Lee – they were singing movie stars, so that was a visual era as well. I began my career during an era of radio artists. Television hadn't figured out how to shoot us yet, and we weren't movie stars, so looks weren't as important then. But with the advent of video, females began to be packaged and promoted for their ability to inspire wet dreams rather than their musical skills. There are lots of talented women working in the visual musical arts now, but the emphasis has shifted and we're seeing more skin. It's gotten more burlesque. Throughout history women have been thrown in the role of the seductress, but things have gotten a bit extreme and lopsided lately. I get lots of letters from kids, and I just got a letter from a 15-year-old boy who didn't like anything on the radio, so his father turned him on to my music. He went out and bought all my records, and he and his friends were really getting into them. I think there's an audience of young people coming up who could appreciate sitting back and listening to records, but these days that experience isn't encouraged by the money men.

Ideally, how should art function in society?

There's nothing wrong with art being decorative, but on a deeper level, I agree with Joseph Campbell, that it's the duty of the artist to be a kind of prophet and bring the lost flock back in.

How would you describe your public persona?

There are several different perceptions of me – some people still think I'm baking bread out in Laurel Canyon – and much of that is the invention of the media. At a certain point I did try and take control of my image. When you're a performer you discover fairly quickly that the romance between an audience and a star is tenuous – the public gets sick of you. Just like people can't keep their own personal relationships together for too long, they can't maintain a good relationship with an artist for long either. As my career picked up steam I became increasingly aware of the imbalance of this audience-star relationship, so I decided to test it. You're in love with an image here – let's see if you can be in love with a person, just like in a one-on-one situation. Get to know me a little bit, see if you can accept my faults. That approach is the antithesis of pop because in pop you don't show your weaknesses – you always try to be bigger than life. But I wanted a truer relationship with my audience, like a better love – a love that thrived in spite of my foibles, or maybe even because of them. And I was happy to discover that a truer relationship is possible and really works.

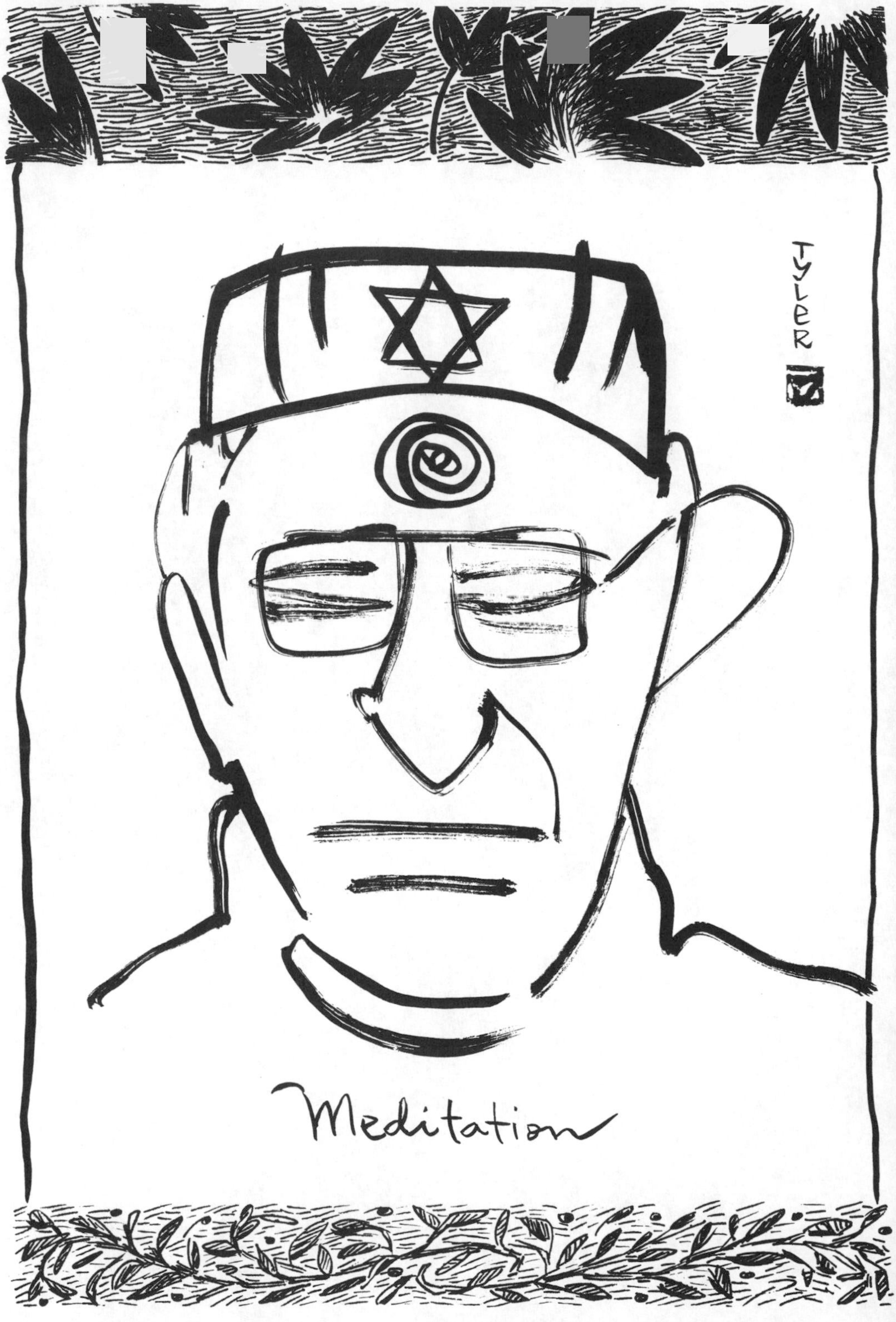
TYLER
Meditation

Jonathan Omer-Man

Jonathan Omer-Man is a British-born rabbi who opened Metivta: A Center for Contemplative Judaism, in West Los Angeles in 1991. Loosely affiliated with the Jewish Renewal Movement, an approach to Judaism that began to coalesce in the mid-'60s and has its roots in the Hasidism of Martin Buber, Metivta welcomed Jews that have traditionally been marginalized – women, gays, converts – and encouraged the rediscovery of Jewish mystical and meditative traditions that have long lain dormant. Spearheaded in America by Rabbi Zalman Schachter-Shalomi, The Jewish Renewal Movement is a more holistic, less rigid approach to Judaism that encourages the cultivation of wisdom rather than blind obedience.

Jonathan Omer-Man is one of the great teachers of this tradition. Born Derek Orlans in Portsmouth, England in 1934, Omer-Man discovered his childhood was over when he was sent to an anti-Semitic boarding school at the age of eight. A miserable adolescence ensued, and in 1955 he moved to Israel where he settled on a kibbutz. His life changed dramatically when he contracted polio late in 1956; two years of convalescence followed, and he never regained the use of his legs. As physical labor was no longer an option for him, his kibbutz sent him to train to be a teacher at Hebrew University in Jerusalem; subsequently, he returned to the school to study Jewish mysticism and the Kabbalah. Omer-Man found these classes exciting but overly intellectual, so he sought out teachers in Jerusalem's old haredi neighborhood, Meah Shearim. The teachings of Rabbi Nachman of Bratzlav became a beacon to him, and at that point he seemed to be moving in the direction of orthodox Judaism. There was, however, an inflexibility in the Orthodox community that he found restricting, so he refrained from putting roots down there either.

In 1981 Omer-Man moved from Israel to L.A. at the invitation of several members of Los Angeles' Jewish community, and he became a kind of minister-at-large for the spiritually alienated. In 1987 he was ordained as a rabbi, but he never aspired to be a pulpit rabbi and he was already laying the groundwork for Metivta. The Center was finally up and running four years later, and it absorbed most of his time and energy during the '90s. I'm not a Jew, but I attended classes there from 1995-2000, and felt enormously privileged to do so, because Omer-Man is a remarkable person.

The subject of two books by Rodger Kamenetz – The Jew in the Lotus, published in 1994, and Stalking Elijah, in 1997 – he's an urbane man able to speak knowledgeably about music, literature and visual art, and he carries himself with the reserve characteristic of the British. He's resolutely skeptical about the touchy-feely manifestations of the New Age movement, yet he's an intensely emotional, intuitive instructor with an unorthodox approach to teaching that places him on the fringes of the mainstream Jewish community. He punctuates his lectures with quotations from a far-flung cast of characters that included Rumi, the Dalai Lama, Picasso and Thomas

Pynchon, among many others, and his unconventional approach to religious study serves as a subtle illumination of the fact that at their best, art, culture, and spirituality share the common purpose of elevating the human soul. During my years at Metivta, he led his students through Dante's Inferno in a class called Spiritual Poetry, taught Jewish meditation, hosted a seminar on William Blake's Jerusalem, and gave spectacularly original lessons on the Jewish High Holidays.

In 1997 Omer-Man began splitting his time between Northern and Southern California, and was on and off planes every week in order to fulfill his teaching commitments. A series of health scares brought that regimen to a halt in 2000, at which point he stepped down as director of Metivta. I visited Omer-Man at the house in the Berkeley Hills he shares with his wife, Nan Gefen. He's reduced his teaching schedule considerably, and devotes a good deal of his time these days to mastering classical Arabic and studying Islam. "I spent much of my life in the Middle East, yet learned very little about this rich culture, and it's time to correct that," he explained. "It's also thrilling to discover the places where it overlaps with that part of the Jewish tradition that I love so much."

What's your earliest memory?

They say you don't remember your earliest memory, but I do have a few general memories of childhood. I'm the eldest in a family of three boys, and my mother was a sunny person who also had dark clouds that occasionally overcame her; I think I inherited some of her darkness, although it has largely dissipated over the years. Both my parents were liberal Jews and were the children of immigrants who'd come to England from Eastern Europe. As such, they had a definite idea of where they wanted to go in life; they wanted to be English, and were concerned with upward social and economic mobility. My father was a hard working dentist and a serious person who went off to the army for five years while I was growing up. My childhood was quite fractured by the Second World War. I have vivid memories of the Blitz, and when my father left I was sent off to boarding schools, which were absolutely horrible. George Orwell once said that people who go to English public schools either love the experience or hate it for the rest of their lives, and I fell into the latter category. My younger brothers didn't suffer the anti-Semitism in the public schools that I did, but for me, fear of what the bullies could and did do to me was a constant companion for many years. I was in school during a terrible time when the British were still occupying what was then called Palestine, and I remember the day when two British sergeants were hanged in retaliation for the hanging of a Jewish Palestinian fighter. My fellow students gave me a very bad time.

How did growing up in an anti-Semitic environment affect you?

In different ways. I compensated for the fact that I was a member of an excluded and despised minority group by regarding myself as superior. However, a more important coping mechanism was that I learned to live inside myself. In those days British public schools were a world of bullying, beating, and competitive sports, and I withdrew as much as I could and developed my own inner life. It was rich, but it couldn't sustain itself indefinitely because there was no input – it was like a secure little garden where all the plants were going rotten for lack of fertilizing.

How did the Holocaust mark your consciousness as a young man?

Nobody spoke about it, so it didn't enter my consciousness until after I moved to Israel in 1955. I'm not entirely certain why it wasn't discussed prior to that, but I think it was in part a reactive response. After a great trauma there comes a point when you have to start looking towards the future, and people were struggling to deal with the many problems faced by the state of Israel in its early years. So, the Holocaust didn't really come to the fore until the time of the Eichmann trial – one of the purposes of which, by the way, was to educate people who hadn't been through the war. We were aware of it, of course – it was impossible not to be, because there were so many people with the bluish tattoos on their forearms – but the scope of the information that came out during the trial had a very deep impact on me. The question of vulnerability, and the presence of such great evil in the world moved to the foreground of our thinking at that point. Prior to the trial the question of how the Jews of Eastern Europe could've agreed to be led to the slaughter like sheep was in the air, and the Eichmann trial answered that question. It described the mechanism by which the Jews were completely demoralized, separated and beaten down before they were actually led off to be killed. It's such an enormous, complex subject.

In your work as a teacher you maintained a policy of refusing to discuss the Holocaust. Why?

Because it's too big, we don't yet have the language to discuss it, and it's generated too much glib rhetoric. Sometimes we need the perspective of a hundred years to understand phenomena, and we're still at a point where all we can do is describe what happened. I'm certainly interested in the evolution of European anti-Semitism and how it culminated as it did, and I'm concerned about contemporary manifestations of anti-Semitism, but I have a great aversion to the theorists and theologians of the Holocaust. It's a subject I want to stay clear of.

In Ron Rosenbaum's book of 1998, Explaining Hitler, *he suggests that meaning was Hitler's ultimate victim because it's impossible to find coherent meaning in this episode of history. Do you agree?*

I agree that Hitler was a destroyer of meaning, at least old meanings, but anti-Semitism preceded Hitler and has outlasted him. He was, however, unique in the scope and the totality of his demonic vision, and he employed all the apparatus of a centralized state to implement his plan. Prior to Hitler, anti-Semitism was much more local and anecdotal, although he certainly wasn't the first person to use the powers of the state as a force for anti-Semitism. The Czars did it, as did many other rulers. However, they weren't consumed by it, and their efforts resulted in persecution rather than mass murder.

Can you recall the first time you sensed divine presence?

In clouds, sitting and watching clouds float by. I was a dreamy kid and there's no shortage of clouds in England, especially in the summer. In looking at them I sensed a different dimension of reality, although of course I couldn't name it then. My first explicit experience of the divine, that I could name as such, was when I was studying for my bar mitzvah. Prior to that God didn't exist for me as a meaningful concept, in part because everyday at school I heard Christian prayers and I couldn't relate to their basic assumptions. I didn't know whether there was a God, but I was quite certain that Jesus wasn't his son. One year I was taken out of boarding school – the year of my bar mitzvah – and the rabbi who instructed me became an important character in my life. He offered a completely opposite model to the teachers at school. He was a gentle man with a softness about his being, and I felt something as I studied with him. Suddenly there was something coming through the letters – not necessarily from the words of the text, but light flowing from the letters themselves. I remember weeping with joy because I felt a deep recognition of something I knew was manifestly true and was important for me.

What happened in the years following your bar mitzvah and prior to your move to Israel at the age of 21?

For several years I was a poor student at school – so bad that I had to repeat the tenth grade. Then things got better and I went to medical school for three years, primarily to satisfy my parent's expectations. I didn't particularly want to be a doctor if I was to be anything less than the brilliant brain surgeon who was publicly thanked by Winston Churchill for saving his niece's life. Actually that's not the whole story. I had some kind of breakdown while I was at school. I lost all sense of direction and didn't like the other students, and I finally left England and never returned, except for short visits. That was almost 50 years ago and it's strange that people still describe me as British, despite the fact that I have three citizenships; British, Israeli and U.S.

In reflecting on your move to Israel, you've said, "When I went to Israel I discovered redemption through land." What did you mean by that?

It was as if the private drama I'd carried within me for years was suddenly a shared drama. Physical labor and contact with the soil of that land brought new dimensions of meaning into my life, and I felt part of a new, more integrated reality. It was a return to my people and to an ancestral home, and I sensed that intensely from the moment I got off the boat. I felt very happy and complete in a way. But at the same time, there was a nagging reality that wouldn't go away, and that was the question of the native Palestinians. I had no solutions as to how the problem should be addressed, I was just aware of it. We were living quite close to the border, and we knew there were refugees on the other side, but there the matter ended.

Did many Israelis feel guilt about displacing the Palestinians?

Guilt is too strong a term. Israel was very fragile and its survival wasn't guaranteed. There wasn't guilt, but there was an increasing awareness of responsibility, which grew very slowly. It started coming out much more in the late '60s and '70s.

How did falling ill in Israel change you?

I got polio 18 months after I arrived and basically the entire context of my life changed once again. One day I was an agricultural laborer and part-time cowboy working on a kibbutz in the upper Galilee, and the next day I was flat on my back in bed for six months, and in hospital for a year. On one level it gave me an acutely focused sense of purpose; to be rehabilitated as completely as possible. At another level, I was learning to come to terms with the fact that I would remain disabled for the rest of my life. It also gave me an enormous amount of time to read. I got through all the Russian classics in that year and there was always a pile of books on my bedside table. In a way, being ill made me very self-centered in that for two years I focused almost entirely on myself.

Your previous comment regarding your feelings about a career in medicine suggests that as a young man you had a hungry ego and needed to do something heroic. The possibilities for heroism changed dramatically with your illness; were you aware of that at the time?

That's very perceptive. I would never have described the person I was before I became ill as in quest of the heroic, but it's true that as a young man I tried to identify with the aggressors and be "like them." Not that I aspired to be a macho bully, but I did want to be someone with some power over his own life. The illness gave me a sense of my own soul work, and yet that period was completely non-religious. That came back slowly, at different stages, through subtle signs and experiences, which often took the form of chance encounters that were extremely powerful. Occasionally you meet people who open a door for you and say, "This is your path," and I've had several such encounters which were crucially important. Religion returned to me through those subtle signs, as well as through literature. English poetry, Hebrew short stories, Thomas Merton, Hebrew mystical literature, Sufi and Buddhist texts – the list of writings that were important to me is long, and literature gave me a new vocabulary to understand the inner life. I was particularly moved by Dostoyevsky and his willingness to explore the complexity of the religious soul with all its quirks. However, I had no entry point into the Jewish world then, because during the late '50s in Israel, religion seemed to me to be controlled by a narrow, power-hungry orthodoxy obsessed with politics. I never found it attractive.

Could you describe one of the chance encounters that played a role in your spiritual development?

There was a man I met in Jerusalem who had the most wonderfully acute sense of reality and the way things are on all levels. He was an illiterate person who never read newspapers or anything like that, but he could see people and events. He was a carpenter and he knew where to put the hammer and how to shave the wood – he was incredibly present. There was another man I met on one of my first visits to the United States when I started coming here on lecture tours. He was a Native American who knew how to be in the space that he occupied. During our brief encounter, I asked him a barrage of questions and he said to me quite firmly, "Stop talking and just look." That stayed with me in a powerful way.

Have you had pivotal episodes of shattering insight along your spiritual path, or has it been more of a long, slow slog?

It's been both. Wonderful insight means nothing unless there's been a slog beforehand and afterwards, but yes there have been powerful moments of discovering new coordinates of existence. And having experienced one of those moments, you continue on the same path but you understand it in a completely different way. There is danger in having those dazzling moments – you can get hooked on the high and devote yourself to getting the next one – but one should really regard them as anchoring points. Real life takes place between the high points, and focusing on them too much impoverishes the totality of one's life.

Were Jewish esoteric traditions suppressed in Israel while you were living there in the '50s and '60s?

I don't think they were suppressed, but they were certainly beyond my horizon. You look over there and see a group of people dressed in black wearing hats, but you have no idea what's going on in their minds. Israel's always been a place for people on spiritual journeys going in different directions, however, and I succeeded in carving out a path for myself. My sense of quest was growing extremely strong when almost by chance I discovered the world of Kabbalah. I was working as chief editor of general scholarship at a publishing house that was producing the *Encyclopaedia Judaica*, and one day my boss took me aside and said, "We've got a cash flow problem and we're closing your division. Would you mind being the revising editor of the *Encyclopaedia Judaica*?" What that job boiled down to was reading every page of the encyclopedia before it was printed, and it was then that I discovered Kabbalah. I went on to study with Gershom Scholem's students and subsequently edited a few of his books. Scholem was a great scholar with tremendous ambivalence towards traditional observance, and he was a creative genius who changed the world he inherited. As a person, he was a magisterial man with a remarkable scope of knowledge and zero tolerance for error, and he helped me see the place of mysticism in Judaism, and understand the nature of Jewish mysticism. Through him, I realized I wasn't just a solitary pilgrim and that I was on a well-walked path that others before me had taken. However, the introduction to Jewish mysticism he gave me was an academic one, and after a while I needed to experience this quest for the divine in a less intellectual way. Nevertheless, this academic foundation helped me a great deal in sifting the essential from the inessential, and it provided me with a first set of tools to grapple with the big questions I was wrestling with – exile and alienation, spiritual yearning for wholeness, redemption, and the essentially untainted nature of the human soul.

That view of the human soul has parallels with Buddhism's notion of Buddha nature, which refers to the enlightened self that resides dormant within us all. Are the concepts the same?

I wouldn't use that language, but belief in an untarnished essence is central to Jewish practice. An important part of a religious Jew's morning prayers is the acknowledgment of the untarnished essence that is the human soul. Our work is to chip away the accretions that prevent us from experiencing reality at its most essential level. Those accretions often take the form of false selves that surround us like husks and impair our ability to see the underlying presence of the divine in the world. Spiritual work could be described as the effort to maintain contact with essential being.

In a piece on Gershom Scholem written by Cynthia Ozick and published in The New Yorker in the fall of 2002, Ozick says this of the Jewish community Scholem was born into: "Jewish mysticism was untouchable because it was far out of the mainstream of Judaism, excluded by Rabbinic consensus. Normative Judaism saw itself as given over to moral rationalism: to codes of ethics, including the primacy of charity, and a coherent set of personal and societal practices; to the illuminations of midrash, the charms of ethical lore – but mythologies and esoteric mysteries were cast out. The Zohar, a mystical treatise, was grudgingly admitted for study, but only in maturity, lest it dazzle the student into irrationality. For normative Judaism, ripe sobriety was all." Do you agree?

I don't think there is such a thing as "normative Judaism." The term seems to imply that there's a right way and that certain people own it, and that's not true. Moreover, your understanding of that term depends on where you live and who you ask. There have always been Jews who followed a traditional mystical path, and there's never been a rabbinic consensus; all there has been is our group versus their group. Ram Dass and an entire generation of Jews turned to Hinduism and Buddhism because there was something they needed from Judaism that it wasn't providing. The truth is that what they needed was there, but it wasn't accessible.

Kabbalah presents a conception of God as "ain sof, about which nothing can be said." This feels like a slamming door to anyone struggling to learn. What's the appropriate response to a concept such as this?

That phrase alludes to the need to acknowledge that there is a mystery that the human nervous system cannot grasp that is forever incomprehensible. God is here in this room, in my yard, in my relationships, in people, but God isn't something you can put into your database. You can know and experience the divine, sometimes in the most intimate ways, but you can never comprehend it. People want to talk about the nature of God, but even the concept of God can be an obstacle; the word itself is no more than a symbol and a doorway to an unending corridor. This isn't to suggest that there's nothing at the end of the corridor, however, it's simply impossible for the mind to encompass something of this magnitude. To even approach a glimmering of understanding of it, the mind must cease being active. The mystery of God is impossible to penetrate because God is infinite and the human mind is finite. It's like expecting a frog to understand physics.

Does God ever disappoint you?

I don't understand God in that way at all. If I were to believe in a God that disappoints I'd probably be an atheist. My understanding of the divine has little to do with a historical God that lives within causality, and the question, "Why did God let this happen," makes no sense to my experience of the world. As for being pissed off at the world, yes, sometimes I am, but I don't blame God, whoever God is. I don't think God is something that can be blamed.

Having spent years in Kabbalistic study, has that system come to completely permeate your view of reality?

No. I hope my view of reality is fluid and expanding; moreover, I moved away from Kabbalah several years ago and began studying Hasidism, which is primarily concerned with the drama of the human soul. Kabbalah focuses on the soul of the world, and the spiritual drama of the cosmos, of creation, good and evil, and the nature of God. In my understanding, Hasidism focuses on one's work as a human being here and now, and on reaching a place where we can know the divine, and live a life of service. Service has always been a major part of my understanding of this work.

Is the Kabbalistic cosmology a place you can go to?

It's a place I've been to. In some ways the kabbalistic cosmology is like learning to drive, and at a certain point you just know how to drive. You know the vehicle and the road and don't think about it too much. The kabbalistic cosmology is a way of reconceptualizing the world, and for me it was a corridor I had to pass through in order to discover that it was just a re-conceptualization, and there were places beyond it. I spend very little time now with Kabbalism and feel quite averse to the way it's been popularized.

Why has it become so popular?

On one level I think it's just a fad that will go away, but it also has to do with the fact that other sources of comprehensive meaning that worked for people for decades no longer work. I'm referring to things like socialism and the idea of progress, which was an orienting factor in many people's lives that seems to have evaporated.

What was the last nail in the coffin of the notion of progress?

There have been so many nails! For some people it was the Holocaust or the assassination of Kennedy, but for me it was an increasing awareness of the cyclical nature of existence. Things aren't getting progressively better; rather, there are cycles of birth, maturity, and decline. This isn't to suggest I don't fight for progress. I'm fairly politically active and I believe in trying to make the world a better place, but I try not to identify with the outcome of this struggle. Things might well get worse.

Taking the long view of human history, is there any evidence that we're evolving in terms of consciousness?

It depends on what you mean by consciousness. I believe Claude Levi-Strauss said that the highest level of human consciousness occurred in the New Stone Age. One could certainly make the case that in Europe during the 15th and 16th Centuries we moved from a sense of wonder in creation and saw it as a place to explore and exploit, and we became more centered on ourselves as individuals. The Inquisition, along with other reactionary forces, tried to stop this move towards humanism and to deny the significance of the individual. Paradoxically, although individualism is one manifestation of the evolution of humanity, it incurs a terrible price in that it can lead us to forget the commonality and oneness of all beings.

Have your intense spiritual experiences tended to occur when you were alone?

Mostly, but some occurred while in the company of others. Being with people doing the same work can be a powerful experience.

Have you gone through long periods when you were unable to sense the divine?

I've gone through long periods when I didn't look for it, and that's a kind of despair. I've met people who appear to be conscious almost all the time, but most people are conscious about ten percent of the time.

Has the dark side of your nature subsided over the course of your life, or have you simply learned how to manage it?

Probably a bit of both. Certainly I know how to manage it better, but it's very subtle, like a hydra that's always changing its form. Despair, which I'd characterize as the loss of meaning, is something I do know, and when that feeling descends I wait for it to pass – and time has shown me that it will. But I've also learned that there can be great wisdom in the place of despair, because it's there that one's false personalities grow monstrously and are then stripped away. A tendency to be judgmental is another dark aspect of myself that I've struggled with and tried to refine into something else. My judgmental attitude towards myself and others led me into a quest for excellence that's been an important part of my life. Obviously there can be tyranny in that as well, but it's much less damaging to myself and others. This process of metabolizing darkness and transforming it into something better is a kind of alchemical transmutation.

What's the difference between knowledge and wisdom?

Knowledge is integrating facts and skills, and understanding ways of manipulating the world. Wisdom has more to do with the ability to integrate the sensibilities of our lives, including those from the past that often come through us. Wisdom can be highly developed in some people, and it's often quite invisible. We live in a world in which it's held in very low esteem, probably because it's non-quantifiable and doesn't serve the goals of the economy or the political system.

Why do some people have the gift of faith, and others simply do not? It's not something one can choose.

I can only speak for myself in this regard, but for me, what faith I have – which doesn't include belief in an afterlife – is essentially a way of integrating everything I know, excluding nothing. I experience the divine more than I have faith or believe in it. Belief is an intellectual construct that demands some kind of definition, but experiencing the divine defies definition – it's a kind of intimate contact. Knowledge of the divine is more easily described than defined, and that's why I prefer poetry to philosophy. Poetry permits you to perceive things sharply, and frees you to be inconsistent and to maintain unresolved paradoxes; philosophy, as far as I know, does not.

You say you don't believe in an afterlife; how can we presume to know
anything about what happens after death, when existence is so
fundamentally unknowable?

It isn't that I believe or don't believe, it's just that this area of concern isn't part
of my understanding of the world. I don't get up in the morning and ask myself; do I
believe in an afterlife? Questions like that tend to degenerate into head games. So
much of religious philosophy and what people refer to as belief systems are ultimately
head games that don't have much to do with the experience of the divine.

What is the purpose of religion?

Remember the story of Hansel and Gretel? In its highest form, received religion
is like pebbles along a path left by the great people who went before you. I've always
believed one can learn from geniuses, and following the pebbles is a way of aligning
oneself with people who truly changed the way we conceptualize the world.

Everyone in life is challenged, and people respond to challenge in one of
two ways: either they're embittered and hardened by the difficulties they
face, or they derive wisdom from them and are deepened by them. It seems
that some people simply don't have the equipment to handle what happens
to them in life. Why do some people get to grow and others don't?

The word that comes to mind here is blessing. Blessing is always present, but
sometimes you find yourself locked in a constellation of dark forces that block it out.
But then, the blessing breaks through and reaches you, and it refreshes and heals
you. In some of the most difficult times of my life I've encountered blessing, and
somehow I've been open to it. I don't know what made me that way.

Does everyone have the capacity to love?

I don't like questions about everybody, but I will say that I know people who are
so locked up in their false selves and the circumstances of their lives that they can't
reach the joy and the beauty of loving.

With sufficient understanding of the Other, would the impulse to kill be erased?

I don't think the impulse to kill is rooted in the lack of understanding. There are
many other sources – fear, the projection of one's own darker self onto the Other, and
economic insecurity, for instance. Economic insecurity is a powerfully destabilizing
force that has a horrible effect on people's lives.

Can a religious tradition that condones killing be a viable path?

That's a terribly general question. Of course, the answer is no, but I'm not a
total pacifist either, and I think there are times when a person has to use force. The
fighters of the Warsaw ghetto rose up and said, "They're gonna kill us, but we're
gonna get as many of them as we can first." Maybe that wasn't very enlightened, but
then again maybe it was. Religion sometimes uses myth as a point of entry, and these
myths can be very powerful, sometimes elevating and liberating, other times enslaving
and destructive. Myths should function as doorways to light and truth, but if people
get stuck in the myth then the religion that produced them is undeveloped. Many of
the popular aspects of world religion today are stuck in myth, and this is something
Judaism is presently struggling with.

Why is Judaism so enthralled by its own mythology and history?

Because in the beginning its mythology was one of the most insightful ways of
seeing reality that anyone had come up with. It was revolutionary. But Judaism must

move away from seeing God as a force in history and into the God of now if it is to flourish – and that means moving away from the concept of the chosen people. Jewish identity is much too much involved in its own history.

What are the earmarks of a person with a viable spiritual practice? How can one recognize such a person?

It's a certain way of being richly in the world and involved with its bounties and its grief, without losing sight of an essence within the world that's often lost to many of us. Someone with a spiritual grounding isn't buffeted by external events and is able to transcend the drama of his own life. We all must wrestle with false selves that obstruct the expression of the soul, and a spiritually grounded person manages to overcome those false selves without denying their existence.

Many spiritual practices advocate a monastic lifestyle that involves removing oneself from the earthly realm. Is this wrong? Do spiritually developed people have a duty to remain amidst the fray and work to improve things?

My path has never espoused the monastic tradition, though I've occasionally been drawn to it, and it certainly has its uses. Thomas Merton is one of my heroes, and he's an example of someone who needed to go to Gethsemane for an extended period before he was able to emerge and serve in the world. A religious tradition is an ecology of many niches and one of those niches involves isolation from the world – not as a form of escapism, but because it's one of many practices that enrich the tradition.

Meditation is a central part of your practice. Do you regard meditation as a form of work?

No. It's a practice of refinement and a way of moving from the powerful to the subtle. I've always felt that there's more truth in the subtle than in the powerful, and I tend to distrust people who advocate powerful religious experience, as opposed to simply living with subtle ones. For me, meditation is a way of living with the subtle.

Leonard Cohen once made the comment, "There's only one important achievement in life, and that's the acceptance of your lot." Do you agree?

The acceptance of your lot is like cleaning your window, and until you do it you can't see what's on the other side. It's an absolutely necessary preparation, but the real work comes later.

Why are sexuality and spirituality so often at odds with each other? It seems most spiritual traditions have a hard time integrating these two energies.

Those energies aren't intrinsically at odds with each other, but it's true that one of the major themes in the history of civilization has been the management of sexuality. Nobody's got it right yet, either – which isn't to say it's unmanageable. Sexuality is one of the greatest gifts given to mankind, and as to why it's such a volatile issue and we're so cautious about it, I don't think it's because of shame. It's simply because it's something extremely private.

In your work as a teacher you've often said that the purpose of spiritual study isn't to find answers; rather, the point is to refine one's questions. "The questions get bigger," you've said, "and then comes the real biggie: what is the question for which my death is the answer?" How would you answer this question?

The question is less daunting now. Previously it was a great mystery to me that this mind and this body of mine that have done and known so much will one day disappear, but it no longer is. I'm now concerned with a different question: how do I complete my work and maintain my clarity and my path in the face of declining health and power? As I move into old age I'm entering a period of my life I've never been in before, and though I know various ways not to do it, it's basically uncharted territory. I used to be fascinated by King Lear, who seemed to do everything wrong, or at least his timing was awful, but I find myself looking to The Tempest's Prospero as a better model because he knew how to relinquish power. I'm in a period of relinquishing power and reflecting on my life. The capacity to reflect is, in fact, a gathering of power, but it's power of a very different kind.

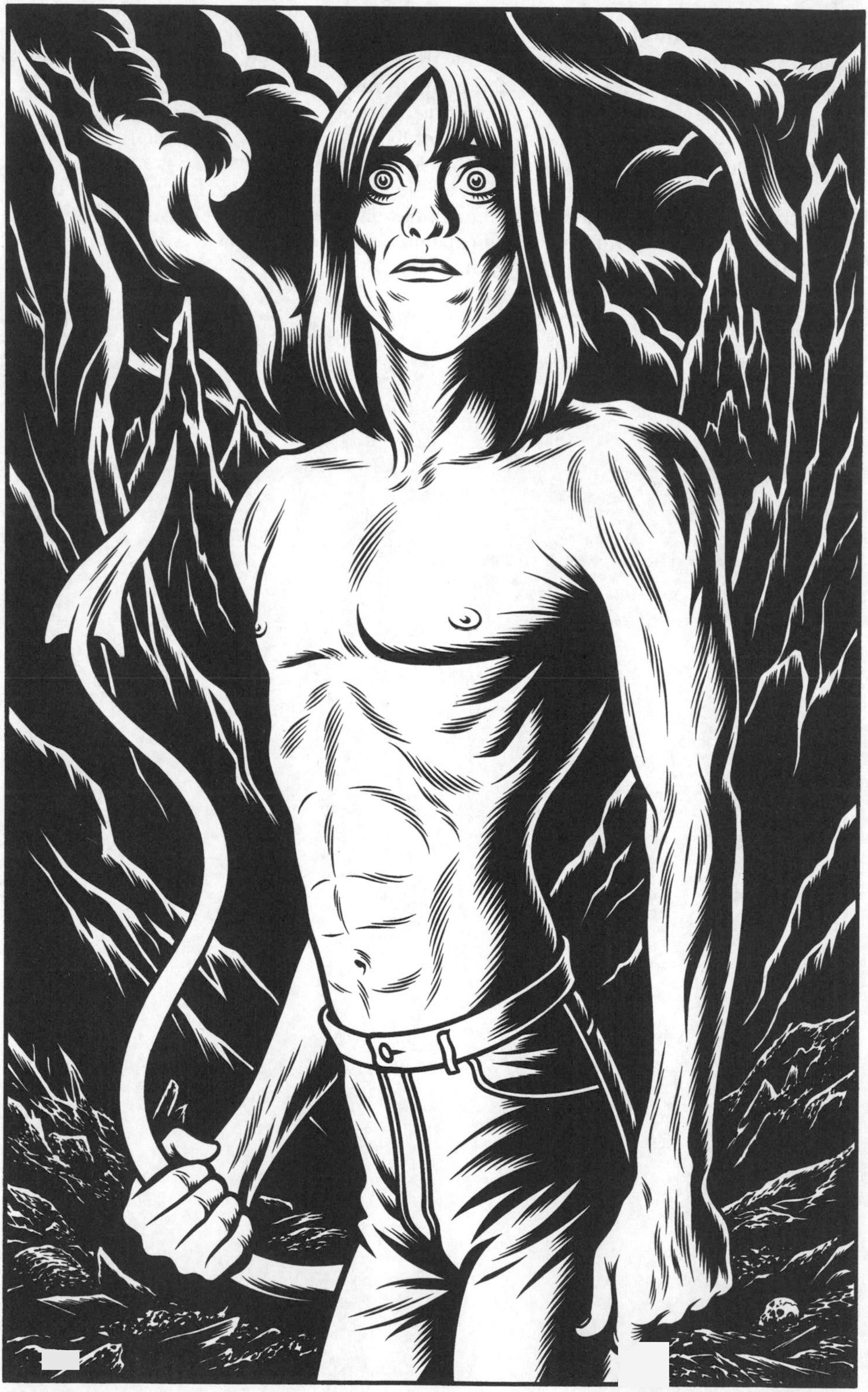

Iggy Pop

If you've never read Iggy Pop's 1982 autobiography, I Need More, do yourself a favor and go out and buy it. It's a totally inspiring book. Talk about triumph of the will! There he was, Jim Osterberg, a slightly built, asthmatic only child growing up in a shabby mobile home in a sleepy Mid-western town during the '50s. The chances of his metamorphosing into a rock avatar who would channel the id of an entire generation were not good. But Jim came in with an extra hit of the life force, and that's exactly what he did.

Perhaps I should backtrack for a moment and recap the story so far. James Newell Osterberg was born on April 21, 1947, in Muskegon, Michigan. His father, Newell Sr., was an English teacher, and his family lived in a trailer park in Ypsilanti Michigan. When he was 15 he formed his first band, the Iguanas, which is how he wound up with the stage name Iggy. He was playing drums at the time, and after three years of practice and local gigs, the Iguanas recorded a single; the year was 1965, and the song was "Mona", backed with "I Don't Know Why." A short time later he joined the Prime Movers Blues Band, an experience that prompted him to head for Chicago to serve some kind of apprenticeship with real blues guys. Eight months later he'd come to the conclusion he was barking up the wrong tree, so he returned to Ann Arbor and formed the Psychedelic Stooges with Ron and Scott Ashton. They played their first gig on Halloween in 1967.

It was then that Iggy began redefining the parameters of rock 'n' roll with a show unlike anything that had been seen before. Synthesizing elements of shamanic ritual, blues, Artaud's Theater of Cruelty, psychedelia, and performance art, Iggy invented a frightening and transformational form of musical theater that soared into the stratosphere. A crucial ingredient in his show was his extraordinary body – a perfectly constructed skeleton with an overlay of muscle in a wrapping of taut skin – which he deployed to maximum effect. He was also hilarious. All of Iggy's work has been inflected with a bracing current of self-deprecating humor that makes him very easy to love. Describing himself in the early days of his career in I Need More, he says 'you gotta' understand that I was still like Top Cat, the cartoon character. I was very lazy and happiest dozing in a garbage can.' Who can't relate to that?

The Stooges were extreme and definitely weren't for everyone, but incredibly enough, they were signed to Elektra Records just a year after they debuted. The next five years were a tornado of wild gigs, drugs and escalating conflict, and at the end of 1973 Iggy quit the band. His downward spiral gathered momentum, and in 1975 he suffered a breakdown that resulted in several weeks of hospitalization. His longtime fan David Bowie helped him relocate to Berlin, got him back on his feet, and produced his first two solo albums, The Idiot and Lust for Life.

It was shortly after that, in 1979, that I interviewed Iggy for the first time. We met in his tiny room at the now defunct Tropicana Motel, and to tell the truth, I was afraid *of him – his reputation at that point was rather formidable. He surprised me, though. He came across as a somewhat reserved, well-spoken man who'd clearly thought long and hard about the world and his place in it. At the end of our meeting, he said 'if I have any goal it's to be an unchanging beacon in this world full of health foods and good vibes. I wish not to change.'*

I spoke with Iggy again in the summer of 2003 on the occasion of his reunion with the Stooges. Iggy spent most of the '80s and '90s in Manhattan, then in 1999 he moved to Miami following his divorce from his companion of 16 years, Suchi Asano Osterberg. Miami appears to suit him; he seemed strong, focused and 'an unchanging beacon in this world of health food and good vibes.'

What is the source of your strength?

Whatever strength I have is probably the result of the fact that I made some good emotional investments at an early age. I went for a certain kind of music and maintained the naïve belief that I could do something wonderful in music, and that that would help me move towards what is wonderful in life. I looked like I was nuts at the time, and those beliefs caused me a lot of grief for a while, but it paid off for me big time.

What gave you the courage to make those choices early in life? Something that comes through clearly in I Need More is what extraordinarily loving parents you had. Did they play a significant role in setting you on the path you've taken in life?

Yeah, I definitely had some killer parenting. My parents were really great, spiritually glowing people whose love and protection really set me up in life. I'm getting the credit for a lot of stuff they did. Losing my mother was one of the most painful things I've experienced. [Louella Osterberg died in 1996.]

In reflecting on your childhood in I Need More, you say, 'we were very good dreamers, which is mostly what my dusty Midwest is all about. The land that time forgot. At this time, in the fifties, America was a beautiful, virgin land with green meadows and room for everyone. It was a calm and verdant land.' Where did that world go?

Unfortunately, most of it has been paved over. Sometimes I'll be motoring through Ohio on the way to work somewhere and I'll see what I think might be a glimpse of it, but in general, the U.S. has lost a great deal of its charm. A certain rigidity has set in now that we have imperial capitalism unbridled by other isms – it was nicer when we had communism to balance the capitalism. Here in Florida there's a little more land and a few more wild creatures walking around, but the pavement is coming, and I think that's a contributing factor to things like Columbine. The problem isn't just that there are guns available. It has a lot to do with the fact that things have become so systematic in a kind of binary code, rectangular way that it makes everybody kind of tense.

Are you proud to be an American?

Oh yeah, among other things, though. I wouldn't say it's my proudest thing – I'm more proud that I've made some decent music.

What's the worst thing that ever happened to you?

I once woke up in an abandoned building in L.A. puking weird, green bile and decided I better check myself into a neuro-psychiatric hospital. At the time I felt like a pet who'd been put into one of those animal carriers for a plane flight – you know how they'll whimper for the first few minutes, but after that they don't want to waste the energy. The thing that led me to that moment in that building was heroin, so maybe the worst thing that ever happened to me was the first time anybody offered me heroin and I took it. We had an ex-junkie roadie we'd neglected to take along on a West Coast trip and he was pissed off at us about that, so I think he decided to turn us into junkies and fuck up the band – and he did. I don't know what happened to that guy. I'm not in touch, let's put it that way.

What was the first record you ever bought?
A Johnny & the Hurricanes album I bought at Woolworth's for 99 cents that had a regional hit on it called "Red River Rock." This group was from Toledo, Ohio and was what was referred to as a greaser band. They had greased up pompadours, matching skinny suits, and the leader played sax.

Name a song that always makes you cry?
"Walk on By" is a pretty deep one, but only Dionne Warwick's version. The others are all terrible. There's also an old jazz standard, "The Night We Called It A Day"; that makes me a little misty.

You once said, 'what I heard John Coltrane do with his horn I tried to do physically.' Could you describe precisely what that thing is?
The first time I heard Coltrane the cut was "A Love Supreme," and that's an extremely simple three note bass line that repeats without variance throughout the duration of a very long piece. I was a novice unfamiliar with that sort of jazz, and I heard him run through the gamut of emotions on his horn, from tender to angry to kind of bluesy, to just fucking insane, to where it actually sounded offensive to me – until later. I liked the way he was dancing, over, above, under, within and without this rock solid motif that didn't change, and that three note motif established a trance world where he could do all those things. It seemed timely, spiritual and earthy all at the same time. I was 20 at the time, and was just starting to play gigs with the Stooges when I heard Coltrane, and I heard him at the home of a prospective new manager who was an older hipster on the local scene named Jimmy Silver. He was a good friend of John Sinclair's – in fact, he probably got the record from John, because it was very much a reflection of the nexus John was establishing between free jazz, indigent criminality, and rock'n'roll.

Why was this the right time to work with the Stooges again?
We had to wait until everybody was hungry enough for it that we were able to transcend our more crappy parts – but I didn't know that going in. The way it happened was I wanted to work with multiple people on this record, so I made a list of possibilities, then when I looked at the list I thought 'the Stooges are the coolest people on this fuckin list!' I didn't know what it would be like though, and I think we were all surprised at how good it was. But we had something going for us in that we had a good bunch of songs we'd written a long time ago, and all the playing we'd done a long time ago was right there for us too, like money in a bank. It was the same, because we'd done all those fucking gigs and because we'd lived in that house together. An added plus was that we were working towards a recording instead of just doing a reunion tour to play old songs and lap up some bread – not that we didn't lap up a little bread. But we had the recording first, and that's the lifeblood of anything that's gonna have any currency to it. So we laid it out there, and people can say this shit is cool or it sucks, and going through that process makes your togetherness more timely. At this point the Stooges play with the authority of two old sharecroppers. There's some serious authority in their sound, but they still sound dangerous and appropriately childish.

You toured with Junior Kimbrough shortly before he died. What did you learn from him?

To slow down musically. I also learned that Fat Possum is the only decent record company in this country. They're the only ones putting out consistently good product, and their shit is the only new shit I listen to for pleasure. I'll go out and buy the White Stripes because I think I should hear the new White Stripes album, but if I want to listen to something for pleasure or genuine interest, I go to Fat Possum.

You once made the comment, 'the longer a person lives the more useless he becomes.' Do you think that's true?

I have to reverse myself on that, although it's certainly true I'm not gonna make a primal album again. There were certain things I could do when I was at a certain age and you can't do those things when you get older. You can be worth other things to people, though. There's a certain fascination to anybody who's older who isn't just sucking eucalyptus leaves on the porch, because young people wonder hey, what happens later?

It's not as if you're doing a lounge act now. In fact, the show you do today is largely the same as the one you did when you were 20.

It is related, but if you looked at film you'd spot differences. I never really thought much about it, then or now, though. The main thing is you've got to be in that song, and then everything will come from there. If you're not inside it you can exhaust yourself but it will be shit. You gotta remember to obey the song.

Are there songs you're no longer able to get inside of?

Lots of them, but you never know until you try it out at a show and it doesn't click. I haven't been doing "Lust For Life" for a couple of years, maybe because of all the film and advertising usage, but I do "The Passenger" from that album. I tried "Knockin' 'Em Down (in the City)" the other day but it wasn't happening, and I just learned "I Snub You", which was a gas. I was doing "Five Foot One" for years and I did it to death, which does happen.

Speaking of film, how did you feel about Ewan McGregor's portrayal of you in Velvet Goldmine?

I didn't see the movie but I did see the trailer, so I saw him singing "T.V. Eye". My first impression was, "Dude, you're a little pudgy aren't you?" After that I thought it was pretty cool that somebody was singing "T.V. Eye", and at least they got it right that he stood at the microphone and sang it. I'd read the script for the film and had a brief conversation with Todd Haynes, who is an estimable filmmaker, but I didn't want to see the movie because I thought it was a confused piece. I did O.K. their use of my songs, though.

I'm a big admirer of your performance in Jim Jarmusch's 1996 film, Dead Man. ***[Hunkered down around a campfire in prairie drag, Pop gives two grubby associates a bible lesson.] Was your scene improvised?***

It was improvised around a rough structure, but I came up with my own lines. Jim worried that I'd gotten too carried away talking about Nero and the dogs, so in the version released to theaters he cut my monologue back to a story about the three bears. Later on he had an attack of conscience and he reinstated my lines in the video release.

You once made the comment, 'it's very rare that an individual actually has anything to say.' Is this because people lack the courage to speak out,

or because they lack the imagination to come up with anything worth saying?

Probably the latter: The times we live in are not very conducive to the use of the imagination. Everything's pretty wired in just about now. It's pretty bad.

What's the closest your average, middle-class American comes to experiencing shamanic ritual?

If you're talking about an actual journey, I guess there were many years when the movies served that function of taking people into the dark underworld and into heaven. I don't know what they're doing out there now because it's been so long since I've been an average American.

How have you maintained your connection with your animal nature?

I try to stay near rocks because they have a nice energy, and old objects have a better energy than new objects – my house is old, my cars are old, I'm old. I like plants to be around, and I pay attention to animals and enjoy watching them. I try to stay near the sea, and I have these funny exercises I do, this Tai Chi shit – all these things lead you in that direction.

Do you believe in God?

No.

What do you think happens after death?

Probably the better it goes the quieter it is. If it's a hard one it's probably like those dreams you have just before you wake up, but I imagine that one eventually settles down. After that, one can come back as anything from a worm to a member of the Bush family. I can't quite say that I believe in reincarnation, but some sort of regeneration makes sense to me. There must be some sort of weird, viscous, soul goop – some sort of anima that persists.

You once commented, 'the natural instinct of every person you meet will be to use you.' Are we all craven opportunists sizing each other up as a meal?

I'm afraid so. Either that, or they look and think 'no meal there' and that's the end of the interest. A lot of us don't want to know this about ourselves, though.

What's the purpose of chaos?

Chaos is the sound of one hand clapping.

What seemed terribly important to you as a young man that no longer seems quite so pressing?

When I was young I wanted girls and music, those were the two things. The chick thing has played itself out, but there are still lots of things I want to do with music I haven't gotten to yet. I was never interested in being famous, not even as a highly confused youth.

Is fame infantilizing?

You can definitely spoil yourself, and as long as you're aware of that you can cut that back in certain ways. I was fighting with my guitar player [Whitey Kirst] on some airstrip in Brussels the other day because he was drunk, and he turned to me and said 'you're spoiled!' I got really mad and said 'I'm not spoiled, you're spoiled, I've worked hard, blah, blah, blah...' Then I went back to my room and thought shit, he's right.

What's the most widely held misconception about the life of a famous person?

That it's easy. The hard thing is dealing with the choices – one has tremendous choice thrust upon you constantly, but the choices aren't really yours to make, and you have to make them whether you're ready to or not. And, the choices are couched in terms that may or may not be appropriate to your fame. And do you want to even allude to that? How healthy is that? What do you get out of it? Do you care what you get? Should you always be getting? Is this shit cool? Is it for real? It gets pretty fucking complicated! Sometimes they're not the choices you want either. All of a sudden you're in a position where you can do something for somebody, or not, they think. You can hurt somebody, or not, they think. It gets pretty intense trying to figure out what you want.

So, what do you want?

Funny you should ask. I've got a Tai Chi master who functions as sort of a guru for me, and he's written a book I've been reading, and in the book he organizes life into pyramids of desire. Some people want money, others want health, some want to find God. I haven't had sex in four days, so today I want sex. I have it all the time with a super-specimen named Nina.

Are you in love?

Oh my god! Yeah, I love her. I'm in love sometimes, then other times you're fighting. You know how it is – hey, gimme that soup bone.

In a recent interview you were asked how you envision yourself 15 years from now and you said, 'probably playing music and hanging out with a chick a lot younger than me. I'm an American guy so I prefer young pussy.' Why is young pussy better?

It's probably the same with dick. You've got me pacing the room now! I'm sweatin' this one! Gee, let's see. I think it might have something to do with the fact that when chicks get older they worry more about what they're doing, and inevitably the boyfriend is gonna get involved in that; like 'I need to be fill-in-the-blank and you're not helping me with that.' The younger they are the more air seems to be available to fill their heads.

In Kiss My Blood, a film of a performance you gave in Paris in 1991, there's a sequence where you interact with a few girls in the audience who seem to be completely under your spell. It looks as though you could've persuaded those girls to do anything. Do you take pleasure in the power you're able to exert over women, or is that something you've thoroughly explored?

I've lived out everything I needed to experience with women in that regard, and I don't get a charge from that kind of thing any more. Some people might say 'hey, I've been this way for a while and it's too much hassle to change,' but around the time I turned 50 that died down as a motivating factor, and I don't have a plural attitude towards relationships any more. I really want to be with one person at one time. Sometimes I do encourage audience participation of the sort you just mentioned, but if it gets too sexy it become embarrassing to me as a musical artist, because the music must remain paramount at all times. If the other thing starts to climb on top you'll be on Hollywood Squares in three years. There's sexual energy in the world and we all want to be attractive to members of the other camp, but that's something I'm choosy about because it's an important thing who you're with. I didn't really use to care. It was more like I want a chick; this seems like a good one, hey, now I haven't got that one, but look, there's another one. Now, I'm really surprised [laughing] but they actually become people.

Do you consider yourself sexist?
Everybody's sexist when they're young, especially in America. With me, it had more to do with the fact that I had something I wanted to get done and I couldn't think of anybody else. I didn't even think of myself as a person much. Whenever I did, it usually got in the way and made me get drunk.

Physiology aside, what's the most significant difference between men and women?
The need to love and be loved appears to be more of a focal point for women. Whether they actually live that out, or simply use that as a weapon in the temporal world is another thing. For men that's less of a primary drive. Men are more apt to define themselves in terms of work or some sort of achievement in the gorilla world.

You've been quoted as saying 'all boys are queer.' Do you really think that's true?
Kind of, in that all boys want to impress other boys and all boys get crazy if they think some other boy is lording it over them. It's not a sexual thing – it has more to do with having an ego-driven obsession with your peers.

Why does love die?
Business and daily practicalities get in the way, and familiarity does breed contempt. The only way to get around that is to cultivate your familiarity, choose the more enchanting varieties and weed out the vulgar. Familiarity is necessary between people – if you don't have that you're all alone – but uncultivated, it will breed contempt. Everything from saying 'hey, while you're up can you bring me...' to bring up the toilet paper, to fart jokes, to money worries can kill the mood. I just read an article in the New York Times about a couple of limited means who spent so much money on their wedding that it put them in debt for years and killed the marriage.

Is money the same thing as power?
No. Health and sound judgment give power. A healthy, balanced person is more capable of exercising sound judgment, and that can lead to the mastery of the tools of power, one of which is money. Money is definitely something that's unfortunately not to be spit at.

You've said that, 'on a daily basis in my life I tend to avoid people.' Have you always been this way, or is it a behavior that's come with age?
Nah, I've been lurking since kindergarten. Being in a band there are periods where you're always surrounded by people, and one of the toughest things I've had to do is deal with the necessity of immersing myself in a bunch of musicians in order to accomplish something musically. It's really hard because everybody's got their little trip. I did the live-in thing pretty steadily until I was around 31, and that was enough.

Everybody talks about how tough you are. Do you feel tough?
No. I feel fairly well disciplined in certain areas, and sometimes I kind of surprise myself and get results that would imply that I'm tough, but that's never been a motivating factor. I must've been some kind of fool to do some of the things I've done, but I seem to be the one cockroach in a large bunch that didn't get squished by the

boot of infamy. Then, when I was in my late 20s I met some people who were more worldly than I was when I went through my English rock star phase with David Bowie. I learned a lot from the people I met through him – 'oh, so this is how you defend yourself, and this is how you act at dinner with Mick Jagger' and so forth.

How would you describe your state of mind today?

A little bit crafty, a little bit getting away with murder. I'm livin' in Miami Beach with a couple of Rolls Royces and no nine-to-five, goin' to the beach when I want to, feelin' good because my album's done and it sounds pretty bitchin. I'm kind of sneaking and lurking around like I do.

What did you do last night?

I was quiet, basically. I was at the beach until twilight, just looking at the waves and thinking, then I cooked myself a steak sandwich, which I muffed badly by under-cooking it, so I shared it with a feral cat I entertain. Then I did a little reading of a book by my Tai Chi master called Elixir, and picked up some tips on a couple of breathing exercises I want to try. I had a glass of a '98 Saint-Estephe red Bordeaux, called Nina and said goodnight, then watched TV for an hour, something about Mike Tyson called *Beyond the Glory*, that focused on his troubles, and I was in bed by ten. I'm a seriously conservative person. I'm ready to throw money away, and I'll do and say things that piss people off, but I'm always in bed between 9 and 11:30 at night, I don't smoke cigarettes, I don't run around chasing affairs, and I keep my attention on the ball. I don't have my nose to the grindstone, but I move the ball right along.

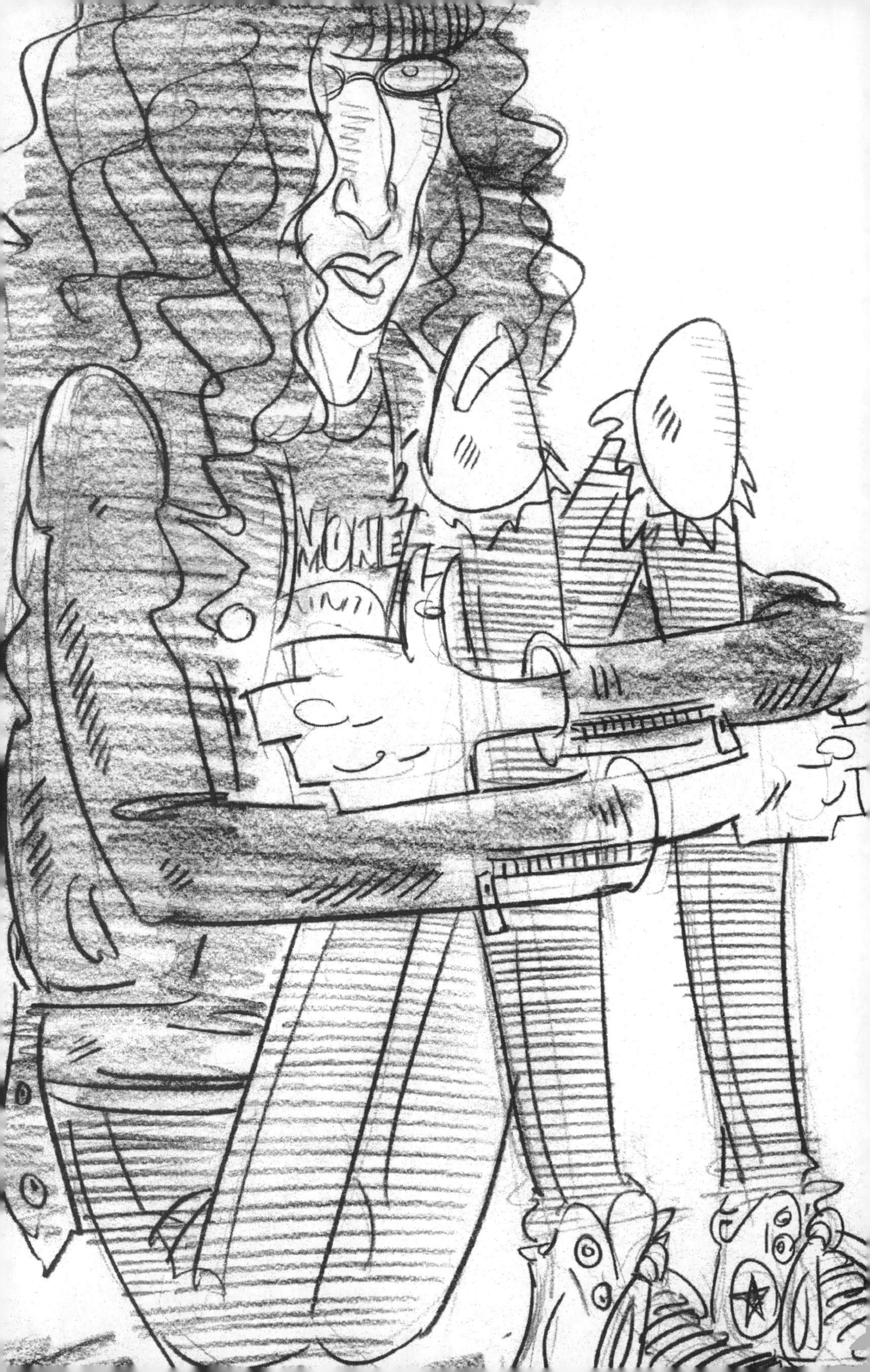
MONE

Joey Ramone

When Joey Ramone died of lymphatic cancer on April 15, 2001, he was 49 years old, but he still had a healthy relationship with his teenage identity crisis. The pimples, the pizza, the raging hormones, the torn blue jeans, the black leather attitude – they were with him up to the moment that he drew his final breath. One of the four eternal teen-agers known as the Ramones, minimalist geniuses widely hailed as the founding fathers of punk, Joey Ramone helped perfect a brilliantly simple approach to rock built around explosive chords played at the speed of light. Formed in 1974, the Ramones were the first punk group to be signed to a record deal, and their self-titled debut album – which was recorded in less than two weeks on a budget of $6,000 – was released in 1976. They put out 20 more albums during their 22 years together, and their defiantly fundamental music still sounds great today.

Born Jeffrey Hyman in the Forest Hills section of Queens, New York, in 1951, Joey Ramone claimed that his musical career began when he was eight years old and sent away for a toy drum kit being offered as a promotion by Kellogg's Corn Flakes. When he was 13 he got a real drum kit and began forming bands, and he had a brief foray into glam rock in the early '70s working under the name Jeff Starship. In the early days of the Ramones, Joey was the band's drummer, but as the tempo of their songs grew increasingly frantic he had a hard time keeping up, so he switched to vocals. The unlikeliest of rock stars, Joey was built like Olive Oyl, had a bouncy pageboy with heavy bangs, and lousy posture, and yet he was an unforgettable presence at the microphone. He always stood the same way – shoulders rounded, one hip cocked, belly thrust forward. He always wore the same thing, too – black leather jacket, worn T-shirt, seriously ragged jeans, and shades – and there wasn't a great deal of variety in his performances either. He wasn't a wildly emotive singer, and there wasn't much jumping around with Joey. But he was a total powerhouse who manned the microphone for more than two decades and always delivered. Rock 'n' roll was a calling for Joey, and not rising to the occasion simply wasn't an option for him.

I interviewed Joey in 1990 and can testify that there was no hidden agenda with him, nothing at odds with his public persona. The funny, generous, irreverent person he was onstage is the person he was all the time. Fourteen months after Joey's death, bassist and chief songwriter Dee Dee Ramone also died, of a drug overdose, in Los Angeles. Sad to say, it seems the Ramones have finally left the building for good.

Did the Ramones invent punk rock?

Yeah. There was no such thing as punk rock before us. When we came along in the mid-'70s there was a huge void in music. It was the beginning of disco and corporate rock, and bands like ELP, Pink Floyd and Boston were passing themselves off as rock 'n' roll – no way is that rock 'n' roll! We stripped it down to the bone and reassembled it with the excitement, guts and raw energy rock 'n' roll is supposed to have – basically, we made it fun again. When we went to England for the first time in 1976, the big thing there was pub rock, but the word was out about us and tons of kids came to our sound check at Dingwalls. John Lydon and Joe Strummer were there that day, and they later told us we were directly responsible for inspiring them to form their own bands.

What did punk accomplish? Did it bring about any long-term change in the music business or society?

Punk changed everything – music, culture, philosophy. The world changed 360 degrees.

If punk changed everything, then how do you explain the wave of extreme conservatism currently sweeping across America?

You'll always have your mainstream, but on the other hand there's a minority of artists doing great things. The Chili Peppers, Guns 'n' Roses, the rap artists – there's a real strong underground on the left, and it's not that far underground. Faith No More is very inventive and unique. They're taking different styles of music and doing something exciting and fresh with them. Music is in its healthiest period ever right now.

The Ramones' music is about teen-age frustration, yet you all stopped being teen-agers years ago. What does it mean to you to sing these songs now? Do you still relate to them?

Yeah, because everybody relates to frustration. Of course you realize you're getting on a bit, but being in rock 'n' roll keeps you young. For one thing, our audience keeps getting younger – most of our fans are around 16 years old. A few original fans still show up – I guess the arthritis hasn't set in for them yet – but for the most part our audience is very young.

It's generally thought that bands need to move in new directions in order to remain vital, but the Ramones haven't tampered with their original style at all. Why?

Because we created a unique trademark style and sound, which is something everybody tries to achieve but very few accomplish. Less than ten bands since the inception of rock 'n' roll have created a unique sound: Buddy Holly, Led Zeppelin, the Rolling Stones, the Beatles, Elvis Presley, the Who, the Byrds – and the Ramones.

What's the greatest live act you've ever seen?

The Who, the first time they played America in 1967. They had so much aggression and they were so visual and had such character and great songs – they really blew my mind. Unfortunately, when Keith Moon died a bit of Pete Townshend died as well, and he's never been the same since. And now, with his aches and pains and hearing problems – he shouldn't go around complaining like that. I mean, you're in or you're out, you know what I mean?

How do you maintain the physical stamina your show requires? The Ramones are a pretty high-energy band.

You have to take good care of yourself and we're very health-conscious. We like pizza and beer but we don't live on that stuff and we're careful about what we eat, and try to get enough sleep and take vitamins. Being in this band is a big responsibility, and you have to be able to hold up your end. There's no room for slouchers in the Ramones.

Your music does much better on the European charts than on the American charts. How do you explain that?

Because there's so much politics in the American music industry. Plus, Europeans have a deeper appreciation of rock 'n' roll. American kids are spoiled and take things for granted because there are lots of different media and entertainment outlets here. Over there they don't have that much. Don't get me wrong, I love America – it's my home, I'm happy to be here and I have all the conveniences. But it's a lot of bull here when it comes to music.

Do you envision a day when you'll have outgrown this band?

To be truthful, yeah. I don't know whether it means I've outgrown them already, but I've been wanting to do a solo record for a while now. A lot of people would interpret my doing a solo record as a sign I've lost interest in the band, but that's not the case. There's no reason you can't do all kinds of things, and I'll always enjoy the Ramones because performing with this band taps into something inside me that's so intense I can't explain it.

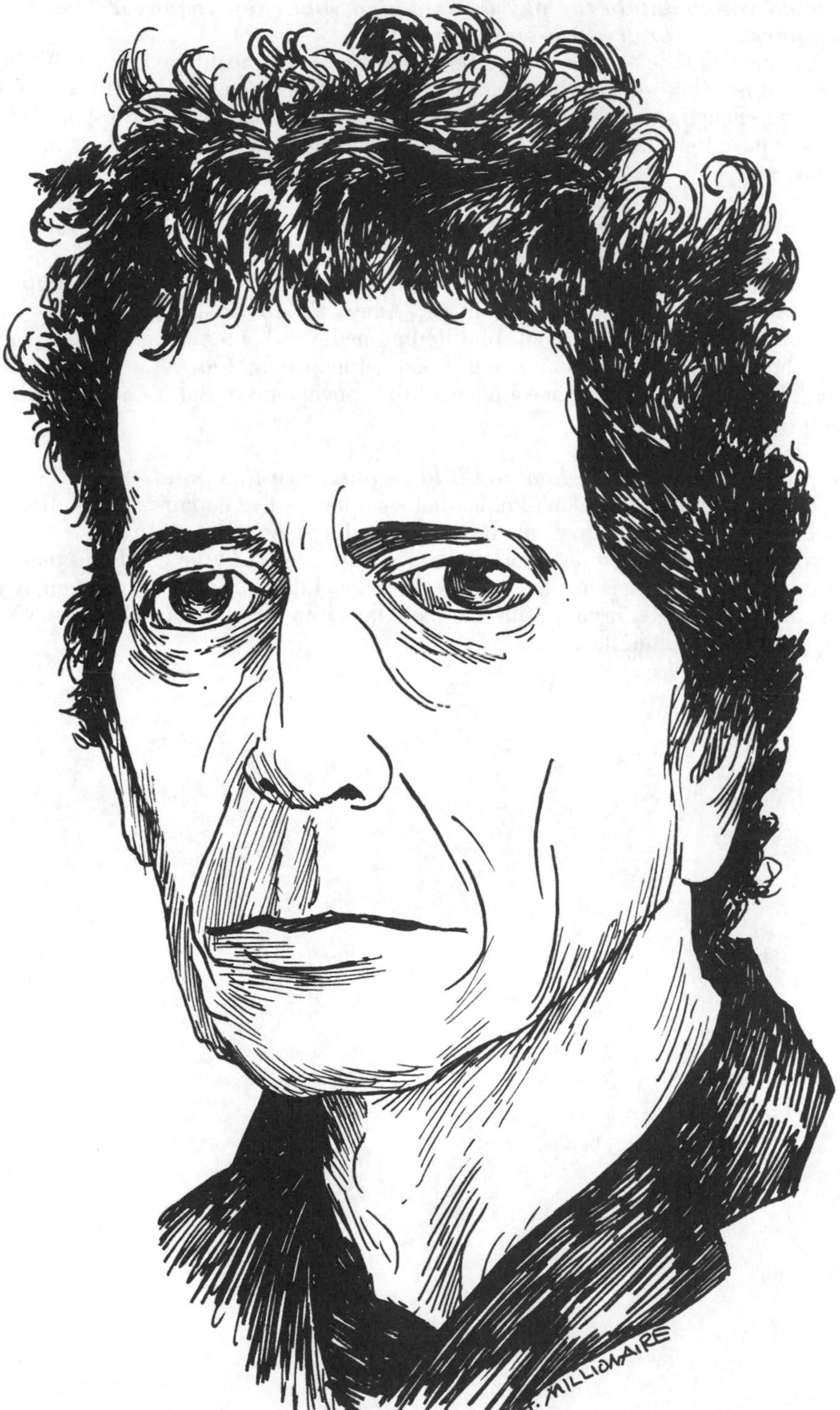
T. MILLIONAIRE

Lou Reed

....

Lou Reed was born in a middle-class neighborhood in Brooklyn in 1939, but by the time he'd reached adulthood he'd reinvented himself as the quintessential urban punk. The guiding light of legendary '60s avant-garde outfit, the Velvet Underground, Reed perfected a musical blueprint that continues to inspire young players, and his influence has been pervasive. Brian Eno once made the observation that although the Velvet Underground sold a mere 5,000 copies per album, everyone who bought one of their records eventually started his own band.

Exploring themes previously considered taboo in pop – heroin, suicide, street hustles, sexual deviance, the ennui of the terminally hip – Reed demolished long-held ideas as to what could serve as appropriate subject matter for pop songs. Musically, Reed's tunes are simple, almost primitive, but they're distinguished, and immediately recognizable as his, by virtue of his uncanny ear for dialogue. The characters in his songs seem vibrantly authentic because they talk the way real people talk. Reed's vocal style – a flat, reportorial snarl – is well suited to the vernacular of the outsiders he writes about, and the tone he assumes with the heroic fuck-ups who people his songs is casual, bitchy and sentimental. Hope does spring eternal, and no matter how vehemently Reed tried to deny it, he could never quite manage to extinguish it in himself. That spark is what makes his music so powerful. He's made quite a lot of music, too; as of this writing, Reed has released 23 solo albums, in addition to the five that he completed with the Velvet Underground. That's quite an impressive track record when you consider the fact that Reed has never pandered to the marketplace. The guy is tough.

The first time I interviewed Reed was in 1984. We spoke in his tour bus parked outside a concert hall in Santa Barbara, California, and he was so ill tempered that it was funny. "Sometimes you meet a person and you just don't like them," he hissed at a certain point, and I thought to myself, gee, I guess he just doesn't like me. Consequently, I was surprised several years later when his management offered an interview with Reed to the Los Angeles Times, with the stipulation that I be the journalist to do it. I figured maybe he was just having a bad day that afternoon back in Santa Barbara, and that he actually didn't think I was a total jerk. But when we met again, this time at Le Mondrian Hotel on Sunset Boulevard in Los Angeles, he behaved exactly the same way! With the distance of time, these have become two of my favorite interviews – I think they're hilarious. And nobody can accuse Lou of sucking up to the press.

What's the most significant change you've observed in yourself in recent years?
I hope somebody told you I don't like to answer personal questions. I consider that a personal question.

Uh…okay. What do you consider to be your chief strength as an artist?
I never thought about it, and that's not a question I could answer glibly off the top of my head.

In 1977 you made the comment, "I came through because I have a demented sense of humor." Is that still your most valuable survival tool?
I don't comment on past quotes, which are secondary information at best. I don't know where the quote came from – if it's real or not. And anyway, if it's something I said seven years ago, what do I care?

How do you define the contract between audience and performer?
The contract? I don't think of it as a contract and never have. I think of it as seeing an old friend.

So, that relationship has never been an adversarial one?
I sometimes feel that we haven't understood one another.

Do you think the public enjoys seeing its heroes suffer or self-destruct?
I wouldn't know what the public thinks. Do you know what the public thinks? Neither of us has any way of actually knowing the truth about this, but it does seem to me that the public has certain ghoulish appetites. People who go to car races probably don't mind seeing a crash now and then.

Do you think video is having a good effect on your music?
I refuse to get involved in an argument about whether videos are good or bad for music because that doesn't remotely interest me. Video is here to stay. It can bring music to the attention of people who might not be exposed to it otherwise, and I think the video I recently made for my song, "Suzanne," made some people aware of me who hadn't previously heard my music. So video had a good effect on my music. Personally – and I can only speak for myself, I can't speak for other people – I see video as an ad for the album, and thats how I approach it.

What's the biggest disadvantage of fame?
I'm not famous enough to have to worry about that. I don't consider myself famous.

But you do acknowledge that a certain legend has developed around you?
I'm told.

Is that something that you can distance yourself from and play with, or has it been a problem in your life?
It hasn't been a problem per se. How seriously can anybody take something like that? Not seriously at all.

You recently told the Los Angeles Times that you're treated with greater respect in Europe than you are in America. Why do you think that is?

I didn't say that, and I can't respond to quotes given to other people. I sell more records in Europe because Europeans are interested in America and they listen closely to people who seem to them to be representative of this country.

Do you feel distinctly American, and feel a strong sense of connection with this country?
I don't feel a strong connection with this country, but I do feel a strong connection with New York.

Do you continue to find New York a creatively stimulating place?
Sure.

You recently commented, "How seriously will people take a rock 'n' roll record? Not very seriously at all." Can you elaborate on that?
I've always felt that most people have a basic contempt for the form and consider the field to be populated by inarticulate idiots. I've always believed that there's an amazing number of things you can do through a rock 'n' roll song, and that you can do serious writing in a rock song if you can somehow do it without losing the beat. The things I've written about wouldn't be considered a big deal if they appeared in a book or a movie.

Do you see that situation changing? Is the thematic range of rock broadening?
Some of the rap groups coming out of New York are touching on things that interest me, and I think there's some pretty good writing to be found in rap music. I don't know who it's by, but there's a song I like called "We Became Lovers Before We Became Friends," and I think "30 Days," by Run-D.M.C., is great. "The World is Tough," by the C.D. 2 or something like that is good. I can't keep the names of those groups straight.

Do you see much live music?
Almost none, because I don't much like going to clubs. I did go see Tina Turner and Springsteen, recently, though. Springsteen put on the best rock'n'roll show I've ever seen.

Better than yours?
I don't see mine. And I don't see why anybody would want to compare things.

What qualities do you find consistently compelling in people?
What an odd question. I know right off the bat whether I like somebody, and it has nothing to do with the qualities in them. Sometimes you meet somebody and without a word passing between you, you like them. Then you meet other people and you just don't like them regardless of what qualities they might have. You just don't like them.

I see. Are you an easily enchanted person?
What?

In other words, are you the kind of person who goes in to see a movie willing to let it cast whatever spell it might be capable of over you, or do you struggle to remain skeptical?
If I see a movie with my wife, it's hard to fall under a spell, because with Sylvia it starts with whether or not the movie's in focus. Sylvia's really into movies, and I've learned a lot about them from watching them with her.

Seen anything good lately?

I just saw *Terminator* and thought that was great fun. It was kind of like "Road Warrior," which was another movie I really liked. I also liked "Tender Mercies," and one of my favorite movies is "Chan Is Missing." It was inscrutable.

What aspect of your work do you find the most difficult?

Not second-guessing or perfecting your work to death – and that's something I've learned to avoid. When you're really tired, you can't allow yourself to start thinking, "Oh jeez, I don't know." I have great faith in the basic thing I started out with, and I usually won't be moved on it.

Do you have structured writing habits?

I used to worry that I'd lose the capacity to write because sometimes I'd sit down and nothing would happen. But I finally realized that writing is an ability I have, that the mechanics of it are always operating in the back of my head for my own fun and amusement, and that I can draw on it when I need to. I can write very quickly. Sometimes I'll take a title and let it loose in my head and just write out a song, and it's really fun when it goes like that. On the other hand, a song like "My Friend George," which is one of my favorites of the things I've written, required much more effort. Normally I just let a song go where it will – if it comes back, fine, but if it doesn't, to hell with it. But I really liked the little bit that I had of "My Friend George," so I had to spend a couple of hours figuring out some chords for it. I finally got the chords and I couldn't sing it and play it at the same time! That song took a long time – by a long time, I mean a couple of hours; all afternoon, all night with the thing, then the next day going over it again.

Have you ever considered writing a play?

Yes, but I haven't done it yet. One of my strong points is that I'm good at dialogue and can do two things with it: I can make it sound like something someone said, or I can have it really be exactly like something someone said. A lot of my stuff sounds like the way people speak, when, in fact, it's not; it's sort of a polished version of the way people speak.

It's a popular theory that an artist must be in some kind of conflict or turmoil in order to do good work. Do you think there's any truth in that?

No, I think that's an unfortunate concept, that one.

Do you think that once a person has experienced certain extremes of despair and survived them, they never have to go through it again? Or can life repeatedly throw you back to point zero?

I can't answer questions like that and that's not the kind of thing I should answer. I don't know any more than you do. Who's qualified to answer a question like that? A good friend might be.

How rare are good friends?

I guess that depends on the person, doesn't it?

You recently told the L.A. Times: "I want my music to get funkier, more danceable. That's what interests me now." Why does that idea appeal to you?

I never ask myself things like that because I couldn't care less why. I never think, "No, don't go over there – I want you to go over here." It goes where the fun goes, and I follow.

What do you consider your best work?

I always like my most recent album best, and that applies to every single one of them. I'm always excited about the last one when I get out of the studio, and then having heard it so much, I'll suddenly get very sick of it and won't listen to it for a year or so. I always find that I don't discover what the songs are really about until maybe a year or so later.

How do your early songs feel to you now?

I like every single one of my songs or I wouldn't have recorded them. The ones I didn't feel that good about I didn't record.

Have the social and sexual taboos operating in American culture when you started making music in the '60s changed?

I'm a rock 'n' roll person and I'm not interested in answering questions like that. It's true I've addressed certain subjects as a writer, but that's in the work. People are always asking me if there's a realistic validity in my work. "Did you really do that? Can we really believe it?" I always keep my mouth shut about these things because I don't want to be put in the position of having to actually do something in order to write about it. I don't believe in that.

Why is popular music obsessed with the idea of romantic love?

It's not just popular music – everything is obsessed with that because love is so important to people's lives. They want to hear it, sing about it, listen to it being sung about, see movies about it, write poems to it, dance to it, and think about it.

What would you like to change about your life at this point?

I wouldn't want to change anything about my life.

Are you surprised at what you've achieved in life, or did you feel from the time you were a child that you were destined to leave your mark on the world?

I never thought about that or thought into the future that way. I just wanted to write and I really liked rock 'n' roll.

Do you believe in luck?

I believe in bad luck, so I guess I believe in good luck. But really, what's the point in a question like that?

–1986–

For many years you were very open with the press, whereas now many areas of your life are off-limits to reporters. What caused this change in attitude?

I simply decided that certain things were nobody's business but mine.

What subjects do you feel are appropriate to a dialogue between a person such as yourself and the press?

That's a question? I don't know. Anything that regards my personal life is inappropriate. We should talk about music.

During the time you were with the Velvets, did you have the sense that you were making important music that would have a lasting impact on popular culture?

We were having a lot of fun and had basic goals in mind, which we stuck to very carefully.

Do you remember that period of your life fondly?

Sure. I wouldn't have missed that for the world. I don't know how old you are, so I don't know whether you know what it was like then, but when we took the show across the country, rock 'n' roll clubs didn't really exist yet, so we made our own places to play. We played at museums just to have a place to play.

Is music culture as exciting now as it was then?

It's exciting for me in a different way now. I get a thrill from playing with people that I get along with and whose playing I admire, and I enjoy using all the gadgets in the studio. But the basic payoff in music is still playing for a live audience and I still love touring and playing for people – although I don't like the accoutrements of touring. The travel can be a real grind and I don't think anyone likes that. It's quite complicated to play these days. You have to have sound, lights – this whole mechanism gets going.

What was the last music you heard that excited you?

I've been listening to an Ornette Coleman album that I like a lot.

What's your favorite Elvis Presley song?

"That's Alright Mama," or "Mystery Train," which has great guitar on it. I didn't much care for his middle and late stuff.

What was the first record you bought?

I can't remember the exact first one but it was probably a doo-wop record. It might've been "Ain't That a Shame" by Fats Domino, or a Carl Perkins record, and I still love that music. There's this great record of Little Richard's outtakes that I really love. He had so much talent as a piano player, it's just amazing – I'd recognize his touch anywhere. I saw that movie he was in – Beverly Hills something or other – just to see what he was up to. I love Fats Domino too. The first record of his that I bought was this thing called "The Fat Man," and it's still one of my favorite records; great piano playing. Jerry Lee Lewis is a pretty fantastic player too. I love all those old boogie-woogie players like Meade Lux Lewis and Albert Ammons.

Why is the idea of originality so valued in music?

I don't know that I'd agree that there's that high a premium placed on originality. I don't know how many original things there are to do, and I personally value something in terms of how well it's done.

What aspect of your work comes hardest to you?

Finding the right people to work with. Playing and writing are easy for me – it's the outside things that I struggle with. I'm firmly convinced that I'm only as good as the people I'm around, and my records are truly a team effort. I can't stress enough how important it is for me to have the right people around me.

You've managed to use video fairly successfully. What quality is it in you that enabled you to employ that form efficiently?

I don't think I've used video successfully and I don't usually enjoy making videos because I don't like to lip synch. In fact, I can't lip synch – it's really difficult for me. I told the directors of my last video, no lip synching, no models running around, and women getting beat up, and they made a video built around a robot of me, which was sort of designed after the robot they made for Herbie Hancock's "Rockit" video. I am much more attractive than my robot is. Are you very serious today?

I'm always serious when I interview people.
Oh, are you? Are you depressed? You seem depressed.

I appreciate your concern. You have a very passionate relationship with motorcycles – you write about them, and even made a television commercial for them. What is it about them you find so compelling?
Next to playing the guitar, motorcycles are the most fun you can have. The sound of the engine – I just love everything about them. I ride as often as is humanly possible and I'd like to drive from New York to Los Angeles – I've never made that drive and it's something I've always wanted to do. Riding on a motorcycle you see things you wouldn't notice if you were in a car. I don't drive cars very well because I don't pay attention.

Is the ability to create a happy life for oneself a talent or skill one can acquire, or, for example, is a melancholy child doomed to be a melancholy adult?
I never thought of happiness as a talent and questions like that make my skin crawl. I can't take them seriously and I don't see the point of them.

The point of the question is to find out how much control you believe a human being can exert over the self-destructive aspects of his own nature.
Oh, I see – you want to know if I'm a determinist. Some people call that fatalism, that "you're doomed to be right-handed" kind of thinking, but I believe you can learn to do practically anything you want to do, particularly here in America. I know a lot of people may not believe that, and they might say, "Sure, that's easy for you to say, but within the parameters of your abilities you can do anything." Like Clint says in *Dirty Harry*, "a man's got to know his limitations." Beyond that, if you want to learn to swim or fly or speak a foreign language – it's all possible. You can make yourself better or worse or leave it alone.

Have you always had that much faith in your power to shape your life, or is it an attitude you've acquired over the years?
I branched out from music and writing, which are like living things to me, and came to understand that what I could achieve in music and writing I could accomplish in other areas of life too. But you have to start someplace.

What's the most insidious idea currently being peddled by popular culture?
I don't like this PMRC business [rating and censorship of records]. I think it's a bad idea and something to really worry about. You start censoring music, and books and movies aren't far behind, so you have to be very careful about things like this. I honestly believe that whatever excesses we have to deal with are really worth it in the long run because what we're talking about here are basic freedoms. And who are the people who are going to decide what you can hear? Who's in charge of that? I don't want anybody deciding those things for me, and as far as children are concerned, that's what parents are for.

Were you exposed to anything as a child that in retrospect you wish you hadn't seen?

That's very possible. I saw a movie called *Cat People* that really terrified me when I was a kid. I don't know if I'm permanently twisted from it, but you never know what might set a person off.

The PMRC is part of a swing to the right that this country presently seems to be experiencing. Do you think this mood of conservatism will run its course and disappear like previous political regimes, or is this one dangerous in a different way?

I don't know. I kept hoping that if you didn't mention it and acted like it wasn't there it would go away, but that hasn't happened. It hasn't gone away and I think people are going to have to think about possibly exerting themselves a little to maintain basic freedoms.

What do you see as being the dominant characteristics of America?

The most noteworthy thing about America is that you can do anything you want here. If you have the opportunity to travel around the world as I have, you come to understand what a rare thing that is, and you see that in many ways America is still the Wild West. America is the home of the free, and even though things like the PMRC pop up here periodically, that too is an example of people exercising their freedom. There's a lot of economic tyranny that goes on here, but despite that you can still go out and travel around.

Are there places in America that you've yet to see that you have romantic notions about?

I want to drive through the Grand Canyon on my bike, and I'd also like to drive through the Rockies.

What's the most widely held misconception about fame?

That money goes along with it.

Are the Seven Deadly Sins listed in the old proverb moral issues that man continues to wrestle with, or has the world changed to such a degree that new and different evils are currently stalking the globe?

It's interesting that rock 'n' roll people get asked questions like that. People expect so much of music. They look to musicians expecting them to have all the great answers and solutions.

I haven't singled you out as a "rock 'n' roll" person as someone who should be able to handle the tough questions – all of us must address these questions. And, as a person of great and varied experience, I thought perhaps you might know something about life that I don't know and could be of use to me.

Of course I do! And I put those things in my songs, quite clearly. To answer your question, I'd say that even though technology has changed things a lot, things aren't remarkably different. People are still fighting over basic things that you'd think we'd no longer even need to speak about, much less fight about.

Would you describe yourself as an angry man?

No.

What's the mark of a true friend?

A true friend will tell you the truth. And, having told you the truth, a true friend will be on your side even when you're wrong.

Do you feel you owe anything to the people who've followed your music and supported it?

Owe them anything? I've never thought of it that way, although I probably wouldn't be around today if they hadn't supported me. I've gone for years without getting any airplay and if people hadn't supported my records the record companies would've dropped me.

You have very staunch fans.

I'm a very staunch artist.

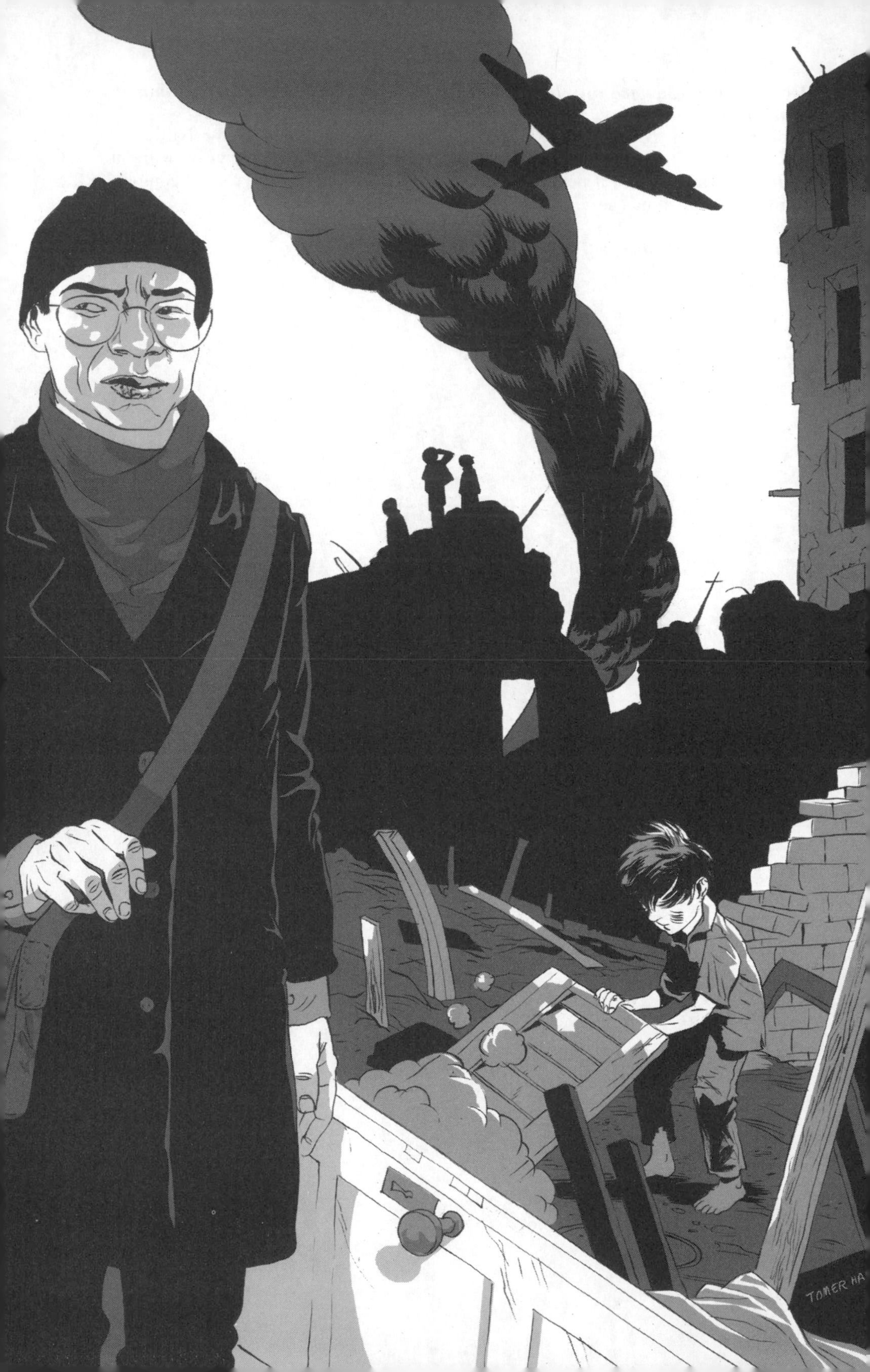
TOMER HA

Joe Sacco

When Art Spiegelman began serializing the graphic novel Maus, his chronicle of his father's experience under the Nazis, in the pages of RAW magazine in the early 1980s, it was clear that comics had the capacity to handle the big subjects. No one has blazed further into the territory Spiegelman pioneered than Joe Sacco, a political reporter who uses his cartooning skills to chronicle his experiences in the Middle East and the Balkans.

Born in Malta in 1960, Sacco spent his childhood in Australia and his early teenage years in Los Angeles. After earning a degree in journalism at the University of Oregon in 1981, he hit the road and lived in Europe as he worked towards finding his own creative voice. In 1991 he made his first trip to Palestine, and at that point the form and content in Sacco's work coalesced into his mature style. Sacco's experiences in the Occupied Territories resulted in Palestine, a deeply moving account of daily life during the first Intifada that was published by Fantagraphics Books beginning in 1993. That same year Sacco visited Sarajevo and it's surrounding areas just as the Bosnian War was winding to a close. His experiences there can be found in Safe Area Gorazde: The War in Eastern Bosnia, 1992-95, a wrenching study of a Muslim enclave in a state of siege.

In 2003 Sacco published The Fixer – A Story From Sarajevo, which examined the aftermath of the Bosnian War as embodied in a man named Neven, a former member of one of the paramilitary groups that simultaneously protected and terrorized Bosnian civilians during the war. Also out that year was Notes From A Defeatist, a collection of Sacco's early work that serves as an illuminating chronicle of his artistic evolution. In September of 2003 Sacco returned to Portland, after having spent a year living in a small Swiss farming village. He's presently working on a story about Chechen refugees, and a longer piece about Gaza.

Why are comics a better vehicle for your work than straight journalism?
I've been doing comics since I was six years old, so it's a medium that's been with me for a very long time and I think there are advantages to it. It's accessible and immediate – right away, the reader is thrust into a small town in Bosnia. I can make the crane that allows me to hover above a city – I don't have to hire a helicopter to get the picture – and I can take the reader into someone's past. I can ask visual questions that allow me to render it as faithfully as a film director.

Which artists have been important for you?
Robert Crumb and Brueghel the Elder – he's a big influence on me. I love the solidity of the people in his paintings, and his work provides a window into daily life in Flanders during the 16th Century in a way the Italian Renaissance simply doesn't. When I first got to Gorazde it looked like the Middle Ages because there were hardly

any cars running and the electricity was mostly off, and I thought wow! I can draw just like Brueghel! I really got into drawing people doing things like chopping wood.

Why are you so sensitive to global politics?

It could have to do with the fact that my parents went through World War II in Malta, and I grew up hearing about it. We lived outside Melbourne when I was a kid, and all their friends in Australia went through the war, too. Whenever they got together that's all they talked about.

In 2003 Fantagraphics published a collection of your early work, much of which is quite light-hearted compared with the work you're known for. When did you turn the corner into the serious work you do now?

From 1988 to 1992 I did a comic series called *Yahoo* and in the course of that series I went from short, satirical pieces that were supposed to be funny, to more involved autobiographical pieces, to autobiography mixed with politics, and then eventually to telling the story of my mother's experience during World War II. I found out what my strengths were doing that series. However, the first time I visited Palestine I didn't have some notion in my head that from then on I'd be doing "important journalism."

What compels you to spend time in war zones as a source for your work?

It's not as if I want to be in places where there's shooting going on. Those particular situations – Bosnia and Palestine – are of great interest to me, and I want to put my two cents in because the media hasn't portrayed those situations very accurately. I don't blame the media for perpetuating this conflict, but in failing to fully inform the electorate they prevent people from bringing their influence to bear on these situations, because they don't know what the hell is going on with them to begin with.

Your first book of political reportage was Palestine. Prior to actually going to Palestine, how did you know the media was portraying that situation inaccurately?

With Palestine, that was easy to know because there are so few Palestinian voices in the media. The obvious reason for that is U.S. interests lie with Israel, and our media reflects that.

Having spent a good deal of time there, what do you think it will take to resolve that conflict?

I don't see it resolving any time soon. I was there several times over the past year, and during that year the level of violence went way up on both sides. It's no longer a question of jeeps coming around shooting a few rubber bullets – it's tanks and aircraft now. It looks increasingly likely that there won't be a viable Palestinian state, and that these two peoples will be forever conjoined in some way that might result in an apartheid situation. Israel knows that removing the settlements would do a great deal in terms of moving towards a just solution, but it would take considerable will amongst the Israelis to do that, and it would be messy – at least fifteen per cent of the Israeli population would oppose it tooth and claw. The U.S. has played a lousy role in this situation all the way through, and should be pressing Israel harder to make concessions. But I hardly consider the U.S. the "honest broker" it claims to be.

For decades different ethnic communities lived side by side in the former Yugoslavia, then a fierce sense of tribal identity flared up and separated

people; what caused this to occur?

It occurred because some politicians saw it could be exploited in their quest for power. For all the good [Josep Broz] Tito did, he created problems in not allowing people to talk about crimes that had been committed among these ethnic groups at various points, particularly during World War II. [Tito was a revolutionary communist who ruled Yugoslavia from 1945 until his death in 1980.] There was no truth and reconciliation commission, and many people weren't brought to justice. These are things politicians can use, and that's what Milosevic and Karadzic did.

How do you explain the atrocities committed during wartime? Do some people have the capacity to switch gears and take pleasure in killing?

There are always a limited number of sadists in any war, and a few hardcore sadists can turn a group around. They tend to make sure the people around them get blood on their hands, too, so everyone has a vested interest in continuing the killing. It's hard to get anyone involved to speak openly about those things, of course. Every now and then a journalist is around one of those people whose star is rising, who feel like they can do anything they want. But when I was there in 1995 the Serbs appeared to be on the losing end of the Dayton accord and The Hague Tribunal had been set up, so people weren't bragging about things they'd done during the war.

What finally made the people in the Balkans stop killing one another?

Sheer exhaustion was part of it, but international pressure also had a lot to do with it. And, a lot of what the Serbs wanted out of the war was accomplished in that they cleared vast areas of the Muslim population.

You returned to Gorazde in 2001; had the city begun to recover?

No. They fixed up some houses at the center of town and painted them garish colors, but the outskirts of town were still wrecked. Gorazde is a dying city. Little by little, all the people are leaving Gorazde.

Are people capable of recovering from the extreme trauma they often suffer during war?

There are always individuals who are just too fucked up, but generally I think people do recover. In Gorazde, there were two girls who dreamed about a new pair of 501 jeans, and that's a beautiful thing – the fact that they were hanging onto anything as normal as that was good, because it shows that people just want to be a part of the world, in all its silliness.

Your 2003 book, The Fixer, ***is about a fixer named Neven; what is a fixer?***

There are many kinds of fixers, but generally they're people who can translate well, are knowledgeable about the local scene, and can make introductions and make things happen for you. With Neven, I could've said, "Take me to the 5th Army Corps and get me an interview with a general," and he probably could've arranged it. A fixer can really influence a journalist's story in that his or her politics can determine which stories they introduce you to. They can steer you in a particular direction or not translate specific things, and there's no way you can know they're doing it. One point I wanted to make with this book is that journalists are dependent on these people, for good or for bad. I can't know for sure if Neven was always telling the truth, but my tendency was to believe him, and I think he gave me an accurate overall picture of what happened. However, I always had to remember that it was through Neven's filter.

Why does someone become a fixer?

They're often people who enjoy talking to foreigners and want to improve their English, but mostly it's money that makes them do it. When I was in Bosnia a fixer could make $150 a day, which was more than most people there were seeing in a year.

Do you consider Neven a sympathetic figure?

It's hard to describe him with a single adjective because he's complicated. I didn't know anyone in Sarajevo on my first visit, and Neven was the first person I spoke to. In his way he took me under his wing, and I appreciated that because he was a tough guy and I was a little afraid when I was there. It was good to be around this guy because it felt like his street credibility was rubbing off on me on some level. It wasn't until later that I learned he didn't have street credibility with everyone. Sarajevo didn't have an army, so when it came under attack it needed people like Neven to step into the breach. Without people like Neven, Sarajevo probably would've fallen, and who knows what the consequences of that would've been. Neven considered it a tragedy that the paramilitary groups that defended Sarajevo were crushed, but they definitely had to be stopped. Ultimately, Neven was someone who was able to thrive for a time in a very chaotic circumstance, and then it turned against him and he was back to being caught up in it.

Who is responsible for intervening when genocide is being committed? As the strongest military power in the world, is that America's responsibility?

I don't know if you can make a blanket statement like that because every case has to be judged individually. I don't think America is obliged to be the policeman of the world. However, you could certainly make the case that situations on the scale of what occurred in Rwanda must be addressed, and truth be told, America is the country with the equipment and manpower to do these sorts of things.

Are there other areas of the world that are of particular interest to you?

Almost any place can interest me but I have to chain myself to a desk and work right now. I'd be interested in going to Iraq, but I'd have to be sent there because I couldn't finance a trip like that on my own, and I'm not sure who to approach. It's unlikely I'd approach an American paper because they end up hammering you about "their style" and things that seem trivial to me.

Do you go into these projects prepared to lose your life?

No. Obviously this work is risky on some level, and I know that something can happen, but I try to be very careful. I'm not a war photographer running into streets taking pictures of rolling tanks.

Does making this work depress you?

Occasionally. When you see a bombing in a café in Tel Aviv, houses being demolished and people getting killed by tank shells, it's depressing as hell. But I channel those feelings into a sense of purpose – I'll think O.K., I'll sit at my drawing table and start working, and three years from now there'll be a book coming out about this. I'd get more depressed if I wasn't doing this work.

Having made a first-hand study of war, what conclusions have you drawn about human nature?

You see extremes of humanity in places like Palestine and Bosnia – you see enormously good people who'll give you the shirt off their back despite the fact that they have nothing, and you see incredible cruelty. Mostly what you see is innocent people being crushed beneath the wheels of history.

LIFE
U.S. SUPER-ROAD SYSTEM
GROWS AND GROWS
SALADS, HEARTY AND LIGHT
EVA MARIE SAINT
FROM TV TO STARDOM
IN MOVIE 'WATERFRONT'
20 CENTS
JULY 19, 1954

Eva Marie Saint

Eva Marie Saint lives in an apartment in Los Angeles, but the minute you enter it you know she's a New York person. Furnished with the tasteful modernity of a pied-a-terre on Central Park, it's a modest home decorated with mementos of the New York theater community, original sketches by her friend Andrew Wyeth, and family photographs. There's no sign whatsoever that an Academy Award winning movie star lives there, nor does Saint herself make much of that fact. She's an extraordinarily graceful woman, with a sweetness and authenticity much like that of the character she plays in Elia Kazan's masterful film of 1954, On The Waterfront. Alfred Hitchcock once referred to Saint as a "calm beauty," and it's an apt description.

Saint was born on July 4, 1924, in Newark, New Jersey. She had one older sister, and spent her childhood and adolescence in two small towns – Elsmir and Delmar – outside Albany, New York. Her father was a Quaker and a traveling salesman, and she studied acting at Bowling Green University. In 1946 she moved to New York and began laying the foundation for what's proven to be an amazing career as an actress. She's been directed by Alfred Hitchcock, Elia Kazan, John Frankenheimer, Vincente Minnelli, Edward Dmytryk, and Otto Preminger, among others, and done love scenes with Paul Newman, Gregory Peck, Marlon Brando, Cary Grant, Montgomery Clift, and Warren Beatty. Saint is humble about her body of work, though, and gives much of the credit for all she's achieved to her husband of 52 years, director Jeffrey Hayden.

–2000–

What's your earliest memory?

It was something in the house where we lived in Jackson Heights, New York. That house had a back yard with a seesaw, and I remember seesawing with my sister in that little yard. I loved being in that house, maybe my folks seemed particularly happy there.

What were your parents like?

They were very strong people, and in our family you didn't show anger or tears – you went to your room for those things. I'm sure one of the things that drew me to acting is that I needed to put those emotions somewhere. My dad grew up in Marshalltown, Iowa, and he had four brothers and two sisters, all of whom died of influenza within a period of two years. His mother died when he was ten, and his father got a mail order bride, so he left home when he was 16 and wound up working as a salesman for B.F. Goodrich until he was 65. He worked six days out of seven and traveled all the time. My mother had been a teacher prior to meeting my father, but that stopped once she got married because women simply didn't work then. Both my parents were very conservative. They didn't like F.D.R. and they loved Ronald Reagan, so I always avoided talking politics with them.

Early in their marriage my parents were very social, and I could always tell when they were having company because there would be a Baby Ruth candy bar cut up in pieces in a cut glass dish. If company was coming my mother would take the spread off their bed and replace it with this big lavender spread covered with a beige piece of lace, and the doilies would suddenly appear, too. The earlier days of their marriage seemed happier because they had a social life, but as they got older they had fewer friends.

Which isn't to suggest they weren't wonderful people, because they were. One of my fondest memories is of coming home from school in the afternoon on really hot days. My mom always had the shades drawn on hot days so the house would be cool, and I'd walk in and she'd have prepared a beautiful little lunch, probably a chicken salad sandwich. I knew even then how lucky I was to have such a wonderful mother. She made everything we wore all through high school, and everybody said the Saint girls were the best-dressed kids in town. She was a very refined woman who sewed beautifully and she could've been a designer had she been driven that way.

It sounds as if you were rather glamorous as a young girl. Were you?

Absolutely not: Men come up to me when I'm with my husband and say, "I've been in love with you since *On the Waterfront*," but I assure you I didn't have that effect on men in high school. I was painfully shy when I was young, and I don't know why I was, because my parents were very encouraging. I played the violin in the school orchestra, and I was in chorus, modern dance, and was on the hockey team, but when it came to relationships and dances I always felt like I was on the outside looking in at the fast kids who were smoking, drinking, and carrying on sexually. My dad was a Quaker so our family was strict, and because of how I was raised I didn't want to participate in any of that – not that I felt I knew how. I didn't think I was bad looking, but I never considered myself a great beauty and I had just one boyfriend during high school. My sister was the popular one. She was a gregarious redhead, and she'd be in the parlor holding court with five or six guys, and I'd be in the next room doing my homework. She was two years older, and I think I was really jealous of my dear sister because she seemed so much more worldly than I.

When did you finally grow out of your shrinking violet phase?

I guess you could say I blossomed when I got to college. I was chosen to be the May Queen and the Valentine Pin-up Sweetheart Girl, and while I was in college I became engaged to a man named Otto Shepler. He was very German, and the first time we visited his folks in Pennsylvania, his mother mentioned that she'd never sat in her own living room before! That made me a little nervous. Then, after the war started, the fact that he was German made me uncomfortable, partly because my dad had been badly wounded in World War I. He was in the Argonne the day after the armistice was signed, and the news that the war was over hadn't yet reached them when most of his company was wiped out. He lay wounded in a trench for seven days, then he was in a hospital for months. Before leaving for the front he'd become engaged to a girl who lived in New Jersey, and when he returned on crutches she broke up with him. My father never talked about the war, but every year on Memorial Day he cried the whole day. I never saw my dad cry other than that, and my mom would take my sister and I out of the house on that day to give him some privacy. He's buried at Gettysburg now along with my mother.

Did you love movies while you were growing up?

I wasn't interested in celebrities, but I did love movies. When we lived in Delmar we'd go to the movies every weekend at this place we called the Stink-Box because it was a movie house that had been built on a dump. They tried to perfume the place so it didn't smell but it always did, and after you came home from seeing a movie there your clothes would reek of the place. I used to love to be scared and liked things like *Dracula*, and I loved Charles Boyer and Norma Shearer. Every New Year's Eve we'd go see the stage show at the Palace Theater in Albany, and my mother loved radio soap operas, so I grew up listening to *Stella Dallas*, and *The First Nighter*. Whenever I came home from a movie I'd stand in front of the mirror and try to reenact some of the scenes I'd just seen, but I never thought of myself as a person who could be a performer.

When did you become interested in acting?

I went to Bowling Green State University planning on becoming a third grade teacher, then when I was in my sophomore year someone dared me to try out for a play called *Personal Appearance*. I don't know why I took the dare, but I did, and I played a Hollywood sex pot in a slinky gown. There was something about transforming myself into someone completely different from how I perceived myself that I absolutely loved. The house father in the sorority where I lived was a professor of speech and theater named Eldon T. Smith, and he was a mentor to all of us, so I wrote to him over the summer after my sophomore year. I said, "I just have these feelings. What would it be like to be an actress and pursue this?" I asked him what he thought my chances were, and he wrote me a beautiful letter that I still have about the possibilities for me in theater in New York. He felt I could take the rejection, so after I read the letter I felt encouraged enough to ask my parents what they thought. They said whatever you do, do your best, and I was off. We all have pivotal moments in our lives when we receive a crucial bit of encouragement, and in my case it was that one sentence from my parents and the letter from Eldon.

My folks were living in Flushing by the time I finished college and I'd done a bunch of plays by then. I wanted to be financially independent, so I gave myself one year of living with my folks and making the rounds in New York trying to get acting work. During that same period I started studying at the Herbert Bergoff Studios with Herb and Uta Hagen, then I went over to the Actors Studio and continued to study there until 1956, when I moved to Los Angeles. Everybody was in my class at the Actors Studio – Lee Strasberg, Ben Gazzara, Paul Newman, Joanne Woodward. Annie and Eli Wallach were there too, and they were our best friends. I remember going to their apartment one Sunday morning to work on a scene with Eli, and when I arrived they were still in bed with their baby. I'll never forget the vision of these two talented actors with a little baby between them. It was such a beautiful scene and I said to myself, "Yeah, you can have it all."

At what point did your career begin to take off?

In 1948 I auditioned for my first play on Broadway, which was the first production of *Mr. Roberts*, directed by Josh Logan and starring Hank Fonda, and I got the part. There was only one female part in the play and I got it! The rehearsals went really well and I was deliriously happy, then just before the play opened Josh Logan took me aside and said, "Eva Marie, we're a little nervous. This is going to be a big hit and it's your first play, so we're going to replace you with another actress. We would, however, like you to stay on as understudy." I said fine, I'll think about it, but the minute I got to my dressing room I burst into tears, and on the ride home that night I was devastated. I'd never been rejected that way, and I thought to myself I don't know if I can take this. Maybe I should become a teacher. I decided that by the time

I got to Flushing I was going to resolve either to leave acting and become a teacher, or to pursue acting, but never allow myself to feel the way I felt that day again. I could be disappointed, but never sick to my stomach with a pounding heart, because I couldn't survive a lifetime of feeling that way. By the time I got to Flushing I'd decided I was going to try to be an actress and never let myself be destroyed by a disappointment, and I've been able to do that. However, I don't think I could've done it if I hadn't had Jeffrey.

We met in 1947 on the third floor at NBC. He was doing radio research and I was always on that floor, and Jeff had seen me in my purple corduroy raincoat carrying my big black modeling book that said Eva Marie Saint on it in big letters. We were finally introduced to each other by a mutual friend, and the next time we ran into each other Jeff invited me for coffee, but I told him no, I don't have time. I was very serious about my work and wasn't looking for a guy because I felt I had to really buckle down if I wanted to do this. But he was persistent, and the third time he asked me to lunch I told him I'd love to. We didn't marry until four years later, in 1951, and those years were hell on wheels. We'd date, we wouldn't date – I can't remember what sorts of things we'd break up over, so they obviously weren't that important, but every time we did I knew there was an underlying love that would get us through. We were both in analysis so we got a lot of the bad stuff out that would've been with us had we married. During those years I was living in a one room apartment on 110th Street with a girl who worked in radio and you couldn't have liquor, men or cigarettes in the building where we lived. So Jeff and I would sit in the cold foyer of the building and have long talks about life. We both wanted each other's dreams to come true, and we've continued to feel that way about each other for 50 years.

Getting back to the '40s, I stayed with *Mr. Roberts* as an understudy, and watched Hank Fonda every night but I never got to go on. Many years later I did *First Monday in October* with Hank and it was like a dream come true. Every night after the performance he'd put his arm around me and we'd walk to our dressing rooms, and one night I said to him, don't we have the most wonderful lives? I didn't know it at the time, but he'd been diagnosed with cancer and hadn't told anyone. I adored him. He was so giving.

So, Mr. Roberts *doesn't really qualify as your big break.*

You're right; you can't really call it that! After *Mr. Roberts* I started doing Admiral commercials on live television, and got a part on a running radio series that aired five days a week. It took me one whole year to get the part, and the only thing I said week after week was, "This is your long distance operator. Number please." One day I was working on a scene from Chekov at the Actors Studio and I had to leave to try out for an Admiral commercial. I said to Lee Strasberg, "You know, it's really hard for me to go from Chekov to do this stupid commercial," and he said, "What's stupid about it? You want to eat, don't you? You can't go through life doing scenes from Chekov at the studio and going to friends' houses to work on scenes because that's not life." He was, of course, absolutely right.

What made Elia Kazan cast you in On the Waterfront?

In Kazan's autobiography he says he cast me after seeing me in a production of the Horton Foote play *The Trip to Bountiful*, that was done live on television. I actually didn't have much of a part – it really is Lillian Gish's piece, and she's wonderful in it. I play a girl whose husband has just gone off to war, and I spend most of my time listening to Lillian. It's hard to just listen in a piece and it's something I can do, so I guess Gadge saw some potential there.

Did you sense that On the Waterfront ***was an important movie as you were making it?***

No, you never know that. It was my first film and I was with Kazan and all these wonderful people, but the work was the thing and it was exciting doing it. We were shooting outside on the docks in Hoboken which was very cold, so that sort of stimulated everybody, and there were real longshoremen there. I'd seen Brando in *A Streetcar Named Desire*, and around the Actors Studio, and while I certainly admired him, I'm never in awe of an actor because that's what I do. Starring opposite Brando in a film didn't give me pause, nor did it make me nervous to star opposite Cary Grant. They're actors. They're not doctors who've found a cure for cancer. We live in a culture that tends to view actors as godlike creatures, but they're just people. So, I was comfortable working with Brando, although I certainly had difficult moments. There's a scene where Brando breaks in on me while I'm in bed in a slip, and I found that incredibly hard. I'd never been in a slip on stage or in live television and I felt so vulnerable I might as well have been naked. The feelings I was having were good for the character and for the scene, but only to a point, and Kazan could see how awkward I felt. So, he walked over and whispered my husband's name in my ear, and somehow that helped me relax. That's the kind of director he was – he just knew how to push the right button. He really was the finest film director we've ever had, largely because he went so deeply into the writing. As he got older it was hard for him because many people held the blacklist thing against him, but I never did. Everybody had to do what they had to do, but I wasn't involved in any of that. I knew what was going on at the time, of course, but New York's theater community was less affected by the blacklist than the film community was. I loved my experience with Kazan, and remember that period of my life with tremendous gratitude. I won an Academy Award for my work in the film on March 31, 1955, then two days later I gave birth to my first child.

It was only a few months later that you went back to work, starring with Montgomery Clift and Elizabeth Taylor in Edward Dmytryk's film of 1956, Raintree County. ***How do you recall that experience?***

That got to be sort of a drag because it was all on the MGM lot and the shoot just went on and on, partly because poor Monty Clift had a terrible car accident when we were halfway through shooting, so they couldn't replace him. His face was disfigured by the accident, and film buffs can really tell the before and after. Monty was a dear man and he was wonderful to work with, but he and Liz were very close, so he and I never really spent time together off the set. I invited him to have lunch with me one day in my dressing room, but I felt so shy I didn't know what to say to him, and he didn't know what to say to me either, so we just sat there. I couldn't wait for lunch to be over! I wasn't aware of his problems because when I work with people I put on my blinders. I don't get involved and don't want to know too much because it's distracting. There's always loads of private turmoil churning away on movie sets, and there was quite a bit of it on *Raintree County*, which was a difficult shoot. In fact, I threw the one tantrum I've thrown in my career on that set. My husband was in France working on a film, and I was counting the days until my shoot was finished so I could go join him. I thought I was going to be finished on a Friday, only to be told, "Miss Saint, it's going to be another few weeks." I marched into Dore Schary's office and said "I can't go on!" I couldn't handle those waist cinchers one more day.

That same year you made what can only be described as a surprising choice, coming as it did on the heels of On The Waterfront; ***you co-starred with Bob Hope in*** That Certain Feeling. ***What attracted you to that project?***

I thought the script was funny. I adored Bob Hope and thought my character sounded fun. I'm drunk in one scene and get to run around with a lampshade on my head, and I did have a great time making that film. The first day I arrived on the set I thought I'd made a mistake because it was so different from what I experienced with Kazan. He maintained a closed set where you didn't fool around or talk because it would dissipate your energy, and the atmosphere was intensely serious. That first day on Bob Hope's set there was a football team hanging around waiting to watch us shoot. Strasberg always said, "We have our instrument, take care of it so that when somebody asks you to do something you can play that instrument." So I thought O.K., here I am with my instrument. I'm going to have to do what the director wants in spite of the presence of that football team. But by the end of the day I loved it. I worked with Bob again in 1972 on *Cancel My Reservation* – it wasn't a very good film, but we had fun making it. I'm sure this doesn't come as a surprise to anyone, but it's generally more fun being on the set of a comedy than a drama. *The Russians Are Coming*, [1966], for instance, was an incredibly fun set – how could it not be fun with Carl Reiner, Alan Arkin, Jonathan Winters, and Theodore Bikel in the cast. We were shooting at Fort Bragg, and there was one point where we were completely fogged in for a week and couldn't shoot anything. We all loved Norman Jewison who was directing the film, so we decided to put on a show for him in the local town hall, and Norman would screen the rushes for the entire town. That was the most fun set I've ever been on and it shows in the movie. The thing is to find a balance, and sometimes you need to do a comedy. After that first film I did with Bob Hope I made *Hatful of Rain*, with Fred Zinneman. I play a young mother who doesn't know that her husband is a dope addict, and it was a very emotional piece.

One could make the case that the signature role of your career was your performance as Eve Kendall, the icy blonde femme fatale in the 1959 thriller, North by Northwest, which was the 30th film directed by Alfred Hitchcock.

That was great fun, and I've always wanted to play Eve Kendall again. Hitch was my sugar daddy and he took me to New York to have all those beautiful clothes made – the clothes in that film are so fun. Part of the pleasure of movies is that they allow people to escape into a fantasy of perfect lives and perfect people, and Hitch understood that. He once said to me, "Eva, I don't want you to make any more sink-to-sink movies." I said what are sink movies, and he replied, "They're black and white movies where you're at the kitchen sink and dressed accordingly. Do you think people want to see their leading ladies dressed like that? They want to see you how you look in *North by Northwest*," and he was right.

Hitch was a playful, facetious man, and he never really said actors are like cattle. He had great respect for actors and he was certainly fascinated by women. Of course, the women who worked with him all had very different experiences. For instance Tippi Hedren hadn't done much when she was cast in *Marnie*, and she was very vulnerable. Hitch kind of had her in his grip, and she finally had to break her contract because he had too much influence over her – it was as if he was trying to mold her. By the time I did *North By Northwest* I'd done a lot of work and I was married, so I wasn't looking for a father figure and my experience with him was completely different. I felt Hitch really nurtured you, and although he didn't give you much direction, he was there for you, as was Cary Grant. The first thing Cary said when we met was, "You don't have to cry in this picture – we're gonna have fun with this one," and we did. It wasn't a serious thriller, you know – it was a spoof, and Eve Kendall was fun to play because she was so devious. And Cary was an incredibly giving co-star. He had a rider in his contract that allowed him to control the photos of him that were released to the press, and on *North By Northwest*, he rejected several really wonderful shots of himself because I didn't look good in them – that's how giving he was. He was a sweet man and a great gentleman, although he did of course charge 25 cents for his autograph. It went to the Motion Picture Home, he said. The most torrid love scenes I ever did were the ones with Cary in that film. They're cool, torrid, but they are torrid – you don't have to be all over one another for a love scene to be torrid.

Is it hard to kiss people in front of a camera?

No, I love it. If I'd been married to a jealous husband it probably could've created problems, but Jeff is a director so he understands. It would be hard to be in this business with a husband who wasn't in it too. I never dated an actor because they're simply too neurotic. Not many actors last together, either – there are very few couples who have.

In 1960 you made the most politically volatile movie of your career, Exodus, Otto Preminger's film adaptation of Leon Uris' chronicle of the Palestine/Israeli conflict. Preminger had a reputation for being very difficult to work for. Was he?

He was a very talented man who made good things – *The Man With The Golden Arm*, for instance, and *Advise and Consent* – but he did scream, not at the actors, but at the underlings. That creates a bad atmosphere because if you're one of the stars you feel responsible. He was the only screamer I've ever worked with, and every day at some point there would be screaming – it was as if he had to have some kind of daily catharsis. The title of the film refers to a refugee ship, and many of the extras in the film had been on the real Exodus and said that making the movie for fifty cents a day, which is what they were paid, was more difficult than being on the real Exodus. I play a nurse in the film, and there's a scene when she has to give injections to a bunch of kids. The first time we did the scene all the kids were screaming because they thought they were really getting a shot, but by the fourth take they weren't screaming any more because they knew it was make believe. Finally we did a take and the kids were crying so hysterically I could hardly get through it, and I subsequently found out that Preminger told those kids before the scene that they would never see their mothers again, just so he could get the shot. I found that unconscionable. I was pleased when I was cast in that film but it wasn't until I got to the set in Israel that I realized how important it was. Suddenly it was more than just a role and I felt a tremendous responsibility in helping tell that story. Paul Newman never mentions his performance in that film because he was never happy with it, but I thought he was very good in it.

One of your lesser known performances that's one of my favorites is your portrayal of Echo in the John Frankenheimer film of 1962, **All Fall Down,** *which was based on a script by William Inge.*

It's so sad Frankenheimer's gone. He was such an attractive man, and as a director he was incredibly well prepared. I know I sound like Pollyanna, but the fact is that I've been extremely fortunate to work with really talented people. Warren Beatty had done maybe one or two films when we did *All Fall Down* together and he was good in it, and good to work with, too. Brandon DeWilde was also in the cast, and he's the one I really adored – he was about 14 when we shot that film, and we became inseparable. That film is a favorite of mine, and I feel very tenderly towards Echo, who was one of those Blanche DuBois characters who's simply too fragile to survive. I met Andy Wyeth shortly after that film came out, and the first thing he asked me was where I got the coat and the car I have in *All Fall Down*, which he loved. I worked with John

Frankenheimer again in 1966 on *Grand Prix* and co-starred Yves Montand. Yves had that wonderful twinkle in his eye and I just loved him, as did my daughter. She was eight at the time and when my husband brought her to the set she and Yves just hit it off. In fact, he wrote to her years later just to say hello. I play the other woman in that film, but that's the only time I was ever cast as that sort of character. When I made *The Sandpiper* with Richard Burton and Liz Taylor in 1965, I said to Vincente Minnelli, who directed it, "Why can't I play Liz's part and be the home wrecker? I don't want to play the little wife waiting at home." Vincente said, "I'm sorry, but blondes never break up marriages." Just as Hitchcock had this thing about icy blondes, Vincente had a thing about brunettes.

What's the most widely held misconception about the life of a famous actress?

That they're not human. Shortly after Jeff and I got married we were living on West 9th Street and we appeared on *Person to Person* with Edward R. Murrow. At one point he said to me, "Miss Saint, can we see the shoes you wear when you go on auditions?" I show my little shoes as if there's something extraordinary about them, but really, I'm just a person and these are just my shoes. I remember being in the bathroom at Sardi's in New York years ago, and while I was in one of the stalls two women came in. I heard one of them say, "Did you see Eva Marie Saint? She's much taller than I thought." "No," said the other one, "I think she seems shorter. She looks good for her age though, don't you think?" "I don't know," said the other one, and they went on and on. Finally I emerged from the stall and said "Hi. You see, we're human like everybody else," and I walked out. It's strange to be the object of that kind of interest, but I certainly don't hold anyone's curiosity against them. I have compassion for people. I don't know how you could be an actor without feeling compassion for people.

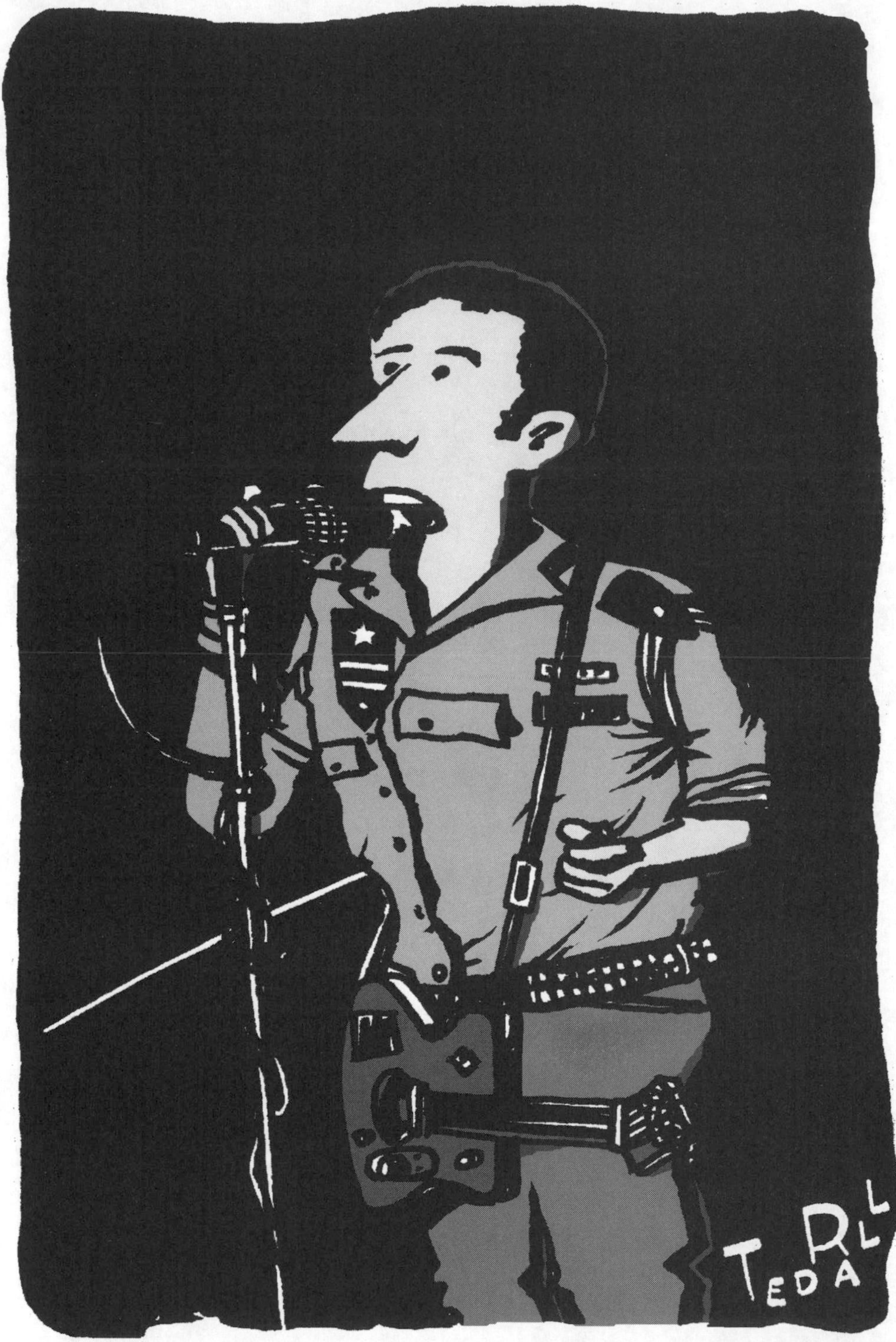
TED RALL

Joe Strummer

....

When the Clash first burst on the scene in 1977, I dismissed them for the same reason I've always hated U2. Their music struck me as humorless, self-important political blather that wasn't remotely sexy or fun; definitely not for me. Nonetheless, being a dedicated punk I had to check them out when they made their Los Angeles debut at the Santa Monica Civic on February 9, 1979, and what I saw that night changed my mind – just a little, though. As expected, Mick Jones came off as a typical rock fop who clearly spent far too much time thinking about neckerchiefs and trousers. Joe Strummer, however, was something else. With the exception of Jerry Lee Lewis, I'd never seen anyone that furiously alive on stage. Legs pumping, racing back and forth across the stage, singing with a frantic desperation that was simultaneously fascinating and puzzling, he was an incredibly electric presence.

At the press conference following the show that night, L.A.'s ranking punk scribe, Claude Bessy, jumped up and snarled, "This isn't a press conference – this is a depressing conference!" (Jeez, tempers always ran so high during that first incarnation of the punk scene! Who knows why the hell we were all so crabby!) I remember that Strummer looked genuinely hurt by the comment. Mind you, he was a working-class Brit so he wasn't about to start sniffling in his sleeve, but he didn't cop an attitude either. I was touched by how unguarded and open he was – and I was certainly impressed by the man's vigor. I wasn't surprised when I subsequently learned that Strummer ran three marathons without having trained at all. His preparation? "Drink ten pints of beer the night before the race and don't run a single step for at least four weeks before the race."

That first show at the Santa Monica Civic didn't transform me into a Clash fan but Strummer interested me, so when the band showed up in 1981 in Manhattan, where I was living at the time, I decided to see what he was up to. The Clash had booked a nine-show engagement at Bond's, an old department store on Times Square in Manhattan, and this turned out to be not a good idea. The place wasn't designed to handle the crowds the band drew, and the engagement turned into a nine day standoff between the band and the fire marshals. I attended three nights in a row and can't recall them ever actually making it to the stage and performing. But then, that was business as usual during the glory days of punk, when gigs were forever being shut down, aborted, abruptly canceled. This was political theater, not just music, and nobody embodied that idea more dramatically than the Clash.

Cut to June 14th of the following year and I finally saw the Clash succeed in completing a full set at the Hollywood Palladium in Los Angeles. By then, I'd finally begun to appreciate the breadth and fearlessly experimental nature of the band's music, and Strummer was at the peak of his powers as a showman at that point. The huge hall was packed, and it was as if Strummer was a maestro conducting this undulating mass of sweaty people, and could raise or lower the pitch at will. Boots, beer bottles and articles of clothing flew through the air, and people leapt on stage then leapt back into the arms of their friends, while Strummer stood at the microphone stoking the fire. Somehow he managed to keep the proceedings just a hairsbreadth short of total chaos for two hours. It was a commanding display from a man who clearly knew his job and knew his audience.

Following the break-up of the Clash in 1985, Strummer charged head-on into a busy schedule of disparate projects. He acted in several independent films and composed six film soundtracks, including one – for Alex Cox's lousy film of 1988, Walker – that was remarkably beautiful. I wrote an admiring review of the score for [now defunct] Musician magazine, and a few months after it was published Strummer was passing through L.A. and invited me to lunch in appreciation for the supportive words. We were to meet at a Thai restaurant on Sunset Boulevard, and though I was nervous on the way there, he put me at ease the minute we met. Strummer was such a genuine person that it was impossible to feel uncomfortable around him – I know it sounds corny, but he truly was a man of the people. He was funny and generous in his assessments of people, but he didn't sugar coat things either. He had no trouble calling an asshole an asshole when it was called for. The thing that ultimately made Strummer such a spectacular human being, however, is so simple that it barely seems worth mentioning: he was interested in people. He wanted to hear your story and know what was going on in your neighborhood, he asked how you felt about things and was an empathetic listener – he paid attention! The other thing I immediately loved about him was that he was an enthusiast and a fan.

Just how big a fan he was became clear to me a few months later when he guest hosted a radio show I had at the time on Santa Monica radio station KCRW. My show was at midnight on Saturday, and KCRW's studio is hard to find, so our plan was to meet behind the Foster's Freeze at Pico and 14th at 11:00 P.M. He roared into the parking lot exactly on time in a car with four pals, and the lot of them tore into the record library at the station looking for the records on Strummer's play list. His plan was to play all the records that shaped his musical taste as a teenager in the order that he discovered them, and the show he put together was equal parts history lesson and autobiography. Included in the far-flung set were tracks by Sonny Boy Williamson, Lee Dorsey, Captain Beefheart, Bo Diddley, Hank Williams, and loads of fabulous, rare reggae and dub. His loving introduction to the Beach Boys' "Do It Again" brought tears to my eyes. Several fans crashed the studio when they heard him on the air and realized he was in town, and he welcomed them all. It was a wonderful night. He had fun too, and as he thanked me and said goodnight, he kissed me on the cheek and I blushed.

Strummer spent the next ten years struggling to re-start his career post-Clash and stumbling repeatedly. "The only thing that got me through was sheer bloody-mindedness – I just won't quit!," he told me when I interviewed him in October of 2001. We were talking on the occasion of the release of his second album with his five man line-up, the Mescaleros, Global A Go-Go, which was rightfully hailed as the best work Strummer had done in years. He was happy with the record, and when I saw him perform at the Troubadour a few weeks after we spoke, he seemed happy in general.

"I've enjoyed my life because I've had to deal with all kinds of things, from failure to success to failure again," Strummer told a journalist from Penthouse magazine in 2000. "I don't think there's any point in being famous if you lose that thing of being a human being."

That's something that was never a danger for Strummer. During that last interview, I asked him what the great achievement of punk rock had been, and he replied, "It gave a lot of people something to do." I loved the complete lack of self-importance in that answer, however, this isn't to suggest Strummer ever broke faith with punk. "Punk rock isn't something you grow out of," he told Penthouse. "Punk rock is like the Mafia, and once you're made, you're made. Punk rock is an attitude, and the essence of the attitude is 'give us some truth.'

"And, whatever happens next is going to be bland unless you and I nause everything up," he added. "This is our mission, to nause everything up! Get in there and nause it out, upset the apple cart, destroy the best laid plans – we have to do this! Back on the street, I say. Turn everything off in the pad and get back on the street. As long as people are still here, rock 'n' roll can be great again."

The following conversation took place on the eve of Strummer's final U.S. tour, during the winter of 2001-2002. He died of a heart attack at the age of 50 on December 22, 2002.

You say the great achievement of punk rock was that "it gave a lot of people something to do." What was its great failure?

That we didn't mobilize our forces when we had them and focus our energies in a way that could've brought about concrete social change – trying to get a repressive law repealed, for instance. We're stuck in a kind of horrible holding pattern now, and it seems to me that the only way to change it is if we get hipsters to stay in one place long enough to get elected. The problem is that no hipster wants to get elected.

I saw the Clash several times during their U.S. tours of the late '70s and early '80s, and I remember the sense that something profoundly important was at stake at those shows, that they were about something much larger than pop trends. What was at stake?

In the rush of youth you assume too much – and so it should be – but we felt that the whole machine was teetering on the brink of collapse. Some amazing things went down in Britain during the '70s – the government decided they could disempower the unions by having a three-day week, for instance. Can you imagine that? Monday morning you wake up, and suddenly there's only a three-day week, from Monday to Wednesday. There were garbage strikes, train strikes, power strikes, the lights were going out – everything seemed on the brink, and looking through youthful, excitable eyes it seemed the very future of England was at stake. Obviously, that's very far from the feeling these days, when everything's pretty much smugly buttoned down.

Has England recovered from the Thatcherism that dominated the country during the years you were with the Clash?

It will never recover – and now we've got Blairism. We are so completely confused. If you think of England as a patient lying on the couch in a shrink's office I'd say it's time for the straitjacket. Imagine the party we had in England when Blair got into office after all those years of Thatcher. Everyone was cheering, "This is the dawn of a new day," but since then we've had no vision or justice. The Blair administration just wants to get into bed with the richest corporations, and the very notion of labor has vanished into the mist. Obviously, the worse it gets, the better it gets for artists, so culturally England is doing OK. But politically, it's total mixed-up confusion.

What's the proper course of action when everything around you is falling apart?

It's not a good idea to run away. You gotta smile, whistle, look self-assured, and try and fix things up a bit.

Given that the Clash's music grew out of a situation specific to England, did it strike you as odd that it was embraced in America?

No, because everybody feels the same on a certain level. The Zeitgeist is a real force of nature, and although we don't know how it's transmitted, it's like an invisible tidal wave.

How would you characterize the Zeitgeist now?

I think people are feeling a bit cheated and frustrated. They've come to realize that voting is basically useless because either side you vote for has no more than a shade of difference from the other side, and ultimately politics is about nothing but the mighty dollar. So "OK," say the people, "let's forget politics and get into drugs or skateboarding" – anything that passes the time and gives you some sense of freedom. People want to feel free, and it's a hard feeling to come by in this world. People have a right to change their consciousness, too, and in the back of their minds they know they have that right. So people are gonna flout the laws established to prevent them from smoking marijuana or experimenting with Ecstasy, because they know that nobody – especially a politician half pissed on gin – has the right to tell you what goes on in your mind.

You say it's hard to experience the feeling of freedom: do you feel free?

No, I do not. If I invited nine friends over to my house and put on an acid house record, and we stood in the garden listening to it, we'd all be arrested and fined a thousand pounds each, because in the United Kingdom it's illegal for ten or more people to listen to repetitive beats – this is in the statute books, "Repetitive beats!" People in Britain are much less free than people in many other counties because we've got really repressive laws. All bars there must close at 11:00 P.M., for instance. As to why I continue to live there, I really think all British people have a streak of sadomasochism. I live in the middle of nowhere, so you'd think I could get away with playing a record, but such is not the case.

Why do you live in the middle of nowhere?

I've got no idea! If you wanted to be harsh you could describe the area where I live as nothing but an agribusiness abattoir – all you see are people wearing masks, riding tractors and spraying god knows what onto the ground. I'm a townie, and I don't know what I'm doing out there, although it is nice being able to see all the stars in the heavens at night.

As a rule, people tend to resist change; why is this so?

Because they're afraid of the new and the unknown, and familiarity is comforting. For instance, when you live out in the middle of nowhere as I do, you really appreciate small things, and one of the things I'd come to appreciate was this small bar not far from where I live. The guy who ran it was cool, he kept the lights low, and there would always be interesting jazz playing when you popped in there. In the middle of nowhere, that's like a gold mine. I popped in the other day and the music was gone, it was brightly lit, and a smiling woman chirped, "Can I help you?" The bar had been sold, so the place I knew no longer exists. Arthur Rimbaud said, "Some destructions are necessary," and that's a lesson I'm really trying to learn.

An overriding theme in all of your music is personal and political conflict. Why can't people get along?

I think fear is the corrupting agent, and I don't know how we can eliminate that. Of course, there's no way to eliminate the most terrifying reality – that we all have to die – but at least the sun shines, and we've got a bit of time, so it's not all sniveling. Maybe if every child in the world was shown a really good time, a new breed of human beings would appear. On the other hand, I believe some people are just born bad – I've met a few of them, too. Whether they were born bad, what happened to them was bad, or it was a combination of the two, by the time they're teenagers you can see they're gonna flip. No matter who loves them or what happens to them, they're gonna smash up the room.

Do you believe in karma, or do some people get away with smashing up the room?
Surely karma must be one of the few things we can believe in. Even if it were proved to me that it wasn't in play here on Earth, I'd still hope that in another dimension, in the spirit world, it does exist. I do think it operates in this world.

What forces played a role in shaping your sense of morality?
My mother was Scottish, and a no-nonsense kind of woman, and maybe I got some vibes from her.

What's been the most difficult year of your life?
I took a long breather after the Clash broke up, and I had a really hard time about half way through that. I needed a rest, so I was kind of grateful for the break, but at a certain point I became overwhelmed by a sense of self-doubt. In the music business, an eleven year layoff is like a hundred and eleven years, and I felt like I'd blown it and would never get up there again. The only thing that got me through was sheer bloody-mindedness – I just won't quit! Every time I think, "You've had your lot, now just shut up," a larger part of me says, "No, there are things you can say better than anyone, and you must say them." The other thing that carried me through that period was the fact that I had a lot of responsibilities – I'd managed to have children, and both my parents died during those years.

How were you affected by the death of your parents?
I wasn't close to them, because when I was eight years old I was sent to a boarding school, where I spent nine years. I saw my father once a year between the ages of nine and twelve, then twice a year from then on. As to whether I felt cheated by his absence, I didn't bother with that, because I was in a hard place. You know Tom Brown's *Schooldays*? Imagine being in a second-rate boarding school in South London in 1961. You had to punch or be punched, so I became hard and ceased being a mama's boy pretty quickly.

You've been referred to in the press on several occasions as "the son of a diplomat who dropped out of art school to be a bohemian." Is that an accurate description?
No. In my first ever interview in *Melody Maker*, when I was suddenly regarded as "somebody," I said that my father was a diplomat simply because I wanted to give him his due for one time in his life. My father was an excellent eccentric who liked nothing better than dressing up for a party, and he was great fun, but he was basically a low level worker in the hierarchy of the British embassy, and we actually had fuck all. A four-room bungalow in Croyton was all he managed to accrue during his life, and Croyton is not much of a salubrious suburb.

When you were twenty years old, your older brother, David, committed suicide. How did that mark you?

I was deeply affected by it, and I don't know if I've come to terms with it yet, because it's a mysterious thing to try and understand. We were only separated by 18 months, but we were opposites: whereas I was the loudmouth ringleader who was always getting everybody into trouble, he was quiet and never said much. When we were teenagers in the '60s, there was a load of shouting about Rhodesia, and that led to his becoming a member of the National Front in 1968. At the time, I was too busy listening to Jimi Hendrix to really understand what was going on with him, but I don't think his politics had anything to do with his suicide. I think it had more to do with his shyness.

What's the most valuable thing you could teach your children?
I don't think I've taught them anything, and don't feel like I've been a very good father. My first marriage split up after 14 years when my two daughters were still relatively young, and you feel guilty about that forever. They get born, and suddenly the thing they were born into is pulled apart. It eats away at my mind, particularly since my parents stayed together.

You married again in 1995; what's the secret of a successful marriage?
You have to love your partner more than you love yourself – and I do.

What's the most widely held misconception about you?
That I'm some kind of political thinker: I definitely am not. I think about politics all the time, but it's become increasingly difficult to know what's going on in the world. I grew up hearing my parents go on about World War II, which was an episode of history that seemed very clear: Hitler = bad, everyone else = good. People are basically lazy and we want to see a good guy and a bad guy. Obviously, nothing is black and white, yet we yearn for that beautiful clarity, but I'm finding it more and more difficult to come to those kinds of conclusions – possibly because we're getting more information and we have to sift through it. I used to believe it was possible to learn what was going on in the world by reading the newspaper, but that began to change around the time that the Balkans thing kicked off. Either the newspapers aren't up to snuff or I'm losing my mind, but I found it very difficult to get a grasp on what was going on there.

Do you believe music has a responsibility to address social and political issues?
I do, but I would add that the climate of the times dictates the way people write.

How are you evolving as a songwriter?
Oh god, backwards man! I'm trying to be less idiotic. Every writer likes to feel that when he sits down to write he's gonna zoom off into a new field he didn't even know existed, but the truth is that writing is basically a process of blundering in the dark, and there's a lot of luck that comes into play.

Are there specific issues that are particularly well suited to being addressed in music?
Love – because with music, you have the extra dimension of melody to communicate things that are beyond language.

Name a song that never fails to make you cry.
Hoagy Carmichael's "Georgia." It has a quality of yearning and reminiscence that is incredibly moving to me.

What was the last record you bought?

The Call, by Alan Skidmore, who was a be-bop saxophone player who could probably be described as washed-up, not to be too rude. He went to South Africa and hooked up with a group called Amampondo, and they made this record together that's basically a bunch of crazed drumming with a be-bop guy free falling all over it. It's not bad, but when I put it on everyone else leaves.

What's your favorite Clash song?

I really like the song, "If Music Could Talk," which is on side 21 of *Sandinista!* [Laughs.] I like it because it's quite weird, and it shows we were willing to try stupid things all the time.

What do you miss about being in the Clash?

That was so long ago that it's all faded, and I'm never on the nostalgia tit, but we did have a very good camaraderie and an extremely acute sense of humor. It was fun being in the Clash.

Was there ever a time when you believed the myth of the Clash?

No, and that's why I managed to survive. They say you should never read your press, and that comes in handy when they're saying you suck.

Does the adversarial nature of the music press help keep musicians honest, or does it simply undermine them?

On several occasions it's definitely knocked me for six, but then I'd grudgingly get up and dust my clothes off, and say, "Better that than the other way." The press is harsher in England than it is other places, but I think it's a good thing because it keeps you on your toes and prevents you from getting too pretentious. Yes men tend to collect around famous people, so the conditions are really conducive to becoming pretentious. So you might as well get the mean guys in to flay you alive.

How has fame been of use to you?

It obviously has its uses, but it's really more of a liability than an asset to anyone interested in writing. If you want to write, the first thing is, you've got to experience life like everyone else experiences it. Secondly, you need room to think. If you're incredibly famous, all you can think about is, "Oh my God, has that person over there recognized me, and did I bring enough bodyguards to the supermarket with me." By accident I managed this quite well, because the Clash never went on television in Britain. If you wanted to see the Clash you had to actually get up and go out to one of the shows. Consequently, I'm able to move about Britain without being recognized for the most part.

Are fame and money invariably corrupting?

Definitely. The Clash never had to struggle with the latter of those two things, however, because we never got any money. The music business is a bad racket, and the people on the first crest of a wave never get paid. I don't like to moan on about money, but you have to realize that although you might've heard of the Clash, we didn't sell any records. Nobody sends me five pounds every time somebody's heard of the group. We never had any real power, either, other than in an abstract, poetic way. What I wrote on a piece of paper might influence someone somewhere down the line, and that's something I still take great care with. Not writing things that are stupid, or easily misconstrued is something I keep onboard at all times. But it would've been nice to have the power to say, "50,000 people down to the Houses of Parliament now!" We might've been able to get 1,500 people at the height of our power, but ultimately, it's the big money men who have the power. Then again, I suppose somebody must've seen us as some kind of threat back in the day, because we were constantly being arrested for petty shit. We'd go to play small towns in the North of England and you could almost hear them thinking, "Here they come, those punk rockers from London – we're not having any of that!" So they'd pull over our cars, search us, shake down our motel rooms – it was all very petty.

Does the legacy of the Clash continue to get in your way?

Not any more, because enough time has passed, but certainly, for ten years after the group broke up, I found it difficult to deal with. But I managed to chill long enough that it's allowable for me to come back and knock in a few good albums. It's not pissing anybody off.

You've traveled quite a bit as a touring musician; what's the scariest place you've ever been?

Mozambique. There was a war going on there, and I was only there for a day, but the entire time I was there I was nervous about who might be lurking in the bushes along the roadside. It was also a little unnerving playing Ireland with the Clash, but you have to laugh. You fly in there, you check into the Europa Hotel in Belfast, and the clerk cheerfully informs you that this is the most bombed hotel in Europe. Twenty-eight bombings so far! Then you go up to your room where you ask yourself, "Should I crawl under the bed? Do I dare stand at the window?" We were quite pragmatic and decided to just get on with things, because we couldn't see how either side could gain anything politically by blowing up a rock 'n' roll show. It wasn't as if the whole world was saying, "Oh wow, the Clash are in Belfast." The only people who cared that we were there were the other scrawny punk rockers walking around Belfast.

In A Riot of Our Own, the 1999 book about the Clash written by Johnny Green and Garry Barker, everyone in the band comes off well, with the exception of Mick Jones, who's depicted as being ridiculously obsessed with his wardrobe. Is the book accurate?

Yes it is, but you need some of that in a rock 'n' roll band! If Paul Simonon hadn't been in the Clash I doubt that we would've been as successful as we were, because you need to look stylish. People don't think of Bob Dylan as a glamorous guy, but he was actually pretty good looking. When you think of his Cuban heel phase, with the curly head, the Carnaby Street clothes, the polka-dot tab collars, the tight jeans, the boots – he was pretty styling.

Rumor has it that Bob's had a face-lift.

That's probably a good idea. You have to remember, this is show biz, and it's not as if Bob's a merchant banker or a film critic or something. If he wants to go out on the road for another 20 or 30 years, he's gonna want to tuck it up a bit. It's not as if we're novelists who can hide in our studies like J.D. Salinger and never have our photos taken. It's easy for those people to say, "What the heck." You don't know what it's like having photos taken of yourself all the time. It's appalling to regularly see the destruction of age marked out sharply on your face in photos, videos, and on television. This is a visual thing we do. Johnny Cash dyes his hair, and I think it's only right that we try and scruff up a shambling face.

At what point did you become an adult?

Are you kidding?! I'm nowhere near becoming an adult.

What do you think you represent to the people who admire you?
Maybe they see a good soul.

Tell me about someone who inspires you.
Bo Diddley is inspiring. When he was a young musician starting out he needed some maracas, so he went to the local scrap yard, got some of those floating balls that sit in the tank of a toilet, filled them with black-eyed peas, then used them to invent a whole new kind of music. That's heroic and inspiring.

What's the biggest obstacle you've overcome in your life?
I wouldn't say I've overcome it yet, but it's my sheer laziness. I'd rather sit and watch Popeye cartoons than do anything. Nowadays I'm into *The Simpsons*, *South Park*, and *SpongeBob SquarePants*.

The second album by your current band, the Mescaleros, is dedicated to the late Joey Ramone. What was the nature of his genius?
A sharp intelligence. People think of spirit when they think of the Ramones, but the more I listen to those records the more I'm struck by how smart they are.

Where do you think Joey is now?
He's in heaven.

Do you believe in heaven?
Maybe not for me, but certainly for Joey Ramone.

What's the most one can hope for in life?
The sense of having accomplished something – and I don't have that feeling yet. Being in the line of work I'm in, you hold yourself up against the real greats like Dylan, Ray Davies, Jagger & Richards, Paul Simon, Lennon & McCartney, and John Fogerty. I'm not in that pantheon yet, but I'm gonna get there.

Verlaine in "WHALE TALE"

THE CONCEPT OF **SUCCESS** IN AMERICA IS VERY **STRANGE**.

I THINK IT'S POSSIBLE THAT **TELEVISION** CAUSES THE **UNCONSCIOUS** TO CONFUSE **IMAGE** WITH ACTUAL **HUMANNESS**.

THAT'S WHAT THE **HOLY GRAIL** MYTH IS ABOUT— SOMEBODY WITH A **WOUND** OR **MISTAKE** IN HIM!

HEROIN IS A **MOTHER** DRUG. IT PUTS YOU IN THE WARM SAFETY OF THE **WOMB** WHERE EVERYTHING'S **FINE**.

IF YOU'RE PERSONALLY **INVOLVED** WITH SOMEONE, YOU'RE GOING TO ENCOUNTER **IRRECONCILIABLE** PROBLEMS.

THE LAST **RECORD** I BOUGHT WAS A RECORDING OF **WHALES**.

The END

Tom Verlaine

When Tom Verlaine persuaded Hilly Kristal to book rock acts in his Bowery bar, CBGB, back in 1974, the wheels of American punk rock began to roll. It was there that Verlaine unveiled his band, Television, whose music pivoted on his considerable gifts as a writer, singer, and guitarist. Verlaine has an unusual approach to his instrument that allows him to produce clanging, angular slabs of sound that are simultaneously stark and magisterial. It's a massive sound, and nobody else plays remotely like him. Verlaine is a distinctive vocalist too, and his terse, stuttering singing style is well suited to the very odd songs that he writes.

Born Tom Miller in Delaware in 1949, Verlaine grew up listening to classical music and jazz, and fooling around on the saxophone and the piano. An indifferent student who kept to himself, he was voted "Most Unknown" by the high school in his home town, which he left behind for good in 1968 when he moved to Manhattan. He landed a job in New York at now defunct bookstore the Strand, and in 1971 he formed his first band, the Neon Boys, with his old high school friend Richard Hell. By that point Verlaine was a guitarist of considerable skill, and when the Neon Boys broke up shortly after they'd formed, he embarked on a series of solo performances on electric guitar. In October of 1973, guitarist Richard Lloyd caught one of those performances and immediately recognized that he and Verlaine had compatible musical sensibilities. By March of the following year, Television had officially come into existence, and the group began an extended residency at CBGB, where they played every Sunday night. By 1977, when Television's magnificent first album, Marquee Moon, came out, they were almost famous. The record was hailed as a masterpiece in Europe, and American critics loved it too, but Television broke up the following year after releasing a second album, Adventure. Verlaine continues to make records as a solo artist; the most recent one, Warm and Cool, was his eighth. Released in 1992, it was his first instrumental record. Two years later he took the logical next step and began composing film scores, the first of which was the soundtrack for the 1994 film, Love and a .45. Beginning in 2001, Verlaine began to occasionally do live performances accompanying screenings of silent films.

I interviewed Verlaine twice in the early '80s, when the heat around his career was at its most intense. We met in cafés on the Lower East Side for both interviews, and he struck me as a very odd fellow each time we met. He's not a terribly warm person, and he has a peculiar sense of humor. He's remained admirably true to his own muse, however, and there's no arguing with the music he makes, which is breathtakingly beautiful.

How have you changed over the past few years?

I used to be a lot more wide-eyed about things. You listen to those old blues singers and hear clichés about the world; well, it's all true and it goes on to this very day. Five years ago I was aware that there were people that would come into your apartment at night and steal things, but I didn't believe that people I'd known for years could be thieves. Then I realized that I'd involved myself with people who didn't regard themselves as thieves, but had an inflated sense of their own worth. They considered themselves worth anything they could get. Now I know there are people like that and I've become more cautious, and I think that's a definite change for the good.

Do you feel you've been lucky in life?

On the way here to talk to you today I was thinking that if you're lucky in the music business it's usually the result of two things; one is a certain sort of specialized support offered by kind hearted women, and the other is thieves who help you while taking more than they're entitled to. As to whether I feel I've been lucky – I think everybody gets what they deserve. But then, I just heard on the news that some black civil rights leader has been shot and it's hard to imagine that he deserved it. So maybe that invalidates my claim that people get what they deserve.

Why do you make records?

The obvious reasons; it's fun, it's some kind of art form, and it can be financially rewarding.

Do you tend to see things in terms of good and evil?

No – more in terms of helpful and unhelpful...

Did you have a religious upbringing?

Yeah, Catholic... Catholicism was a real '50s thing. I had to go to mass, confession, all that stuff. Breaking away from it wasn't traumatic, though, because the idea of it never really appealed to me. I can't really say if any of the Catholic doctrine has stayed with me – maybe it has. I recently read a history of the Christian church and what happened was, it became a political structure about 200 years after Christ died and it's been that way ever since. Nobody really knew who this Christ guy was and his words have all been changed over the years to the point that what it's all come down to is oatmeal. But I'm sure it has a soothing effect for some people.

I guess everyone needs to join a club and that's one club you can join.
I suppose rock 'n' roll is another one.

I don't see rock 'n' roll as a club.

I'm referring to Jung's idea that man has a need for some kind of tribal identity.

Did Jung say that? He said there was a collective but he also said there were men who differentiated themselves from the collective. The Greeks supposedly invented the gods to protect themselves from too much "collectiveness" – they created forces that were greater than man. So if a man was a thief he was under the influence of Hermes, who was an interesting god. He was also associated with mirrors, quick thinking, and all sorts of other things.

Are you superstitious?
No, I can't think of any superstitious habits I have.

What are your responsibilities as a pop artist? For instance, do you feel obliged to be informed on current events, or keep up with trends in popular music?
No, and I don't think you can call these things that happen in the newspapers for two weeks trends. A trend is a much larger thing. What did you think of that movie *Network?*

I thought it was heavy handed and obvious.
Maybe so, but it was true. I agree with McLuhan's theory that television has replaced the hearth in the modern home. Everyone knows it's utter trash but people are still hooked on it. When I was growing up I didn't like it. My brother watched it but I never did – I was outside rompin' instead. We lived in the suburbs but there were still places I could go, polluted rivers I could play by. But, back to television, if you take a child, who is like a clean slate, and allow him to become hooked on TV, I think it does hurt his ability to respond. I think it's possible that television causes the unconscious to confuse image with actual humanness.

Did you go to college?
I went to two colleges within six weeks then I quit. This was in 1967. Then I bummed around Delaware for a while then came to New York in the fall of '68. I never liked school in general and never went to classes. I'd go outside and smoke cigarettes instead. The only way I managed to graduate high school was, I had a friend who talked to all my teachers on my behalf. She told them I had a rough family life and was disturbed.

Were you disturbed?
No, although I did find it hard to relate to people at that point in my life.

What sort of non-musical sounds appeal to you?
In Scotland there's this legend of "second hearing" that refers to people who hear not just voices, but all sorts of extrasensory sounds. In fact, Mohammed, before he became a so-called prophet, would wake up in the middle of the night hearing things. He was afraid he was going mad. Then he started hearing books and that's how the Koran came to exist. It's what is known as a revealed book. A lot of people view the whole thing as just a cranky guy who heard voices and got a following. It could certainly be argued that anyone who hears voices will get a following.

Is it necessary to be ambitious and self-serving to be successful?
The concept of success in America is very strange. This culture tends to be very technique oriented, so I don't know if the term self-serving applies. That's a foreign idea to me. Who's an example of a self-serving person?

Iggy Pop makes no bones about the fact that he always comes first.
That might just be his routine. People in rock 'n' roll tend to develop routines. I suppose it's possible that if you perform a routine enough times you come to embody it, but getting back to the original question, to me success is something I feel when I've finished working in the studio or writing. An activity can be successful in and of itself and that's all that matters to me.

Are you interested in making a lot of money?

I'm not gung-ho to make millions. If I had a lot of money I'd probably get a really spectacular apartment in New York, but other than that, possessions don't really interest me. There aren't many objects that I feel any personal attachment to. Objects seem to have a life of their own, and some have pain in them.

How could fame be of use to you?

The poet Robert Graves said, "Fame is good if you want to get something across the border once in a while." Really, what is it good for?

Well some artists use it as a canvas of sorts – I think Bowie has.

I don't think he uses it. I don't mean this against him, but if anything, it probably uses him. He may be completely in control of it but if he's sincere in his professional goal of wanting to be a public figure – well that strikes me as completely naïve. Nixon had a similar goal, and most people who aspire towards that sort of public life fail to assume the responsibility of it.

What's the most overrated idea currently held by Western culture?

There are a lot of them. The "life of the artist" is certainly an overrated notion. And that phrase sheds even more light on what I'm saying. It is a life – not a product one can acquire, which seems to be attitude held by the middle class. Take a poetry class and you're an artist. Most people really have no idea what being an artist is about – and I'm not saying I do either. But, it does seem to be something you're born to, whether you're born to it at day one or when you're 23. Whichever, it's something that ought not to be taken up arbitrarily.

How do you see your music evolving?

I don't see an evolution – I see it going through the same thing in different ways. It's been said of Beethoven that his music wasn't "about" anything but qualities – his music was the voice of qualities and that's something I can understand. I like strong simple beats, although at the moment I'm thinking about doing something without drums.

What do you think about the Brian Eno School of ambient recording?

His first album had a few neat things on it, but the ones after that – there's a desperate grasping for ideas in that school of music. Eno's music certainly has its own sound, but ideas, ideas, ideas! Basically I'm just not all that attracted to that music.

Do you have any heroes?

There are people I admire but I wouldn't call them heroes. I admire Robert Graves. There are guitar players whose work I've liked over the years; John McLaughlin when he first came to New York and was playing with Miles Davis, Michael Bloomfield when he was playing on Dylan's records, the guitar player in the Band – that was a group I really liked.

Do you believe in the myth of romantic love?

I don't think romantic love is a myth. I think it can have a redeeming quality, although I don't think it can transform a person's behavior for more than six weeks. It's all commitment. It may be a gift you receive and if you want to keep it you have to work at it, like anything else.

Is charisma an absolute quality or is it always subjective?
In the '70s it seemed to be a thing people tried to put on like a suit of clothes.

What qualities do you look for in people?
It's easier to define what turns me off in people. There are some people who put no limits on themselves and think they can carry their behavior as far as they like, and I don't care for those types of people. Heavy heroin users tend to be that way. I've been close to a few heavy heroin users and there's no question that drug creates completely selfish people.

Are you then attracted to disciplined rather than reckless people?
I don't think of heroin as reckless. I like spontaneous people but you don't encounter them too often because most people are programmed to behave in particular patterns, and live by beliefs they're not even aware they hold.

What is the ultimate act of courage?
Personally I find patience to be the quality I most need and most lack. They say there are seven deadly sins and seven heavenly virtues – it's an old proverb but it still holds true today. Greed, sloth, gluttony, lust, pride – all of those things are still fouling up the world. But courage – one's definition of that is always very personal, and it's something you need every five seconds of the day.

–1982–

IDLE WORSHIP
I honestly can't believe that people worship rock stars. When people go to bed at night they don't feel that musicians are religious figures who change history the way Mohammed did. For most people music is just a good time and a way to release tension. I mean, do you really think people took cues from Dylan?

WRITING
Every writer reveals something of his life in his writing – maybe he reveals some part of his death. Some people manage to assemble songs in a very detached way, but if that detachment is forced I don't think you'll get a good song. You're most apt to get a good song when any notions you might have about "good writing" have collapsed. I've always felt that good writing has to involve another person, not necessarily as a subject, but as someone you're involved with.

ROAD TO REALITY
Genuine life is one inch gone in retreating. Genuine life is the one you find without looking for it.

PICKS TO CLICK
The last record I bought was a recording of whales. It's a beautiful record – I found it for 49 cents so I picked it up. I don't have a record player but I'm getting one tomorrow, I hope.

BOWIE'S KINGDOM COME
I didn't go along with the Bowie version of "Kingdom Come" myself but it's always a thrill to hear someone else interpret your work even if you don't like what

they do with it. I'd love to hear Ray Charles do that song – I bet he'd do a great version.

ADVICE TO THE LOVELORN
If you don't relate at all you won't have problems. But if you're personally involved with someone you're going to encounter some irreconcilable problems.

IRELAND
I'd like to see Ireland. Ireland has the lowest suicide rate, the lowest of all self-destructive rates of any country, plus it has a mythology and sense of history. I have a feeling the mythology is still alive there right down to the grass growing on the ground. I've read a little about the old Irish poets and there's a legend of a real poet who lived before the Christian influence who could rhyme rats to death. That was part of becoming a poet then, and that idea is so beyond anything that's called poetry today.

DRUGS
I have these theories about the uses of various drugs. Drugs have two sides, a healing side and a destructive side, and to me, heroin is a mother drug. It puts you in the warm safety of the womb where everything's fine. I've noticed that people with heroin troubles frequently have problems with their mothers. I've taken heroin but I'm not a junkie, nor was I ever a junkie, even though some people thought I was. Why did I take it? Well hell, why not? I didn't shoot the jazz up because I'm not into that sort of self-image and it didn't affect my work at all. I took the stuff because I got beat up and these guys broke my rib. The first time you take it it's a great painkiller, but the second time you have to take twice as much to get the same effect. Actually it doesn't kill pain – it just creates this womb effect of warmth and safety, and maybe people who didn't get that feeling when they were growing up need that feeling. That feeling becomes paradise for them and they become addicted to it. Maybe I had a good family that gave me the basics so that I don't crave that sensation. But then maybe other people got the basics too but want more. There is greed in the world and it operates in all sorts of ways.

THE HOAX OF THE NEW
Pablo Casals said that, "The desire for innovation leads to greater aberrations in art than would acceptance of what's already there." I think he's definitely got a point.

MORAL OBLIGATION
If you have a friend who's being set up and you have a friend who's a judge then maybe it's your job to go in there and say, "Hey, this is way off." I've never been in that position myself, but a guy does have an obligation to do what he can. I'm beginning to think that things have always been and always will be corrupt, but then, I don't know history well. Somebody recently told me that the Renaissance culture was not corrupt and that there were periods in India when the caste system was a successful thing. You do need people to make wheels and there are people who are happy doing that stuff. But between the post-war years and the '60s there was a real turning point away from and disdain for handwork. I can see it in my own family, in my father's generation, the idea that it's beneath you to work with your hands.

MAX ERNST
I've been reading some things written by the painter Max Ernst. It's a book I've looked for for years that includes a little bit of his writings. It's not a serious book of

aesthetics by any means – I find I can't read that stuff at all. Ernst had a sense of humor and wrote about his life in a very interesting way. He was a funny guy – I guess you might say he was an artist.

THE PAST

I don't feel nostalgic about the New York music scene of the '70s, but I might when I'm 50 years old. Who knows? I recently realized that Television has influenced a lot of English bands. Echo and the Bunnymen, U2, The Teardrop Explodes – it's obvious what they've listened to and what they're going for. When I was 16 I listened to Yardbirds records and thought, "God, this is great." It's gratifying to think that people listened to Television albums and felt the same.

FASHION

On the way over here I saw these two guys who were probably in some type of English band like Adam & the Ants, and I realized that whenever I've met people who project a very stylish appearance they've always turned out to be disappointing. People who draw attention to their physicality as being something other than physicality are disappointing in even half-assed intimate situations. Style to me is incidental. The British are very adept at creating it for its own sake, but the best style is incidental. John Coltrane had a style but it was totally incidental to what he was.

RECIPE FOR REDEMPTION

Sometimes old songs will run through my mind and I'll think, "Oh, that line isn't right." But a little bit of failure can be a good thing. In India, when they weave marriage blankets, they make them perfect until they get to the end, then they put in this little screwed-up thing. They say that little mistake is what lets you in. That's what the Holy Grail myth is about – somebody with a wound or "mistake" in him. I think you just have to accept that wound because it might contain its own healing factor. Accepting that wound might be the first ingredient in some kind of recipe.

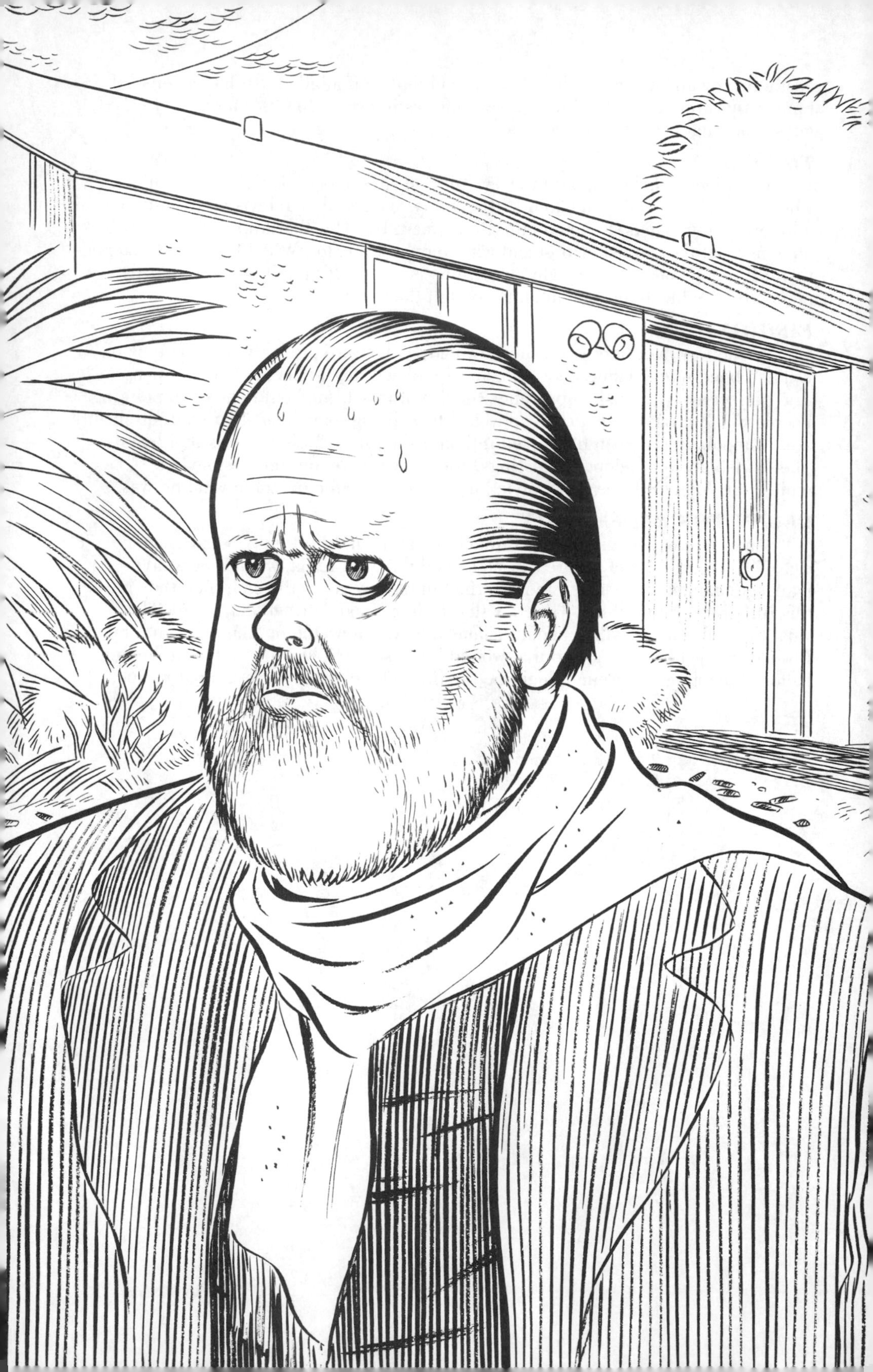

Orson Welles

....

*In 1984 I met a guy named Bob Kensinger. A graduate of the Rhode Island
School of Design, he'd moved to Los Angeles from the East coast to pursue a career as
a filmmaker, but he was working for a catering company when our paths crossed. Food
catering was decidedly less exotic than Kensinger's previous job as personal assistant to
the great Orson Welles, but that was a job he chose to leave. Welles was not an easy man
to work for. He was, however, never dull, and every time I ran into Kensinger I'd beg
him to tell me stories about the time he spent at Welles' house on Wonderland Avenue.
Kensinger had a real gift for recounting the ignominious closing chapter in the life of
this great man; he had a good eye for telling detail, and he told his stories with a
pleasing mixture of tenderness and humor. In 1993 I finally sat Kensinger down and
spent several hours interviewing him in order to preserve his stories for posterity. In the
interest of brevity I've eliminated my questions to create the following first-person
narrative.*

In 1978, when I was 22, I moved to L.A. to break into the movie business. I
arrived here with zero money and no place to live, and for a while I drove a meat
truck. Then one day early in 1979 a neighbor of mine told me she knew someone
who'd been working for Orson Welles, so I tracked the guy down. He didn't say a
word about how hard it was to work for Orson, he just asked me if I was interested,
and I said definitely.

Citizen Kane had been out of circulation for most of the '50s and '60s, but it came
back in a big way when I was a film student at the Rhode Island School of Design in
the mid-'70s. There were posters for it plastered all over the campuses at Brown and
RISD, and I remember thinking that it looked like a really cheesy production, but I
went to see it anyway and was blown away. We were used to seeing European movies
in film school, which were great, and Hollywood movies, which were almost uniformly
lousy, but *Citizen Kane* was something entirely different. The camera work was
amazing, and something about it was so inventive that I made a point of seeing all of
Welles' other films. By the time I graduated I had it in my head that I wanted to work
for him.

This guy who'd worked for Orson gave me a number to call, and after several
attempts to reach someone I was told to go to KCOP where Orson was taping a
talk/magic show with Burt Reynolds and Angie Dickinson. Orson had rented the studio
space and was footing the bill for the shoot, but he wasn't there when I arrived, and I
ended up talking to Burt Reynolds and Orson's companion, Oja Kodar. They knew
why I was there and I got the feeling I'd have the job if they approved of me. After
about ten minutes of small talk they handed me the keys to Orson's huge Chrysler

convertible parked outside in the lot, and told me to go up to his house and get him.

Orson always rode around with the top down, and he'd had the seats electrified so he could get in and out easily. He hadn't driven in about 15 years because he'd been ticketed so many times for speeding that he'd permanently lost his license. He claimed he'd driven to the studio in a horse and carriage for a while. I drove this boat of a car up to his house on Wonderland Avenue in Laurel Canyon, and when I got to his place I couldn't believe where he was living. He was renting a crummy little tract house, one of those early '60s sloped hard-edged buildings – it was such a shabby, unemotional piece of architecture. I rang the bell, and as I stood there waiting I looked around and noticed there were hundreds of cigars piled up in the garden, which was mostly weeds and dead plants. I later learned that whenever Orson went into the house he'd throw his cigar in the yard, creating these mounds of cigars everywhere. He only smoked Macanudos, which cost a fortune, and he'd smoke them only halfway before tossing them in the yard.

After what seemed like a long time, the door opened a crack, a hand jutted out holding a pair of shoes, and a voice said, "Please put these in the car." I followed these instructions and returned to the door. This time some clothes on hangers were thrust out and the voice said, "I'll be right out." I waited in the car for a while before the door finally opened and there he was. His face was a complete blank as he walked to the car, and he didn't say a word after he got in. I said hello, he said, "Hello." Then he said, "Shall we go?" I tried to make small talk as we drove along, but he said, "Can we please not talk?" I thought, "Oh man, this sucks, I'm gonna quit today." But after we got to the studio and he'd done an interview with Burt Reynolds, he came over to me and was the soul of amiability. "Please come back tomorrow," he said, so I did. I started working for him in February of 1979, and at the end of my first week on the job he sent me a note requesting that I address him as Mr. Welles. I did that for a while, but after a few weeks I went back to calling him Orson and he didn't seem to mind.

In general, he was pretty vague about what I was supposed to be doing for him and I found that frustrating. I definitely didn't want to be his valet, and fortunately those duties fell to another guy who was working for him. Alan was a young guy from the San Fernando Valley who only knew Orson from talk shows and commercials, and was only working there to save enough money to buy a car. He never stopped bitching about Orson, who meant absolutely nothing to him. Orson was definitely a major pain in the ass, but I was still awed by his talent. Alan talked about him with zero reverence, and he did really malicious things to him. If Orson was looking for a shirt from the cleaners and Alan was too lazy to go get it, he'd tell Orson the cleaners had lost the shirt. On one of my first days working with Orson, we were all sitting in the front room and Orson asked Alan to bring him a pair of scissors. It was hard for Orson to get in and out of chairs, and Alan, who was just flipping through a magazine, hollered back, "What for?" Orson looked at me, then he looked at the kid, and answered, "So I can stab you with them."

Orson hired me because he hated this other guy and wanted me to replace him, but I made it clear I didn't want to be an errand boy. Orson said, "Fine, I'll keep you with me and put him on shit duty." So the other guy did the shopping and took care of his clothes, and I was with Orson all the time. Orson paid me well – I got about $400 a week, which was pretty good at the time – and I was always paid in cash. He never used checks or credit cards because his finances were a mess. The way he spent money was one of the most eccentric things about him – he'd blow it right and left. He wasn't materialistic, but he never hesitated to get anything he wanted at any given moment, and he'd spend until his money ran out, then do something to get some more. Almost every penny he spent went toward his work. At the time I was working for him he'd just made a ton of money on those Paul Masson wine commercials. I think he got half a million dollars for them and he did them in three weeks.

My usual routine was to show up at his house at nine or ten in the morning. Orson worked every day and was never idle, and although he was around 60 then, he still had stamina like you wouldn't believe. This was doubly impressive when you consider that he weighed 350 pounds. He seemed to be in good health, but he went to a doctor once a week. He had back problems, which he never complained about despite the fact that he was often on his feet for 12 hours when we were working, and he had high blood pressure. But he just kept on slugging away. He never took any prescription medication that I knew of, or any other kind of drug. He wasn't supposed to drink, but he'd often knock back three double zombies with dinner. I never saw him drunk, though – he held his liquor very well. He once told me that when he was shooting *Touch of Evil* in Venice, California he'd had to do a scene where he fell into one of the canals. "If you think the water in those canals is dirty now, you should have seen it then – it was absolutely filthy," he said. He fell in headfirst and inhaled all this disgusting water, and when he got out he was so miserable that he got a fifth of gin and downed the whole thing. "I felt so polluted," he explained, "that I had to clean out my system." I thought it was funny that he cleaned out his system with a fifth of gin.

I was supposed to have two days off a week, but Orson would call at any hour of the night or day if he wanted something. He'd often say, "I have something to do tomorrow – I'll call you in the afternoon." It drove me nuts because I never knew when I'd be free, and some of my friends made fun of me for being Orson's "slave." But I never got over how surreal it was being 24 years old and living in Hollywood, and having Orson Welles call me every day.

He'd get up at seven each morning, put on his bathrobe and go straight to the typewriter. He had a little sitting area surrounded with books that was by a window in the front of the house and he had a Smith-Corona typewriter there. It was a horrible, claustrophobic little space, but he had a big comfortable padded chair, and he'd sit there typing. He'd type my agenda for the day, and type notes to people who might be interested in putting money into *The Other Side of the Wind*, which was the film he was trying to complete at the time. It starred John Huston as an aging, washed-up Hollywood director, and Peter Bogdanovich, Jack Nicholson, and Oja Kodar were in it too. The film was never released because the negative somehow wound up being owned by the government of Iran, and despite all of Orson's efforts, he could never get it back. So, he'd sit there doing paperwork for that film and sometimes he actually wrote. He had a few scripts going at the time, and he'd completed one called *The Deep* that he wanted to direct and he sent that out a lot. But he was mostly involved in the magic shows and TV specials he was financing on his own. He completed three or four of them, but I don't think he ever sold any of them. Orson was an adequate magician, but his real skill was as a storyteller – he'd take the simplest trick and draw you into it with a wonderful, mysterious story. In fact, the most valuable thing I learned from watching him work is that you can make something from nothing in film and make anything look great if you're creative enough. Orson did some amazing things with nothing – he was great at using black backgrounds, for instance. He often shot people on black, and it would be incredibly dramatic.

Orson's house was small, with a brown carpet, a flagstone fireplace, and a sloped ceiling with beams going across it. There were no mementos and no art on the walls, and it felt almost like a hotel room. He didn't do anything to leave a personal mark on the place. It was very dark and the living room had a reclining Barcalounger where he'd sometimes sit and watch TV. He watched *All in the Family* religiously and thought it was the best piece of TV programming ever – he'd just crack up at Meathead. He never played music at home and if I turned on the radio in the car, he immediately turned it off. He never went to a movie or rented a video, and he never entertained. I got the impression he didn't want people to know where he lived – not because he was ashamed, but because he was cynical about being in Hollywood. He loved Europe and hated L.A., and he often said that if it weren't for the money he'd never set foot here again. He grumbled about the smog in L.A. and called the people in Beverly Hills mummies. When we were driving, he'd look at them and snarl, "Cadavers – there's no sign of life there." But he courted them, of course, when he needed to raise money.

He went to Ma Maison [restaurant] almost every day. Maybe it was because of the European flavor the place had, or because industry people would come up and pay homage to him there, but he loved the place. One day Orson called me and said, "Alan's disappeared with my car" – which was something Alan did regularly – "and I have to go to lunch at Ma Maison. It's very important and I need a ride desperately." I said, I'm happy to take you Orson, but you know I have a Volkswagen bug, and he said, "I know, I know, God! Just get up here!" So I drove to his house, and when he came out and saw me sitting in my car he just shook his head. But he was determined. With a tremendous amount of effort he managed to get into the car, but his chest and stomach were smashed into the glove box. He was obviously very uncomfortable, but he didn't say a word, so I started driving down through Laurel Canyon. The car was leaning so dramatically to the right that I had trouble making the turns. He had a cigar in his mouth when he got in the car, and halfway to the restaurant he decided he had to light it and started fumbling for a match. I told him there were matches in the glove box, which he started struggling to open, and after a good deal of effort on both our parts we extracted some matches from the glove box. He lit the cigar, and for the rest of the ride the ashes dropped down the front of his shirt because he couldn't ash the thing. Finally we pulled into Ma Maison and the valet guys, who all knew him, couldn't believe their eyes. They were all smiles as they opened his door and said, "Hello, Mr. Welles," but as he was getting out of the car his foot got caught in the stretchy map compartment on the car door. He quietly said, "Bob, could you please help me, my foot's stuck," so I got out and helped him lift his foot out of the map compartment. He then proceeded to walk proudly into the restaurant as if nothing had happened.

To the back of the house were Orson's bedroom and bathroom. On his dresser he had a row of fake thumbs that he used for hiding things in magic tricks, his change purse, and a bottle of Jean Nate body splash. When I think of Orson, that's what comes to mind – the smell of cigars and Jean Nate. His closet was filled with 20 or 30 very expensive, identical black cotton shirts with large side and breast pockets that reminded me of Captain Kangaroo. He had them custom-made by an Italian tailor with a shop on Sunset Boulevard across from the Chateau Marmont.

Orson never spoke about his body – it was a taboo subject. People used to say to me, "He must eat all day," but he didn't. In fact, we'd go through ten-hour runs of work and he wouldn't eat a thing. But when he did eat, he ate for five people. Eating was very important to him, and it was a big part of his life. He and Oja never really cooked, and when he was at home he ate lots of Chunky Beef Campbell's Soup and ice cream. When other people were around I think he was a bit embarrassed about his relationship with food, but with me he didn't care and he'd eat whatever he wanted. He loved steak tartar and shark's fin soup, and when he had to have a certain type of food he'd go out of his way to get it. One time we were driving home from work and he insisted that I stop at Baskin Robbins because he had to have an ice cream cone. I told him I'd go in and get it for him, but he said, "No, just drop me off and circle the block, then pick me up." So I left him at this heavily trafficked intersection on Sunset Boulevard, went around the block and came back, and there he was, big Orson Welles, standing on this busy corner eating an ice cream cone.

His bathtub was filled with a heap of old encyclopedias and Bibles. He wasn't religious, but he loved ancient literature and history, and I guess he read those books while he was sitting on the toilet. I think he used his swimming pool as a bathtub. One morning when I arrived for work, the house was unusually quiet and there was nobody around. The car was in the driveway so I knew he had to be there, so I looked around and called his name. When I looked out the window at the backyard I noticed a little beach ball in the pool, and thought to myself, "Why would Orson have a beach ball?" It struck me as odd. After looking around some more I looked out the window and saw the beach ball again, then all of a sudden it started turning at this very funny pace. Just as his face came into view in surreal slow motion, I realized it was Orson wearing this weird colored shower cap. Then he suddenly lumbered out of the pool naked and tiptoed across the yard with this swim cap on. I ran back into the living room and grabbed a magazine so he wouldn't know I'd seen him.

I always thought of Orson as "old intelligence" because he knew the classics and was almost an Elizabethan character himself. It often happened that I'd be talking to him about something and I'd suddenly realize he just wasn't relating to what I was saying. He never expressed any interest in anything I knew about that he didn't know about, and that always annoyed me. It was always a one-way street with him, and I think that was partly attributable to the fact that he wasn't in the contemporary world at all. Being with Orson was like entering a time warp, because he saw Hollywood as it had been in the '40s and '50s, and he did things in 1980 exactly as he'd done them in 1945. He was slightly bitter about the success the young generation of directors was having at the time, but he never disparaged the talent of another director, and felt they deserved whatever success they were having. I think it bothered him a lot that he was cut off from the young generation in Hollywood, but he didn't court them. He often talked about himself as if he were some kind of dinosaur, and he seemed to feel that although his stuff was very artistic and had served a purpose in its time, the art form was different today. In fact, his films still look incredibly fresh. He had a really special way of moving people through a frame, and there was always so much going on in every shot. Next time you see *Othello* or *Touch of Evil*, which are my favorite of his films, look at the backgrounds. It's amazing how beautifully choreographed they are.

Next to his bedroom was a room for Oja Kodar, who was an artist. She made these amorphous, organic-looking plaster sculptures, very late-'60s, Claes Oldenburgish forms, and there were lots of them around the house. She was a beautiful, exotic-looking woman in her early 40s and she and Orson did everything together. I think they really loved each other and that he was faithful to her. He couldn't really get around on his own so he would've had a hard time cheating on her, but I don't think he had the desire to – I think his sex life was essentially over. I have no idea what his sex life was like at that point, because he never talked about sex to me, nor did he ever ask about my personal life.

Even though he lived with Oja, he remained married to his wife, Paola [Mori], who lived in Las Vegas. Whenever she came to L.A. Orson would check into the Beverly Wilshire, so he and Oja were obviously trying to hide their relationship from Paola. Every once in a while he'd send me to Las Vegas to deliver money to Paola – he'd put me on a plane and I'd get there and deliver something to her, then fly right back.

Orson wasn't the kind of person who could be alone, and he needed somebody around at all times. Even late at night after we'd been working all day and he'd done a talk show, he'd often drag me to a restaurant rather than go home, and then he'd sit there making small talk for hours. He seemed to keep his friends on a tether, only pulling them in when he needed company, and in all the time I worked for him I never once saw a friend drop by. His phone didn't ring much because everyone had to call him through his lawyer, and although he had three children I never saw any of them either. As far as I know, they never came around. He never went to parties, although he was invited a lot, but when he was trying to raise money he'd dress up and take people to nice restaurants. These people were mostly dentists and lawyers. Every once in a while he'd have meetings at Ma Maison with people like Spielberg, but essentially he was out of the game and the film community wasn't there for him in any way. I think he was ostracized for a few reasons. Some people hated him because he was a prodigy and sometimes behaved like a show-off, but the thing that really screwed him up was his reputation for not being able to control money. He never had any accounting whatsoever for what he spent, and it was widely known in the industry that he was unreliable when it came to completing his films – in fact, *Citizen Kane* was the only film he ever finished editing. What typically happened was he'd finish shooting a movie, then get an acting job and just take off. From what I heard the footage he shot in South America, which was finally released as the documentary *It's All True*, was mostly worthless, but Orson made it sound as if he were the victim and the film had been taken away from him. It's obvious he was just fucking around and wouldn't admit it.

Orson treated everybody equally, except if you were working for him, in which case he treated you like a tool. As a boss, he was overbearing, demanding and selfish, and on a set he saw everyone as existing solely to facilitate his creativity. At the same time, he was very respectful of actors and actresses. He loved Angie Dickinson, for instance, and was also fascinated by Marlene Dietrich. There were plenty of people he had negative opinions of, though. He disliked Joan Collins, and thought Greta Garbo was completely vacuous. He seemed to have a love/hate relationship with Peter Bogdanovich, and if you brought his name up Orson would chortle and say, "Peter's got some problems." He despised John Houseman after their Mercury Theater collaboration deteriorated into petty competition for roles on and off the screen, and he never forgave the actor Robert Shaw for accidentally burning down his house in Spain and destroying all his personal mementos. When Shaw died Orson said, "I hope he burns in hell." He also disliked Victor Mature, maybe because they were rivals over Rita Hayworth for a while. Orson told me that one time Victor Mature was in a movie he was directing, and there was a scene that called for Mature to fall backwards into a deep mud puddle. He needed somebody to help him get out of the puddle because he was wearing heavy wardrobe. It was the last scene of the day and the sun was setting, and Orson told everybody on the crew that he had a plan. So they shot the scene of Mature falling in the mud puddle and Orson immediately said, "OK, wrap it up everybody, let's get out of here," and they left Mature in the mud.

The most important person in his life was Skipper Hill, who'd been the athletics coach and headmaster at a school Orson attended in Woodstock, Illinois, and he served as a mentor/father figure to him for most of his life. Skipper was 20 or 30 years older than Orson, but they were incredibly close and they wrote four textbooks on Shakespeare together. He was a very theatrical man, and, like Orson, he used a vocabulary nobody in the modern world uses. Orson had been fucked over so many times that he didn't trust anybody else and Skipper was his Rock of Gibraltar. The first time Skipper visited I went to pick him up at the airport, and there he was with his wife – they were quiet, humble, country types who were really polite. But the minute Orson saw Skipper he changed from Orson Welles the figurehead into a child.

It was amazing to see Orson completely let down his defenses and become a real person who didn't have to pretend any more.

Orson's other great love was his dog Blitz, a poodle the size of a baked potato. Orson would spend the day booming in stentorian tones, and the minute he got home and saw Blitz, he'd shift into this high-pitched baby talk. He loved going home to Blitz, and it used to scare the shit out of me when he'd walk in the house because Blitz would run in between his legs while Orson lumbered over to the couch. I'd watch, thinking one false move and that dog is history, but he never stepped on him.

When I first started working for him, I kept asking questions about *Citizen Kane*, but Orson made a rule that I was only allowed to ask one question a week about his past. He rarely answered questions from anybody about *Citizen Kane*. In fact, whenever he did talk shows he'd send a letter in advance instructing them not to bring it up because he wanted to be identified with other films he'd made that he was equally proud of. I once asked him who had played Hitler in the opening newsreel footage in *Kane*. With Orson, every question elicited a long story, and there was a long story about this, too, but the short version is that Hitler was played by a waiter he'd spotted in a restaurant on Hollywood Boulevard. At first the waiter refused to do the part, so Orson went to dinner there every night and harassed him into agreeing. When I asked him about the *Kane* sets, which looked to me like some of the most elaborate sets ever made, he told me, "Those were the cheapest sets I ever had. That was a low-budget film and the sets were cardboard." I also asked him about Bernard Herrmann, who composed the music for *Kane*, and he fumed, "Hitchcock stole him from me!"

Orson told me once that one of his directing techniques was to throw a tantrum during the first day on the set. He said he did it as a way of gaining control and letting people know who was boss, and I saw him do it many times with absolutely no provocation. Barbara Leaming tells a story in her biography of Orson about the actor who played Iago in *Othello*. He walked up to Orson on the set after not having seen him for a while and said, "Hi," and Orson absolutely exploded. "Is that how you greet the director of this motion picture? You just say, 'Hi?'" I witnessed these outbursts directed at unsuspecting targets many times, and it would quiet a set down in seconds. The attacks were reserved strictly for men, however, and even the bimbos he used in his magic shows were treated with kid gloves. He wasn't sexist at all, and he was totally color-blind, too. He loved Hispanic people and felt completely at home with them, and he never had a bad thing to say about any race.

I was the victim of one of his tantrums one night when we were at Lucy's El Adobe having dinner with the crew from a magic show we were shooting. Orson was talking about what an awful actor Dustin Hoffman was and how much he hated method acting, and I said that *Midnight Cowboy* was one of my favorite films, and that I thought Hoffman was great as Ratso Rizzo. Orson always got hostile when he was challenged, and he put down his fork and screamed, "Don't you ever make another cuntish comment like that again!" I stood up and said, "That's my opinion," threw the car keys on the table and walked out. After a while, he came outside and sheepishly handed me the keys and got in the car, but I refused to say a word all the way home. When we got to his house he invited me in, and I said, "I'm going home because I'm hungry and tired." He reached in his pocket and handed me 50 dollars and said, "Go have a really great dinner on me." That was the closest he could come to apologizing.

After I'd been working for Orson for about eight months, I quit because I'd been offered a job doing a rewrite on a Roger Corman film. I told him I was going to work on a movie because I had come to L.A. to direct, and he said, "Bob, don't waste your time – you'll never be a director. YOU WILL NEVER DIRECT!" I was shocked and I flashed him a look of contempt that he obviously saw, because he added, "It's my duty to tell you how impossible it is to get that job in this town. If you want to direct, go to some small town and make your movie there, but don't waste your time here." I quit anyhow, and on my last day at his house he said, "I'll tell you what's going to happen. You'll work for these people, and whatever job you came in with is the job you'll be stuck with – that's the only way they'll ever see you." He was absolutely right, of course. Though I'd been promised various things by the Corman people, they let me go after they'd wrung what they wanted out of me.

A year later I found myself with nothing happening, so I called Orson and asked him if he needed anybody and he hired me again. That was at the beginning of 1980, and I worked for him until the fall, then quit again for good. I just couldn't take the phone calls in the middle of the night any more. One night shortly before I quit, I took Orson over to do the Carson show, and at the end of the evening he was hungry and wanted to go get something to eat. When I brought the car around he said, "Somebody stole my money out of the dressing room and now I have no money to eat with." One of the wonderful things about Orson was that as cantankerous as he was, he let any situation roll off his back. "I was robbed," he told me that night, and I never heard another word about it. It was just life as far as he was concerned, and I think that attitude was the result of years of making movies, which is basically nothing more than one problem after another. Anyhow, I told him I had 12 dollars and he said, "Great, let's go to *Pink's*," which was a cheap hot dog stand he liked. As we were driving along he suddenly asked me to pull over and said, "I have an extra pair of pants in the truck and there's probably some money in the pockets." He found another eight dollars and said, "Then it's the *International House of Pancakes*." We were just about to pull into the parking lot when I suddenly remembered that I'd received my first credit card in the mail that day. He was ecstatic. "Why didn't you say so!" he said. "That means it's *Don the Beachcomber!*," which was his favorite restaurant. So we went to Don's and when we walked in everyone greeted him, he was shown to his favorite table, and they brought him his gold, engraved chopsticks, which were enshrined in a case in the middle of the room with the chopsticks of other famous people. After he ordered, he said to the waiter, "My son here would love to have the same thing as me" – he was in a very generous, emotional mood.

As we were eating we noticed a family across the room staring at us, and eventually the father sent his son over for an autograph. Orson was cordial and he waved to the family across the room, then, as we were driving home, we saw the same family walking down Hollywood Boulevard. Orson said, "Look at that family. They all love each other and they're all together – what lucky, lucky people," and he didn't say another word for the rest of the ride home. He was incredibly melancholy that night, and I saw a side of him I'd never seen before. I realized at that point what a heavy price he'd paid for the things he'd accomplished in his life. I think he always wanted a family, but his ambition drove him in a way that made that impossible. With some people the creative drive is so strong that it forces you to forego everything else, and I think that's how it was with him. His need to create made him give up a lot.

He was very distraught the second time I quit. He said, "What's the problem this time," and I told him I wanted to go write. He said "I'll give you plenty of time to write, we'll make the hours," but I knew the phone calls in the middle of the night would never stop and I couldn't take it any more. I never saw him again after my last day at work in 1981, and I don't know what he did in the four years after I stopped working for him until 1985 when he died. I heard that he moved out of the house in Laurel Canyon and bought a house in Beverly Hills that was said to be bigger and nicer, but I don't think much happened.

The Artists

....

Max Andersson [John Lydon], born in Sweden, made his English-language comics debut with the junk-culture graphic novel *Pixy*. A prolific contributor to the now defunct anthology *Zero Zero*, he now produces the *Death & Candy* comics series. He currently resides in Berlin.

Jim Blanchard [Kristine McKenna] is the cartoonist behind the comics *Bad Meat* and *Cruel World*, and the retina damaging poster art collection *Glam Warp*. He is best known in comics circles for inking 15 issues of Peter Bagge's *HATE*. His recent work includes collaboration with Jim Goad on the hilarious comic *Trucker Fags in Denial*, and the exhibition of psychedelic paintings and portraiture in the finer galleries of the art world.

Charles Burns [Exene Cervenka, Iggy Pop], who cut his teeth in *RAW* during the early 1980s, combines an E.C. fetishist's line quality with the traumas of adolescence and alienation. In 1994 he began the most ambitious work of his career, the horror comic *Black Hole* (the 12th and final issue is scheduled for release in early 2005!). A prolific illustrator, Burns' work includes ads for Altoids, covers for *Time* and *The New Yorker*, and album covers for Iggy Pop and many others. Burns lives in Philadelphia with his wife and children.

Frankie Chan [Chrissie Hynde] currently lives in Los Angeles, CA, by way of Seattle, WA, and Bloomington, IN. After years of making rock posters, he made the jump into comics in 2003 with two minicomix entitled *this is how we party*. Chan is now working on a full-length graphic novel and in his free time enjoys dj'ing and being a punk.

Dan Clowes [Orson Welles] is the creator of the legendary comic book *Eightball*, as well as the Oscar-nominated screenwriter for the film adaptation of his best-selling graphic novel, *Ghost World*. His most recent work includes *Eightball #23* and his second feature-length film collaboration with director Terry Zwigoff, *Art School Confidential* (scheduled for release in 2005). Clowes lives with wife Erika and son Charles in Oakland, CA.

Bob Fingerman [Joey Ramone], a 2002 Society of Illustrators Silver Medalist, is best known for the 1990s-era comic *Minimum Wage*, for which he won much-deserved recognition with the award-winning re-worked collection, *Beg the Question*. He currently lives in New York City with his wife Michele.

Mary Fleener [Joni Mitchell] is best known for her neo-cubist comic series *Slutburger*, her unique perspective on life in Southern California, from hippie art student, to gigging musician on the lesbian bar circuit, to surfer; also collected in *Life of the Party*. Fleener lives in Encinitas, CA.

Rick Geary [Richard Hell] has appeared in *National Lampoon*, *Mad*, *Spy*, *Rolling Stone*, *Heavy Metal* and many other fine publications. The *National Lampoon* strips have been collected in *Housebound* with Rick Geary. His true crime tales of the last century, *Treasuries of Victorian Murder*, are carefully researched and use a gleeful tongue-in-cheek tone to tell lurid details from the Victorian era.

Tomer Hanuka [Joe Sacco] is an illustrator and cartoonist living in New York. His work has been published in *The New Yorker*, *Time*, *Spin*, *Rolling Stone* and *The New York Times* among others. He also creates the comic book *Bipolar* with brother Asaf Hanuka, published by Alternative Comics.

Tim Hensley [Tom Verlaine] produced amazing work for *Dirty Stories*, *No More Shaves* and the *TCJ* Special Editions, all of which are available from Fantagraphics Books.

Ted Jouflas [Guy Maddin] was born in Utah and raised in California. A contributor to the seminal 1980s anthology *Weirdo*, his most recent work is *APE, Son of Vision Thing*, a 32-page comic that fuses the Bush Administration with the horror films of the 1930s. Look for more of his work in *The Bush Junta* and *The Comics Journal Annual 2005*.

Megan Kelso [Edie Beale] lives in Brooklyn, NY. She is working on a graphic novel called *Artichoke Tales* and also editing an anthology of female cartoonists called *Scheherazade*, due out in fall 2004.

Michael Kupperman [Walter Hopps] is best known for the 2000 Harper Collins release, *Snake 'n' Bacon's Cartoon Cabaret*. Cartoons from the book were adapted for Comedy Central's *TV Funhouse*. His comics and illustrations have appeared in *The New Yorker*, *Fortune*, *The New York Times* and *L.A. Weekly*. He lives and works in New York City.

Roger Langridge [Robert Altman] is known for his comics *Art d'Ecco*, *Zoot*, a six-issue series and the graphic novel *Zoot Suite*. In 2003, Antipodes Publishing released *No More Mrs. Nice Nun*, a collection of Langridge's *Knuckles the Malevolent Nun* strips, and in 2004 Fantagraphics Books released his major work of the last half-decade, *Fred the Clown*.

David Lasky [Eva Marie Saint], former Xeric Grant recipient and self-publisher of *Boom Boom*, is also a cartoonist who writes bad poetry and the co-creator of *Urban Hipster*. A native of Washington D.C., he now lives in that other Washington—Seattle.

Jessica Lynch [contents cassette] is an obsessive doodler living on Guemes Island, Washington. Since 1997, she has operated Slow Loris (Shirts), screen printing limited editions of her work onto clothing and distributing them nationally through boutique shops and slowshirts.com. Most recently, she has opened a combination storefront and art gallery, the Garagesale Gallery in Anacortes, Washington.

Jason Miles [Ralph Gibson] Wyoming (1979-1983), Pacific Northwest (1983-1997), San Francisco (1997), Olympia (1997-2001), Paris (2001), Olympia (2001-2002), Esparto (2002), Los Angeles (2002-2003), Washington Backwoods (2003-2004). Testicular Hernia (1979), Swallowed Penny (1982), Split Chin and Bruised Mouth (1986), Fractured Foot (1990), Heart Failure (2002-2004). See more of his work on Jordan Crane's site reddingk.com and in the *TCJ Annual 2005*, coming out in January 2005!

Tony Millionaire [Lou Reed] grew up in the seaside town of Gloucester, Massachusetts where his grandparents taught him to draw ships and old houses. He now writes and draws the comic book *Sock Monkey* as well as the weekly strip *Maakies*, which have won him four Eisner Awards including Best Writer/Artist-Humor in 2003. Book collections of his strips are available from Dark Horse and Fantagraphics. He lives in Pasadena, California with his wife and daughters.

David Paleo [Rickie Lee Jones] is a cartoonist and illustrator. You can see more of his work in various *Comics Journal Annual* editions, *The Bush Junta*, *Legal Action Comics* #2, *House of Twelve* and toothpaste tubes all over his native Argentina, where he currently resides.

Ted Rall [Joe Strummer] gained the title of "Most Hated Cartoonist in America" with his thrice-weekly strip, going after such targets as 9/11 Widows, firefighters, Pat Tillman, and the still warm Ronald Reagan. His flurry of recent books include *Attitude 2*, an anthology including interviews with fellow alternative cartoonists (NBM); *Generalissimo El Busho*, a collection of essays and cartoons about George W. Bush (NBM), and *Wake Up, You're Liberal!*, an all-prose political manifesto (Soft Skull Press).

Eric Reynolds [Dick Dale] is the publicist for Fantagraphics Books, a sought-after illustrator and a member of several prolific rock bands. He lives with his wife Rhea in Seattle.

Johnny Ryan [Russ Meyer] is best known as the creator of the controversial and hilarious *Angry Youth Comix*. He has also contributed to *Nickelodeon* magazine. His first compilation of *AYC* material, *Portajohnny*, was released in 2003, and he is working on a second collection, as well as a book of his weekly *Blecky Yuckerella* strip, and a second edition of his widely beloved sketchbook series *Shouldn't You Be Working?* He lives in Los Angeles.

Greg Stump [Jacques Derrida] is a freelance artist, writer and teacher in Seattle. His comic strip, *Dwarf Attack*, appears in *The Portland Mercury*. His collaboration with David Lasky, *Urban Hipster*, earned a Harvey nomination for Best New Series in 1998.

Carol Tyler [Jonathan Omer-Man] made her home in anthologies such as *Weirdo*, *Drawn & Quarterly*, *Street Music* and *The Comics Journal* Special Editions. Over a decade after her first book collection, *The Job Thing*, 2005 will see the release of her second one. She is also working on a new book-length story about her family. She lives in Cincinnati with her husband, the cartoonist Justin Green, and their daughter, the aspiring cartoonist Julia.

Mack White [Allen Ginsberg] is a cartoonist, illustrator, writer and investigative journalist whose work has appeared in *Details*, *Heavy Metal*, *Zero Zero*, *Strapazin* and *Stripburger*. Past projects include *The Mutant Book of the Dead* and *Villa of the Mysteries*. 2004 will see the release of the political anthology *The Bush Junta*, which he co-edited and to which he contributed several stories. He lives in Austin, TX.

Jeff Wong [Elvis Costello] has been creating caricatures and humorous illustrations for a variety of national and international magazines since 1985. He has also produced character designs and storyboards for television and film. His work can be seen weekly in *Sports Illustrated*, for Bill Scheft's column, "The Show."